University of Michigan Publications

HISTORY AND POLITICAL SCIENCE

VOLUME XVII

THE EVOLUTION OF THE ZOLLVEREIN

THE EVOLUTION OF THE
ZOLLVEREIN

A Study of the Ideas and Institutions Leading to German Economic Unification between 1815 and 1833

ARNOLD H. PRICE

OCTAGON BOOKS

A division of Farrar, Straus and Giroux

New York   1973

Reprinted 1973
by special arrangement with the University of Michigan Press

OCTAGON BOOKS
A DIVISION OF FARRAR, STRAUS & GIROUX, INC.
19 Union Square West
New York, N. Y. 10003

Library of Congress Cataloging in Publication Data

Price, Arnold Hereward, 1912-
    The evolution of the Zollverein.

    Reprint of the ed. published by the University of Michigan Press,
    Ann Arbor, which was issued as v. 17 of the History and Political
    science publication of the University of Michigan.

    Bibliography: p.
    1. Zollverein.   I. Title.   II. Series: Michigan. University. Uni-
    versity of Michigan publications. History and political science,
    v. 17.
HF2103.P7   1973   330.9'43'07   73-12446
ISBN 0-374-96566-8

Manufactured by Braun-Brumfield, Inc.
Ann Arbor, Michigan

Printed in the United States of America

To
ALICE

PREFACE

THIS book is an outgrowth of a proseminar paper which revealed to me the possibility of further fruitful research on the Zollverein and particularly on the rôle it played in the rise and development of modern Germany. In 1938 I began my investigations for this work with the purpose of analyzing and evaluating the movement for German economic unification during the founding and early years of the Zollverein, and especially during the somewhat neglected period 1834-48. As the subject unfolded, however, the developments before 1834 presented a challenge far greater than could have been anticipated by glancing through the extensive treatment the period had already received, and hence the scope of my undertaking had to be reduced to cover only the founding years of the Zollverein (1815–33). I completed this task in 1942, and the present text differs from the dissertation I submitted then only in that minor changes of phraseology were made.

The credit for making this study possible must go chiefly to the staff and the facilities of the University of Michigan. I acknowledge gratefully the advice and help I received from my thesis committee, and in particular from its chairman, Professor Howard M. Ehrmann, who was responsible for my methodological training. The other committee members, Professors Arthur E. R. Boak, Benjamin W. Wheeler, and Dwight C. Long, of the History Department, as well as the late Professor John W. Eaton, of the German Department, also gave me the benefit of their guidance, in class and outside.

My work was greatly facilitated by the fine collection of material in the University of Michigan libraries. I appreciate fully the infinite patience and interest with which the staffs of the General Library and of the Legal Research Library helped me in finding half-forgotten pamphlets and dust-covered books. While I was collecting my basic material in the summer of 1938 many privileges were afforded me by the Harvard University Library, the Yale University Libraries, and the Library of Congress.

A graduate student depends to a large extent on those who take personal interest in him.   In this connection I am deeply indebted for help and encouragement to the late Professor Arthur L. Cross, of the History Department, to the late Professor Morris P. Tilley, of the English Department, and to Dr. Robert H. McDowell, formerly of the University Museums.

I was generously assisted by many people in the technical preparation of this work. My thanks go to my parents, Hereward and Elizabeth Price, each of whom went through the manuscript several times. I am indebted to the editor of the University of Michigan Press, Dr. Eugene S. McCartney, for transforming the thesis into a book, and to Mr. Wilfred B. Shaw, Director of Alumni Relations, for the drawing on the title page, which shows an 1833 Bavarian coin commemorating the founding of the Zollverein. I am more than grateful to the University of Michigan Press for sponsoring this publication, and particularly to Dr. Frank E. Robbins, its director, for his interest. I should like to thank also the many others who have helped and advised me.

ARNOLD H. PRICE

Kensington, Maryland
February 19, 1949

CONTENTS

NOTE ON CITATIONS

Full or shortened titles of works referred to by *op. cit.* will be found within the chapter in which this abbreviation occurs.

A number of long titles are frequently cited in condensed form, but complete collations are made in the Bibliography. The following shortened forms of reference are used after the first mention of one organization and four works:

League = Deutscher Handels- und Gewerbsverein.

Nebenius, memorandum [1819], 1833 ed. = Nebenius, Carl Friedrich, anonymous manuscript memorandum of about 1819, reprinted in the 32-page appendix to Nebenius, C[arl] F[riedrich], *Denkschrift für den Beitritt Badens zu dem zwischen Preussen, Bayern, Württemberg, den beiden Hessen und mehren andern deutschen Staaten abgeschlossenen Zollverein.* (See p. 276.)

Oncken and Saemisch = Oncken, Hermann, and Saemisch, F. E. M. (eds.), *Vorgeschichte und Begründung des deutschen Zollvereins 1815–34 Akten der Staaten des Deutschen Bundes und der europäischen Mächte.* (See p. 270.)

[Prussia, Staatsrath] Gutachten . . . 1817 = [Prussia, Staatsrath] Gutachten des preussischen Staatsrath über den Entwurf eines neuen Steuergesetzes 1817. (See p. 269.)

Treitschke, *Deutsche Geschichte* = Treitschke, Heinrich von, *Deutsche Geschichte im neunzehnten Jahrhundert.* (See p. 283.)

CHAPTER I

INTRODUCTION

THE German Question, or the problem of how to organize the German people, dates back to the early nineteenth century, when Germany's feudal structure was swept away by the forces released through the French Revolution. From 1815 to 1945 the world witnessed an ever-increasing concentration and centralization of Germany's political power, paralleled by an equally dynamic expansion and integration of her economy. With Germany defeated in World War II, the German Question entered another critical period, and a study of the origin of her economic unification may therefore be considered of more than academic interest. The Zollverein, the organization which supplied this unity, contributed greatly to the economic basis and fiscal stability of Bismarck's Reich, as well as to its constitutional pattern.

The German Zollverein (1834–71) provided an economic union of most German states without impairing their political independence, and so constituted the first nonpolitical union among independent states. The system worked so well that it was continued, with slight modifications, by the Reich until 1919. Thus the Zollverein not only was important for its influence on international organization, but also contributed to the development of coöperative federalism in Germany. Until 1933 the German constitution afforded a considerable amount of decentralization within the framework of the federal administrative machinery, and the history of the Zollverein is filied with references to the old problem of centralization versus coördination.

The present investigation tries to present a critical history of the origin and growth of the ideas and institutions which led to the foundation of the Zollverein in 1834. It may be considered a case study of the influence ideas exercise on historical developments, specifically, on the origin and rise of institutions. Thus two different lines of development are followed through. A critical analysis of pertinent contem-

1

porary thought, as well as a detailed examination of the technical and administrative history is given. So far as possible, particular attention is paid to all occasions when these two lines of development cross. This work attempts to describe not only the intellectual background of the period when the Zollverein was founded, but also the extent to which already existing concepts and new ideas influenced the establishment of German economic unification. Its main emphasis is upon ideas, whether they occur in speeches, pamphlets, or documents. Neither the extent of these ideas nor other problems of public opinion, however, form the major task of this treatise, and so they are discussed only incidentally.

The work is limited primarily to those ideas which deal directly with economic unification. Contemporary economic theory, economic conditions, and political thought and events are touched upon only briefly and only when bearing on the main theme. For this reason the reader should not expect a continuous account of political and economic thought and actions in the period under consideration.

An effort is made to deal with the period of 1815–33 as a unity and to place ideas in their relationship to specific and general contemporary thought. As a rule, the description will proceed from the age, its philosophic outlook, its theories and ideologies, and its experiences, to the individual, with his policies, schemes, and interests, and finally will arrive at the institutions and their perfection.

The organization of the subject is approached without any effort to make the material conform to preconceived theories. Since the study deals with thought, ideas furnish the main principle for arranging the material. The first three chapters describe the development of ideas which took place between 1815 and 1825. Before 1815 German economic unification was discussed as a by-product of political unification; between 1815 and 1820 it became an issue in itself, and it was then superseded by the plans for a separate regional union. This last idea was elaborated in South Germany by 1825 so as to contain the essential principles of a customs union. Its growth was paralleled by the rise of two institutions in North Germany, the modernized Prussian customs administration and the Prussian Zollanschluss system. The years 1815–20 saw a great deal of interaction between the people and the governments. The actual founding of the Zollverein, however, was the exclusive work of the cabinets. Between 1827 and 1833 they took over and combined the achievements the preceding decade had accomplished in the South as well as in the North. Even though popular thought did not participate in this final and technical development, its history is important for the understanding of the whole period, and it is for this reason that it is discussed.

Although both the scope of this study and the approach to it are original, it must be explained why the author feels justified in choosing a topic which has been dealt with by many other treatises. In spite of the voluminous literature on this subject, the material has never been integrated, and many points still remain unsettled. Moreover, most of the historians who studied the field during the latter half of the nineteenth century wrote for the benefit of one region. Thus Beck[1] and Böhtlingk[2] argued Baden's cause, while W. Weber[3] defended Bavaria, and Treitschke[4] glorified Prussian policy. Treitschke's extensive account, though brilliant, is biased. He derides any opposition to Prussia and evaluates Prussia's pre-Zollverein policy with the standards of an 1871 Prussian patriot, being frequently unable to understand the spirit and temper of the period he is describing. During the

[1] J[oseph] Beck, "Karl Friedrich Nebenius in Beziehung zur Geschichte Badens und des deutschen Zollvereins," *Unsere Zeit. Jahrbuch zum Conversations-Lexikon,* VIII (1864), 35–69; Jos[eph] Beck, *Carl Friedrich Nebenius. Ein Lebensbild eines deutschen Staatsmannes und Gelehrten. Zugleich ein Beitrag zur Geschichte Badens und des deutschen Zollvereins* (Mannheim: J. Schneider, 1866), 128 pp.

[2] Arthur Böhtlingk, *Carl Friedrich Nebenius. Der deutsche Zollverein, das Karlsruher Polytechnikum und die erste Staatsbahn in Deutschland* (Karlsruhe: Friedrich Gutsch [1899]), 119 pp.

[3] W. Weber, *Der deutsche Zollverein. Geschichte seiner Entstehung und Entwickelung* (2d ed.; Leipzig: Veit & Comp., 1871), x.+ 503.

[4] Heinrich von Treitschke, *Deutsche Geschichte im neunzehnten Jahrhundert* ("Staatengeschichte der neuesten Zeit," Vols. XXIV–XXVIII. Second edition, Leipzig: S. Hirzel, 1879–89), Vols. I–III. (Third edition, Leipzig, 1890–95), Vols. IV–V. This work will hereafter be cited as Treitschke, *Deutsche Geschichte.*

first decades of the twentieth century historical knowledge of the early Zollverein advanced considerably. A number of excellent monographs, like Brinkmann's on Prussia,[5] Doeberl's on Bavaria,[6] Menn's on Nassau,[7] Köhler's on List,[8] Baasch's on Hamburg,[9] Suchel's on Hesse-Darmstadt,[10] and Borckenhagen's and Bab's on public opinion,[11] added to the understanding of the period. Since the publication of the great documentary account of the foundation of the Zollverein by Professor Oncken and Dr. Saemisch in 1934,[12] German historiography has declined rapidly. Dr. Olshausen,[13] for instance, tried to study the List of 1819–20 by superimposing the concepts of the *Führerprinzip*, and it is more than significant that the best general account of the Zollverein

[5] Carl Brinkmann, *Die preussische Handelspolitik vor dem Zollverein und der Wiederaufbau vor hundert Jahren* (Berlin: Verein Wissenschaftlicher Verleger, 1922), vi + 242.

[6] M[ichael] Doeberl, *Bayern und die wirtschaftliche Einigung Deutschlands* ("Abhandlungen der Königlich Bayerischen Akademie der Wissenschaften, Philosophisch-philologische und historische Klasse," München. 1915), xxix, Part II, 1–117.

[7] Walter Menn, *Zur Vorgeschichte des deutschen Zollvereins, Nassaus Handels- und Schiffahrtspolitik vom Wiener Kongress bis zum Ausgang der süddeutschen Zollvereinsverhandlungen 1815–1827* (Greifswald: Ratsbuchhandlung L. Bamberg, 1930), 159 pp.

[8] Curt Köhler, *Problematisches zu Friedrich List. Mit Anhang: Lists Briefe aus Amerika in deutscher Übersetzung* (Leipzig: C. Hirschfeld, 1908), x + 259.

[9] Ernst Baasch, "Die deutschen wirtschaftlichen Einheitsbestrebungen, die Hansestädte und Friedrich List bis zum Jahre 1821," *Historische Zeitschrift*, CXXII (1920), 454-85.

[10] Adolf Suchel, *Hessen-Darmstadt und der Darmstädter Handelskongress von 1820–1823* ("Quellen und Forschungen zur hessischen Geschichte," No. 6; Darmstadt: Hessischer Staatsverlag, 1922), vii + 109.

[11] Fritze Borckenhagen, *National- und handelspolitische Bestrebungen in Deutschland (1815–1822) und die Anfänge Friedrich Lists* ("Abhandlungen zur mittleren und neueren Geschichte," No. 57; Berlin: W. Rothschild, 1915), 83 pp.; Bernd Bab, *Die öffentliche Meinung über den deutschen Zollverein zur Zeit seiner Entstehung* (Doctor's dissertation, Berlin, 1930), 98 pp.

[12] Hermann Oncken and F. E. M. Saemisch (eds.), *Vorgeschichte und Begründung des deutschen Zollvereins 1815–1834 Akten der Staaten des Deutschen Bundes und der europäischen Mächte* ("Veröffentlichungen der Friedrich List-Gesellschaft E. V.," Vols. VIII–X; Berlin SW, 61: Reimar Hobbing, 1934) 3 vols. This work will hereafter be cited as Oncken and Saemisch.

[13] Hans-Peter Olshausen, *Friedrich List und der Deutsche Handels- und Gewerbsverein* ("List-Studien," No. 6; Jena: Gustav Fischer, 1935), x + 357.

is the recent work of Dr. W. O. Henderson, an Englishman.[14] Dr. Henderson's survey emphasizes political and economic factors and constitutes an excellent introduction to the subject, since he has consulted and handled both published and unpublished material in a thorough and competent manner. Although there is a wealth of material on various aspects of the early history of the Zollverein, no one has ever attempted to relate and integrate the ideas on economic unification with the origin of the Zollverein as an institution.

The author of the present study has used a large number of contemporary pamphlets, and he probably had available all those that are important. He is indebted to the generosity of the late Mr. Philo Parsons, of Detroit, who donated an excellent collection of nineteenth-century German economic tracts to the General Library of the University of Michigan. Professor Oncken and Dr. Saemisch's *Vorgeschichte und Begründung des deutschen Zollvereins,* as well as the statute books of various German states, contains the major portion of the official documents used. The recent editions of Görres' and List's works[15] were helpful in studying these two publicists. The author has attempted to use all pertinent historical treatises, and he was able to gain access to all but a few of them. The monographs dealing with political history did not, however, yield as much supplementary material as he had hoped.

Though having a large body of publications as its basis, this work does not attempt to give a comprehensive picture of the political or economic developments leading to the foundation of the Zollverein. Its main subject is the intellectual history of the origin of the Zollverein, a theme which is brought out in describing the interplay of ideas and interests, the interaction of personalities and situations, and the interrelationship between thought and action.

[14] W[illiam] O[tto] Henderson, *The Zollverein* ("Cambridge Studies in Economic History"; Cambridge: University Press, 1939), xvi + 375.

[15] [Johann] Joseph [von] Görres, *Gesammelte Schriften,* ed. by the Görres-Gesellschaft (Köln: Gilde-Verlag, 1926–), Vol. I–; Friedrich List, *Schriften/ Reden/ Briefe,* ed. by Friedrich List Gesellschaft E. V. (Berlin SW. 61: Reimar Hobbing, 1927–35), 10 vols.

CHAPTER II

THE BACKGROUND OF GERMAN ECONOMIC UNIFICATION UNTIL 1815

THE era of the Napoleonic Wars left Germany torn and divided between the memories of the past, the forces of the present, and hopes for the future. The old Empire was still well remembered, in spite of all its shortcomings. Napoleonic institutions as well as revived nationalism had spread during the period preceding the Congress of Vienna, but neither of them had been able to win general approval. While the Wars of Liberation had been won by the popular support of many sections of the country, the postwar reconstruction was taken over entirely by the cabinets. Events had followed each other rapidly; the dissolution of the Empire and the rise and fall of Napoleon's supremacy in German affairs had occurred within a single decade. Old institutions had been shaken to their foundations, and new reforms had hardly gained a foothold. The French Revolution and other subsequent upheavals had impressed their mark on everybody's mind, though to a certain degree the traditional outlook persisted.

These cross currents gave the thought of the years 1813–15 their peculiar pattern. Political ideologies were not developed to any extent, nor were there definite political camps. Progressive leaders still cherished the institutions of the old Empire, but the new nationalism had not altogether taken the place of the cosmopolitan ideals of the prewar period. Although the recent national awakening had swept over whole sections of the population and although it seems to have been the predominant force of the period, not everybody agreed with this new conception of German national destiny, and there were still many who sympathized with the French.[1] The leading men of the age were products of the

---

[1] Adolf Rapp, *Der deutsche Gedanke, seine Entwicklung im politischen und geistigen Leben seit dem 18. Jahrhundert* (Bonn: K. Schroeder, 1920), pp. 53-54; Hermann Meerwarth, *Die öffentliche Meinung in Baden von den Befreiungskriegen bis zur Erteilung der Verfassung (1815–1818)* (Doctor's dissertation, Heidelberg, 1907), p. 31.

eighteenth century, and one should not measure them by the standards of the subsequent century. The movements which were to become typical of the nineteenth century, like its nationalism, its historicism, or its liberalism, had scarcely begun to take shape in 1815.

In this transitory period of 1813–15 old and new ideas were flourishing together. Ardent leaders of the national cause, such as Stein, remained cosmopolitans.[2] There were men like Arndt who desired popular representation, but still in the form of the old estates.[3] The new nationalism was inseparable from the old Imperial patriotism. The romanticists had not yet split into liberals and conservatives,[4] and the reactionary cabinets and popular movements had not dissolved their alliance against the national enemy. An emotional difference had already begun to develop between the two groups. A new school had grown up which regarded political unity as an essential of national unity,[5] in contrast to earlier thought, which had limited itself to cultural unity.[6] This new group, which included future reactionaries and liberals alike, emphasized the emotional value of the state.[7] The older school, on the other hand, was still following eighteenth-century rationalism and looked upon the state from the standpoint of political realism and professional diplomacy. Metternich was a typical representative of this school of thought.[8]

---

[2] Friedrich Meinecke, *Weltbürgertum und Nationalstaat. Studien zur Genesis des deutschen Nationalstaats* (7th ed.; München: R. Oldenbourg, 1928), p. 164.

[3] Karl [Theodor Albert] Wolff, *Die deutsche Publizistik in der Zeit der Freiheitskämpfe und des Wiener Kongresses 1813–1815* (Doctor's dissertation, Leipzig, 1934), p. 49.

[4] Wilhelm Roscher, *Geschichte der National-Ökonomik in Deutschland* ("Geschichte der Wissenschaften in Deutschland, neuere Zeit," Vol. XIV; München: R. Oldenbourg, 1874), p. 822.

[5] Meinecke, *op. cit.*, pp. 93–94, 110–11.   [6] *Ibid.*, pp. 54–59.

[7] *Ibid.*, p. 140; Tim Klein (ed.), *Die Befreiung 1813· 1814· 1815, Urkunden Berichte Briefe mit geschichtlichen Verbindungen* (Ebenhausen bei München: W. Langewiesche-Brandt, 1913), pp. 500–2, quoting from Ernst Moritz Arndt, *Über künftige ständische Verfassungen in Teutschland* (1814): "Die Stiftung *grosser* Reichsgerichte mit dem *Glanz* und der *Majestät* der Gerechtigkeit, dass beide die *Heiligkeit* der *höchsten* Angelegenheiten des Volkes erscheine, und die geschwindeste Schlichtung der Zwiste und Händel möglich sei." (Italics are mine.)

[8] Heinrich *Ritter* von Srbik, *Metternich, der Staatsmann und der Mensch*

A generation which had suffered much for its political sins was inclined to think of political security first and to put economic questions in the second place. The people limited their interest in economic problems to a general dislike of Napoleon's Continental System and of all excessive state paternalism. Though business men would not hesitate to voice local grievances, they remained, with few exceptions, totally unaware of fundamental economic issues. This condition was in part due to the relatively undeveloped state of German economic life.

On the other hand, since many administrators, publicists, and professors had studied economics, economic thought among the educated had acquired a certain standing. Undoubtedly Adam Smith had exercised the greatest influence upon this class; his doctrines were taught at a number of universities, and thus his ideas had spread in many official circles.[9] There were still some remnants of mercantilistic doctrines, and among the romanticists the beginning of economic conservatism was discernible.[10] The achievements of the eighteenth century in administrative practices had been kept alive, for this field of applied economy was also taught in the universities. Academic interest therefore confined itself primarily to economic theory and to administrative practices, paying little attention to an analysis of existing economic conditions. Economics as a field had not yet fully developed, since it remained closely tied to philosophy, history, and the eighteenth-century disciplines of cameralism and administrative law (Polizeiwissenschaft.)

The main criticism which can be made of German eco-

(München: F. Bruckmann A.-G., 1925), I, 194–99, 224–29; Wilhelm Adolf Schmidt, Geschichte der deutschen Verfassungsfrage während der Befreiungskriege und des Wiener Kongresses 1812 bis 1815, ed. by Alfred Stern (Stuttgart: G. J. Göschen, 1890), pp. 35–36.

[9] Karl Rathgen, "Die Ansichten über Freihandel und Schutzzoll in der deutschen Staatspraxis des 19. Jahrhunderts," Die Entwicklung der deutschen Volkswirtschaftslehre im neunzehnten Jahrhundert (Memorial volume for Gustav Schmoller's seventieth birthday; Leipzig, 1908), II, No. 17, 4; Wilhelm Treue, Wirtschaftszustände und Wirtschaftspolitik in Preussen 1815–1825 ("Vierteljahrsschrift für Sozial- und Wirtschaftsgeschichte," Beiheft No. 31; Stuttgart: W. Kohlhammer, 1937), p. 242; Carl William Hasek, The Introduction of Adam Smith's Doctrines into Germany (Doctor's dissertation, Columbia University, 1925), pp. 60–94.

[10] Roscher, op. cit., pp. 763–78.

nomic thought in 1815 is that the theorists had derived most of their knowledge from books, whereas the men with practical experience had not risen above details or arrived at general conclusions. There were, however, some intellectuals who had enjoyed both theoretical training and practical experience, and so were capable of synthesis; but they were primarily administrators and not scholars. When they were confronted with an immediate problem, they had to work it out by themselves, since there was no ready-made solution. Theoretical thought remained too abstract to be of help in such cases, and it often followed in what Professor Brinkmann terms a "compilatory eclecticism."[11] For such reasons Adam Smith's ideas had produced very little direct results by 1815; mercantilistic practices continued to flourish throughout Germany, as they did all over Europe.[12]

Both the economic and the political thought of 1813–15 reflected the transitory character of the period with its complex mixture of ideas. The past with its ideas of stability, the youthful forces of change, and the realities of the present all claimed their ideological share in the minds of contemporaries. The suddenness with which the new problems arose did not allow sufficient time for proper integration. Thus, at the end of the Napoleonic era, Germany's economic and political thought showed a number of serious and general weaknesses.

German economic unification was also handicapped by two particular deficiencies. In all her history Germany had never constituted an economic unit, and the types of existing and known economic unions were limited. There had been no instance of economic unification among independent states which did not constitute at the same time a political federation or union.

Economic unification, generally speaking, had till then been limited to individual states, like France, to federal unions, like the United States; and to personal unions, like the United Kingdom. In all these states economic unification was incidental to political unification. Likewise, mon-

---

[11] *Die preussische Handelspolitik,* p. 7.
[12] Rathgen, *op. cit.,* pp. 16–17.

archies had never formed a federal state in the modern sense, and the only federalism which had been developed institutionally to any extent was unitarian federalism, in which almost all federal matters were administered by federal officials, whereas coöperative federalism, in which many federal matters were executed by state officials—as they were in Germany from 1871 to 1933—was as yet unknown.[13] Moreover, there existed none of our modern international unions for nonpolitical services, such as the Postal Union. Perhaps the only mutual arrangement of this type was the collection of the Rhine octroi, in which a local technical problem had been solved through international coöperation.[14] At the time of the Congress of Vienna, international as well as federal institutionalism had not been developed to a point where it could have provided Germany with a workable pattern for economic unification. There had as yet been no customs union.

Although Germany had formed no economic unit before 1815, economic unification had been considered from time to time. The old Empire had a very peculiar customs system, which prevented the Empire, as well as the territories, from pursuing an independent economic policy. The Empire did not have a single customs of its own,[15] but it had definite control over the customs policies of the territories. No new customs house could be erected by the territories and no tariff rate increased without the formal consent of the emperor and the electors.[16] These regulations had not always been followed, so that a number of customs houses existed illegally.[17] There was, however, no provision to prevent individual territories from completely closing their boundaries against any number of commodities.[18] The net result was an irregular distribution of customs houses all

---

[13] The term "federalism" as used here refers to a federal state, not to a confederation of states.   [14] Infra, pp. 100-1.

[15] Johann Stephan Pütter, Historische Entwicklung der heutigen Staatsverfassung des Teutschen Reichs (Göttingen, 1787), III, 264.

[16] Loc cit.; [Johann Friedrich Böhmer] Das Zollwesen in Deutschland geschichtlich beleuchtet ("Geschichtliche Beleuchtungen des deutschen Staatsrechts," Vol. I; Frankfurt am Main, 1832), 2, 30-39.

[17] Ibid., p. 8; Pütter, op. cit., I (1786), 226.

[18] Roscher, op. cit., pp. 949-50.

over Germany, especially along the rivers, with the greatest possible variety of tariffs.

The ensuing constitutional deadlock and its result, the lack of a national commercial policy, were often recognized, and occasionally changes were suggested. The most famous of these was the attempt of the Reichstag in 1523 to establish a customs line around the Empire. No customs union, in the technical sense, was proposed, since the money was going to be both collected and used by the Empire.[19] Although the resistance of the cities foiled the scheme,[20] it nevertheless remains an important milestone in the history of German economic unification.

The subsequent centuries saw the rise of territorial power in Germany, and economic unification was removed even further out of the range of possibilities than before.[21] However, the Empire still inspired a certain patriotism, and men grieved at the decline of Germany as an economic power. In the second half of the eighteenth century, Möser deplored the state of German commerce and pointed back to the time of the Hanseatic League to show what Germany had been able to do commercially.[22] He doubted that Germany would ever recover that position[23] and suggested the formation of a new Hanseatic League.[24]

The decades following Möser's writings saw the introduction of Adam Smith's ideas into Germany. During this period economic theory rose to a higher scholarly level, and cosmopolitanism spread through Germany. A unique product of this period was Fichte's scheme for a "closed commercial state." This state was to have a minimum of commercial contacts with other states, and it was to be autarchic in

---

[19] Bill for the regulation of an Imperial toll [Nuremberg, January–February, 1523], [Holy Roman Empire] *Deutsche Reichstagsakten*, "Jüngere Reihe," ed. by the Historische Kommission bei der Königlichen Akademie der Wissenschaften [at Munich], III (Gotha: F. A. Perthes, 1901), 622–41, No. 108. A mixed commission of six was to administer this system.

[20] Oncken, in Oncken and Saemisch, I, xii–xiii.

[21] For contemporary authors discussing the problem of German economic unification during this period see *ibid.*, xiv; Doeberl, *Bayern und die wirtschaftliche Einigung*, p. 5.

[22] Justus Möser, *Patriotische Phantasien*, ed. by J. W. J. v. Voigt (New and enlarged ed.; Frankfurt, 1780) I, 7–21, 258–63.

[23] *Ibid.*, p. 260.   [24] *Ibid.*, pp. 263–65.

the modern sense, with such modern institutions as a double currency, a state board to control imports and exports, and restrictions on foreign travel. At that time Fichte was not motivated by an extreme nationalism, but he proposed this plan in order to establish internal and external peace.[25] Even after his turn toward nationalism Fichte was opposed to German commercial expansion in other countries.[26] The most important development of the opening years of the nineteenth century was the beginning of a modern commercial and tariff policy in various German states. After the dissolution of the Empire in 1806 the surviving territories regarded themselves as sovereign and assumed all those rights which had been exercised by the Empire.

During the period of French domination more attention had been paid to such problems as free trade and protection versus prohibition, than to a discussion of national economic problems. Jahn, in his book called *Volkstum* (1810), asked for a unified standard of measures and coinage[27] and followed Seume in his fight against internal excise taxes.[28] Seume opposed the existing anarchy in the collection of internal revenue[29] and wrote a long poem on the dangers of the contemporary system of taxation.[30] This was in line with the thought of other writers of that period who were generally opposed to the obstruction of trade by the governments, although they were not necessarily in favor of absolute free trade.[31]

The period after 1800 saw the slow growth of nationalism in Germany, which increased the longer Napoleon's rule

---

[25] Johann Gottlieb Fichte, *Der geschlossene Handelsstaat* (1800), reprinted in *Johann Gottlieb Fichte's sämmtliche Werke* (Berlin, 1845), III, 421, 443, 476, 497–500, 508, 512–13.

[26] H[elmuth] C[arl] Engelbrecht, *Johann Gottlieb Fichte. A Study of His Political Writings, with Special Reference to His Nationalism* ("Studies in History, Economics and Public Law," ed. by the Faculty of Political Science of Columbia University, No. 383; New York: Columbia University Press, 1933), p. 120.

[27] Fr[iedrich]-[*sic*]L[udwig] Jahn, *Recherches sur la nationalité, l'esprit des peuples allemands et les institutions qui seraient en harmonie avec leurs mœrs et leur caractère*, trans. by P. Lortet (Paris, 1825), p. 92.

[28] *Ibid.*, pp. 62–67.

[29] J[ohann] G[ottfried] Seume, *Prosaische und poetische Werke* (Berlin [1875]), X, 226–27.   [30] *Ibid.*, V, 135–37.

[31] Roscher, *op. cit.*, pp. 648–49, 679–80, 694; Brinkmann, *op. cit.*, p. 8.

lasted. Soergel was a lone and early (1800) advocate of German economic unification,[32] and it was not until 1813, when liberation was nearer than ever before, that this problem again received attention. The question remained, however, a secondary one, political unification being the main problem. It was, nevertheless, discussed by diplomats and publicists alike, and through experience a few statesmen became aware of the complexity of the problem.

The three main aspects which should be considered for this period (1813–15) in the history of German economic unification are: (1) the attempts to establish a general impost along the North Sea and the Baltic; (2) the failure of the Congress of Vienna to provide directly for economic unification; and (3) the attitude of the writers of the period.

The first of these aspects was important as a contemporary experiment in customs unification. As the war progressed and French influence in northern Germany decreased, the Prussian government and the Central Administration which had been set up by the allied powers for the conquered German territories attempted to collect an impost along the coast of northern Germany. Prussia introduced the impost on April 15, 1813,[33] after having abolished Napoleon's Continental System on March 30, 1813,[34] and repealed it on May 16, 1814.[35] Stein tried to extend the impost to the coast under the control of his Central Administration, but apparently his attempts never succeeded.[36]

There is no indication that the impost was planned and executed as anything more than a provisional measure to collect money for the conduct of the war.[37] Thus it did

[32] Paul Sick, Übersichtliche Geschichte der Entstehung des grossen deutschen Zollvereins (Doctor's dissertation, Tübingen, 1843), p. 6.

[33] Jahresberichte der Geschichtswissenschaft 1888, XI (1891), Part II, 430.   [34] Rathgen, op. cit., p. 15.   [35] Loc. cit.

[36] K. Mamroth, Geschichte der preussischen Staats-Besteuerung 1806–1816 (Leipzig, 1890), pp. 728–74; Alfred Zimmermann, Geschichte der preussisch-deutschen Handelspolitik (Oldenburg: Schulzesche Hof-Buchhandlung und Hof-Buchdruckerei, 1892), p. 7; Stein to Hardenberg, Paris, May 12, 1814, Karl Freiherr vom Stein, Briefwechsel, Denkschriften und Aufzeichnungen, ed. by Erich Botzenhart (Berlin: C. Heymann [1933]), IV, 644–45.

[37] Rathgen, op. cit., p. 15; Stein to Czar Alexander I, Breslau, March 16, 1813, "Der Ursprung des deutschen Verwaltungsrathes von 1813," Historische Zeitschrift, LIX (1888), 300.

not aim at economic unification, and it cannot be regarded as a predecessor of the Zollverein.[38]   Nevertheless, some of its personal and technical aspects were important.   It was an attempt, although in a limited way, to coördinate German customs policy.   The problem of free trade versus protection was extensively discussed among Prussian officials, especially by those who were to influence later developments.[39]

Stein labored temporarily under a number of misconceptions, the most serious of which related to the establishment of an impost just along the coast, without surrounding the hinterland with land customs.[40]   But by December of 1813 he was already advocating a customs line around Germany,[41] and in the spring of 1814 he finally gave up his plan of collecting an impost and deferred the question until the time when Germany should have a general customs system.[42]   He had probably realized the complexity of the problem he was dealing with.   He stood firm in his belief in customs duties, although they were opposed not only by free traders pure and simple, but by all those who had suffered under Napoleon's Continental System.   He was warned that a customs line would be looked upon as an act of "French tyranny."[43]

Stein was also among the statesmen who contributed their advice to the allied governments on the economic problems connected with the reconstruction of Germany. As early as April, 1813, he recognized the problem,[44] and in his memorandum of August, 1813, he made some suggestions for an Imperial financial administration.[45]   This

---

[38] Rathgen, op. cit., p. 15.

[39] Jahresberichte der Geschichtswissenschaft, XI, Part II, 430; Brinkmann, op. cit., pp. 36–41.

[40] Stein to Czar Alexander I, Breslau, March 16, 1813, "Der Ursprung . . . ," Historische Zeitschrift, LIX, 300; Carl J. H. Blume, Hamburg und die deutschen wirtschaftlichen Einheitsbestrebungen 1814–1847 [Hamburg, 1934], pp. 9–10.

[41] Clemens Theodor Perthes, Friedrich Perthes' Leben nach dessen schriftlichen und mündlichen Mitteilungen aufgezeichnet (Gotha: F. A. Perthes, 1896), I, 258.

[42] Jahresberichte der Geschichtswissenschaft, XI, Part II, 430.

[43] Blume, op. cit., p. 9.

[44] G[eorg] H[einrich] Pertz, Das Leben des Ministers Freiherrn vom Stein (Berlin: G. Reimer, 1849–55), III, 665.

[45] Dated Prag, Schmidt, op. cit., pp. 59–67.

memorandum did not penetrate very deeply into the political problems of the German Question; Stein approached the problem from the past, taking as an ideal the German constitution of the tenth to the thirteenth century,[46] and adding to it proposals for institutions which he thought might be good and eliminating what had proved to be disastrous. He wanted an Imperial treasury established, to be located at Ratisbon.[47] The relation of the emperor to this treasury remained obscure.[48] Stein provided also for an Imperial minister of finance. Only military, judicial, and diplomatic officials were to receive a salary from the Empire, but the minister of finance was to have central as well as local offices.[49] The various states were to retain, as a rule, their jurisdiction over finances,[50] but taxes were to be used for Imperial needs.[51] This same lack of clarity is noticeable in Article XXIII, which dealt with tolls. It read, simply: "Matters of coinage and customs belong to the Reichstag. All territorial customs agencies (*Territorial-Zoll-Einrichtungen*) are to be abolished, and boundary customs are to be paid for the account of the Empire."[52] The first sentence had a somewhat flexible meaning, if one considers that in the old Empire coinage and customs had also been under Imperial jurisdiction. The sentence that followed indicated, however, that Stein did not want a return to the old conditions. But what did he have in mind? On the one hand, he proposed that all territorial customs agencies should be abolished and, on the other, that customs duties be maintained, but he did not make it clear by whom. If he wanted the Empire to do the collecting, then why did he specify that the duties were to be paid to the account of the Empire? Why did he not provide salaries for Imperial customs officials? He does not seem to have had any clear conception of federalism or of the division of power between central and state governments.[53] This, then, was the reason for the vagueness in his provisions concerning the collection of

---

[46] Art. IX, *ibid*.   [47] Art. XIX, *ibid*.   [48] Art. XVI, *ibid*.
[49] Art. XVII, *ibid*.   [50] Art. XXIV, *ibid*.
[51] Art. XXV, *ibid*.   [52] *Ibid*.; my translation.
[53] Thus in Article XXV (*ibid*.) he gave each state the right to determine how much it desired to contribute to the Imperial treasury through direct or other taxes.

customs. However, so far as can be gathered from his ambiguous terms, he proposed two important things: the fiscal independence of the Empire and the end of internal customs lines. He suggested boundary customs, but differentiated between sea and land customs, indicating that he advocated a higher degree of fiscal unity rather than commercial unification in the modern sense.

Stein broadened his views, however, on German economic unity, influenced perhaps by his experiences in directing the Central Administration. The stress remained on boundary customs under central control.[54] He became very outspoken in his opposition to internal customs lines.[55] Although he still differentiated between boundary and coast customs,[56] he began to understand that a customs policy must be conducted for the whole country and not in one region alone.[57] In the subsequent period, during the discussion of the German Question, he opposed internal tariff lines, favored boundary tariffs,[58] began to realize the importance of a large customs area,[59] and always advocated that the Empire or Federation should have jurisdiction over customs, coinage, and similar matters.[60] He kept in mind the importance of a financially independent central government.[61] In spite of all weaknesses, Stein's proposals of 1813–15 were noteworthy for three reasons, namely: he did not overlook the economic question; he demanded greater unity; and he experienced great difficulty in dealing with the technical aspects of the subject.

Other leading statesmen also elaborated their views on the reconstruction of Germany. Humboldt studied the

---

[54] Stein to Stadion, Freyburg, December 25, 1813, Bruno Gebhardt, "Zwei Denkschriften Stein's über deutsche Verfassung," *Historische Zeitschrift,* LXXX (1898), 257–72.

[55] Memorandum, Chaumont, March 10, 1814, Schmidt, *op. cit.,* p. 132.

[56] *Loc. cit.*

[57] Perthes, *op. cit.,* I, 258; *Jahresberichte der Geschichtswissenschaft,* XI, Part II, 430.

[58] Stein to Oppel, June 21, 1814, Karl Freiherr vom Stein, *op. cit.,* p. 5.

[59] Stein's commentary on Hardenberg's Forty-one Articles, Schmidt, *op. cit.,* pp. 175–76.

[60] *Loc. cit.; Jahresberichte der Geschichtswissenschaft,* XI, Part II, 430.

[61] Stein's commentary on Hardenberg's Forty-one Articles, Schmidt, *op. cit.,* p. 184; Stein's commentary on Humboldt's draft of a German constitution, *ibid.,* p. 322.

problem for the Prussian government, and his memorandum of December, 1813, included a solution of the economic question. He proposed to curtail the newly gained sovereignty of the various states in customs matters through a general commercial treaty between all the German states which should set a maximum for all tariffs to be collected in interstate trade.[62] That is to say, he wanted something similar to the system in the old Empire, in which the territories collected all the customs but were restricted in their fiscal policy. He also thought of establishing a common department of finance and commerce to further coöperation among German states in these matters.[63]

Although Humboldt had regarded his proposals as a minimum, in his next memorandum he took, under Münster's influence, another step toward decentralization by not allowing any financial independence to the central government.[64]

In his final draft of a German constitution in July and August, 1814, Hardenberg followed Humboldt by proposing that restrictions should be placed on the commercial absolutism of the various states.[65] He suggested that customs and postal matters should be regulated in a reasonable way and that trade and commerce should be facilitated and promoted among the various states. Internal German tariffs were not to be abolished but kept within certain limits. He also proposed a common standard of coinage and a German legal code.[66] His plan was opposed, however, by Bülow, who suggested, according to Professor Brinkmann, "a German or North European customs union" against the French system of prohibition.[67]

Though the official Prussian proposal did not offer much for economic unity, an Austrian scheme of December, 1814, which called for a federation without Prussia, stated that

[62] Art. XXXI, ibid., p. 121.   [63] Loc. cit.

[64] Abstract of Münster's memorandum, Dijon, March 30, 1814, ibid., p. 140; Humboldt's memorandum, April, 1814, Art. XIX, ibid., p. 152.

[65] Hardenberg's Forty-one Articles, Art. VIII, ibid., p. 175.

[66] Loc. cit.

[67] Dated Hirschberg, September 24, 1814, Brinkmann, op. cit., p. 45. I have found only this reference on the matter. I am skeptical whether Bülow actually conceived the idea of a customs union.

federal legislation would provide for freedom of commerce and trade.[68] This idea was not without merits, since laws were to be passed by a majority vote.[69] But freedom of trade did not mean economic unity.

In all these proposals, and during all the negotiations of the Congress of Vienna, economic problems were dealt with as secondary matters. Political interests dominated the scene and were responsible for all major decisions. Because no one thought of economic unification without political unification, general economic provisions for a reconstructed Germany strikingly reflected the lack of political unification.

Two factors were mainly responsible for this situation. The Austro-Prussian dualism, or the rivalry for leadership in Germany, rose again, as did the traditional opposition of the other German states to any central authority.

The rivalry between Austria and Prussia was accentuated by the divergent interests which linked these powers to German affairs. In 1815 Austria received a well-rounded territory with a simple boundary separating her from the rest of Germany. She acquired a unity of her own, retaining only indirect interests in the remainder of Germany. Prussia's territory, on the other hand, was scattered all over northern Germany with a complicated boundary which associated her interests inseparably with those of her German neighbors. It was for this reason that Austria was not much concerned about German unification in 1815. The general as well as the specific differences between Austria and Prussia—the Saxon Question might be mentioned here —prevented these powers from forming a united front and made it possible for the other German states to assert their sovereignty at Vienna, which they were not slow to do.

Ever since the close of the Middle Ages the various territories had enjoyed an increasing independence, but it was not until 1806 that those which survived became sovereign states. In 1815 the desire of the various German governments to remain independent was as strong as ever.

The difficulties which were made by some states in

[68] Dated December, 1814, Art. XVe, [Congress of Vienna, 1814–15] *Acten des Wiener Congresses in den Jahren 1814 und 1815*, ed. by J. L. Klüber (2d ed.; Erlangen, n.d.), II, 5, No. 1.   [69] Arts V, IX, *ibid.*, p. 2.

ratifying the Acts of Confederation bore this out. Bavaria objected to the first draft of Article XIX, which reserved to the members of the Confederation the right to *decide* matters of common commercial interest at the first meeting of the Diet, because this was endangering *iura singulorum,* that is, state rights.[70] The article was subsequently changed, and in its final form stipulated that the governments should only *deliberate* about these matters instead of *deciding* them—which was exactly what happened later.[71]

The main factors blocking any political unification in Germany lay in the rivalry between the leading states and in the desire for independence among the smaller ones. Economic unification had to reckon, in addition, with the different financial and economic interests of the various governments and of the regions they represented.

The people did not participate in the foundation of the German Confederation, and the publicists did not exercise any visible influence on diplomatic negotiations. Although the desire for German unity was widespread, expressions in favor of it were neither forceful nor specific enough to be effective.

Many writers were demanding that common coinage and common measures be introduced and trade restrictions be abolished.[72] Frequently, however, as these very general demands were repeated, different ideas were associated with them. Arndt, without having economic unification in mind, advocated these measures in order to effect a better political unity.[73] A typical position was that of Lips, who demanded the abolition of internal restrictions, but did not propose any system of an external customs line,[74] so that it

---

[70] Congress of Vienna, protocol for the second conference on the German Confederation, May 26, 1815, *ibid.,* p. 69, No. 31; Joint Austro-Prussian draft of the Acts of Confederation, May 23, 1815, Art. XVII, *ibid.,* p. 322, No. 30: "Die Bundesglieder behalten sich vor, . . . die zweckmäsigen [*sic*] Anordnungen zu treffen."

[71] Acts of the German Confederation, Vienna, June 8, 1815, Art. XIX, *ibid.,* p. 613, No. 41: "Die Bundesglieder behalten sich vor . . . [i]n Berathung zu treten."

[72] Wolff, *op. cit.,* p. 81; Olshausen, *Friedrich List,* p. 13.

[73] *Schriften für und an seine lieben Deutschen* (Leipzig, 1845), II, 90.

[74] [Michael] Alexander Lips, *Der Wiener Congress oder was muss geschehen um Deutschland vor seinem Untergange zu retten* ... (Erlangen, 1814), p. 44.

is difficult to say to what extent such a writer was advocating free trade rather than economic unification.[75]

It was also argued that it would cost too much for the small states to collect tariffs. One writer wanted a European league with free trade, common coinage, and common measures.[76] There were, however, some like Karl Ernst Schmidt who desired a customs line around Germany, abolition of all internal restrictions, and the establishment of an Imperial treasury which was to receive all customs money.[77] While a number of publicists did not touch the question of German import duties, a few were already bitterly opposed to such measures. Haller and Hess, from Hamburg, were especially prominent in this dispute. Both were interested in commerce, and both opposed tariffs as endangering Hamburg's commercial interests. Haller in particular saw the dangers which lay in a policy of artificial protection and prohibition.[78] Hess took liberty as a basic requirement for commerce,[79] and argued that the independence of the Hanse Towns would guarantee free trade and therefore also Germany's prosperity.[80] Both writers represented Hamburg interests, which centered around political independence and free trade.

Among the German periodicals of those years the *Rheinischer Merkur* was the most important. It advocated national unity, and the German Question was discussed extensively in its columns. Since independent newspapers of a definitely political nature at that time were rare in Germany, Görres, obviously in editing the *Rheinischer Merkur,* had to do a considerable amount of pioneering. The paper had many weaknesses which were common during those years, but in perspective it stood above the average publication of that time. Although Görres wrote most of the articles himself, he had important collaborators, and

---

[75] Wolff, *op. cit.,* p. 81.

[76] Mallinckrodt, cited from Heinz August Wirsching, *Der Kampf um die handelspolitische Einigung Europas, eine geschichtliche Darstellung des Gedankens der europäischen Zollunion* (Feuchtwangen: Sommer & Schorr, 1928), p. 4.   [77] Cited from Schmidt, *op. cit.,* p. 214.

[78] Baasch, "Die deutschen wirtschaftlichen Einheitsbestrebungen," *Historische Zeitschrift,* CXXII, 455–57; Blume, *op. cit.,* pp. 22–23.

[79] *Ibid.,* p. 25.   [80] Baasch, *op. cit.,* pp. 457–59.

varying opinions were frequently expressed on the same subject.

Among these contributors, Görres was the first to write on the problem of economic unification.[81] Germany was to be one nation economically. Customs and tolls separating the Germans from each other were to be abolished, so that each region could produce those goods in which it naturally excelled and send them to the other regions. Görres did not want an economic separation which would "create vineyards along the Baltic, grainfields in the Harz Mountains, or sheep farming on the hills along the Rhine." He therefore did not believe that agricultural or industrial enterprises should be created by such artificial means as tariffs. Since he did not apply this doctrine to international economic relations, he made only a limited use of a basic free-trade argument in order to advocate economic nationalism and self-sufficiency. He was not guided as much by economic theory as by his desire for political unity. In addition, he advocated a common system of taxation for Germany.

Some two weeks after the appearance of this article by Görres the *Rheinischer Merkur* contained a pseudonymous contribution which showed a practical interest in Franco-German economic relations.[82] The author wanted financial independence for the Empire, abolition of internal customs lines but also a customs boundary around the Empire, and measures of retaliation against French trade restrictions in order to avoid an unfavorable balance of trade. He also proposed that a national fashion of dress be introduced in Germany in order that no more money might be wasted on French fashions.[83]

Another article warned against the dangers which threatened German industry if it did not take precautions against

---

[81] "Teutschlands Ansprüche," *Rheinischer Merkur*, 1814, No. 76 (June 23), facsimile reprint in Görres, *Gesammelte Schriften*, Vols. VI-XI.

[82] "Germanicus Eremita" [pseudonym], "An Teutschlands Fürsten und Völker," *Rheinischer Merkur*, 1814, No. 82 (July 5), and No. 83 (July 7), *ibid.*

[83] These ideas are similar to ideas already expressed by Jahn and Luden (Treitschke, *Deutsche Geschichte*, II, 390–93; Roscher, *op. cit.*, p. 648).

English competition.[84] The commercial interests of the Hanse Towns were attacked, because they profited by promoting the import of English goods, a complaint to be repeated for many decades. It was also demanded that foreign goods imported through these ports should pay import duties, which raised a problem that was to be settled only after many years.

Protection was also advocated by Benzenberg.[85] He suggested that Germany, through a customs line around her borders, should protect her industries. Thus he wanted Germany to produce her own beet sugar. One should note, however, that he admitted that free trade was the best measure for Europe from a theoretical and cosmopolitan point of view, but as long as England and France kept their customs systems Germany should follow them and have her own national customs system. He realized that high tariffs were regarded as "unjust" and that they promoted smuggling. He therefore favored low tariffs.

Another article that appeared toward the end of 1814 analyzed the beginnings of the controversy between the commercial interests in free trade and the industrial interests in protection, demonstrating to what extent each group promoted its own interests and to what extent the common good.[86] This article also discussed in detail the introduction of a common standard of coinage and measures into Germany.

The articles in the *Rheinischer Merkur* have been discussed at this length because they showed the characteristics of popular opinion in those years. The idea of economic unity developed slowly, but remained a by-product of political unity. The discussions contained a mixture of ideas. Imperial patriotism and eighteenth-century cosmopolitanism

[84] [Anonymous] "Politische und merkantilische Bemerkungen über einige Verhältnisse Teutschlands zum Auslande," *Rheinischer Merkur*, 1814, especially No. 96 (August 2) and No. 97 (August 4), in Görres, *Gesammelte Schriften*, Vols. VI–XI.

[85] B[enzenberg] "Teutschlands Gewerbe und Teutschlands Zölle," *Rheinischer Merkur*, 1814, No. 126 (October 1), *ibid.*

[86] Aurelius B[?], "Mancherley," *Rheinischer Merkur*, 1814, No. 143 (November 4), No. 144 (November 6), No. 146 (November 10), No. 147 (November 12), *ibid.*

stood side by side with the new nationalism and the recent reforms, while future problems like retaliation, protection, free trade, and common economic institutions were already considered by a few.   Occasionally future party lines became discernible, but ideological campaigning was rare. The problems to which the new era had given rise had to be recognized before they could be solved.   It was a difficult process for Germany to realize exactly what her interests were.

The years 1813–15 were filled with fresh hopes and were looked upon by contemporaries as the beginning of another era.   They produced a number of writers with wide perspectives who made a serious attempt to solve the economic and political problems of the period.   The obstacles, however, proved too great.   The decentralizing forces of the old Empire continued in a different form, but with the same vigor.   The lack of practical experience in dealing with a nation-wide political economy was supplemented by the preference the age showed for abstract theories.   The past had not been relegated to its proper place, nor had the new ideas been sufficiently analyzed and absorbed.   These handicaps were not overcome, even by the leaders of the nation.

CHAPTER III

THE IDEA OF GENERAL GERMAN
ECONOMIC UNIFICATION, 1816–20

THE hopes of those German patriots who had been looking forward to national reconstruction were deeply
disappointed by the Vienna settlement. The German
Confederation was set up which had the character of a
permanent alliance of all the German states; but it provided
for neither political nor economic unity. Each state remained sovereign in tariff matters, and no restrictions, such
as maximum tariffs, which had been frequently demanded,
were established.

The foundation of the German Confederation also marked
the end of the era of good will which had existed between
the people and the governments. The new order did not
evoke popular enthusiasm, although many patriots resigned
themselves to these conditions with the hope that the governments would develop the Diet of the Confederation into
an effective institution. Since the cabinets continued to
control national affairs, political leaders began to concen-
trate on local problems. By promising a constitution to each
German state the Acts of Confederation furthered this tendency and even supplied the liberal movement with a program. Within a short time the progressive forces in many
sections of Germany organized themselves as political parties
which fought primarily for liberal institutions in their home
states.

Many of the older leaders of the national resurrection
of 1813–15 withdrew to purely local or private affairs. Only
groups like those under Jahn or like the Burschenschaften at
the universities carried on an open agitation for greater
German unity and for the development of German "na-
tionality."[1] Their approach was dogmatic and emotional,
and their importance lay in the fact that they kept national
sentiment alive among youth, a sentiment which was never

[1] Referring to Jahn's term *Volkstum*.

to be extinguished in student circles and which was to influence the majority of the educated class in a later period. Even between 1815 and 1818 their actual understanding of political realities was very meager. Many of them were unable to overcome their war psychosis and to adjust themselves mentally to problems which the new settlement brought. Jahn, for instance, continued his extreme hatred of the French,[2] and even suggested that whole boundary districts be laid waste in order to eliminate foreign ininfluences.[3] From this quarter one expects no understanding of the political and economic problems of the German nation.

The peace settlement of 1815 had been based on the reactionary philosophy of the restoration, and these principles were to influence the policies of the German governments to an ever-increasing extent. Many cabinets and many courts began to treat with suspicion all those who did not strictly follow the conservative party line. The change was noticeable in Prussia, where a man like Stein was never again entrusted with important tasks. The recently restored governments of Hesse-Kassel and of Hanover adopted from the beginning an ultraconservative policy, completely forgetting the popular forces which had fought to bring them back again.

Once the old powers had been securely reëstablished most German governments hesitated to introduce the constitutions they had promised to every German state. Even when a government granted a constitution, it would rarely adopt at the same time a liberal policy.

By 1816 the first persecutions began. Early in that year Görres' *Rheinischer Merkur* was suppressed by the Prussian government.[4] It was not until 1819–20, however, that a supreme effort was made by the reactionary governments to stamp out all liberal and national movements.

The alliance between the cabinets and the popular movements under whose auspices the Wars of Liberation had

---

[2] Carl [Philipp] Euler, *Friedrich Ludwig Jahn, sein Leben und Wirken* (Stuttgart: Krabbe, 1881), pp. 483–84.   [3] *Ibid.*, pp. 488–89.

[4] Görres, *Rheinischer Merkur*, 1816, announcement following No. 357 (January 10); reprint in Görres, *Gesammelte Schriften*, Vols. VI–XI.

been fought was dissolved with the advent of peace, and within a few years the former allies became bitter enemies. These years of increasing animosity between the parties (1815–19) constituted a complete break with the preceding era of good will. The best political talents were absorbed by local problems, and none of the mature leaders continued to develop his opinions on German unity in public.

While political unification was thus wished for by many and spoken of by only a few enthusiasts, force of circumstances made economic unification one of the major questions of the period. Prior to 1815 economic unification had been considered a corollary of political unification. After 1815 it was asked for primarily as a necessity. A postwar depression aroused many peaceful citizens to demand action from their governments. When, however, conditions grew worse in 1819, business organized itself and demanded general German economic unification. It was able to put enough pressure on the cabinets to make them consider this measure seriously, but the political structure of Germany rendered it impossible to introduce general economic unification. As soon as this was realized in 1820, the plan was abandoned for good. Nevertheless, the history of this idea is important for the understanding of the origin of the Zollverein and will be traced in detail in the subsequent sections.

THE FORMATIVE YEARS, 1816–18

THE period following the Napoleonic wars was one of transition and readjustment. The years from 1816 to 1818 represented a time of orientation with regard to German economic problems. It was also distinguished by disunity of thought among its publicists. That is to say, although many valuable ideas and suggestions on economic unification can be found in the writings of those days, there was no publicist who was able to put theory and reality together in order to offer a general solution in a systematic and coherent way. None of the issues was so formulated as to present clear-cut party lines, and most writers gave a hopeless mixture of major and minor points, remaining vague on many matters because they lacked realistic concepts.

The Napoleonic era and the Congress of Vienna had been

responsible for numerous reforms in Germany. Nevertheless, many medieval and early modern institutions, practices, and ideas persisted beyond 1815. Although the various states were to be sovereign, some of them continued to be limited in their full control. Postal matters were administered in a number of the smaller states by neighboring governments or by the house of Thurn and Taxis. While these interstate relations had lost their feudal content and had become pragmatic, the constitutional practices of several German states preserved a great number of older elements intact. Many members of the German Confederation were not unified and centralized, but consisted of various subdivisions which were so autonomous that they resembled states within the state. In several sections of Germany, the economic dependence of whole agricultural classes, the administration of rural districts, and the representation by estates remained essentially feudal. The absolutism of the preceding century still flourished in many of the smaller states. Thus the financial administration was frequently conducted with no public accounting, and occasionally the taxpayer was not even informed about the existing rates.[5]

The economic life of the nation was still at the stage of early capitalism. Germany was primarily an agricultural country, and her industry had not developed to any point of importance. Contemporaries thought in terms of cities when they speculated about economic progress, and they hoped that the flow of goods on the main highways would bring prosperity. They did so because they still remembered the Hanseatic League and the days when the trans-Alpine trade flourished. Moreover, the cities often retained many of their trading and manufacturing monopolies, and the large fairs remained as living symbols of their economic strength.

Germany's backward economic system had suffered during the wars of the Napoleonic era, but it was to receive more severe blows with the peace that followed it. There were all those difficulties which arose through the demobilization and through the change to peaceful conditions. The former soldier had to find his place in the economic system; trade

---

[5] Brinkmann, *Die preussische Handelspolitik*, p. 121.

and production had to adjust themselves to new demands; commerce had to seek new connections, and reorganization and reconstruction were on their way all over the country.

The various customs lines in Germany were as much of an obstacle to German trade as to foreign competition. Most states were not able to enforce their customs laws owing to the size and shape of their territories, and hence smuggling became a predominant occupation in many regions. Furthermore, the overthrow of Napoleon had brought about the fall of his Continental System, and with it went the protection many newly developed industries had enjoyed from British competition. England, finally seeing that her old continental markets were reopened, flooded German states with the goods she had stored up for a long time. Since the various German tariff barriers, so far as they existed, were ineffective and since the British sold at low prices, German production fell off considerably. Moreover, all the major European countries, with the exception of Prussia, continued their old policies of prohibition and protection or soon set up a system of high tariffs. Germany's new western frontier became almost instantly a new trade barrier, and exports met increasing difficulties.

This commercial decline was aggravated by a famine during the winter of 1816-17. It had rained for months in 1816, and the whole harvest was destroyed in many parts of Germany. In addition, technical facilities to relieve the situation were poor. The roads were in bad condition, the governments could not agree on a common action, many of them, especially in South Germany, prohibited all exports of foodstuffs, and there was no strong credit system capable of bringing relief.[6]

Such distressing conditions slowly drove the people and the governments to seek new means of remedying the situation. The years 1816–18 constituted a period of orientation in a general way and of experimentation on a relatively small scale. The impact of the realities of the crisis with the theories and sentiments which dominated this age was overwhelming. The strain which this conflict exercised on the

---

[6] Treitschke, *Deutsche Geschichte*, II, 172–73.

contemporary mind was well reflected in the weird pattern of ideas and plans during this formative period of 1816–18.

Economic thought was still dominated by Adam Smith's program of free trade, and many authors paid homage to his ideas. The extreme paradox was presented by a Bavarian customs official who proved in a thorough discussion that any tariff was detrimental.[7] Some publicists supported free trade because they were convinced of the rational economic basis of this theory. There were, however, others who wanted free trade to be established as a fundamental right similar to the right of choosing one's residence, which the Acts of Confederation granted.[8] Free trade was also demanded as a partial fulfillment of the obligations incurred by the powers of the Holy Alliance.[9] Another author advocated free trade for its valuable effects on religion; he expected that with free trade confessional differences would disappear.[10] Although this type of sentiment prevailed among many writers, the possibilities of free trade were clearly understood by some. It was pointed out that universal free trade was possible only under a world government or under a "universal despotism," as it was put.[11]

The greatest difficulty for the free traders arose out of the fact that the only way Germany could be assisted against foreign competition was by some degree of protection, especially since protection had averted the worst in these other countries. This dilemma was sidetracked by many publicists who asserted that free trade was to remain the final goal, but that it was to be achieved by retortion, that is to say, they

---

[7] Hans Caspar Brunner, *Was sind Maut- und Zoll-Anstalten der National-wohlfahrt und dem Staatsinteresse?* (Nürnberg, 1816), vii + 136.

[8] [Anonymous] "Deutsche Staatssachen, Vorschläge, Deutschlands künftigen Handel betreffend," *Allgemeiner Anzeiger der Deutschen*, 1815, No. 209, quoted from List, *Schriften/Reden/Briefe*, I, Part II, 983.

[9] [Anonymous] "Meinungen verschiedener Völker über den gegenwärtig bedrängten Zustand des Kunstfleisses und Handels, und Vorschläge ihm abzuhelfen," *Europäische Annalen*, 1817, No. 8, p. 211.

[10] Oncken and Saemisch, I, 303.

[11] Böttiger, in *Allgemeine Zeitung Augsburg* of October 21, 1816, quoted from Hans Friedrich Müller, *Die Berichterstattung der Allgemeinen Zeitung Augsburg über Fragen der deutschen Wirtschaft 1815–1840* (Doctor's dissertation, München, 1934), p. 21. For Adam Smith's influence in Germany see Hasek, *The Introduction of Adam Smith's Doctrines into Germany*.

wanted Germany to force the other nations through economic reprisals to give up their trade barriers.[12]   Some free
traders, however, were not willing to allow any compromise,
and one went so far as to say that manufacturers who were
unable to compete were bad citizens and should either "dig
ditches" or emigrate.[13]   This opinion was even then regarded
as carrying a principle too far and was bitterly resented.[14]
Further, the claim that Germany was gaining by buying at
such low prices from the British was opposed by those who
said that there was no exchange of goods and that thus
money was drawn out of Germany.[15]

The number of writers who had remedies to propose
was much larger.   Their suggestions ranged from minor reforms in the local markets to vague schemes for the whole
of Germany.   Adam Müller, then in the Austrian consular
service, suggested that the public auction of British goods
should be prohibited, a suggestion which was followed in
some of the major commercial centers.[16]   It should be noted
here that Müller was in favor of some action to overcome the
crisis, although at the same time he discouraged the formation of a general association of business men.   Ernst Weber
had conceived this idea, but had asked the advice of Müller,
who told him that German business men could only act together while attending a fair and that a permanent organization crossing state lines would be impossible.[17]   At the same
time when Weber's attempt to unite German business men
into a nation-wide organization failed, local movements

---

[12] [Anonymous] "Entwurf einer Rede die von einem der deutschen
Gesandten am Bundestage zu Frankfurt am Main bey Wiedereröffnung der
Sitzungen desselben am 3. November 1817 gehalten werden sollte," *Euro-
päische Annalen,* 1818, No. 3, p. 340.

[13] "... sie möchten zum *Spaten greifen,* oder *auswandern...,*" *Nürn-
berger Handlungs-Zeitung,* No. 250, quoted through [Anonymous] "Meinungen...," *Europäische Annalen,* 1817, No. 8, p. 206.   The italics in the
quotation are substituted for the spacing of letters in the original.

[14] *Loc. cit.*   [15] *Ibid.,* p. 205.

[16] Memorandum by Adam Müller, December 6, 1819, Oncken and
Saemisch, I, 359, No. 182.

[17] *Ibid.,* pp. 359–60; [Anonymous] "Meinungen...," *Europäische Annalen,* 1817, No. 8, p. 204; Olshausen, *Friedrich List,* 14; Johannes Falke,
Die Geschichte des deutschen Zollwesens (Leipzig, 1869), p. 357; Wilhelm
Roscher, "Zur Gründungsgeschichte des deutschen Zollvereins," *Deutschland,* 1870, p. 147.   It remains doubtful, however, to what extent Müller's
influence was decisive.   Another attempt to found a *Verein* was made in
1817 (Müller, *op. cit.,* p. 121; Weber, *Der deutsche Zollverein,* p. 4).

against foreign goods sprang up in various parts of Germany. Clubs were organized whose members pledged themselves not to buy any foreign goods. Those who signed up were mostly business men. Although these clubs were frequently organized spontaneously, they were unable to influence public opinion so as to create a popular movement and to bring about an effective boycott.[18]

In addition to forming local unions, people endeavored to improve conditions by sending petitions to the government. Although bitter necessity compelled many to resort to this action, no attempt was made to put organized pressure on the governments, nor was more than a special interest, either local or regional, represented. The governments were only too often expected to develop the overall policy as well as to determine the administrative details which were to remedy the petitioner's grievances. There was a certain enthusiasm for Germany's economic welfare, but not enough persistency to carry out plans. It does not seem to have required much effort on Adam Müller's part to discourage Ernst Weber. Petitions and formation of local clubs were the only direct actions undertaken by the business men of those years. Furthermore public opinion on the problem also lacked force and unity, but was nevertheless rich in sentiment and speculation. Perhaps no depression was ever commemorated by its victims in a more poetical form or in more elegant language than the decline of German industry after the Napoleonic wars. A poem which called on the manufacturers to drape their machines with mourning bears the palm as a typical outgrowth of the prevailing sentiment.[19] There was hardly a writer who was not guided by some sentiment of this kind, and it is often difficult to distinguish between the various schools of thought, since all used similar expressions.

Although little action was undertaken or even visualized,

[18] Ritthaler, in Oncken and Saemisch, I, 301; [Anonymous] "Meinungen...," *Europäische Annalen*, 1817, No. 8, pp. 212–17; F[riedrich Willibald Ferdinand] v[on] Cölln, "Keine Accise mehr?! [*sic*]" reprinted from *Freimüthige Blätter*, XIII (1816), 514–16; Müller, *op. cit.*, pp. 23–25.
[19] "Umhängt mit Flor..." Version I, [A. Storck] *Über das Verhältnis der freien Hansestädte zum Handel Deutschlands* (Bremen, 1821), p. 12; Version II, Philipp Schnell, *Das Frankfurter Handwerk von 1816–1848, ein Beitrag zur Wirtschaftsgeschichte* (Doctor's dissertation, Frankfurt am Main, 1933), p. 9, n. 4.

many suggestions were made. These schemes, which were designed for the betterment of the economic situation, were more speculative than systematic in their approach, and more wishful than programmatic in their intentions. However much these ideas lacked unity, the individual suggestions were often of value. Not all of them were original, but many undoubtedly influenced the later development, if only by keeping contemporaries conscious of the issue. Some of the original ideas were forgotten and remained without influence.

Most plans provided for the abolition of internal German customs lines or at least proposed their modification. A scheme of this type was not always and necessarily tied to the idea of a common customs line around Germany. There were some, therefore, who seem to have wanted only this internal free trade.[20] Others advocated that a system of retortion and reprisals be set up against those foreign states which did not abolish their restrictions on German goods,[21] but they usually failed to point out what form these reprisals should take, and it can therefore be questioned to what extent these writers had any conception of how a customs system functioned. Most of those publicists who were more specific in their proposals expected that the Diet of the Confederation would be the agency to effect the economic unification of Germany and the establishment of a common customs system.[22]

It should be noted, however, that the ability of the Diet to bring about such reforms was already questioned. Two

---

[20] E.g., [Friedrich List] "Kritik des Verfassungs-Entwurfs der Württembergischen Ständeversammlung mit besonderer Rücksicht auf Herstellung der bürgerlichen Freiheit in den Gemeinden und Ober-Ämtern," *Württembergisches Archiv*, 1817, quoted through List, *op. cit.*, I, Part I, 242.

[21] [Anonymous] "Entwurf . . . ," *Europäische Annalen*, 1818, No. 3, p. 340.

[22] [Anonymous] "Teutschlands Forderungen an den ersten teutschen Bundestag, Handlung und Schifffahrt betreffend," *Württembergisches Archiv*, quoted through Friedrich Lenz, *Friedrich List, Der Mann und das Werk* (München: R. Oldenbourg, 1936), p. 63; Johann Heinrich Moritz Poppe, *Deutschland auf der höchst möglichen Stufe seines Kunstfleisses und seiner Industrie überhaupt. Vorschläge, Wünsche und Hoffnungen zur Vermehrung des deutschen Wohlstandes* (Frankfurt am Main, 1816), p. 38; Petition of Rhenish industrialists to Friedrich Wilhelm III, Rheydt, April 27, 1818, Oncken and Saemisch, I, 69–71, No. 13.

articles tried to show how Germany could achieve economic unification in such a way that the Diet would not be in absolute control. One proposed that "German commerce should be separated from the governments" and welded into a unity. A chamber of commerce was to be in charge of German trade and was to have the right to pass laws, that were to be executed by the Diet, which, in turn, was to appoint a supreme commercial court.[23] Although this idea lacked practicality and clarity, its significance lay in the fact that it might be interpreted as an early understanding of how political factors constantly interfered with commercial interests and of how the difficulties might have been solved through a separate treatment of the commercial problems.

The other article wanted customs only as reprisals and did not seem to have seen the difficulties which would arise out of an attempt to have the Diet settle the matter alone, but was more concerned with the fact that not all German states bordered on foreign countries. These states, as this anonymous writer felt, would be put in a disadvantageous position if all internal tariffs were abolished and if reprisals against foreign trade were enforced along the boundary of the Confederation. For this reason, he argued, the "German customs houses were to be common institutions, like the Central Commission in charge of the Rhine octroi."[24] This argumentation illuminated one point: that for those who used them terms like "reprisals" and "retortion" and phrases like "retaining a customs line along the boundaries of the Confederation" were by no means always identical in meaning with a unified Confederate customs system. The article was, however, not clear about the way the system suggested here was to operate in detail. Should the whole administration be centralized and be placed in the hands of a Confederate commission? Or should only the central office be in common, the local offices being administered by state authorities who were to act as agents of the central commission?

---

[23] *Allgemeiner Anzeiger der Deutschen* of August 12 and 14, 1815, quoted through Borckenhagen, *National- und handelspolitische Bestrebungen,* p. 31.

[24] [Anonymous] "Teutschlands Forderungen...," *Württembergisches Archiv,* quoted through List, *op. cit.,* I, Part II, 983–84.

The latter arrangement was followed by the Central Commission of the Rhine, which was specifically mentioned, and it was the system of separate state administrations which eventually became an outstanding feature of the Zollverein.

Further aspects of an active commercial policy were discussed in those years. Common standards for measures and coinage were demanded,[25] and the construction of interstate highways and canals was proposed.[26] Furthermore, attention was given to overseas shipping; a German fleet was demanded especially for protection against the Barbary States;[27] even a German flag was proposed.[28] An Anglo-German treaty of navigation was also suggested, in order to put German shipping on equal terms with British shipping. It was recognized that Germany would have to bargain collectively with Great Britain if it was to break down British trade restrictions.[29]

These maritime aspirations led in 1819 to the foundation of the Antipiratical League in Hamburg,[30] and later to the establishment of an export company, the *Rheinisch-Westindische Companie*.[31]

Such attempts as these, which were made to better economic conditions in Germany, contained definitely national elements. The reforms proposed were designed to improve conditions all over Germany and not just in one particular region. In many circles emotions ran high against foreign competition, and against the practices and policies of foreign traders. This national movement did not merely continue that of the Wars of Liberation. It was not so specifically anti-French as it was anti-British; nor did it preach an exclusive nationalism, but it retained many international elements, especially since free trade was the fundamental doctrine of most publicists. Its theoretical aim was equality and coöperation with other nations. In economic affairs it

---

[25] [Anonymous] "Entwurf ...," *Europäische Annalen*, 1818, No. 3, p. 342; [German Confederation] *Protokolle der deutschen Bundes-Versammlung* (Frankfurt am Main, 1818), IV, 67, "Eingabe" No. 328.

[26] [Anonymous] "Entwurf ...," *Europäische Annalen*, 1818, No. 3, p. 342.   [27] *Ibid.*, p. 341; Treitschke, *op. cit.*, II, 175.

[28] Baasch, "Die deutschen wirtschaftlichen Einheitsbestrebungen," *Historische Zeitschrift*, CXXII, 461–62.

[29] *Loc. cit.*   [30] *Ibid.*, pp. 468–70.

[31] List, *op. cit.*, I, Part II, 1054–55; Olshausen, *op. cit.*, p. 169.

showed more practical sense. While Jahn and his followers
had proposed to introduce a German fashion, this went further by demanding that German material be used for German clothes.[32]

In judging political matters, however, many mistakes
were made. The character of the Confederation especially
was not yet correctly estimated. One writer argued that,
after the political unification had been achieved, economic
unification was due.[33] It was also denied that the Diet
would help German commerce, since its members owned
large estates and would therefore represent the landed interest.[34] Others saw more realistically the difficulties which
were founded on the rivalry of the various states.[35]

Although national sentiments were predominant, some
authors were of an essentially different opinion. There were
outright defenders of the English commercial policy.[36]
Others were opposed to German economic unification because it would be unnecessary for Germany's welfare and
because it would only create a superficial or fictitious unity.[37]
There were those who predicted revolution,[38] and similar
menacing thoughts against the existing régime were expressed. The particular charge was made that the Napoleonic System had taken better care of material interests,[39] and
one patriotic writer went so far as to interpret the whole

---

[32] Cölln, *op. cit.*, pp. 514–15; Müller, *op. cit.*, pp. 24–25; Serviere,
*Versuch einer Beantwortung der Frage: Wie können die Deutschen sich vom
Joch des englischen Küstenmonopols befreien?* (Frankfurt a. M., 1817),
quoted through Baasch, *op. cit.*, p. 461. For the differences between Jahn
and Cölln see Treitschke, *op. cit.*, II, 394.

[33] Poppe, *op. cit.*, p. 38.

[34] [Anonymous] "Meinungen . . . ," *Europäische Annalen,* 1817, No. 8,
pp. 204, 211–12.

[35] [Anonymous] "Über Kurzsichtigkeit in vaterländischen Angelegenheiten," *ibid.* 1818, No. 5, p. 271.

[36] [Anonymous] "Meinungen . . . ," *ibid.* 1817, No. 8, p. 205.

[37] [Anonymous] "Über Englands Reichtum und Deutschlands Wohlstand
in Beziehung auf staatswirtschaftliche Gesetzgebung," *ibid.* 1816, No. 7,
pp. 28–29.

[38] [Anonymous] "Meinungen . . . ," *ibid.* 1817, No. 8, p. 219.

[39] [Anonymous] *Unterthänigste Vorstellung, der Bundes-Versammlung zu
Frankfurt, von Deutschlands Fabrikanten und sämmtlichen Arbeitern, dem
engl. Handelssystem Einhalt zu thun, zutrauungsvoll zugeeignet,* reprinted
from *Stafette* ("Germania, im Sommer 1817"), 15 pp. I doubt very much
that this petition was ever sponsored by any larger group. I could find no
record showing that it was ever filed with the Diet.

problem as the old struggle between England's colonial system and continental interests.[40]

The Diet, however, attempted in those years to deal with the situation, but did it so inadequately that the saying *Dum Romae deliberant, perit Saguntum* was applied to it.[41] Not until the spring of 1817 did the Diet of the Confederation take cognizance of the situation[42] and start negotiations for lifting the prohibitions on foodstuffs the trade of which the governments had restricted in order to combat the shortage created by the bad harvest. The committee which was appointed by the Diet to consider this question[43] suggested that the prohibitions put on interstate trade in foodstuffs should be abolished. Export tariffs, however, were to remain, and transit tariffs should not be excessive; restrictions on foreign trade were to be regulated later by common agreement. Although the whole proposal was intended to become a general provision, it allowed retortion against German states which would "prefer to continue the restrictions."[44] The negotiations were as a whole kept within the scope of these ideas,[45] except for Bavaria's proposal to include also those provinces of member states which lay outside the Confederation.[46] Bavaria touched on a very difficult problem, although

---

[40] [Anonymous] "Entwurf ...," *Europäische Annalen*, 1818, No. 3, pp. 352–53.

[41] [Anonymous] "Meinungen ...," *ibid.* 1817, No. 8, pp. 211–12, n. It is here accredited to a contemporary German statesman.

[42] Buol had already remarked on Article XIX at the session of the Diet on November 11, 1816. What he meant when he said that Article XIX would alienate the German states seems to need further clarification. Cf. Treitschke, *op. cit.*, II, 146–47.

[43] Protocol, session of May 19, 1817, [German Confederation] *op. cit.*, III, 45–49, No. 180.

[44] Protocol, session of June 2, 1817, Oncken and Saemisch, I, 315–16, No. 162.

[45] Protocols, sessions of June 6, 30, July 3, 10, 14, 1817, [German Confederation] *op. cit.*, III, 310–13, 333–38, 356, 394–97, 431–33, Nos. 269, 278, 293, 319, 337.

[46] Treitschke believes that Bavaria's intention was to defeat (*vereiteln*) the negotiations (*op. cit.*, II, 173), while Weber claims that Bavaria only wanted to secure the import of Hungarian grain (*op. cit.*, p. 7). Treitschke gives the impression that Bavaria had opposed a concerted diplomatic action of the other members. There was, however, no unity among the other states. (Blume, *Hamburg*, pp. 30–31; Ludwig Karl [James] Aegidi, *Aus der Vorzeit des Zollvereins. Beitrag zur deutschen Geschichte* [Hamburg: Noyes & Geisler, 1865], p. 14; Metternich to Franz I, Wien, May 13, 1820, Olshausen, *op. cit.*, pp. 291–2, No. 126.)

at that time she was probably not aware of its ramifications. The negotiations dragged into the middle of July, when the prospect of a good harvest made emergency measures unnecessary and the matter was put aside for the time being.[47]

The Diet of the Confederation attempted to improve the situation by abolishing the symptoms, in this case the temporary export restrictions, but it failed to penetrate to the causes. It did not think of economic unification.

LIST'S AGITATION, 1819-20

THE negotiations at the Diet of the Confederation had been discontinued before they led to any result whatsoever. By the spring of 1819 public opinion forced the Diet to reconsider Article XIX of the Acts of Confederation. Economic conditions had not improved, and the Prussian law of May 26, 1818, which introduced a system of boundary customs into Prussia had made matters worse for the smaller states. It was in such distressing circumstances that the nation turned for the last time to the Diet for a remedy for its economic grievances. Never before had the need for economic unification been so generally recognized.

There had been many complaints in Germany up to that time of the intolerable economic conditions, but no attempts had been made to unite public opinion on a definite program of reform and thus exert pressure on the governments. A change set in at the Frankfurt Fair in 1819, when Friedrich List and a number of German business men founded the German Commercial and Industrial League,[48] which set as its aim the economic unification of Germany. Its program demanded the abolition of internal German customs lines and the erection of boundary customs with protective tariffs for the Confederation. Its ultimate aim was European free trade, which was to be achieved through retortions. This program was submitted to the Diet and to the various governments by List and his followers through petitions, memoranda, and personal interviews. They set up a network of correspondents all over Germany, printed pamphlets, and published their own periodical. No other private organiza-

---

[47] Protocol, session of July 14, 1817, [German Confederation] *op. cit.*, III, 431–33, No. 337.

[48] *Deutscher Handels- und Gewerbsverein.* This organization will hereafter be referred to as League.

tion in Germany was so active in propagating its ideas as the
League of business men. List himself wrote numerous petitions and articles for the good of the cause, stressing in
particular the economic foundations of his proposals. It
was undoubtedly due to his influence that the governments
were stirred out of their lethargy and began to discuss the
problem seriously.

Although the general program of the League can be
easily understood, List's ultimate aims and deeper reasons are
difficult to fathom. This is partly due to the fact that he
often distorted his ideas and employed sophisms in order
to make his proposals more agreeable for one government
or the other.[49] For these reasons he often hid his patriotic
motives, although it seems certain that he was mainly inspired by a desire for national unity.[50] He had, however, no
clear conception of the geographical extent of the economic
unification he was proposing or of the details of its organization. On the one hand he wanted the Diet to create this
economic unification; on the other hand he had in mind
the inclusion of Switzerland, which was not under the jurisdiction of the Confederation.[51]

When it became obvious that the Diet was not capable
of setting up a general customs system, List modified his plan
by suggesting the farming out of customs duties to a private
company.[52] A Confederate commerce commission, appointed by the Diet, was to supervise the company. The
suggestion has been severely criticized by contemporary as
well as by modern authorities.[53] It should be said that the
idea of farming out public institutions was not yet entirely

---

[49] Perhaps the best example of this type is List to League committee,
Nürnberg, June 12, 1819, List. op. cit., I, Part II, 496–504, No. 18.

[50] Cf. List and League to Diet of Confederation, Frankfurt, April 14,
1819, List, op. cit., I, Part II, 492, No. 17; List's memorandum, Wien, February 15, 1820, ibid., p. 543, No. 25.

[51] Basel Chamber of Commerce to Commercial Directory of Schaffhausen,
Basel, December 23, 1819, Olshausen, op. cit., pp. 270–71, No. 72; Aargau
Commercial Council to Schaffhausen Commercial Directory, Aarau, Decem-
ber 27, 1819, ibid., pp. 271–72, No. 73; ibid., pp. 51–57.

[52] Confidential report of League representatives about their Berlin mission [November–December, 1819], ibid., p. 265, No. 64; List's memorandum,
Wien, February 15, 1820, List, op. cit., I, Part II, 546–47, No. 25.

[53] Ibid., p. 1002; Olshausen, op. cit., pp. 129–30.

antiquated,[54] and List's proposal should be interpreted as indicating that he realized that political circumstances prevented the Diet from administering the customs itself and that he was trying to find some other general solution on a lower level than that of the Confederation. The weakness of his plan is apparent; but was there a better one?

Since the final decision concerning all these matters lay with the various state governments rather than with the Diet, List and other representatives of the League tried to induce these governments to support their plans. The methods employed for this end are open to many criticisms. The real feelings of the petitioners were often difficult to grasp because of their sophistic argumentation, and therefore the seriousness both of the proposals and of the authors become questionable. Such difficulties arise at once in the understanding of the first petition to the Diet. Here List condemned the new Prussian customs system as most detrimental to German trade, and on the same page praised it as a step towards "complete free trade."[55] This same arbitrary interpretation of Prussia's intentions can be found in a petition to Friedrich Wilhelm III which claims that the idea of a general commercial system was the basis for her new customs law.[56] List, moreover, appealed in this petition to the "German spirit" of the Prussian monarch.[57]

In dealing with Austria, however, List carefully avoided terms which might be interpreted as revolutionary. He quoted official declarations made by Austria in the Diet and thus stressed a modified Imperial patriotism.[58] The most peculiar parts of these petitions submitted by the League

---

[54] [Johann Ludwig] Klüber, *Das Postwesen in Teutschland, wie es war, ist, und seyn könnte* (Erlangen, 1811), pp. 195–207; *Köhler, Problematisches zu Friedrich List,* p. 96; Köhler claims List got the idea from a Belgian precedent; Gustav Fischer, "Über das Wesen und die Bedeutung eines Zollvereins," *Jahrbücher für Nationalökonomie und Statistik,* II (1864), 320, n. 6; Fischer mentions that privately owned customs existed in Germany after 1815; List, *op. cit.,* I, Part II, 1002–3.

[55] List and League to Diet of Confederation, Frankfurt, April 14, 1819, *ibid.,* pp. 494–95, No. 17.

[56] Dated, November, 1819, *ibid.,* p. 509, No. 20; cf. List to Hardenberg, Karlsruhe, August 15, 1819, *ibid.,* VIII, 147, No. 59.

[57] "Sinn," *ibid.,* I, Part II, 511, No. 20.

[58] List to Franz I [Wien], January 30, 1820, *ibid.,* pp. 520–21, No. 22.

to Franz I were the passages in which extraordinary privileges were offered to Austria, privileges which would have
left Austria almost independent in customs matters and
which would have been incompatible with any general system of German economic unification.   According to the first
petition of January 30, 1820, those parts of the Austrian
monarchy which did not belong to the Confederation, especially Hungary, were to be excluded from the proposed common customs system.   List, however, expressly conceded to
the Austrian emperor the right to regulate all tariffs with
Hungary, in order to further the importation of Hungarian
wines and tobacco into Germany, where they would find no
obstacle after the abolition of all internal tariffs.[59]   Another
concession was made in the petition of March 2, 1820.   Austria was to retain her customs system, along with the proposed Confederate system, until she was sure that the new
system was satisfactory.   In this transitory period, however,
the Austrians were to tax only non-German goods,[60] but in
his next petition List proposed that this temporary Austrian
line should also be used for protecting Austrian industry
against the importation of certain goods made in the rest of
Germany.[61]   He said at the time that he was not proposing a new system, but that he wanted "the extension of the
Austrian mercantile system over the whole of Germany."[62]
It is not difficult to see the inconsistencies of these proposals
with the general program of the League, inconsistencies
which can be only partially explained as being desperate
measures to save a lost cause.

This last argument cannot be used to explain why so
early as the spring and summer of 1819 List and the League
were trying to win the support of the South German governments by describing the League as anti-Austrian and anti-
Prussian.   Bavaria and Württemberg were asked to form a
separate "union against customs" in order to force Prussia
and Austria to give up their hostile systems and establish
free trade.[63]   Although List's ultimate aim remained to effect

[59] Ibid., p. 518.   [60] Ibid., p. 522, No. 23.
[61] Dated Wien, April 20, 1820, ibid., p. 524, No. 24.
[62] Ibid., p. 523.
[63] List to Wilhelm I, Stuttgart, April 29, 1819, ibid., VIII, 132, No. 46;
Schnell to Max I, quoted by Doeberl, Bayern und die wirtschaftliche Einig-

a solution for the whole of Germany, the advocacy of a separate union within Germany might have been very detrimental to the cause of general German economic unification. Such an idea poured oil on the fire lit by all those who wanted the complete independence of the medium and smaller states preserved. The fact that later on the Zollverein was actually founded through separate negotiations did not give this idea a different connotation.[64]

Apparently, List and his followers had really an unfriendly attitude toward Austria and Prussia. In 1817 he had already declared that the king of Prussia and the emperor of Austria represented foreign interests in Germany, since they controlled possessions outside the Confederation.[65] What was the reason for List's antagonism toward the two leading German powers? Was it the fact that they controlled non-Germanic peoples? That might have been of some influence; but List wanted to include Switzerland, which was not entirely Germanic either, nor was it German in a political sense. Was List opposed to Austria and Prussia on account of their absolutism? This attitude might have influenced him, although it remains doubtful whether he would ever have preferred local liberal institutions to national unity. List, however, did not advocate trialism, yet he represented interests which were closely connected with South and Central Germany. The League was primarily organized in these regions, and the interests of these districts received a special consideration from him.[66] But this is only a partial explanation, since he was not a mere agent of vested interests. In 1819 he might have been called a South German nationalist, a position which should be distinguished from trialism. He felt for the whole of Germany, but he retained and intermixed with this feeling a consciousness of his regional background.

---

ung, pp. 13–14; List to Wilhelm I, early July, 1819, List, *op. cit.*, I, Part II, 514, No. 21; smaller committee of the League to List, Nürnberg, September 5, 1819, Olshausen, *op. cit.*, p. 250, No. 39.

[64] For a different view cf. *ibid.*, p. 83.

[65] [List] "Kritik des Verfassungs-Entwurfs . . . ," *Württembergisches Archiv*, quoted from List, *op. cit.*, I, Part I, 242.

[66] Cf. Olshausen, *op. cit.*, pp. 345–50, who gives the geographical distribution of the correspondents appointed by the League.

Another difficulty presents itself when the various statements made by List and his followers on the problem of free trade versus protection are examined. Some aspects of this problem have already been touched upon in pointing out how List advocated on the one hand a union against customs and on the other the introduction of a mercantile system into Germany. The political aspect of this problem has been shown. There remains the economic side and, specifically, the question: To what extent were List and the League pleading the cause of commercial interests and in what degree did they represent industry? In dealing with this problem it must first be noted that the process of modern capitalistic specialization had not developed in Germany so far as to separate banking, trade, and industry clearly from each other. It was common for a manufacturer to market his own products and for a well-established business man to be a trader, manufacturer, and banker at the same time.[67] Merchants, with the exception of importers, were therefore as a rule vitally interested in the welfare of local production. The members of List's League belonged to this class.[68] In the course of its first year the League became more and more outspoken in demanding protection for industry. It should be understood, however, that it never altered its program of ultimate world-wide free trade, which was to be enforced through retortion.[69] But what can be observed is a change in emphasis. During all the spring and summer of 1819 the idea of free trade or commercial liberty was stressed,[70] while with the beginning of the fall of 1819 and during all

---

[67] Werner Sombart, *Die deutsche Volkswirtschaft im neunzehnten Jahrhundert und im Anfang des 20.* [sic] *Jahrhunderts* (5th ed.; Berlin: Georg Bondi, 1921), pp. 202–08; Olshausen, *op. cit.*, pp. 340–50.   [68] *Loc. cit.*

[69] List's memorandum, Wien, February, 1820, List, *op. cit.*, I, Part II, 539, No. 25; List, Inwiefern ist der Grundbesitzer und also vorzüglich der grossbegüterte Adel bei einem Prohibitivsystem interessiert? MS [May, 1820?], *ibid.*, pp. 586–87, No. 33.

[70] List to Wilhelm I, Stuttgart, May 29, 1819, *ibid.*, VIII, 132, No. 46: "auf völlige Handelsfreiheit zu dringen"; List to Wilhelm I, early July, 1819, *ibid.*, I, Part II, 514, No. 21: "die Sache der Handelsfreiheit"; this passage was used again, with minor changes, by Schnell and Weber in their petition to the Grand Duke of Hesse-Darmstadt, Darmstadt, July 18, 1819, Olshausen, *op. cit.*, p. 242, No. 32; Georg of Mecklenburg to League, Neustrehlitz, August 20, 1819, *ibid.*, p. 245, No. 35.

the following winter the emphasis was placed on industrial interests and protection. The more general term "manufacturing"[71] gave way to such expressions as "industry" or "factories." Special care was taken to get in contact with industrialists, and the welfare of industry always received preferential attention in the discussions.[72] During his stay in Vienna List himself became interested in industrial exhibitions as a measure of helping German manufacturers.[73] For the same reason he advocated a German patent law.[74] This trend of giving increasing consideration to industrial interests should not be taken as a sign that in 1819–20 Germany was a predominantly industrial nation in the modern sense. It shows, however, the intimate connection which existed between commerce and industry and how depressed both were through the crisis. The longer this depression lasted the greater was the interest concentrated on immediate measures of relief, which in this case was afforded by protection. Protection had also the advantage of being more obvious, since the loss on the home market through foreign competition was one of the chief complaints made by the manufacturers. It was a different task to find foreign markets for agricultural products. Moreover, the List of 1819-20 had not yet developed his system of economic theories. He had

---

[71] *Gewerbe.*

[72] List to Friedrich Wilhelm III, November 1819, List, *op. cit.*, I, Part II, 508–12, No. 20, a petition stressing industrial needs; List to Franz I, Wien, January 30, 1820, *ibid.*, pp. 516–19, No. 22, a petition dealing with possible advantages for Austria's industries; List's second calling list for Vienna, 1820, Olshausen, *op. cit.*, pp. 282–83, No. 187, a list containing more factory owners than traders; List's memorandum, Wien, February 15, 1820, List, *op. cit.*, I, Part II, 545, No. 25: "wo es die deutsche Industrie vom Tode zu retten gilt" (the original passage is spaced); List to Metternich, Wien, February 18, 1820, *ibid.*, pp. 549–50, No. 26; List denied here that trade and industry are incompatible with each other, but distinguished between trade which promotes national industry and trade which destroys it; List to Metternich, Wien, March 9, 1820, *ibid.*, p. 553, No. 27: "in der *Angelegenheit der deutschen Industrie*" (italicized words are spaced in the original); List to Franz I [Wien], April 20, 1820, *ibid.*, pp. 523–27, No. 24. List asked here for the extension of the Austrian mercantile system over Germany; List, "Gegen die Feinde der deutschen Nationalindustrie," *Organ für den deutschen Handels- und Fabrikantenstand* 1820, No. 17, p. 77, listed *ibid.*, IX, 292, No. 118; List, Inwiefern ist der Grundbesitzer . . . , MS [May, 1820?], *ibid.*, I, Part II, 585–89, No. 34.

[73] *Ibid.*, pp. 1009–13.   [74] *Ibid.*, pp. 999–1000.

become an advocate of economic unification because he saw the practical needs for it and not because he wanted to test the application of a well-developed theoretical system of his own.[75] This explains many of his inconsistencies.

List's attempts to promote German industry did not, however, remain unnoticed in those commercial circles which were primarily interested in trade. A nation-wide controversy arose.[76] The merchants in Bremen, Hamburg, and Leipzig especially were among those who defended their interests and attacked List and the League. These differences were not new, but never before had the matter been argued so extensively on both sides. The tone of the controversy was bitter, but did not go to the extremes it subsequently reached. It was not so much a clash of clearly formulated systems as it was the conflict of unsystematized theories, business interests, and emotions. Many sophisms, rationalizations, exaggerations, mistakes, and inconsistencies can therefore be found on both sides of this controversy. List was never quite clear as to the amount of protection and retortion he wanted, and it was therefore relatively easy to attack him by supposing he wanted something like Fichte's "closed commercial state." Moreover, he had somewhat neglected the political and especially the fiscal aspects of the problem. The technical practicality of his tariffs and prohibitions was therefore frequently questioned.[77] Hardly

---

[75] Borckenhagen, op. cit., pp. 81–83.

[76] For the history of this controversy see List, op. cit., I, Part II, 596–646, 1029–50; Baasch, op. cit., pp. 462–78; Blume, op. cit., pp. 48–54; Lenz, op. cit., pp. 64–66; Borckenhagen, op. cit., pp. 12–16; Müller, op. cit., pp. 122–33; A[rwed] Emminghaus, Ernst Wilhelm Arnoldi. Leben und Schöpfungen eines deutschen Kaufmanns (Weimar: Böhlau, 1878), p. 132; [Karl Gustav Adolph Gruner] Über das Retorsions-Princip als Grundlage eines deutschen Handels-Systems (Leipzig [1820]), 84 pp.; Ernst Weber, Deutschlands Retorsions-System als Nothwehr und nicht als Zweck. Zur vorläufigen Erwiederung [sic] der Schrift: "Über das Retorsions-Princip etc." (Gera, 1820), 59 pp.; [Anonymous] Schutz der einheimischen Industrie, eine Municipal-Massregel und keine Kriegs-Erklärung, als Antwort der in Leipzig erschienenen Schrift "Über das Retorsions-Princip etc. etc." (Hamburg, 1820), 30 pp.

[77] [Gruner] op. cit., pp. 26–42; Benzenberg to List, Brüggen bey Crefeld, August 20, 1819, J[ohann] F[riedrich] Benzenberg, Über Preussens Geldhaushalt und neues Steuersystem (Leipzig, 1820), pp. 314–20; Benzenberg's letter, although critical, had the nature of a friendly inquiry.

any of his opponents were capable of constructive criticism on this point. Many of the standard arguments against protection were used in attacking List: Artificial industries cannot live, protection damages the consumer's interests, industrialists act against their better interests by supporting protection, and so forth. Perhaps the most powerful argument for the case of the purely commercial interests was the assertion that their trade was a vested right and that it was wrong to divest them of this right in order to create arbitrarily a monopoly for industry.[78]

List met charges of this kind by accusing his opponents of pressing their private interests to the detriment of national interests. He described those engaged in intermediate trade as British agents who were working for a "pitiful gain."[79] It was also often implied that traders in Bremen, Hamburg, Leipzig, and Frankfurt were really "Englishmen."[80] This charge was not left unanswered,[81] and it introduced an element of tension into the discussion. List had argued that way because he was convinced of the national benefit of his cause and because his deeper motivation was really political.[82] He not only had the welfare of industry at heart, but also wanted to promote commerce and communications, including oversea shipping, although he desired the latter in order to export German goods. He wanted to find a *modus vivendi* for both.[83] He was therefore not an extreme industrialist who employed phrases of nationalism to further the economic advantages of the class he was representing; neither was he an unscrupulous political agitator who exploited the distress of the manufacturers for mere propa-

[78] [Gruner] *op. cit.*, p. 83.

[79] "Traurigen Gewinn" List, "Handelskonsulent Dr. Gruner und Kammerrat Ploss in Leipzig als Gegner und Ernst Weber in Gera als Verteidiger der deutschen Industrie," *Organ für den deutschen Handels- und Fabrikantenstand*, 1820, pp. 117 ff., 121 f., 129 ff., 141 ff., reprinted in List, *op. cit.*, I, Part II, 599, No. 36.

[80] Miller quoted through *ibid.*, p. 1029; Baasch, *op. cit.*, p. 466.

[81] *Ibid.*, pp. 466–67, 477–78.

[82] Cf. Borckenhagen, *op. cit.*, p. 34.

[83] Baasch, *op. cit.*, pp. 468–71; [List] "Wozu soll der Ertrag einer gemeinschaftlichen deutschen Douanenlinie verwendet werden?" *Organ . . .*, 1820, pp. 102–4, reprinted in List, *op. cit.*, I, Part II, 591–93; *ibid.*, IX, 293–94.

ganda.[84]   The instability of his thinking, which has been
pointed out, did not mean that he was fundamentally in-
sincere.   He saw that other nations which had their industries protected were flourishing.   He saw German industry
struggling against overwhelming odds.   Why could not Germany solve her own problems as the others did?   Such considerations actuated List in his agitation for economic unity.
Neither purely political nor purely economic aspirations were
dominant in him.   His personality, which was both complex
and forceful, can easily be misunderstood.   There is, however, no question about his devotion to the cause of national
welfare, for which he made many a personal sacrifice.

THE DIPLOMATIC NEGOTIATIONS, 1819–20

THE agitation which had been carried on by List and the
League showed its effects on the German governments.
Most cabinets retained a wholesome respect for popular
opinion, even though they were frequently not at all liberal-
minded.   Naturally the governments had not remained unaware of the economic crisis, but it was not until they felt
popular pressure that they began to take the problem seriously into consideration.

These questions were, however, not brought up at the
Diet of the Confederation, where economic matters were increasingly less discussed.[85]   The cabinets had realized the
inefficiency of that institution, and when they were confronted with a serious political situation decided to go over
the head of the regular machinery of the Confederation by
calling special conferences.

By 1819 the German governments believed that Germany needed systematically to combat those nationalistic
groups which had remained active.   National aspirations
among university students had remained alive ever since
the war of 1813–15.   The *Wartburgfest* of 1817 had already
stirred the more reactionary governments.   In the spring
of 1819 Kotzebue, a German writer in Russian service, was
murdered by a student belonging to one of the radical circles.

---

[84] Cf. Borckenhagen, *op. cit.*, p. 34.
[85] Cf. [German Confederation] *op. cit.*, VIII (1819), 15–19, 156–59,
193–94, 259, 291–92; IX (1820), 57–58, 231; X (1820), 112–14; XI (1821),
123–25, 138–40; XII (1821), 7–9, 100–1, 205–6.

This act, especially, caused Metternich to believe that a general conspiracy was at work and to do his utmost to suppress the "revolution."   The measures taken by Austria, Prussia, and other German states in this direction inaugurated the period of reactionary predominance.   The national movement was driven underground, and liberalism had to suffer many restrictions.   The result was that the antagonism between the opposite parties increased and that this new political element was injected into the discussion on economic unification.

Conferences were held at Karlsbad in August, 1819, in order to set up a system of policing all of Germany against the "threatening" revolution.   Further conferences were held at Vienna between November, 1819, and June, 1820, to work out the Acts of Confederation in more detail than had been possible in 1815.   The Final Acts of 1820 elaborated in these conferences interpreted and supplemented the original Acts of Confederation, but did not as a whole fundamentally change the nature of the Confederation or of the Diet.   These Vienna Final Conferences were not so much the scene of ideological struggles as of continual clashes of actual political interests.

Such was the political background against which economic unification was discussed at Karlsbad as well as at Vienna.   Again the economic problems received secondary attention in an atmosphere that was not very conducive to the consideration of popular demands.   Nevertheless, the Vienna Final Conferences were the last instance of all German governments deliberating together about general economic unification.   No agreement was reached, since the obstacles proved too great.   The difficulties lay, first of all, in the political jealousies and ambitions of the individual states and, secondly, in the difference of economic interests among the various governments.   Many cabinets had been anxious to achieve some result.   By 1819 most of them had studied the problem and formulated their position.   Some went so far as to make a detailed inquiry into the wishes of their people,[86] while others asked their experts for memoranda.

---

[86] Cf. the Bavarian survey [October, 1819] as given in Oncken and Saemisch, I, 347–48, No. 177.

During the Vienna Final Conferences it soon became apparent that it was impossible for the governments to agree on general German economic unification. By the end of the Conferences this was so generally understood that, when it was finally moved that the matter be referred back to the Diet, the attending diplomats burst out laughing.[87]

The diplomatic history of these attempts to establish general German economic unification, their relative preponderance during the winter of 1819–20, and the abandonment of the whole scheme in the spring were important landmarks in the development of German thought. It was not until trial had proved it to be impossible for all German governments to adopt a general plan for economic unification that the period became conscious of the limitations and factors underlying the situation. After this was once understood, the way was opened for other methods of approach. The policies and attitudes of the major governments predetermined the checkered pattern of the ensuing diplomatic negotiations and for this reason will be discussed individually.

Austria's decision not to participate in general German economic matters had the most serious consequences and requires special attention. In Karlsbad Metternich had already pointed to the difficulties which would arise if Germany should act as a unit in economic matters; he regarded the sovereignty of the various states as the greatest obstacle.[88] He was not, however, directly opposed to any kind of negotiation, and the problem was to be discussed further at the Vienna Final Conferences. Metternich, before taking a more definite stand at these Conferences, requested memoranda from a number of Austrian experts. He asked to be informed whether Austria would benefit economically by the various schemes which had been proposed. He also wanted to know about Austrian economic interests in general. At the same time he pointed to the fact that Austria was relatively isolated, through her geographical position, from the rest of Germany and that, therefore, Austria's commercial policy was of no concern to the rest of Germany. He said,

---

[87] Aegidi, *op. cit.*, p. 59, describing the session of March 4, 1820.
[88] Karlsbad Conferences, August 30, 1819, *ibid.*, pp. 20–21.

in particular, that the recent complaints in Germany were caused by the new Prussian tariff policy. Another argument advanced by him was the circumstance that any inclusion of Austria in a general German scheme would necessarily divide the monarchy into two parts. And this was regarded by Metternich as suicide.[89]

None of the memoranda Metternich received in answer to his request favored the introduction of a common German customs system as it was proposed by List. Adam Müller in his memorandum pointed to the revolutionary character of List's League and to the illegality of its existence.[90] Another Austrian official, Stahl, also suspected List of revolutionary intentions and questioned List's sincerity;[91] he argued that the League would only create malcontents by arousing hopes which could not be fulfilled.[92] Stahl, moreover, condemned Austrian participation in the general scheme from an administrative and a fiscal point of view by pointing to its practical difficulties and by squarely defending the Austrian prohibitive system.[93] He was supported in his views by Stadion, then minister of finance, who called Germany "those territories which are indicated on maps as Germany."[94] Nor did List's project receive any support from Gentz, who thought it was impractical and could not be executed.[95] Metternich also saw J. J. Eichhoff's memorandum, which was more favorable to the popular aspirations, but which did

---

[89] Metternich to Stahl, November 10, 1819, Adolf Beer, *Die österreichische Handelspolitik im neunzehnten Jahrhundert* (Wien: Manz, 1891), pp. 574–76.

[90] Dated December 6, 1819, Oncken and Saemisch, I, 359–61, No. 182.

[91] Stahl to Sedlinsky, April 2, 1820, List, *op. cit.*, I, Part II, 1040; Srbik, *Metternich*, I, 534–35.

[92] Viktor Bibl, *Der Zerfall Österreichs* (Wien: Rikola Verlag, 1922), I, 236.

[93] Memorandum, March 22, 1820, List, *op. cit.*, I, Part II, 985–86; cf. Olshausen, *op. cit.*, pp. 127–28; Srbik, *op. cit.*, I, 534; Bibl, *op. cit.*, I, 235–36.

[94] Olshausen *op. cit.*, p. 128.

[95] Gentz to Adam Müller, December 15, 1819, *ibid.*, p. 99. The conclusion usually drawn from Gentz's admission that he did not know how economic unity could be achieved seems somewhat exaggerated. Gentz was not an ignoramus in such matters, as some writers have suggested (cf. *ibid.*, p. 153). One may ask whether List himself had been very explicit and consistent about this point.

not subscribe to the whole program, especially the immediate general German economic unification.[96]

Since none of these memoranda favored a general German commercial system, they only strengthened Metternich's opposition to such schemes. His reasons had their origins in his political rather than in his economic views. He was not a defender of the Austrian prohibitive system;[97] he even advocated a modified theory of free trade and did much to promote Austria's foreign trade. Although in this respect he was opposed to the old type of governmental paternalism, his political aims remained the same. He was opposed to high tariffs and prohibitions because he did not favor the sociological consequences of an artificially created industrial preponderance and because he wanted to preserve the agricultural classes.[98]

Metternich was, moreover, obliged to consider Austria's fiscal interests as they had been voiced by a number of high officials. He also saw the political obstacles and difficulties which would have to be met by any statesman who wanted to achieve the general economic unification of Germany.[99] Some of these difficulties and obstacles lay in Austria's peculiar problems, of which Metternich was quite conscious. They arose primarily out of Austria's consolidated geographical location and out of her well-established economic system, both of which rendered her independent of German economic life and therefore evolved into specifically Austrian problems.[100] Metternich also seems to have been opposed on principle to any centralized unification of Germany which

---

[96] Adolf Beer, "Österreich und die deutschen Handelseinigungsbestrebungen in den Jahren 1817 bis 1820," Österreichisch-Ungarische Revue (New Series, 1887), III, 289–92. J. J. Eichhoff, mayor of Bonn, 1801–2, and subsequently general director of the Rhine Commission, has frequently been confused with his son Peter Joseph, later Hofkammerpräsident in Austria. J. J. Eichhoff was the author of the Betrachtungen zum XIX. Artikel der Bundesakte (Wiesbaden, 1820), while P. J. Eichhoff was the Gubernialrat who was sent by Metternich in May of 1827 to Köthen in order to persuade the Duke of Anhalt-Köthen to accept a compromise solution in his feud with Prussia (Oncken and Saemisch, I, 271, n. 1).

[97] Aegidi, op. cit., p. 84.

[98] Srbik, op. cit., I, 531–32.   [99] Aegidi, op. cit., pp. 20–21.

[100] Beer, Die österreichische Handelspolitik, p. 575; Ritthaler, in Oncken and Saemisch, I, 308; Berstett to Ludwig I of Baden, Wien, January 16, 1820, ibid., p. 370, No. 184.

he thought would be incompatible with her confederate nature.[101]

Metternich's objection to an economic unification of Germany did not mean that he was opposed to any aid for German commerce and industry. On the contrary, as early as 1817 he had supported the introduction of free trade in foodstuffs,[102] but had failed to win the Emperor's consent.[103] This plan had at that time received the support of the fiscal authorities,[104] and in 1819–20 many Austrian officials still endorsed similar schemes. Stahl pointed to the advantages which would accrue to Austria by permitting free trade in foodstuffs.[105] Adam Müller went further by advocating that internal German tariffs should be modified, that foreign preponderance be checked, and that a Confederate commerce commission be established.[106] Stadion, however, raised objections to the erection of such a commission.[107] Müller had denounced List's activities as a nuisance,[108] but he nevertheless supported his project for a national industrial exhibition,[109] while other Austrian officials did not share his view.[110]

Metternich was also convinced that something must be done, and in 1820 again tried to obtain the Emperor's assent to a treaty establishing free trade in foodstuffs. He pointed to the economic advantages for Austria and showed how any relief measure like this would take the wind out of List's sails, who had always blamed the inactivity of the governments. He argued, moreover, that Austria would lose all her political prestige and confidence which she had recently gained in German matters and that the Austrian government would have to take the blame if this plan was defeated.[111]

---

[101] Cf. Srbik, *op. cit.*, I, 533–34.

[102] Free trade in this connection means "no prohibition" but not "absence of all tariffs."   [103] Beer, *Die österreichische Handelspolitik*, p. 55.

[104] *Loc. cit.*   [105] *Ibid.*, p. 56.

[106] Memorandum, December 6, 1819, Oncken and Saemisch, I, 361, No. 182; cf. Olshausen, *op. cit.*, pp. 95–96; Olshausen questions the seriousness of Müller's intentions.   [107] List, *op. cit.*, I, Part II, 985.

[108] "Unfug," memorandum, December 6, 1819, Oncken and Saemisch, I, 360, No. 182.

[109] List to Metternich [Wien], March 4, 1820, List, *op. cit.*, I, Part II, 562–65, No. 30; *ibid.*, pp. 1012–13.

[110] Stahl to Sedlinsky, April 2, 1820, *ibid.*, p. 1014; for Stahl's opinion of Müller's abilities see Olshausen, *op. cit.*, pp. 127–28.

[111] Metternich to Franz I, May 13 and 14, 1820, *ibid.*, pp. 291–95, Nos. 126–27.

Franz I, however, again refused to give his consent in this matter. Any agreement which would be reached within the framework of the Confederation by its members would naturally affect only territory of the Confederation. Since only Cisleithanian Austria belonged to the Confederation, only this part would be subject to the proposed regulations. Franz I objected to any such division because he felt that Austria must always remain one body, notwithstanding her adherence to the Confederation.[112] It should be noted that Metternich had argued in these terms against general unification; but this agreement on foodstuffs had rather the nature of a commercial treaty and did not require any common administration.

Franz I had the choice between sacrificing some part of Austrian unity and losing some prestige attaching to Austrian leadership in German affairs. And although Austria was the presiding German power and although his name and family were still closely tied to the old Imperial tradition of Germany, Franz I preferred to follow the interests of his monarchy, even where a great deal could have been gained by a trifling sacrifice.

That the Austrian government was not willing to risk its fiscal system by trying to work out List's still rather undeveloped plan of German economic unification is understandable. No other major government would have taken similar chances. But it can be observed that Austria was much less predisposed to coöperate in any general measure than the other states. Her new boundaries had to a certain degree separated her from the rest of Germany. She could take care of her economic interests alone, and therefore necessity did not compel her to coöperate with other governments. The decision made by Franz I on May 23, 1820, was, however, not so much the inevitable result of Austria's new geographical position as it was a voluntary step in the direction of that complete withdrawal of hers from German affairs which followed in 1866. That is to say, Austria had a choice, and did choose. This decision was by no means

---

[112] Decision, Franz I, Prag, May 23, 1820, *ibid.*, pp. 294–95, under No. 127.

final, but it was to be followed by a series of similar ones.

Austria's policy in German economic matters was of general importance, but her part in the failure to reach a common agreement should not be overemphasized, since there was a great deal of dissension among the other governments on the question.

Baden was probably the outstanding advocate of a common customs system. This was largely due to the prevailing liberalism of her Diet, which gave public expression to its desire for economic unification. When discussing Baden's policy of those years one cannot overlook Nebenius, who was then a councilor in the Baden Ministry of Finance.

As early as 1818 Nebenius had publicly discussed Germany's economic condition. Although a number of concrete ideas were put forward at this time, his conceptions remained vague and uncoördinated, in this way reflecting contemporary thought. Nebenius, however, pointed out that individual actions undertaken by individual states would be of no effect, that it would be difficult to establish a common system, and that the introduction of free trade within Germany would be most helpful and necessary in the case of a prohibition of foreign goods.[113] He kept his interests alive, and in the following year his famous memorandum showed his more advanced views.[114] In this memorandum[115] he discussed primarily German economic unification, and hardly anything can be found which would indicate that he had conceived by that time the idea of a customs union; the

---

[113] [Carl] Friedrich Nebenius, *Bemerkungen über den Zustand Grossbritanniens in staatswirthschaftlicher Hinsicht. Nebst einem Worte über Deutschlands auswärtige Handelsverhältnisse.... Mit einer Übersetzung der französischen Schrift: Über England und Engländer, von J. B. Say* (Karlsruhe, 1818), second page sequence, 100–58, especially, 136–41.

[114] It is for this memorandum that Nebenius has been regarded by some authorities as the inventor or intellectual originator of the Zollverein, a claim which aroused a bitter controversy.

[115] The first complete reprint of this memorandum appeared on the thirty-two pages appended to the main body of C[arl] F[riedrich] Nebenius, *Denkschrift für den Beitritt Badens zu dem zwischen Preussen, Bayern, Württemberg, den beiden Hessen und mehren andern deutschen Staaten abgeschlossenen Zollverein* (Karlsruhe, 1833), 62 and 32 pp. For a detailed account of its origin cf. Appendix A. The memorandum will hereafter be cited as Nebenius, memorandum [1819], 1833 ed.

word "Zollverein" is not once used. He started by stating
three axioms: (1) that Austria alone among all the German
states could protect her commerce and industry successfully
against foreign competition;[116] (2) that any other German
state which should try to do this would do more harm to
German neighbors than to foreign countries;[117] and (3) that
any system of prohibition adopted by a small country would
have more disadvantages than in the case of larger nations.[118]
He concluded that concerted action of all the German governments would suffice and that it would be of no avail if all
agreed to take some action individually.[119]   He therefore
wanted the elimination of all internal tariffs in Germany and
the establishment of a common customs system along her
frontiers, to be administered and directed by the Diet of the
Confederation.[120]   There was to be a common treasury to
bear the costs of the administration and to pay out its surplus
to the governments proportionally according to population or
some other general standard like the military quota.[121]   The
states were to retain some rights in the appointment of officials.   This was not a customs union; Nebenius himself applied the term "German customs constitution"[122] to this
scheme and argued that it was as necessary as the German
Military Constitution and that his plan was designed to execute the Acts of Confederation.[123]   Thus he wanted a Confederate customs administration which would be controlled
by the central political institution of the Confederation.   The
procedure suggested by Nebenius for the appointment of the
officials—about which he remained very vague—and for the
distribution foreshadowed later Zollverein practices.   They
should be explained, however, as necessary corollaries from
the legal character of the Confederation, which was limited
in its financial activities[124] and did not even have a territory

---

[116] *Ibid.*, p. 3.   [117] *Ibid.*, p. 5.   [118] *Ibid.*, p. 6.   [119] *Ibid.*, p. 17.
[120] *Ibid.*, pp. 15–16, 24.   [121] *Ibid.*, p. 24.   [122] *Ibid.*, p. 14.
[123] *Loc. cit.*: "deutsche Militärverfassung," a term applied to the military
system of the Confederation: its fortresses, the army quotas of the member
states, their organization, and their command in the event that a war should
break out.
[124] Johann Ludwig Klüber, *Öffentliches Recht des Teutschen Bundes
und der Bundesstaaten* (3d ed.; Frankfurt a.M., 1831), pp. 151–53, 219–20,
233–35.   The Confederation had a limited number of treasuries, each set up

or citizens or subjects of its own.[125]   Moreover, Nebenius was not quite clear whether the abolition of internal tariffs should be put into effect by a separate agreement.   While discussing this problem of free trade inside Germany, he suggested that each state should join voluntarily and should be allowed to withdraw; the treaties should be concluded for a limited time so as to attract states which might hesitate to join.[126]   The Zollverein later was also based on treaties which had to be renewed periodically; but Nebenius seems to have suggested this item only for the abolition of state tariffs, since he does not mention the right to secede from the common customs administration.   He does not seem to have understood the importance of territorial continuity or to have fully realized the principle that the combination of external customs with internal free trade was essential for a customs union or for any other type of economic unification.[127]   One can conclude that Nebenius wanted German economic unification constructed on the framework of the Confederate constitution, but that he did not as yet visualize a customs union.

Nebenius' scheme suffered from the weakness inherent in all plans which tried to achieve German economic unification through the Confederation.   They overestimated the ability of the Diet to arrive at a concerted action in such matters.   Nebenius' plan showed no greater understanding of the underlying political factors than others had expressed.

Although Nebenius did not in 1819 originate the concept of a customs union, his memorandum is of importance in view of the prominent position he was to occupy during subsequent negotiations.   He devoted considerable space to fiscal considerations.   He advocated low tariffs and a moderate protection of industry;[128] tariffs were, as a rule, to

---

for a definite purpose, which were supported by the shares of the member states.   It did not own any investments, that is to say, it owned fortresses for defense purposes, but not domains for financial purposes.

[125] "Bundesgebiet," *ibid.*, p. 82.   The term *Bundesgebiet* refers here to the geographical extension of the Confederation as well as to the territories over which the Confederation enjoyed special rights.   Klüber (*ibid.*, p. 83) recognized that the Confederation owned land, but he denied the public character of such holdings.

[126] Nebenius, memorandum [1819], 1833 ed., pp. 15–16.

[127] Cf. Fischer, *op. cit.*, VIII (1867), 288.

[128] Nebenius, memorandum [1819], 1833 ed., pp. 18, 20–21.

be levied at the frontier.[129]   He already realized the difficulties which would arise in connection with the revenues imposed by the various states on the consumption of certain
goods, and he advocated a number of restrictive measures to
solve the problem.[130]   He also desired common standards of
measurement and coinage, a common patent law, assimilation
of commercial legislation and coöperation among the states in
their administration of roads, rivers, canals, and the like.[131]
Many of these ideas were not new, but they were thought
out more carefully than usual.   While List's ever-moving
mind had often neglected such details, Nebenius, by turning
his attention to technicalities, had achieved clarity and taken
a more definite stand toward the practical aspects.

While there can be no question as to the relative originality of both List and Nebenius, there arises the problem of the
extent to which they did influence Baden's policy in 1819.
Baden's first Diet under its new constitution was opened formally on April 22, 1819.   On April 30 the representative
Lotzbeck moved that the Grand Duke be asked to take
diplomatic steps in Frankfurt or to approach the German
governments directly for the establishment of free trade.[132]
Lotzbeck reasoned that internal free trade would save administrative expenses and advance economic welfare; tariffs
against foreign countries should be set only on the basis of
reciprocity.[133]   List's first petition to the Diet of April in
Frankfurt, which might have been known in Karlsruhe by
then, seems to be behind this motion.   Officially, however,
his petition was not received by the Baden Diet till May 10,[134]
and he himself visited Karlsruhe around May 15.[135]   He met
Lotzbeck and Liebenstein at that time.   The latter, still under the influence of List, delivered on May 17 in the Baden
Diet his famous speech supporting Lotzbeck's motion.[136]
Its arguments were exclusively political, following liberal and

---

[129] Ibid., pp. 24–25.   [130] Ibid., pp. 26–30.   [131] Ibid., p. 32.
[132] [Baden, Landtag] Übersicht der ständischen Verhandlungen beider
Kammern des Grossherzogthums Baden (Karlsruhe, 1819), I, [53]–54.
[133] Speech, April 30, 1819, ibid., pp. 59–60.
[134] Ibid., p. 123.   [135] List, op. cit., IX, 6.
[136] "Unser Herr Professor List ist seit 8 Tagen in Karlsruhe und arbeitet
mit d[en] Ständ[en] an Reden," Schnell to Arnoldi, Nürnberg, May 23, 1819,
Olshausen, op. cit., p. 232, No. 16.

national ideas.[137]   He voiced in particular those sentiments against the settlement of 1815 which were shared by all patriots.   This had been done before, but seldom had anyone spoken with such vehemence and conviction, and rarely had such revolutionary language been used openly.   Liebenstein declared that the economic conditions would lead to a French Revolution in Germany, that the governments were keeping the economic barriers in order to create hostility among the populations of the various states, and that they were opposing natural forces which would ultimately overcome them.   He also pointed out that the existing economic policy would make the populations lose interest in national affairs and that the governments might therefore find themselves without support in case of foreign invasion.   The revolutionary tone was well understood.[138]   The Baden government acceded to the wish of its Diet[139] and tried to achieve general economic measures in Germany at the Karlsbad Conferences.   Baden put forth a memoir written by Berstett, its foreign minister. This memoir did not go beyond the ideas already expressed by List, Lotzbeck, Liebenstein and referred directly to the desires of the Baden Diet.[140]   It pointed to the necessity of counteracting revolutionary movements by giving economic betterment and described the economic and financial advantages of internal free trade and also the possibilities of a common customs line.   Berstett's memorandum was followed by a decision of the Baden Ministry of Foreign Affairs to pursue the same policy at the Diet of the Confederation,[141] a decision which also showed the influence of Liebenstein's speech.[142]

So far the chain of ideas which first began to be discussed

---

[137] The speech is reprinted in [Baden, Landtag], *op. cit.*, pp. 132–36.

[138] Reigersberg to Bavarian government, May 17, 1819, Oncken and Saemisch, I, 326, n. 1.

[139] Declaration made by Nebenius, June 26, 1819, *ibid.*, p. 327, in footnote 1 continuing from p. 326.

[140] Memorandum, Karlsbad Conferences, August 15, 1819, de Martens [i.e. Georg Friedrich von], *Nouveau recueil général des traités, conventions et autres transactions remarquables, servant à la connaissance des relations étrangères des puissances et états dans leurs rapports mutuels*, ed. by F. Murhard (Gottingue, 1846), IV, 140–47, No. 2.

[141] Karlsruhe, August 17, 1819, Oncken and Saemisch, I, 341–42, No. 174.   [142] *Ibid.*, p. 341, n. 1.

at Karlsruhe with List's visit in May of 1819 and which led to
a reorientation of Baden's policy has been described.[143]
There seems to be very little cause for doubting List's preponderant influence on Baden politicians. It had been frequently claimed, however, that Nebenius' memorandum
played a rôle in this development in the spring and summer
of 1819.[144] Hitherto no idea which has been encountered
could be identified as belonging exclusively to Nebenius.
There were, however, ideas in Berstett's memoir which
were different from Nebenius's beliefs and conceptions.
Nebenius did not discuss the revolutionary aspect in his
memorandum. He also expected that the governments
would be sufficiently reimbursed by the common customs
receipts,[145] whereas Berstett doubted such a result.[146] Berstett, as well as Liebenstein and Lotzbeck, treated the common customs system as a minor point, and it can be argued
that they would have dwelt longer on this point, used some
of Nebenius' ideas, and have referred to Nebenius directly
if they had known his memorandum. There are also other
indications which tend to show that the Nebenius memorandum did not have any influence before the fall of 1819.[147]

Even at the Vienna Final Conferences the influence of
this memorandum was slight. Copies were distributed by
Berstett among various diplomats,[148] who filed them away,
and not even Berstett himself seems to have had much use
of it in his struggle for the fulfillment of Article XIX. He
took a position similar to the one he had defended in Karlsbad,[149] emphasizing political reasons and free trade. Realizing the difficulties German economic unification would have
to meet, he retreated by demanding a minimum fulfillment of
Article XIX, and asked for some measures to relieve the situation.[150] The position of the government at Karlsruhe does

---

[143] Cf. Olshausen, *op. cit.*, pp. 29–30, who arrives at the same conclusion.   [144] Cf. Appendix A.
[145] Nebenius, memorandum [1819], 1833 ed., p. 18.
[146] Memorandum, Karlsbad Conferences, August 15, 1819, Martens, *op.
cit.*, IV, 142, No. 2.   [147] Cf. Appendix A.
[148] Berstett to Ludwig I of Baden, Wien, January 16, 1820, Oncken and
Saemisch, I, 369, No. 184.   [149] *Ibid.*, p. 366, n. 1.
[150] Berstett to Ludwig I of Baden, *ibid.*, pp. 364–69, No. 184; Aegidi,
op. cit., pp. 35–38, 57–58.

not seem to have been determined merely by such practical considerations as financial, commercial, or industrial needs, because it stated that all fiscal achievements for the whole of Germany would be of no value unless general economic unification was supported and carried out by a national sentiment.[151]

Other German governments also supported economic unification, and internal free trade was especially favored. Bavaria had a natural interest in the latter on account of its geographical and economic situation.[152] There was, however, some opposition in government circles to pursuing a national policy of this kind. Some officials were opposed to any general plan which would infringe on state rights and also charged that these schemes lacked all economic foundation. Crown Prince Ludwig's intervention made the government change its position. Up to then Bavaria, jealous of her independence and distrustful of all coöperative schemes, had only favored slight modifications.[153] By the fall of 1819 she had begun to support economic unification.[154]

The Württemberg government proceeded with less enthusiasm in this matter, saw many difficulties, and favored modifications, but was careful enough not to obstruct popular demands squarely. One of its chief concerns seems to have been a possible loss of revenue.[155] Other governments seem to have had similar fears, as for instance, Electoral Hesse.[156] There were, however, some statesmen who, being free traders, were not worried about possible financial losses. This position was held by du Thil, who represented Hesse-Darmstadt at the Vienna Final Conferences, and by Marschall, who was in charge of the Nassau government; both favored free trade in Germany, but opposed a common cus-

---

[151] Decision, Baden Ministry of Foreign Affairs, Karlsruhe, August 17, 1819, ibid., pp. 341–42, No. 174.

[152] Aretin to Max I of Bavaria, Haidenburg, October 30, 1819, ibid., pp. 348–51, No. 178.   [153] Doeberl, op. cit., pp. 11–12.

[154] Instructions for Zentner for the Vienna Final Conferences, München, November 12, 1819, ibid., p. 12, and Oncken and Saemisch, I, 355–56, No. 179.

[155] Du Thil's report No. 49, Wien, January 12, 1820, Heribert [Heinrich Robert] Schmidt, Die Begründung des preussisch-hessischen Zollvereins vom 14. Februar 1828 (Doctor's dissertation, Giessen, 1925), pp. ii–iii.

[156] Ibid., p. ii.

toms system.[157]   While du Thil's conception of economic
matters was fair, Marschall's ignorance was quite obvious.
He was naïve enough to suggest that all internal German
customs erected since January 1, 1814, should be abolished
in order to make Prussia give up her system without the
others having to give up theirs.   Each state which had a
boundary with a non-German country was to be free to
regulate the customs along this boundary as it pleased.[158]
Marschall, although he attacked Prussia's commercial policy,
which was very unpopular in Germany, was an ultraconservative who believed that liberal forces among the lower
officials were to blame for the new Prussian customs system
and that the danger of revolution could be removed only by
a repeal of the Prussian tariff law.[159]   It was therefore quite
natural that he treated List with suspicion.[160]

Here he was following Hanover's opposition against List
and the League.   Hanover's attitude probably originated
from the British interests she represented and was not just
simple conservatism.[161]   It should be pointed out, however,
that the other diplomats attending the Vienna Final Conferences also entertained no favorable opinion of List.[162]

Free trade alone was likewise advocated by Mecklenburg
and some of the Thuringian states.[163]   Hamburg's instruction
for the Conferences went further than this by systematically
defending free trade as such and by opposing any general
customs régime.[164]   Hamburg's government knew what it
wanted and was capable of arguing her case better than
any other German government.   Some members of the
Vienna Final Conferences who had less economic insight
praised these views as something "practical," although they
ran counter to the interests they represented.[165]   Hach, who
represented the Hanse Towns, met, however, some opposi-

---

[157] Ibid., pp. iv–v; Menn, Zur Vorgeschichte, pp. 16, 23, 51, 54–55.
[158] Ibid., p. 57.   [159] Ibid., p. 50; Treitschke, op. cit., III, 31.
[160] Menn, op. cit., p. 43.
[161] Protocols of the Diet of the Confederation, May 24, 1819, Oncken
    and Saemisch, I, 329–32, No. 168, especially n. 2 on p. 329.
[162] Aegidi, op. cit., p. 32.
[163] Ibid., pp. 18, 47–49.
[164] Hamburg Senate to Hach, List, op. cit., I, Part II, 1047–50.
[165] Blume, op. cit., pp. 27–47, especially p. 38.

tion.[166] Hamburg was charged with selfishness and with lack of interest in the whole of German economic life.[167]

Much as many German governments favored general economic unification in theory, frequently the immediate objective was to have the Prussian customs system modified. It was for this reason that the formal negotiations which were conducted during the Vienna Final Conferences for the economic betterment of the nation consisted primarily of a series of diplomatic maneuvers. General measures short of economic unification were not passed owing to the narrow partisanship which looked on the whole problem as offering only the simple alternatives of preserving or abolishing the Prussian customs system.

It has been shown that in the years following the Congress of Vienna the predominant trend of the attempts to better the economic situation was to propose for the whole of Germany a general solution which was usually expected to be brought about by the Confederation. This desire to include the whole of Germany was not so much an outgrowth of an economic rationalism as it was the manifestation of political consciousness. It is true that there existed common material interests, that there was economic pressure, and that there were other factors such as geographical relationship, but the national approach was so general and so definite that it cannot be overlooked. This nationalism was not of a uniform character; it was partly the old Imperial patriotism, it occasionally contained regional elements, it had often retained some of the war enthusiasm, and there was also something which might be called Confederate patriotism. There was, however, no direct relationship with the movements of 1813–15. The desires for general German economic unification grew out of the depression which followed the Napoleonic wars. Although political elements formed the basic pattern for the shaping of these new aspirations, the chief impetus had been economic. The popular movement for general German economic unification

---

[166] Aegidi, *op. cit.*, p. 43.

[167] Berstett to Ludwig I of Baden, Wien, January 16, 1820, Oncken and Saemisch, I, 367, No. 184.

did not attempt to participate in politics, and it tried to enjoy the benefit of political neutrality.

The speculations of the publicists, the campaign carried on by List and the League, and the diplomatic negotiations had certain common characteristics cutting across ideological lines. Lack of judgment and of perspective infested most theorists of German economic unification. None of the schemes proposed was sufficiently integrated to combine the essential elements in economic theory with those found in everyday reality into a unified approach which would have allowed for a comprehensive understanding of the problem. Most of the plans concentrated on one of the four following lines of thought without giving a balanced consideration to all necessary aspects of the question. They were either predominantly philosophical, political, economic, or technical in their appeal. In many instances they contained an unrelated assembly of theories with a miscellaneous assortment of facts. The readiness with which schemes were given up was general throughout the period. These plans lacked substance, primarily because the idea of general German economic unification was in itself not original. It was merely and always a copy of the desired political unity.

The ability of the statesmen and diplomats to arrive relatively soon at a critical understanding of the political realities was not so much due to insight as to inertia. The movement for general German economic unification has to be evaluated historically. Not all who supported this plan were fools, because political factors made such unification impossible. In a similar way, not all its opponents were necessarily farsighted realists. The constitution of the Confederation was still capable of development. Its possibilities of living and growing were not ended until the Final Acts were adopted in 1820. On the other hand, many a statesman refused coöperation in such schemes not so much because he saw actual difficulties arising out of the policies of other states as because he was unwilling to make concessions himself. Moreover, it can be said that the knowledge of the political difficulties which made the Diet incapable of handling the situation had to be gained by experience. That is to say, it was necessary for this wrong way to be tried first before a better one could find widespread approval.

CHAPTER IV

THE IDEA OF A SEPARATE UNION DURING
THE SOUTH GERMAN NEGOTIATIONS
OF 1819–25

THE Vienna Final Conferences of 1819–20 had made clear the impossibility of establishing a general German customs system immediately. During the months when the idea of general economic unification had reached its peak and begun its sudden decline, another movement had gotten under way which also tried to alleviate the economic distress. Diplomats now attempted to form a regional union in South and Central Germany. List and the League had originated this idea of a partial solution in June, 1819. It was taken up by various German governments, and actual negotiations were begun during the Vienna Final Conferences. Although the Conferences never dealt with this matter officially, a number of the attending diplomats discussed it informally and toward the end of the meeting reached a tentative agreement. This convention of May 19, 1820, provided that the South German and certain Central German governments should formally continue the negotiations for a separate union, and it also supplied a program for the subsequent conferences. Accordingly, the various representatives met at Darmstadt in September, 1820, and tried for the next three years to set up a regional union. These negotiations, after they had failed in Darmstadt, were continued during 1824 and 1825 in Stuttgart and other places. The states bordering along the upper Rhine, Baden, Hesse-Darmstadt, and Nassau consulted with each other, and the former two agreed on the Heidelberg Protocol, late in 1824. Bavaria and Württemberg, on the other hand, tried again to conclude a regional union early in 1825, and invited Baden and Hesse-Darmstadt to attend the Stuttgart Conferences which were held for that purpose. Within a few months these negotiations also failed, and thus ended the first period of separate negotiations in South Germany.

Although all these conferences had not brought any relief to the widespread economic distress, they were important because it was here that the concept of a customs union was originated. After the foundation of a regional union had once been suggested by popular demand, it was developed almost exclusively by the diplomats attending the conferences and by their technical advisers. The policies of the participating governments conflicted to such a degree that these differences were the primary cause for the failure of the conferences. The technical aspects of a regional union developed slowly at these negotiations, which endeavored more and more to neutralize the divergent political forces. A knowledge of the political background is therefore essential for the understanding of the technical development of the ideas underlying a customs union. This chapter will therefore deal both with the political factors responsible for the failure of the South German conferences between 1820 and 1825 and with the development of the technical concepts of a customs union. These two main parts will be preceded by a discussion of the idea for a regional union during the summer and fall of 1819, and of the beginnings of the diplomatic negotiations at the Vienna Final Conferences.

The Early History of the Negotiations for a Separate Union, 1819–20

WHEN various members of List's League submitted a petition to the King of Bavaria on June 23, 1819, in which they asked for a separate union, this move was for all practical purposes the starting point of the idea.[1] Although List was not very explicit on the content of such a regional agreement, he and his followers seem to have been the first to advocate the union of a definite region, and they also seem to have had a clear understanding of the geographical elements involved. Their plan showed the same characteristics as the other schemes which List had developed for general German economic unification. It was conceived with the same facility and the same lack of insight and consistency. While his final aim remained a general German solution, he

---

[1] Doeberl, *Bayern,* pp. 13–14; Menn, *Zur Vorgeschichte,* p. 44. Menn mentions Waldeck's proposal for a common action against Prussia made in April, 1819, to various neighboring states. Proposals for a common action, however, should be distinguished from proposals for a separate union.

nevertheless proposed this separate union, which certainly had an anti-Austrian and anti-Prussian tendency. Concerning List's economic ends the following paradox should be pointed out: List and the League apparently wanted this separate union for the abolition of all customs duties, but it was just this proposal which led to the foundation of the Zollverein.[2]

This idea of a separate union, which List and his followers strongly promoted through personal interviews, fell on fertile ground. From July, 1819, on, the problem of a separate agreement was discussed by high officials in Munich and Stuttgart. It was not until the fall of 1819 that the Bavarian and Württemberg governments found their way through the various suggestions, petitions, and memoranda and that each of them had formulated its own policy. In this period of orientation the political side of the problem was mostly considered.

All during these years the policies of the various South German governments can be described by the predominance of one of the following three component factors: (1) Each government cherished a greater or a smaller desire to preserve its political individuality; (2) Many statesmen tried at one time or another to establish a third German power in Central and South Germany in order to counterbalance the Austrian and Prussian domination; (3) Most cabinets understood to some degree the scope of certain common German interests. These three policies were known as particularism, trialism, and nationalism, and their elements went into the making of the policies South German cabinets pursued.

Thus in the fall of 1819 the Bavarian government was advised by its representative at the Diet, Aretin, in a lengthy memorandum, to promote a separate economic union among

---

[2] List to King Wilhelm I, Stuttgart, April, 1819, List, *Schriften*, VIII, 132, No. 46; J. J. Schnell to Max I, June 23, 1819, Doeberl, *op. cit.*, pp. 13–14; List to Wilhelm I, early July, 1819, List, *op. cit.*, I, Part II, 514, No. 21; Schnell and Weber to Grand Duke of Hesse-Darmstadt, Darmstadt, July 18, 1819, Olshausen, *Friedrich List*, pp. 240–42, No. 32; petition to the Duke of Nassau, July 19, 1819, mentioned by Menn, *op. cit.*, p. 64; Ducal Saxon Government of Gotha to League, Gotha, July 30, 1819, Olshausen, *op. cit.*, p. 242–43, No. 33; League to List, Nürnberg, September 5, 1819, *ibid.*, p. 250, No. 39.

the South German governments.   In advocating the union of "purely German states" Aretin definitely followed trialistic lines.   He regarded a common customs system among these states as only a means to bring about a closer union among them.   He also believed that this type of economic union would quiet the popular demand for political unification, since such a union would give all the practical advantages of political unification.   He realized very clearly that the great German powers would not accept a general solution of the tariff question, especially if Bavaria should make a "liberal" proposal for such a solution.   The refusal of these powers to give up their own interests and to submit to the Bavarian proposals was to be used to put all the blame for the failure of the negotiations on them.   If, however, these powers should try to bring about a solution giving the minor states an inferior position, then Bavaria and the other purely German states should stand up for states' rights and charge violation of the Acts of Confederation.   On the other hand, Aretin argued that a separate economic union with a common central administration was compatible with Article XI of the Acts of Confederation.   He foresaw, however, that Bavaria would have to be generous in order to obtain the coöperation of the other medium states for such a union.[3]   Trialistic and clever as this whole scheme was, it was not, however, adopted by the Bavarian government.

Nevertheless, the Bavarian representative at the Vienna Final Conferences was ordered in his instructions to promote a separate union.[4]   This decision, however, was not a mere adaptation of Aretin's suggestion, and there was another and more complicated side to the Bavarian policy.   The instructions which the Bavarian representative received were the result of a compromise between the various forces active at Munich.   The Crown Prince was responsible for the national element in the instructions; it was due to his influence that the Bavarian representative was first to promote general German regulations for the protection of "German goods" and "German industry."   Only if this attempt should

---

[3] Aretin to Max I, Haidenburg, October 30, 1819, Oncken and Saemisch, I, 348–55, No. 178.

[4] Dated München, November 12, 1819, *ibid.*, pp. 355–56, No. 179.

fail was a separate union of the "purely German" states to be supported.[5] At the same time, friendly relations with Austria were to be maintained and particular Bavarian interests taken care of.[6]

Württemberg's policy was also subject to divergent influences. High officials in Stuttgart were quick to realize the importance of List's proposals. By July, 1819, a memorandum was elaborated which developed List's ideas further.[7] While List had only advocated a separate union against customs, the officials at Stuttgart had already conceived the idea of a separate customs system among the South German states. There was to be internal free trade among the member states; a common customs line was to be maintained along the boundaries of this union and was to be administered by a board on which each state was to be represented by two officials. The income was to be distributed among the member states in proportion to their population. The union which was proposed here was not a customs union, since each member state was to give up its own administration and a common customs administration was to be erected. However, the negotiations which were conducted among the South German states during the subsequent years were based upon plans which were substantially identical with the draft worked out by Württemberg officials; and it was not until 1824 that the idea of separate administrations was conceived. This Württemberg scheme seems to have been the first to suggest a union of the South German states for the establishment of a common customs system.[8] It remains doubtful, however, whether this plan, which had been conceived by the government at Stuttgart, had any influence on the actual negotiations for such a union or whether it was completely forgotten when these negotiations were started in the spring of 1820. This scheme was officially called "ideas for a customs and commerce union among South

---

[5] *Loc. cit.*; Doeberl, *op. cit.*, p. 12.

[6] M[ichael] Doeberl, *Entwicklungsgeschichte Bayerns* (3d ed.; München: R. Oldenbourg, 1928), II, 573–74.

[7] Memorandum, Stuttgart, July, 1819, Oncken and Saemisch, I, 335–38, No. 172, and Olshausen, *op. cit.*, pp. 237–39, No. 27a.

[8] List and the League must receive credit for the idea of a separate union only.

German governments."[9]   This seems to be one of the earliest uses of the term "customs union," although, as has been already pointed out, only a common customs system was meant.   Thus the term "customs union" originally had a different meaning and preceded by several years the idea of what is technically known as a customs union.[10]

Moreover, in this document there were reflected political tendencies which were to play a dominant rôle during the following year.   Typical of these tendencies was the argument that the North was profiting unduly from the economic crisis and that the South German governments should therefore pursue their common interests through a separate union.[11]   Anti-Prussian sentiments were voiced, and the cause of the purely German states was taken up.   Although trialistic opinions of this kind were not uncommon in Württemberg government circles, Wintzingerode, her minister for foreign affairs, caused the first draft which contained these elements to be changed into a less provocative form.[12]   A similar caution was observed when the Württemberg government drafted the instructions for its representative at the Vienna Final Conferences.   Nothing was said that might directly be interpreted as a hostile attitude toward the partly German states.   Although general measures to be applied

[9] "Ideen zu einem Maut- und Handelsverein der süddeutschen Regierungen," Oncken and Saemisch, I, 337, No. 172.

[10] "Maut- und Handelsverein" is synonymous with "Zollverein." In the same document (ibid., p. 336) the term "Zoll- und Handelsverein" is used; but it means here a general German customs system.   This also indicates that the special meaning which later attached itself to the words "Zollverein" or "Mautverein" had not yet been developed.   I was not able to find an earlier use of these two words.   Neither List nor Nebenius seems to have been familiar with them before this date (July, 1819).   It is very likely that the word "Zollverein" was formed by analogy with the word "Münzverein," the only earlier connection in which the word "Verein" or union was used for this type of convention.   The word "Münz-Verein" can be found as early as 1739 (J. H. Zedler [ed.], Universal Lexicon . . . , XXII [Leipzig, 1739], cols. 591, 642–43), while the institution can be traced back to the Middle Ages (cf. coinage convention between Constance and Schaffhausen, 1400, Julius [Alfred] Cahn, Münz- und Geldgeschichte von Konstanz und des Bodenseegebiets im Mittelalter bis zum Reichsmünzgesetz von 1559 ("Münz- und Geldgeschichte der im Grossherzogtum Baden vereinigten Gebiete," Part I [Heidelberg: C. Winter, 1911], pp. 391–93, No. 5).

[11] Memorandum, Stuttgart, July, 1819, Oncken and Saemisch, I, 335–36, No. 172.

[12] Memorandum, Stuttgart, July, 1819, Olshausen, op. cit., pp. 237–39, No. 27a.

to the whole of Germany were welcomed in these instructions, it also expressed doubts that the governments would reach a substantial agreement on this matter. It therefore suggested that those governments which had special interests in common should form separate unions, and it mentioned in particular a separate union between Bavaria, Württemberg, and Baden. It also expressly claimed that the various states had the right to form such a union according to Article XI of the Acts of Confederation, and Württemberg's representative was ordered to exploit this right as much as possible. This last point and the fact that a certain amount of secrecy was required seem to indicate that trialistic elements at Stuttgart exerted some influence on the drafting of this instruction.[13]

Bavaria and Württemberg thus took up the suggestion given to them by List and his League and tried to benefit from it politically. There is, however, no evidence that the Baden government studied the idea of a separate union, as the Munich and Stuttgart officials had done. Although it possessed in Nebenius one of the best financial experts, its policy in this matter remained vague and undetermined. Berstett, who was in charge of Baden's foreign affairs, was not familiar with political economy and seems to have learned less about it from Nebenius than might be assumed. Berstett's proposals in case a general solution could not be found centered around the idea of separate negotiations with individual governments. These negotiations were to lead to the conclusion of commercial treaties for the establishment of free trade. This idea can be traced back to Lotzbeck's motion of April 30, 1819.[14] It was taken up again by the official reply made by Nebenius in the name of the government[15] and from then on remained one of the favorite schemes of the Baden government. Several years later it even concluded a treaty of this kind with Hesse-Darmstadt.

It is difficult, however, to determine what the Baden

---

[13] Instruction for Count Mandelsloh, Stuttgart, November 17, 1819, Oncken and Saemisch, I, 357–58, No. 181.

[14] [Baden, Landtag] Übersicht, I, [53]–54.

[15] Baden, Diet, Karlsruhe, June 26, 1819, List, op. cit., I, Part II, 982–83.

Foreign Office meant when it used the term "separate negotiations" in 1819. One can safely say that in June, 1819, it was not thinking of the separate union List was advocating or of a common customs system which other South German statesmen were beginning to develop theoretically. Contemporaries, especially List, interpreted the statement Nebenius made before the Baden Diet on June 26 to mean that Baden was supporting the separate union List was proposing.[16] Whether List suggested his idea of a separate union to the Baden government when he was in Karlsruhe in the middle of July, 1819, cannot be stated with certainty.[17] At about the same time the Baden government was approached by Württemberg and asked about her attitude toward a possible South German union. Baden answered favorably,[18] but nothing came of the move, and it seems to have had little influence in Karlsruhe, since the foreign office continued to pursue the policy Lotzbeck had suggested. The instructions which were sent to Baden's representative at the Diet in Frankfurt leave no doubt that only a system of commercial treaties was intended.[19]

The Conferences for amending the Acts of Confederation which began in the last days of November at Vienna provided new opportunities for the exchange of ideas among German diplomats. It was here that Berstett,[20] Baden's representative, had an opportunity for separate negotiations.

---

[16] Although these references are not definite they have been generally interpreted as relating to this statement made by Nebenius; List to Wilhelm I, Stuttgart, early July, 1819, *ibid.*, p. 514, No. 21; memorandum, Stuttgart, July, 1819, Olshausen, *op. cit.*, p. 237, No. 27a.

[17] I was unable to find any reference indicating that List and the League submitted a petition to the Grand Duke of Baden which was similar to those they used in Munich, Stuttgart, and Darmstadt. List only thanked the Grand Duke and the Baden Diet for their help and asked for further assistance in the matter of general German economic unification (*ibid.*, p. 49). There are also indications that the oral discussions touched only general points (*ibid.*, p. 87; Böhtlingk, *Nebenius*, pp. 43, 46).

[18] Curt Albrecht, *Die Triaspolitik des Frhn. K. Aug. v. Wangenheim* (Doctor's dissertation, Leipzig, 1914), p. 107.

[19] Decision, Baden Ministry of Foreign Affairs, Karlsruhe, August 17, 1819, Oncken and Saemisch, I, 341–42, No. 174.

[20] Berstett's character is the key for the understanding of his rôle at the Vienna Final Conferences. His lack of veracity and loyalty was recognized by some of his contemporaries (Treitschke, *Deutsche Geschichte*, IV, 224–25).

He took part in the informal talks which were conducted by Thuringian representatives and which aimed at the establishment of a free trade area in Southwestern and Central Germany.[21]   The Thuringian governments seem to have carried on a correspondence about common measures previous to the Vienna Final Conferences.[22]   Not very much is known about the relation of these early written negotiations to the oral discussion in December, 1819.   It is also difficult to establish how the negotiations for a regional league started, and one can only guess whether they developed spontaneously among the representatives during the discussion of general measures or whether they can be traced back to earlier developments and ultimately to the petitions List and the League handed in to various German governments during the summer of 1819.   It is improbable that the Bavarian or Württemberg governments took the initiative in these negotiations since they would have based their discussions on a common customs system. Possibly one representative conceived this idea himself, and du Thil, who represented Hesse-Darmstadt at the conferences, has been frequently referred to as the one who originated the idea or at least started the separate negotiations in Vienna.   It has been shown that the idea of a separate union preceded the Vienna Final Conferences.   Moreover, Berstett has been occasionally given the credit for the starting of these negotiations.[23]   The details of when and how du Thil took the initiative have never been given.   The step which brought about these negotiations is nowhere specified,[24] and the relation of the earlier discussions about a free-trade area to the definite program for a separate union around which the negotiations in January, 1820, centered is obscure.   It remains therefore very doubtful whether

---

[21] Berstett, Wien, December 19, 1819, Friedrich [Otto Aristides] von Weech (ed.), *Correspondenzen und Actenstücke zur Geschichte der Ministerialkonferenzen von Carlsbad und Wien in den Jahren 1819–1822 und 1834* (Leipzig: Vogel, 1865), pp. 80–81.

[22] Aegidi, *Aus der Vorzeit*, pp. 65, 72.

[23] W. Weber, *Der deutsche Zollverein*, p. 13; cf. du Thil, report No. 72, Wien, February 2, 1820, H. Schmidt, *Die Begründung*, p. xi.

[24] This is especially true of the sources: Du Thil, report No. 58, Wien, January 22, 1820, *ibid.*, p. ix; Fritsch, report, Wien, May 20, 1820, Aegidi, *op. cit.*, 94, n. 127; Hofmann to Krafft, Darmstadt, March 20, 1828, Treitschke, *op. cit.*, III, 38, n.

du Thil originated the discussions which took place during the last month of 1819 or whether he even started those negotiations with Nassau and Baden, which began early in January, 1820.[25] At any rate, there is no question that du Thil played an important rôle during the early stages of the January negotiations. It was these negotiations which first led to the Punctation of January 13 and subsequently prepared the way for the Darmstadt Conferences.

The events which immediately preceded this punctation are, however, very difficult to reconstruct, since Berstett's and du Thil's reports give two different versions. Du Thil undoubtedly discussed the project of a separate agreement with the representatives of Baden, Württemberg, Bavaria, Anhalt, and Nassau before January 13.[26] Berstett, Baden's representative, reported, however, that he himself started the negotiations by distributing the Nebenius memorandum to the members of the Tenth Committee of the Conferences and to others, after its first meeting on January 12, 1820, had convinced him that it would be a failure. He further claimed to have elaborated the Punctation of January 13 with Marschall, Nassau's representative, and to have sent this punctation to various South and Central German ministers, from whom he subsequently received replies on the matter.[27] It can be shown, however, that he had already distributed copies of the Nebenius memorandum before January 12[28] and that he gave it to the members of the committee during the session and not afterwards, as his report implied.[29] Berstett also had discussed the matter with du Thil before January 12 and must have learned about his

[25] Du Thil seems to have mentioned for the first time the idea of a separate union to his government on January 12, 1820 (report No. 49, Wien, H. Schmidt, Die Begründung, p. i). Suchel (Hessen-Darmstadt, p. 10) maintains, however, that in the middle of December du Thil had already started to negotiate, but Suchel does not explain why du Thil waited until January 12 to ask for further instructions on this point.

[26] Du Thil, report No. 49, Wien, January 12, 1820, H. Schmidt, Die Begründung, pp. ii–iii; Trott to Wintzingerode, Wien, January 8, 1820, Oncken and Saemisch, I, 362–63; Menn, op. cit., p. 65.

[27] Berstett to Ludwig I of Baden, Wien, January 16, 1820, Oncken and Saemisch, I, 368–69, No. 184.

[28] Blume, Hamburg, pp. 37–38; Aegidi, op. cit., pp. 26–27.

[29] Ibid., pp. 35–36.

views.[30]   What was the real nature of these talks?   Trott, one of Württemberg's representatives, stated in his report that the representatives of Baden, Hesse-Darmstadt, and Nassau had expressed their wishes for separate negotiations and also implied that they had undertaken a joint action.[31] Berstett seems to have tried to keep a secret from his government all the negotiations he carried on before January 12.

On the other hand, it is difficult to establish to what extent du Thil participated in the immediate negotiations which led to the Punctation of January 13.[32]   In this case again it was Berstett who tried to suppress any influence du Thil might have had on the development.   Whether this was done with du Thil's consent and knowledge cannot be determined.

Suchel believes that Berstett reported falsely in order to promote his own cause against that of the other representatives.[33]   It might also be suggested that Berstett pursued a personal policy at the conferences and that at the time he tried to give the impression of having followed his instructions and of having conducted affairs dispassionately. Berstett, with his Austrian sympathies, may have feared that his outspoken anti-Prussian policy would cause him to lose favor with Grand Duke Ludwig I of Baden, who sympathized with Prussia.

Whatever the explanation of Berstett's behavior may have

---

[30] Berstett's circular note to various representatives at Vienna, dated Vienna, January 13 (ibid., pp. 66–67) admits "that others have already agreed to give support"; du Thil, report No. 49, Wien, January 12, 1820, H. Schmidt, Die Begründung, p. ii; Berstett to Ludwig I of Baden, Karlsruhe [April, 1825], Oncken and Saemisch, I, 501, No. 253.

[31] Trott to Wintzingerode, Wien, January 8, 1820, ibid., pp. 362–63, No. 183.

[32] Berstett to Ludwig I of Baden, Wien, January 16, 1820, ibid., p. 369, No. 184, and Fritsch, Wien, January 16, 1820, Aegidi, op. cit., p. 68, seem to indicate that du Thil did not take part in drafting the punctation, while du Thil's report No. 58, Wien, January 22, 1820, H. Schmidt, Die Begründung, p. ix, shows the contrary. Since Menn says that the first draft originated with Marschall (op. cit., p. 66) and since du Thil states in his report No. 58 that Berstett drafted the punctation in his and Marschall's presence without giving du Thil a chance to make all the changes he desired, it might be concluded that Berstett and Marschall agreed first secretly and then had another meeting which du Thil attended and during which they pretended to make the original draft.

[33] Op. cit., pp. 15, 18.

been, there is no question that he was counting all the time on du Thil's coöperation. This seems to be particularly obvious if one considers that Baden and Nassau were not neighbors and that the accession of Hesse-Darmstadt would have given the necessary territorial unity to this league.

The general purpose of the Punctation of January 13 was to abolish all tariffs and similar restrictions among the contracting parties. Article III, however, reserved the right of the members of this union to regulate their customs along the boundaries they had in common with foreign countries or with German states which did not adhere to this punctation.[34] Dr. Menn explains the provision as a compromise which was concluded between Berstett, who wanted a common customs system, and the free traders du Thil and Marschall.[35] Du Thil perhaps believed that with Marschall's help he had won Berstett for his idea of free trade,[36] since he thought that Berstett subscribed to the idea of a common customs system as advocated by Nebenius, whose memorandum he had just distributed.[37] But Berstett, to judge from his own behavior during the negotiations, seems to have believed in free trade from the beginning or at least to have been won over without any difficulty. If there was any compromise, it was concluded between Berstett and Marschall, who then got du Thil to accept it. Du Thil claimed in particular that Article III did not represent his opinion, but that Berstett pressed him into accepting it.[38]

Article III of the Punctation of January 13 therefore should not be solely explained as a compromise between two parties, and its peculiar provisions should be regarded as a typical expression of the undeveloped economic thought of that period. It is obvious that the ministers were not too well acquainted with the administration of a territorial system. Although they knew about the possibility of a common customs system, they did not adopt it for their separate union, probably because they did not understand the funda-

---

[34] Punctation, Wien, January 13, 1820, Aegidi, *op. cit.*, pp. 67-68.

[35] *Op. cit.*, pp. 65–67.

[36] Du Thil, report No. 58, Wien, January 22, 1820, H. Schmidt, *Die Begründung*, p. ix.

[37] Du Thil, report No. 49, Wien, January 12, 1820, *ibid.*, p. ii.

[38] Du Thil, report No. 58, Wien, January 22, 1820, *ibid.*, p. ix; cf. Weech, *op. cit.*, p. 89.

mental principles of a modern tariff administration. Ber-stett's paradoxical behavior especially makes this clear. Within twenty-four hours after distributing the Nebenius memorandum advocating a common customs system he supported a punctation with an entirely different program without seeming to realize what he was doing. That du Thil and Marschall gave up their opposition to all customs can be partially explained by a desire to retain a weapon against unreasonable German neighbors.[39]

The Punctation of January 13, however, went beyond the limits of a commercial treaty. The geographical principle seems to have been well recognized.[40] Moreover, they called the institution they were planning a *Verein.* The characteristic feature was the idea of creating a region in which all inhabitants were put on an equal basis in regard to trading rights with each other. This idea appeared much clearer in a revised proposal signed on February 9, 1820, by Berstett, Marschall, du Thil, and Fritsch.[41] This plan of mutual preference was based on a complicated system of certificates of origin. The agreement also mentioned Darmstadt as the place where the negotiations were to be continued.[42]

It was only natural that a scheme like this should find opponents at the conferences. It was soon realized that the ministers who had been promoting these ideas were anything but experts in this matter.[43] The larger states, like Bavaria and Württemberg, were quick to understand that it was in their own interest to continue some kind of customs system. There seems to have been discussion among the ministers of Baden, Hesse-Darmstadt, and Nassau about the extension of their union, before they signed the Punctation of February 9. Du Thil favored a procedure by which an agreement among three or four states should first be reached, after which more states would be asked to join.[44] It was

---

[39] Du Thil, report No. 49, Wien, January 12, 1820, H. Schmidt, *Die Begründung,* p. iv.

[40] Menn, *op. cit.,* p. 65.   [41] Aegidi, *op. cit.,* pp. 72–74.

[42] Before that Frankfurt had been mentioned (Trott to Wintzingerode, Wien, January 8, 1820, Oncken and Saemisch, I, 363, No. 183; Suchel, *op. cit.,* p. 21).

[43] Aegidi, *op. cit.,* p. 74.   [44] Menn, *op. cit.,* p. 65.

with this idea in mind that he tried to prevent Bavaria from participating in these subsequent negotiations.[45] Du Thil, knowing that the Bavarian government was opposed to this free-trade union, had hoped that the smaller states, after having come to an agreement among themselves, could maneuver Bavaria into a position where she would have to accede substantially to their wishes. That this scheme failed —if, indeed, it ever was intended to work—was due to the fact that all political realities had been overlooked. It is not quite clear how du Thil could expect an accumulation of odd territories to force a well-rounded state like Bavaria, that was larger than all of them together, to give up her customs system, which was vital to her existence.

The Bavarian government at first refused even to negotiate a basis for the Darmstadt Conferences at Vienna, and it took a great deal of effort on Berstett's part to persuade both Bavaria and Württemberg to sign a preliminary agreement at Vienna.[46] This treaty of May 19, 1820, and the punctation of the same date meant a complete defeat for the free traders.[47] The program included the erection of a common customs system, and thus modified the old plan completely according to Bavaria's wishes.

It has been suggested that the government at Karlsruhe never shared Berstett's free-trade policy and that Berstett changed his position according to orders from home and that he was not influenced by the Bavarian demands.[48] It is true that the Baden Ministry of Finance objected on February 18, 1820, to Berstett's previous punctation, and it demanded that the treaty should contain provisions about joint actions and excise taxes.[49] But it remains very doubtful whether Berstett was ever ordered from Karlsruhe to in-

---

[45] Du Thil, report No. 72, Wien, February 2, 1820, H. Schmidt, *Die Begründung*, p. xi.

[46] Wilhelm I to Wintzingerode, Stuttgart, April 28, 1820, Oncken and Saemisch, I, 381–82, No. 194; Aegidi, *op. cit.*, pp. 93–97.

[47] *Ibid.*, pp. 100–1; Menn, *op. cit.*, pp. 69–70.

[48] Fischer, "Über das Wesen . . .," *Jahrbücher für Nationalökonomie und Statistik* II, 349; [Carl] F[riedrich] Nebenius, "Über die Entstehung und Erweiterung des grossen deutschen Zollvereines," *Deutsche Viertel-Jahrsschrift*, 1838, Part II, p. 328; Menn, *op. cit.*, pp. 69, 82.

[49] Oncken and Saemisch, I, 380.

sist on a common customs system for the separate union.[50]
What is known about the warning the Ministry of Finance
sent on February 18 seems to indicate that it wanted Berstett
to include common measures against nonmembers, a procedure which was not necessarily identical with a common
customs system.   Berstett's revised draft of March 28, which
was formulated after he had heard the objections from
Karlsruhe, still proposed not a common customs system but
a system of mutual preference.[51]   It is naturally quite possible, although there is no proof for it, that Berstett was
advised from Karlsruhe before March 28, 1820, to demand
a common customs system for the separate union[52] and that
for some reason he did not follow the suggestion.   On the
other hand, there is evidence to show that Berstett neither
changed his position nor supported a common customs system until he heard the Bavarian arguments in its favor.[53]
Before Berstett capitulated completely and accepted the
Bavarian demands he seems to have been slowly weaken-
ing;[54] but this change from supporting a system of mutual
preference to subscribing to Bavaria's demands for a customs
system occurred after March 28 and probably as late as May,
1820.   Berstett explained the change by saying that his government had suddenly realized that it needed the customs
revenues to balance its budget.[55]   If his government had
advised him this way, it would have been natural for him to
tell the other representatives at once.   Instead, Berstett tried
to delay the completion of the old agreement with his neighbors along the Rhine by all kinds of excuses while at the same
time he started negotiating with Bavaria and Württemberg
without informing du Thil.   When du Thil finally pressed
him for an explanation, he told the story about orders from

[50] Weech (op. cit., pp. 94–95) states that the matter was discussed back
and forth by correspondence between Berstett and Nebenius after January,
1820, but Berstett remained unconvinced, and there is no reference to a
definite order for Berstett to change his policy.

[51] Dated Wien, Oncken and Saemisch, I, 380–81, No. 193.

[52] This may have been done by Nebenius in another memorandum (cf.
Böhtlingk, op. cit., pp. 16–17).

[53] Fritsch, report, Wien, May 20, 1820, Aegidi, op. cit., p. 97, n. 133;
cf. Weech, op. cit., p. 97.

[54] Suchel, op. cit., p. 25.

[55] Ibid., pp. 24–25.

home.[56]   In view of Berstett's earlier behavior the truth of
this statement may be questioned, especially if one considers the other circumstances.   Berstett also said that
Baden wanted the separate union to include all of South
Germany,[57] and this statement seems to give the clue to his
behavior.   With his vague economic notions he could have
had only political reasons for his move.   His aim was probably to align as many states as possible against Prussia.   His
subsequent policy also throws light on the nature of the
"compromise" with du Thil and Marschall.[58]

The Political Background of the South German Conferences, 1820–25

AFTER the South German governments had agreed to call
a conference for establishing a separate union, negotiations proceeded in a more regular manner.   Decisions of
policy were made by the responsible central agencies of each
state, and were not left to the intrigues of individual diplomats.   Political considerations determined the policies of the
various governments, and political factors shaped the course
of the negotiations.

It was thus primarily for political reasons that the statesmen were unable to reach an agreement, and it was particularly Bavaria's fault that the Darmstadt Conferences failed.[59]
Rechberg, the Bavarian minister for foreign affairs, pursued a
policy of isolation for his state.   He wanted to maintain
friendly but independent relations with Austria and Prussia,
because he realized that Bavaria herself was too small to
pursue her own European policy, though she was large

---

[56] *Ibid.*, pp. 23–25.   [57] *Loc. cit.*

[58] It has been said that Berstett's change was due to his desire to get
something done in order that he should not have to return to the Baden
Diet with nothing achieved (*ibid.*, p. 26, n. 1; Aegidi, *op. cit.*, pp. 94–96).
Suchel argues that the new orders from Karlsruhe which had been sent out
after the Punctation of February 9 had been known there made it impossible for Berstett to continue this earlier policy. But Suchel (*op. cit.*,
pp. 25–26) overlooks that Berstett's program of March 28 did not propose
a common customs system, though he operated with mutual preferences
and maximum tariffs for the contracting parties.   Suchel also fails to explain
why Berstett at least did not try first to persuade du Thil and Marschall to
change their opinions on tariffs, if he had actually changed his.   Moreover,
in order to achieve something the small union would have sufficed.

[59] Doeberl, *Bayern*, p. 18.

enough to be a welcome ally of a great power. Rechberg believed, moreover, that a union between Bavaria and the small and medium states would only increase their political importance, while Bavaria would not obtain any additional prestige. Such a union might also infringe on Bavaria's independence of action, so that negotiations would be carried out by the union in which the majority of votes would be controlled by governments hostile to Bavarian interests and Bavaria would thus lose all influence.[60] Further, these smaller states would never submit to Bavarian domination and, even if the Bavarian government should enter such a union without any political ambitions, Bavaria would soon arouse suspicion and maneuver herself into a position in which Württemberg found herself while following her policy of trialism.[61] Rechberg's policy was to pursue Bavaria's interests without overestimating her strength. He considered it to be advantageous for Bavaria to continue her membership in the German Confederation and objected strenuously to a confederation within the Confederation.[62] This thoroughly particularistic policy was opposed by Lerchenfeld, who was in charge of Bavaria's finances. During these years Lerchenfeld constantly supported the idea of a separate South German economic union. Whether he subscribed to trialistic ideas is difficult to determine, especially since from 1823 on he strictly confined himself to the administration of his department.[63] His liberal tendencies might have drawn him into a policy of supporting the constitutional South German states against Prussia and Austria. On one occasion he stated that he had begun to like the idea of a purely German association.[64] He was able to entertain a broad view of the situation, for his concern was not limited to the amount of revenue which such a union might yield. By joining a South

[60] Rechberg and Flad to Bavarian Ministry of Finance [Munich], September 26, 1823, *ibid.*, pp. 68–71, No. 5.

[61] Bavarian Ministry of Foreign Affairs, memorandum [February or March, 1822], *ibid.*, p. 63, No. 2.

[62] "Ein Bund im Bunde," Rechberg and Flad to Ministry of Finance [Munich], September 26, 1823, *ibid.*, pp. 69–70, No. 5.

[63] Max, Freiherr von Lerchenfeld, "Lerchenfeld," *Allgemeine deutsche Biographie*, XVIII (1883), 424.

[64] Bavarian Cabinet, protocol, München, May 1, 1820, Oncken and Saemisch, I, 383, No. 195.

German union he hoped that Bavaria would regain economic prosperity. The increasing tariffs of the neighboring states, many of which had been introduced because the Darmstadt Conferences had failed, pressed hard on Bavaria's economic life and hence supported Lerchenfeld's urgent demands for relief through a union.[65]

Although the conduct of Bavaria's foreign policy was in Rechberg's hands, Lerchenfeld was able to see to it that at least the appearance of negotiation was kept up by the Munich government. Public opinion, especially as expressed in the Bavarian Diet, really left them no other choice,[66] and Lerchenfeld's complaints about the poverty of the country could not be overlooked. The policy actually pursued was one of constant delays, diversions, and obstructions. At the beginning of the Darmstadt Conferences it was argued that the principles of May 19, 1820, were not a binding basis for the negotiations. This was legally correct, but not very diplomatic, since Bavaria herself had insisted on the principles.[67] In order that something might be accomplished, the Bavarian representative sided with those who diverted the energies of the Darmstadt Conferences for months to a discussion of free trade in foodstuffs.[68] The reserve shown by the Bavarian representative, the long periods during which he was left without instructions and the unfriendly and dilatory character of those which he finally received were naturally noticed by the other members of the Darmstadt Conferences, and such doings did not make them more confident of Bavaria's intentions.[69] It should

---

[65] Lerchenfeld to Rechberg, München, August 22, 1823, *ibid.*, pp. 450–53, No. 229; Bavarian Ministry of Finance to Bavarian Ministry of Foreign Affairs, München, September 20, 1824, *ibid.*, pp. 458–59, No. 235; Bavarian Cabinet, protocol, München, October 14, 1824, *ibid.*, pp. 462–64, No. 237; Bavarian Ministry of Finance to Bavarian Ministry of Foreign Affairs, München, July 12, 1825, *ibid.*, pp. 510–11, No. 261.

[66] *Ibid.*, p. 426, n. 2; Aretin to Max I, Frankfurt, September 19, 1820, *ibid.*, p. 393, No. 203; Doeberl, *Bayern*, p. 21.

[67] *Ibid.*, pp. 19–21.   [68] Menn, *op. cit.*, pp. 84–85.

[69] Wangenheim, report, Frankfurt, May 25, 1821, Oncken and Saemisch, I, 412–13, No. 211; Aretin to Max I, Frankfurt, May 30, 1821, *ibid.*, p. 413, No. 212; Bavarian Ministry of Foreign Affairs to Aretin, München, July 5, 1821, *ibid.*, p. 417, No. 214; Menn, *op. cit.*, p. 93; Nebenius to Berstett, Darmstadt, April 28, 1822, Oncken and Saemisch, I, 430–33, No. 221; Doeberl, *Bayern*, p. 22.

not be overlooked, however, that the Bavarian experts contributed to the discussions and that the stand taken by the Bavarian government on specific matters was usually in pursuit of her best interests. But this pretense of negotiation should not be taken for a serious interest in a separate union.

The policy followed by Württemberg, the other South German kingdom, differed essentially from that of Bavaria. From the beginning Württemberg favored a South German union, and her aim was to mediate between the conflicting interests.[70] Nevertheless, her policy was also subject to certain fluctuations. Two parties existed among the influential Württemberg officials. One group regarded a separate agreement as the first step toward general German economic unification, while the other party looked at such a regional union as an end in itself. When List first suggested his idea of a separate union in Stuttgart (July, 1819), King Wilhelm I of Württemberg was willing to support such a plan so long as the Confederation did not provide an adequate solution. Under Wangenheim's influence, however, he soon changed his mind and desired a permanent economic alliance among the South German states.[71] Wangenheim, Württemberg's representative in Frankfurt and at the Darmstadt Conferences, remained an ardent supporter of economic as well as political trialism.[72] King Wilhelm I continued to subscribe to trialistic ideas, since it was on his suggestion that the ill-famed *Manuscript aus Süddeutschland* was written. This anonymous pamphlet, which was published just before the Darmstadt Conferences began, was the classical example of trialistic thinking. It failed, however, in furthering the Darmstadt Conferences, since it aroused more suspicion than enthusiasm.

But neither Wangenheim's nor King Wilhelm's views can be regarded as expressions of Württemberg's official policy. Wangenheim was notorious for forming his own policy, and

[70] For instance, Württemberg's proposals for a compromise, Stuttgart, November 22, 1822, Oncken and Saemisch, I, 439–445, No. 226; Schmitz-Grollenburg to Rechberg, München, October 9, 1823, *ibid.*, pp. 453–54, No. 231; cf. Albrecht, *op. cit.*, p. 119.

[71] *Ibid.*, p. 105.

[72] *Ibid.*, p. 109; Wangenheim to Wintzingerode, Darmstadt, September 20, 1820, Oncken and Saemisch, I, 394–95, No. 204.

the extent to which King Wilhelm's trialistic intrigues were identical with the official policy of his kingdom can be gathered from the fact that Wintzingerode was not informed about the origin of the *Manuscript* until after it had appeared. The Württemberg government tried to set on foot negotiations as early as July, 1819, when it sounded out Bavaria and Baden.[73] However, its policy soon became more reserved. It did not take the initiative during the Vienna Final Conferences, and remained in the background in Darmstadt.[74] Wintzingerode never was the trialist that Wangenheim or King Wilhelm was, and it is difficult to determine to what extent financial and industrial interests contributed to the adoption of a more moderate policy. Nevertheless, by 1823 Württemberg had to conform to the political reaction Metternich was extending all over Germany. Wangenheim was dismissed and the trialistic policy abandoned.[75]

Baden, on the other hand, played a leading part at the Darmstadt Conferences. This was primarily due to the fact that her representative, Nebenius, was expert in financial matters. Although the Baden government persistently furthered a separate union of South Germany during the Vienna and Darmstadt Conferences, it refused when these negotiations had failed to join such a South German union or at least made its adherence dependent on conditions which the other states were unable to accept. Baden officials, Nebenius in particular, subsequently claimed that Baden did not join a South German customs system because she always had national economic unification in mind. General German unification, it was argued, would not have been achieved if Baden had helped to give the South German union a better-rounded territory, since the high tariffs demanded by Bavaria and Württemberg would have permanently separated the North from the South.[76] Contemporary records do not support such an explanation of Baden's policy, and Nebenius's statement has to be classed as good propaganda.[77] The patriotic phrases used by Berstett and

---

[73] Albrecht, *op. cit.*, p. 107.   [74] *Ibid.*, p. 109.
[75] Cf. Lenz, *Friedrich List*, p. 114; Suchel, *op. cit.*, pp. 37, 94; Aegidi, *op. cit.*, pp. 96–97; Menn, *op. cit.*, p. 92.
[76] Beck, *Carl Friedrich Nebenius*, pp. 90–91.
[77] Menn, *op. cit.*, pp. 132–33.

other Baden officials in 1819–20 must be regarded with the same skepticism.[78] Berstett was a conservative, and he wanted to abolish all trade barriers because he believed that they were stirring up discontent which would lead ultimately to revolution.[79] Such considerations guided Berstett when he attacked the new Prussian customs law in Vienna and when he instructed Nebenius that he should avoid all contact with List at the Darmstadt Conferences and coöperate with Nassau's representative, who was pursuing an even more reactionary policy.[80] Since Berstett was more and more influenced by Metternich,[81] his policy remained particularistic throughout. Berstett opposed the popular movement for the unification of Germany and believed that, with the increasing individuality of each state, German unity was becoming less likely.[82] It was in line with the principles of this policy that the Karlsruhe government turned away from a South German union as soon as it realized that any trialistic arrangement would curtail Baden's state rights as much as any general unification.[83] Baden even opposed a union with her neighbors along the Rhine, but continued to participate in the negotiations because she did not want to be left out.[84] Baden finally broke up the Stuttgart Conferences by insisting on extremely low tariffs.[85]

Since Berstett did not know much about the technical aspects of the financial questions, he relied greatly on the advice he received from Nebenius. Although it seems to be questionable whether Nebenius was able to develop Berstett's understanding of economic matters, Berstett more than once allowed his financial adviser to influence his policy.

---

[78] Baden Ministry of Foreign Affairs, decision, Karlsruhe, August 17, 1819, Oncken and Saemisch, I, 341–42, No. 174; Berstett to Ludwig I, Wien, January 16, 1820, ibid., p. 369, No. 184.

[79] Menn, op. cit., p. 83.

[80] Berstett to Nebenius, Karlsruhe, September 13, 1820, Oncken and Saemisch, I, 387–90, No. 184.

[81] Treitschke, op. cit., III, 270–71.

[82] Berstett to Nebenius, Karlsruhe, September 13, 1820, Oncken and Saemisch, I, 388, No. 200.

[83] Reigersberg to Max I, Karlsruhe, April 5, 1825, ibid., pp. 499–500, No. 252; Menn, op. cit., p. 139.

[84] Suchel, op. cit., pp. 76, 94–95.

[85] Declaration, Stuttgart, July 4, 1825, Oncken and Saemisch, I, 509, No. 259.

In 1820 Nebenius was not the patriot that some writers have tried to make him;[86] but while sharing Berstett's views on German unification,[87] he seems to have been unable to look beyond his department in this matter of an economic union. Although Nebenius was the best authority on financial administration at the Darmstadt Conferences and although he contributed considerably to develop a working arrangement for a customs system, by unduly promoting Baden's interests he abused the influence he received as an expert. He desired, for instance, that all goods should be cleared as soon as they passed the boundary instead of allowing them to be bonded to their destination in the interior. He also suggested that the net profits of such a common customs system should be distributed according to the mean between the number of inhabitants and the length of the boundaries of each member state.[88] Since Baden's far-stretched territory gave her long frontiers and made her almost completely a boundary district, the advantages she would have received from such a scheme are obvious. The same inability made Nebenius oppose the high Bavarian tariffs and insist on the low Baden tariff, one of the issues on which the Darmstadt Conferences failed to agree. When Baden later adopted a policy of isolation, her action was again determined by the higher revenues her low tariffs could collect for her by attracting intermediate trade and smuggling.[89] This was the time too when Baden returned to Berstett's plans of 1819–20 and tried to establish a free-trade area through a net of commercial treaties.[90] Nebenius seems also to have been influenced by private feelings in this sudden change from coöperation to obstruction, and his personality may have been in part responsible for the failure of his ideas.[91]

---

[86] Cf. Boehtlingk, op. cit., pp. 63–64; Treitschke, op. cit., III, 775.

[87] Ibid., p. 305.

[88] Darmstadt Conferences, protocol of fourth meeting, November 27, 1820, Oncken and Saemisch, I, 399, 402, No. 207.

[89] Reigersberg to Max I, Karlsruhe, April 5, 1825, ibid., pp. 499–500, No. 252; Boehtlingk, op. cit., p. 22; Treitschke, op. cit., III, 304; Menn, op. cit., pp. 132–33.   [90] Suchel, op. cit., pp. 76–77.

[91] Nebenius to Berstett, Darmstadt, April 28, 1822, Oncken and Saemisch, I, 32, No. 221; Reigersberg to Max I, Karlsruhe, November 11, 1824, ibid., p. 466, No. 239; ZuRhein to Max I, Stuttgart, March 11, 1825,

The policy of Hesse-Darmstadt, Baden's neighbor in the north, also underwent a change. When du Thil entered the negotiations in 1820, he tried as a confirmed free trader to fight the Prussian customs law of 1818; but as one conference after another failed, he slowly changed his mind and finally was the first to enter into a customs union with Prussia. As a whole, Hesse-Darmstadt's policy appears to have been steadier and less capricious than Baden's. During the Vienna Final Conferences du Thil refrained from openly campaigning against Prussia,[92] much as he wanted the Prussian customs system changed. It was, nevertheless, an anti-Prussian sentiment which led him, as it did many others, to negotiate for a separate union.[93]

During the negotiations in January and February, 1820, du Thil believed in free trade and was willing to accept a common customs system only as the smaller evil.[94] Such considerations guided him when he signed the preliminary treaty for the Darmstadt Conferences of May 19, 1820. Thus, when these conferences opened in September, 1820, one of the first suggestions he made was to scrap the principles agreed on in Vienna and to negotiate for free trade.[95] In doing so, however, he did not expect to have complete success. He used this stratagem in order to bargain for low tariffs and also in order to show public opinion in Hesse-Darmstadt that he had done his best in the popular cause of free trade.[96]

When his proposal failed, he was honest enough to accept the consequences: either to withdraw from the conferences or to stay and support a common customs system. He decided for a common customs system with low tariffs, and he gave as one of the reasons for his change in policy that this was the only way to enable the smaller states to bargain

---

ibid., p. 493, No. 251; Württemberg to Baden, verbal note, Stuttgart, August 17, 1825, ibid., p. 515, No. 264; Menn, op. cit., pp. 132–33; Treitschke, op. cit., III, 626–27.

[92] Du Thil, report No. 57, Wien, January 22, 1820, H. Schmidt, Die Begründung, p. viii.

[93] Du Thil's memoirs cited by Treitschke, op. cit., III, 305.

[94] Du Thil, report No. 49, Wien, January 12, 1820, H. Schmidt, Die Begründung, p. v.

[95] Aretin to Max I, Darmstadt, September 14, 1820, Oncken and Saemisch, I, 390–91, No. 201.   [96] Suchel, op. cit., pp. 31–33.

with Prussia.   To remain a state without customs duties, he argued, would mean to become a paradise for smugglers. He also expected that the burdensome property tax could be lowered in Hesse-Darmstadt, since a customs system would bring additional revenue.[97]   The Darmstadt government, however, did not accede completely to du Thil's views. But after three years of fruitless negotiations at the Darmstadt Conferences, du Thil was able to take the first step of his revised policy by breaking off the negotiations and introducing boundary customs in Hesse-Darmstadt.   Although all customs were unpopular in the grand duchy and although they could not yield much revenue, du Thil took this action, which he considered a temporary arrangement,[98] in order to have something to bargain with.[99]   This measure really brought some results; a commercial treaty was concluded with Baden which provided that each state should grant preferential tariffs to the other's products.   Nebenius was even thinking of creating an area of mutual preference between the Mediterranean and the North Sea.[100]   However, the system of certificates of origin which were necessary for carrying out such a scheme only created distrust between the two governments, and du Thil even went so far as to charge that Baden had fraudulently abused it.[101]   Thus successive unfortunate experiences compelled him to give up his free-trade beliefs.

During the Vienna Final Conferences du Thil had already shown a special interest in his immediate neighbors along the Rhine.   From the beginning he had favored a small union among these states, and all along he tried to proceed in close coöperation with them.[102]   The Darmstadt government was not opposed to a union with Bavaria and Württemberg, but it was quite conscious of the different interests it shared with its neighbors along the Rhine and therefore

---

[97] Ibid., pp. 37–39.   [98] Ibid., p. 80.

[99] Treitschke, op. cit., III, 624.   [100] Menn, op. cit., p. 123.

[101] Du Thil, cited from H. Schmidt, Die Begründung, p. 15.

[102] Nebenius to Berstett, Darmstadt, April 28, 1822, Oncken and Saemisch, I, 430, No. 221; Hesse-Darmstadt circular, February 24, 1824, ibid., pp. 455–56, No. 232; Hofmann to Nebenius, Stuttgart, November 2, 1824, ibid., pp. 464–66, No. 238; Hofmann to ZuRhein, Darmstadt, August 24, 1825, ibid., pp. 515–17, No. 265; Suchel, op. cit., pp. 45, 77, 79; Menn, op. cit., p. 99; Treitschke, op. cit., III, 624–26.

did not want to join without them.[103]   The lack of common
interests between Hesse-Darmstadt and the South German
kingdoms finally caused du Thil to join the Prussian system.
Du Thil's policy has been described by Treitschke as being
sober and free from political ambitions,[104] which is on the
whole correct.   His attempts to put some pressure on Frankfurt were slight deviations from that policy.[105]   Another
characteristic of his policy was the fact that he always stood
up for the independence of the grand duchy.   It was a
Darmstadt official who introduced into the negotiations the
idea that in a customs union each state should retain its own
customs administration, thus finding a formula which made
it possible for the smaller states to join an economic union
with larger states without giving up any of their sovereign
rights.[106]   Du Thil, although firmly holding his own ground,
tried to avoid any step which might offend the larger states,
especially Austria.

In contrast to Hesse-Darmstadt's businesslike policies,
Nassau pursued a course of intrigue and obstruction.[107]
During the Vienna Final Conferences Nassau's representative had attacked the Prussian customs system and had
already shown his poor judgment in political and economic
matters.   He had attacked Prussia because he believed her
customs law was designed to bring about the revolution
through the discontent it was creating.   His ignorance in
matters of public financial administration went together with
a firm belief in free trade.   However, he did not disapprove
of the Treaty of May 19, 1820, which planned the establishment of a common customs system in South Germany, because he saw in it a means to force Prussia to give up her
tariffs.   But it was not long, before it was realized in Wiesbaden that the anti-Prussian policy had no prospect of success.   Moreover, it became clear to the Nassau government

---

[103] Hofmann to ZuRhein, Darmstadt, August 24, 1825, Oncken and
Saemisch, I, 515–17, No. 265.   [104] Op. cit., III, 305.

[105] Du Thil, report No. 72, Wien, February 2, 1820, H. Schmidt, Die
Begründung, pp. xi-xii; Peter Orth, Die Kleinstaaterei im Rhein-Main-
Gebiet und die Eisenbahnpolitik 1830–1866 (Doctor's dissertation, Frank-
furt, 1936), pp. 15–16.

[106] Hofmann to Weckherlin, Darmstadt, November 24, 1824, Oncken
and Saemisch, I, 473–77, No. 243.

[107] The discussion immediately following is based on Menn's monographic study, which has already been cited.

that it was not Prussia which was to bring the revolution, but that the liberal and constitutional South German states were to be the starting points for the threatening overthrow of the existing order. Thus peace was concluded with Prussia, but no real friendship evolved.[108]

Although as a free trader Marschall was opposed to all tariffs and as an ultraconservative to any union with the South German governments, he nevertheless decided that Nassau was to participate in the Darmstadt Conferences. He did this because he was afraid of popular opinion and because he did not want to see his duchy isolated by Prussia and a South German customs system.[109] Although Nassau participated in the negotiations, she did not refrain from obstructing them; there were the declarations against all tariffs, or against protective tariffs, especially after the Wiesbaden government had found it necessary to introduce a customs system into the duchy.[110] Marschall found other ways of obstruction by promoting a treaty for free trade in foodstuffs[111] and by constantly asserting Nassau's special interests and sovereign rights. Just as in the case of Hesse-Darmstadt, Nassau's economic interests were more with North than with South Germany; and the objections of the Wiesbaden government on that ground were not without justification. But Marschall was not too eager even to join with Baden and Hesse-Darmstadt, with which Nassau had common interests.[112] He approached certain problems in a petty spirit; for instance, he once insisted that straw and fertilizer should be included among the foodstuffs for which a special free-trade treaty was being negotiated, and that only because Nassau needed them for her vineyards.[113] Nassau also tried to preserve her political independence with an extreme jealousy, an independence which was already endangered, according to Marschall, through joining a customs union with protective tariffs.[114] As part of his policy of obstruc-

---

[108] Menn, op. cit., pp. 49–50, 55–58, 73–76, 83, 100.
[109] Ibid., p. 80.
[110] Nassau to Max I, Mainz, March 11, 1824, Oncken and Saemisch, I, 456–57, No. 233; Menn, op. cit., pp. 86–87, 90, 93, 140–41.
[111] Ibid., p. 84.   [112] Ibid., p. 99.   [113] Ibid., p. 85.
[114] Marschall to du Thil, Wiesbaden, November 22, 1824, Oncken and Saemisch, I, 470–71, No. 241.

tion Marschall seems also to have intrigued with Austria in order to break up or to discredit the Darmstadt Conferences.[115]

The other Central German states appear to have participated less in the negotiations. At the beginning Hesse-Kassel was inclined to join if her particular financial interests were considered.[116] There was no opposition on principle against tariffs as such in Kassel, but a great political objective seems to have been lacking.[117] As a rule, petty financial considerations dominated.[118] Lepel, Electoral Hesse's representative in Frankfurt, was under Wangenheim's influence and shared his political views;[119] but the government in Kassel does not seem to have pursued a policy of great ambitions, and it remained in the background during these negotiations. For a long time it hesitated to send a representative and then left him without instructions. When du Thil finally sent Hofmann to Kassel, he received a more cordial response than had been expected. But this interest soon started to wane, and the Kassel government began to obstruct the Darmstadt Conferences. It should be pointed out, however, that its real interests tied the Electorate to its neighbors in Central Germany.[120]

The Thuringian governments desired to coöperate with a South German union, although they opposed a solution which would favor Bavaria's interests or which would further trialistic schemes. They had, rather, a national solution in mind, and after opposing the Prussian customs system for a

[115] Marschall to Metternich, Wiesbaden, September 20, 1820, Olshausen, op. cit., pp. 312–16, No. 152; Handel to Metternich, Frankfurt, September 21, 1820, ibid., pp. 316–18; No. 153; Metternich to Buol, Wien, October 5, 1820, ibid., pp. 320–21, No. 159; Menn, op. cit., pp. 84, 101.

[116] Mülmann, report, Wiesbaden, September 20, 1820, Olshausen, op. cit., p. 315, in No. 152.

[117] Lenz, op. cit., p. 107; Haenlein to Prussian Ministry of Foreign Affairs, Kassel, December 16, 1824, Oncken and Saemisch, II, 76, No. 319; Heinrich von Treitschke, "Die Anfänge des deutschen Zollvereins," Preussische Jahrbücher, XXX (1872), 433.

[118] Mülmann, report, Wiesbaden, September 20, 1820, Olshausen, op. cit., p. 315, in No. 152; du Thil to Berstett, Darmstadt, September 19, 1822, Oncken and Saemisch, I, 438, No. 225; Menn, op. cit., p. 94; Suchel, op. cit., pp. 89-90.

[119] Menn, op. cit., p. 94; Treitschke, Deutsche Geschichte, III, 286, 319, 324.   [120] Suchel, op. cit., pp. 30, 47, 69–72, 77, 89, 90, 94.

while, they wanted some kind of arrangement to include Prussia.[121] Being more industrialized they also favored protection of their industries.[122]

The different economic theories prevalent among the South German statesmen, the conflicting economic interests of the states involved, and, in particular, the political ambitions of each government have been shown so far and they explain only too well why these early conferences failed to reach an agreement. The Darmstadt Conferences started with the largest state opposing any regional solution; two other governments were opposed to all tariffs, one tried to promote its own political schemes of doubtful value, while all of them refused to give up an iota of their own sovereignty and independence. It is therefore almost unbelievable that negotiations were kept up for so many years, and it is easily understood why they failed in their purpose. One result was that minor points were discussed with an energy which might have been used for a better cause. Thus a long debate arose whether snails could be called foodstuffs.[123] This was not so absurd as the proposals to include straw, hay, fertilizer, and lumber among the foodstuffs.[124]

Although many of the original difficulties were overcome during the course of the conferences, there remained obstacles in the fundamental state of mind with which the governments approached the problem and which were never surmounted. At the beginning some statesmen had pursued a dilatory policy, while others had often obstructed the negotiations. This led most of those involved to distrust the intentions of the other governments. The evil was increased through the fact that everybody was thinking first of his own state and hardly anybody ever considered the interests of

---

[121] *Ibid.*, pp. 31, 63, 74–75; Menn, *op. cit.*, p. 93; Fischer, *op. cit.*, pp. 350–51; Aegidi, *op. cit.*, pp. 101–2; Treitschke, *Deutsche Geschichte*, III, 623–24; Borckenhagen, *Bestrebungen*, p. 76; Wilhelm Engel, *Wirtschaftliche und soziale Kämpfe vor dem Jahre 1848 in Thüringen (insbesonderheit im Herzogtum Meiningen)* (Doctor's dissertation, Marburg, 1927), pp. 3–4; Olshausen, *op. cit.*, pp. 172–73; Mülmann, report, Wiesbaden, September 20, 1820, *ibid.*, p. 315, in No. 152; Bernstorff to Bülow and Klewiz, Berlin, June 8, 1822, Oncken and Saemisch, II, 45, No. 300.

[122] Suchel, *op. cit.*, p. 30.

[123] Aretin, to Max I, Frankfurt, May 30, 1821, Oncken and Saemisch, I, 414, No. 212.

[124] Suchel, *op. cit.*, p. 44.

the union they were going to establish, took broad views, or pursued a farsighted policy.

The Technical Achievements of the South German Conferences, 1820–25

ALTHOUGH the governments failed to reach an agreement, the negotiations between 1820 and 1825 were important. At these conferences the political and economic differences which stood in the way of economic unification were discussed, and it was here that the idea of a customs union was developed for the solution of the problems.

The idea of a customs union was indeed evolved; but no detailed scheme of an axiomatic character was worked out. The reason for this was not that there was no discussion of details. On the contrary, from the beginning details were in the foreground, and such questions as that of the tariff which was to be adopted had been argued extensively before the problem of separate or of common administration was attacked.

Moreover, much as certain basic requirements must be fulfilled before the term customs union can be applied, details can vary and can be arranged according to actual needs. The discussion of details was important, but most of them would have to be considered for any customs system. The basic principles of a customs union were then evolved, although some of them were only suggested, and they were not all coördinated. Later negotiations had still many problems to solve in choosing the right suggestions, coördinating them, and arranging the details.

The Punctation of May 19, 1820, drafted by Lerchenfeld, the Bavarian minister of finance, was accepted without any change by the contracting parties.[125] Lerchenfeld, when writing his proposals, knew Berstett's draft of March 28,[126] and there exists a certain similarity in style and content between them as well as between Berstett's previous punctations of January 13[127] and of February 9.[128]

---

[125] Punctation, Wien, May 19, Aegidi, op. cit., p. 101; Bavarian Cabinet, protocol, München, May 1, 1820, Oncken and Saemisch, I, 382–84, No. 195; Max I to Zentner and Stainlein, München, May 2, 1820, Doeberl, Bayern, pp. 60–61; No. 1; ibid., p. 16.   [126] Loc. cit.
[127] Dated Wien, Oncken and Saemisch, I, 371, No. 185.
[128] Dated Wien, Aegidi, op. cit., pp. 72–74.

There was, however, no such similarity between Lerchen-feld's draft and the scheme which had been formulated by the Württemberg government in the preceding summer[129]—except that they both proposed a common customs system—to indicate that it was used directly by Lerchenfeld for his draft. The word "Zollverein" especially, which the Württemberg draft of 1819 had already contained, did not appear in Lerchenfeld's draft. It was not until several years later that first the term "Zollverband"[130] and finally the word "Zollverein" was used more frequently by South German diplomats.[131]

This Punctation of May 19, 1820, already contained a number of valuable principles.[132]   First of all, the economic unification of all parts adhering to the scheme was set up by proposing internal free trade and a common customs line against nonmembers.   To combine these two principles of internal free trade and external customs might seem very elementary, but it was not at all a matter of course in those days.   The external customs were to be administered by union officials, so that each state gave up its own administration and the union established a customs service of its own. The system was therefore a common customs system and not a customs union.   Uniform tariffs were to be fixed by the union and the income from the customs receipts was to be distributed among the members proportionally according to the mean between the population and the extent of each state.   Moreover, road and water toll were to be standardized in order to prevent any government from making the whole treaty illusory by substituting these tolls for the customs they had given up.   For the same reason it was laid down that each state should levy the same excise taxes on subjects of other member states as on its own.   Although

---

[129] Dated Stuttgart, July, 1819, Oncken and Saemisch, I, 337–38, No. 172.

[130] Hesse-Darmstadt circular, Darmstadt, February 24, 1824, ibid., p. 456, No. 232; cf. p. 68 of this volume.

[131] Hofmann to Nebenius, Stuttgart, November 2, 1824, ibid., p. 464, No. 238; Bavarian Ministry of Finance to Ministry of Foreign Affairs, München, July 12, 1825, ibid., pp. 510–11, No. 261.   The term Handels-verein was used by Bernstorff in an interoffice memorandum to Bülow and Klewiz, Berlin, June 8, 1822, ibid., II, 45, No. 300.

[132] Dated Wien, Aegidi, op. cit., p. 101.

free trade was to be recognized in principle for the relation of the member states to each other, one very significant exception, which had already been included in Berstett's draft of March 28, 1820,[133] was stipulated, and that was that each government should retain the right to curtail free trade in salt.   The reason for this exception lay in the fact that in many countries salt was a state monopoly.   Although the Punctation also proposed that each state, after giving due notice, could secede from the union, it did not take over from Berstett's draft the idea that neighboring German states should be admitted to the union on demand.   As a whole, this Punctation of May 19, 1820, expressed a number of important ideas.   Although it was not worked out in detail, one cannot deny that it was the result of clear and systematic thinking.

In conformity with the agreement of May 19, 1820, the Darmstadt Conferences began in the fall of the same year. Nebenius, who represented Baden at these conferences, submitted by the end of November a draft for a South German customs system.   This draft worked out in more detail the system of the Punctation of May 19, elaborating in particular the administrative organization.[134]

Nebenius suggested that two institutions should be set up for running the common customs administration.   There was to be a permanent board in charge of the common administration.   Each participating state was to appoint one member of this board.   Each member was appointed for life and was not allowed to receive instructions or orders from the government which had sent him.   This board was to proclaim the laws agreed upon by the contracting parties, issue executive orders, instruct the customs officials, and, in general, administer the common customs system.

The power of this board, however, was not to be absolute. Once a year representatives of the various governments were to meet in order to check the annual account of the customs board, to approve edicts issued by the board, and to pass laws.   Except for amending the original treaty only an absolute majority was necessary for legislation.   Moreover,

---

[133] Dated Wien, Oncken and Saemisch, I, 381, No. 193.

[134] Darmstadt Conferences, protocol of fourth meeting, November 27, 1820, *ibid.*, pp. 399–402, No. 207.

each state was to have the right to send at any time inspectors to any common customs office in order to check up.   Another interesting feature was the idea that each government could nominate any persons who had passed the qualifying examinations set up by the board to a certain number of vacancies in the customs service.   The board, however, was to install and to promote these appointees.

Among these ideas the following were important in view of later developments.   First of all—and this was the most important contribution—the idea of annual conferences with equal representation was later realized in the Zollverein. And, secondly, there was the valuable suggestion that each government had the right to check all customs officials by its own agents.   Moreover, Nebenius's idea of distinguishing between matters that required unanimity and matters that could be decided by the majority was to be taken up subsequently.

An evaluation of this draft should emphasize that Nebenius dealt more with the administrative than with the political problems involved.   He followed this technical approach from the beginning.   The questionnaire on which he based this draft mostly contained administrative questions.[135] Moreover, his technical suggestions cannot always be praised.   His proposal to give the annual conferences the right to decide many important matters by majority vote might have worked if states of equal size had formed this union.   Under the existing circumstances he was not very farsighted in believing that Bavaria would ever subject herself in this way to her smaller neighbors.

Another criticism which can be made of Nebenius's proposals was his lack of originality.   He seems to have adapted his main ideas, without great changes, from the system employed for collecting the Rhine octroi.   The annual conferences, the permanent administrative board as well as the idea of mutual checking, had their origin with this institution.[136]   Nebenius should not be criticized so much for try-

---

[135] Suchel, op. cit., pp. 35–36.

[136] Eberhard Gothein, Geschichtliche Entwicklung der Rheinschiffahrt im 19. Jahrhundert ("Schriften des Vereins für Sozialpolitik," No. 101; Leipzig: Duncker & Humblot, 1903), p. 35; Eichhoff, Ockhardt, and Wenzel, draft of a temporary regulation, B[ernhard] S[ebastian] von Nau (ed.),

ing to use these ideas—for which he should really be given credit—as for the way he seems to have espoused them without further and deeper consideration.

In discussing administrative details also Nebenius lacked a certain farsightedness. Baden's interests were unduly promoted by such petty means as proposing that the length of the boundaries should be one of the factors in determining the distribution of the common income or that no goods could be shipped into the interior under bond. Nebenius also slipped back into Berstett's earlier ideas by suggesting that each state should retain the right to impose tariffs on goods which were imported into its territory from neighboring nonmember states or exported from its own territory into these nonmember states. This was only a modified version of Berstett's idea of a system of mutual preference with certificates of origin, and incidentally Baden as a boundary state would have profited from it.

The draft which Nebenius had worked out became the basis for all the subsequent discussions at Darmstadt. Some governments were slow to express their views on it, and many replies scarcely scratched the surface of the problem. The Bavarian government was definitely opposed to certain features of the Nebenius draft and therefore proposed changes. Thus it wanted the treaty to include a reference to Article XIX of the Acts of Confederation. This proposal was bitterly opposed by Württemberg, since it might have suggested that the governments did not possess the sovereign right to conclude such unions.[137] Württemberg's viewpoint was legally correct in so far as Article XIX never intended a separate union and therefore could not be used for such a scheme. Bavaria's idea was of interest, however, since this point was to appear again.

Bavaria, moreover, objected to all those points in the Baden draft which violated her interests.[138] It therefore suggested first of all that the various states should be represented at the annual conferences in proportion to their populations.

Beiträge zur Kenntniss und Beförderung des Handels und der Schiff-Fahrt (Mainz, 1818), pp. 108–110; Borckenhagen, *op. cit.*, pp. 35–36.

[137] Württemberg Ministry of Foreign Affairs to Wangenheim, Stuttgart, July 10, 1821, Oncken and Saemisch I, 415–16, No. 213.

[138] Bavarian Ministry of Foreign Affairs to Aretin, München, April 2, 1822, *ibid.*, pp. 426–28, No. 219.

Nebenius's draft had provided that each state should have one vote and that only in certain matters was unanimity necessary. Bavaria's objection to such an arrangement can be understood only too well if one considers how much smaller were most of the other states which were to form the union. However, neither the distribution of votes Bavaria proposed nor any other similar one which was suggested succeeded in solving the underlying problem. This problem of conflicting interests in power and influence was by its own nature not adaptable to be expressed in a mathematical proportion.

The other Bavarian demands did not concern the organization of the union so much as they dealt with relatively minor matters. The Bavarian government suggested that the income should be distributed to the member states in proportion to their population and area, a suggestion which would have been very advantageous to the more thinly populated Bavaria. The Bavarian government also objected to the proposal made by Nebenius that all goods should be cleared as soon as they passed the boundary and that no goods should be admitted into the interior under bond.[139] The advantages of the Bavarian system of a number of recognized storehouses for bonded goods were elaborated in great detail. The problem of bonded goods, the distribution of votes, and the tariff question remained unsolved during the Darmstadt Conferences. Suggestions and countersuggestions were made without introducing a new approach to the problem, and no agreement was reached.

How relatively unimportant most of these differences were can be seen from the fact that in the fall of 1824 Baden and Hesse-Darmstadt gave up in principle their former objections to bonded storages, unequal distribution of votes, and even to high tariffs, when it appeared more than probable that Bavaria and Württemberg would reach an agreement without the smaller states.[140]

The Heidelberg Protocol of November 19, 1824, where these concessions were proclaimed was, however, more notable for the way it tried to solve the political side of the problem. Here, for the first time during the South German

---

[139] Joerres, comments, Darmstadt, November 10, 1821, *ibid.*, pp. 420–24, No. 216.   [140] Menn, *op. cit.*, p. 126; Köhler, *Problematisches*, p. 23.

conferences, the principle of independent administrations was announced. Up to then these diplomats had operated with the idea of establishing a common customs administration. It was now proposed that no such common administration should be created, but that each state should through its own officials administer the customs in its own territory. This feature was to become one of the main characteristics of the Zollverein and was to remain in use with the German customs administration until after World War I.

The credit for having introduced this idea into the South German negotiations goes to Hofmann, an official in the Hesse-Darmstadt government. He put forward his proposal with a clear analysis of the political desires of the smaller states. These states feared nothing so much as the loss of their independent rights.[141] Submission to a common customs system which would take over the whole customs administration of each member state would in the eyes of many German governments have amounted to giving away a vital part of their sovereignty. The first duty of a sovereign government was, according to Hofmann, to preserve its independence, and a country which allowed a foreign authority to exercise official powers in her own territory was endangering her independence. Hofmann also claimed that a common administration would only lead to quarrels between the various governments. Moreover, a number of technical advantages were pointed out. Every branch of a government depended on the coöperation of the other branches for functioning efficiently. A state would be able to uphold its own customs officials through its own courts, police, and other government agencies and thus give the administration in its own territory a uniform character. The officials employed by a common customs system would necessarily lack this support. Furthermore, the subjects of the various member states would prefer to deal with officials of their own state and not with foreigners, and they would resent having to go abroad in order to present their claims to the higher officials of the common administration. It was essential that all internal tariffs should be abolished and that a uniform customs system should be erected. For this the member states had to

---

[141] For this and what follows see Hofmann to Weckherlin, Darmstadt, November 24, 1824, Oncken and Saemisch, I, 473–77, No. 243.

agree on a common tariff, customs law, administrative organization, and uniform rules of enforcement; but, according to Hofmann, it was not necessary that the execution of this system should be in the hands of a common customs administration. Each state should continue to have its own separate administration, which was to execute the common tariff and customs laws.

Each state in particular was to retain the right of appointing and dismissing all officials within its own territory, to direct and supervise their activity, to make temporary agreements in disputed cases, to collect and temporarily keep the incoming revenues, and to pardon or commute offenses committed against the common customs law within its jurisdiction. Each state, however, was responsible to the union for all losses caused by the irregularities of its own officials. The common administrative board was to be a bureau of information and of checking. It was also to be used for settling urgent disputes.[142]

It has often been asked whether Hofmann had originated this idea independently. There is no doubt that the South German statesmen did not discuss the idea of each state retaining its separate administration before Hofmann brought the point up in the fall of 1824. It is also well established that from then on his idea was never forgotten. But the idea was not entirely new and had been expressed before. Nassau's representative, Mülmann, had suggested such a solution to the government of Electoral Hesse as early as 1821.[143] This suggestion probably was soon forgotten, although the possibility remains that it might have influenced the later development.

As early as 1822 the idea of separate administrations was proposed again. This time it was embodied in the agreement reached by the Thuringian governments at the Arnstadt Conferences.[144] A copy of the treaty draft was sent to the Hesse-Darmstadt Ministry of Finance, and this fact makes it more than likely that Hofmann had seen it when he came forward with the same proposal.[145] But even if Hofmann took the idea of a separate administration from

---

[142] Based on Menn's summary (*op. cit.*, p. 128).   [143] *Ibid.*, p. 127.
[144] Georg von Viebahn, *Statistik des zollvereinten und nördlichen Deutschlands* (Berlin, 1858), I, 142–43.   [145] Suchel, *op. cit.*, p. 74, n. 3.

the Arnstadt draft, he must be given credit for developing it, since the scheme proposed by the Thuringian governments was by no means a customs union.   So far as can be gathered from Suchel's uncritical description of this agreement,[146] it seems to have been similar to Berstett's muddled schemes of mutual preference.   Berstett's drafts of 1820 always presupposed that each contracting party was to retain control over its own customs administration.   The nature of these schemes was such that no really permanent, uniform customs system was set up.   They mostly centered around two ideas: The contracting parties were to grant mutual preference to each other's goods and they were to abstain from certain practices against each other.   These schemes were to operate through certificates of origin and maximum tariffs, and in a sense were therefore nothing more than an expanded commercial treaty.   Each government fulfilled its provisions individually, and no uniform measures in the way of a common tariff against nonmembers were contemplated.   Commercial treaties have always been executed individually by the contracting parties, and for this reason Berstett's drafts of 1820 followed common usage.

Although the Arnstadt draft did not contemplate a customs union and although it remained obscure on certain points, at least so far as can be gathered from Suchel's description, more importance must be attached to its provision for separate administrations.

First of all, it is significant that the principle of common commercial legislation with its separate execution by each member state was openly proclaimed.[147]   For two years the South German governments had negotiated for a common customs administration, and now these Thuringian states tried to establish a union without that feature.   Although they do not seem to have intended to keep their separate administrations when entering the South German union,[148] they must have been conscious of wanting something different.   Apparently they did not realize the possibilities of their new

[146] *Ibid.*, pp. 74–75.
[147] Cited from Viebahn, *op. cit.*, I, 142: ". . . in Hinsicht auf inneren Verkehr und auf den Handel mit dem Nichtvereine ein Ganzes und einen in sich geschlossenen Handelsstaat unter gemeinschaftlich zu verabredender Handelsgesetzgebung und besonderer, jedem Vereinslande zustehender Verwaltung."   [148] Suchel, *op. cit.*, p. 75.

idea. The commercial legislation which was mentioned seems to have limited itself to common measures of retaliation against nonmembers.[149] For this reason the scheme cannot be called a customs union, although it was already something more than a mere system of mutual preference. Naturally, a union which made this mutual preference as its basis and allowed each member relative freedom in collecting duties should not have a common treasury.[150] Hofmann may have taken over this principle and applied it to his more advanced scheme.

It has frequently been claimed that Hofmann developed his plan for separate administrations on the analogy of the similar arrangement by which the Rhine octroi was collected. Hesse-Darmstadt participated in that scheme, and there is no reason to believe that an official in Hofmann's position should not have known about it.

The various territories along the Rhine had for centuries received a profitable income from the tolls levied on passing ships. This toll and other restrictions became so burdensome that commerce on the river began to decline.[151] The system was not changed until after the French Revolution. The *Reichsdeputationshauptschluss* of 1803 abolished all tolls with the exception of those dues which were necessary for the upkeep of the river and for paying certain other obligations. This levy was known as octroi.[152] A Franco-German treaty of 1804 fixed the scale of the octroi as well as the places where it should be collected.[153] After the Vienna settlement the collection of the octroi, which had been performed by a centralized administration during the Napoleonic period, was taken over by the individual governments. The Congress of Vienna set up the principles by which the octroi was to be collected and left the details to

---

[149] *Ibid.*, pp. 74–75.   [150] *Ibid.*, p. 75.

[151] Christian Eckert, *Rheinschiffahrt im XIX. Jahrhundert* ("Staats- und socialwissenschaftliche Forschungen," ed. by Gustav Schmoller, No. 81; Leipzig: Duncker & Humblot, 1900), p. 5.

[152] Reichsdeputationshauptschluss, February 25, 1803, Art. XXXIX, [Central Rhine Commission (ed.)] *Rheinurkunden. Sammlung zwischenstaatlicher Vereinbarungen, landesrechtlicher Ausführungsverordnungen und sonstiger wichtiger Urkunden über die Rheinschiffahrt seit 1803. . . . Rijndocumenten* (S'Gravenhage: Martinus Nijhoff, 1918), I, 4–5, No. 1.

[153] Dated, August 15, 1804, *ibid.*, pp. 18–20, No. 4.

a further treaty of the governments interested. One of the principles was the arrangement by which each state was to collect the octroi along its own banks in accordance with the general provisions which were binding on each state.[154] Thus without general assent it could not change the rate of the octroi, erect new places for collections, or modify the general regulations. It was also bound to share the surplus with the other members according to a definite scheme. There was no common treasury into which all revenues were to go, but only a central accounting agency. By 1820 Baden and France had already regulated by treaty their octroi administration according to these principles.[155] A general agreement, however, had not been reached by 1824.

Obviously, the essential points of this scheme were identical with Hofmann's proposal. Hofmann himself did not indicate the source of his ideas. He may have failed to do so for personal reasons or because the connection seemed to him only too apparent. He also may have avoided mentioning the Rhine octroi since this institution showed only too clearly how difficult it was for governments to manage a union of this kind.[156]

Furthermore, it should not be overlooked that, from whatever source Hofmann may have taken the basic idea, he must be given credit for thinking out this theory and developing it. He did not apply it blindly, but must have given it a great deal of consideration. The success of his presentation is also a fair test of its evaluation. From then on the provision for separate administrations remained the *sine qua non* condition of the smaller states.

Hofmann's plan was, however, not able to exercise much immediate influence on the Stuttgart Conferences. At first the Württemberg government received these proposals unfavorably since it suspected obstructionism behind them. This government was, however, soon convinced of Hofmann's serious intentions and began to consider his idea in earnest.[157]

---

[154] Treaty, Vienna, June 9, 1815, Art. VI, *ibid.*, p. 44, No. 41.

[155] Franco-Baden treaty, Mainz, August 25, 1820, *ibid.*, pp. 165–77, No. 57.

[156] Cf. Doeberl, *Bayern*, p. 11; League to List, Nürnberg, September 5, 1819, Olshausen, *op. cit.*, p. 250, No. 39.

[157] Du Thil to Berstett, Darmstadt, December 14, 1824, Oncken and Saemisch, I, 477–78, No. 244.

Bavaria's representative found himself suddenly isolated,[158] and the first Bavarian draft for the Stuttgart Conferences had to be modified.   Württemberg insisted on a list of rights which were to be reserved by the contracting parties.   The Bavarian government, anxious to proceed with Württemberg, gave in.[159]   For this reason, the basic draft of February 16, 1825, contained a mixture of old and new ideas.   The decisive words on the central administration apparently remained unchanged.[160]   This authority was to act as an administrative board with executive and advisory functions and was to be independent of the participating governments.   The board was to be composed of eleven members, Bavaria furnishing three, Württemberg and Baden each two, and the others the remainder.[161]   The board was bound by the customs procedure, customs law, and other instructions.   The governments retained the right of legislation, of general direction, and of general supervision, which they were to exercise through an annual conference of plenipotentiaries.[162] The governments, moreover, were to exercise a certain control over the common administration.   Each state was allotted a proportional share of positions in the customs service and had the right to appoint the officials for these positions. The officials remained under the jurisdiction of the government which had appointed them, and this personal jurisdiction was to be exercised by each government over all its appointees, regardless of the place of their employment.   On the other hand, each government was to have a territorial jurisdiction over all the officials of the common administration working within its boundaries.[163]   The draft gave no details of the working of such a complicated system.   Even if it had been elaborated, it probably could not have worked satisfactorily; there were too many conflicts of jurisdiction.

   This compromise did not satisfy either side.   Bavaria and

[158] ZuRhein to Max I, Stuttgart, November 29, 1824, *ibid.*, p. 479, No. 245.   [159] *Ibid.*, p. 483, n. 1.
   [160] "Der Vollzug der gemeinschaftlichen Zollordnung wird einer Zentraladministration des Vereines übertragen," basic draft. Stuttgart, February 16, 1825, Art. IV, *ibid.*, p. 485, No. 284; cf. ZuRhein to Max I, Stuttgart, November 29, 1824, *ibid.*, p. 479, No. 245.
   [161] Basic draft, Arts. IV, V, *ibid.*, pp. 485–86.
   [162] Arts. V, XXVII, *ibid.*, pp. 486, 489.
   [163] Arts. VI, VII, *ibid.*, pp. 486–87.

Württemberg still wanted a more centralized régime,[164] while the other governments insisted on separate administrations.[165] Toward the end of the conferences a last attempt was made to reach a compromise. These modifications were transmitted to the Bavarian representative by the Hesse-Darmstadt official, Hofmann.[166] Each state was to have a separate administration and was to appoint all officials except the comptrollers, who were to be attached to each first-class customs office. The customs administration of each state was to be directed by an intermediate office, which was to be organized by that state. These intermediate offices were bound by the common customs law and obliged to follow the advice of the central authority in dubious cases. This central board was to supervise the whole customs administration, check accounts, receive reports and enforce uniformity. The central authority had certain administrative functions in technical matters. There were a number of checks on the separate state administrations through the central authority as well as through individual officials delegated to the offices of the other member states for that purpose. The scheme reflected the genuine interest of the Hesse-Darmstadt government in a workable solution. It would have been a possible solution if political factors had not ended the conferences shortly afterward.

In a way similar to Hofmann's idea, Nassau's minister Marschall added another element to this growing concept of a customs union. Nassau had not participated in the Heidelberg Protocol of 1824, but Marschall was given a chance to state her position. He took this opportunity to demand that all the major states should be equally represented at the general conferences. Only small states like the Hohenzollerns, which were completely enclosed by other states, were to have no vote. Moreover, the majority were not to have the right to pass regulations to the detriment of any single member. Marschall argued for the equal vote by saying that the larger members would have natural prepond-

---

[164] Stuttgart Conferences, protocol of first meeting, February 28, 1825, *ibid.*, pp. 491–93, No. 250.

[165] ZuRhein to Max I, Stuttgart, March 11, 1825, *ibid.*, pp. 493–95, No. 251.

[166] ZuRhein to Max I, Stuttgart, May 16, 1825, *ibid.*, pp. 503–6, No. 255; Hofmann to ZuRhein, Stuttgart, May 20, *ibid.*, pp. 506–7, No. 256.

erance through their greater size. If this natural preponderance should be increased through a legal preponderance,
that is to say, if the larger states should have more votes at
the general conferences, then the smaller states would lose
all influence in the common union.[167]   The idea of equal
representation was not new; Nebenius's draft had contained
it, and the working of the natural preponderance of the larger
states had also been understood before.   This preponderance
was to work through the threat of the larger states to withdraw from the union and thus break its backbone.   However, Bavaria had at the time rejected Nebenius's distribution of votes and suggested an "ideal" distribution according
to the importance of each state.   The smaller states had
accepted Bavaria's proposal in principle and the significance
of Marschall's move lay in the fact that this was the first
definite counterproposal the Bavarian demands had to meet.
For some time Bavaria continued to negotiate on the basis of
unequal representation, especially since Marschall gave in
on this point.[168]   Marschall also demanded that each state
should have a central customs office which would regulate
the relation between the local offices and the common union
office,[169] a proposal to which Baden and Hesse-Darmstadt
acceded.

Hofmann's and Marschall's suggestions have been condemned by Treitschke as blackest particularism.[170]   It is
true that Nassau did not exactly underestimate her importance,[171] but that is beside the point.   The problem of German unification was one of coördination and not of subordination.   Although Treitschke objected so strenuously to the
desires of the smaller German states to preserve their independence, he never would have favored a solution by
which Prussia would have had to give up her identity in
favor of another state.   Moreover, if the purely German
kingdoms had been able to consolidate the smaller German
states into a Third Germany, how willing would they have
been to accept a Prussian solution?

[167] Marschall, comments on the Heidelberg Protocol, Wiesbaden, November 24, 1824, ibid., pp. 467–69, No. 240.
    [168] Menn, op. cit., p. 131.   [169] Ibid., pp. 130–31.
    [170] Treitschke, Deutsche Geschichte, III, 625–23.   [171] Ibid., p. 627.

Although the South German negotiations of 1819-25 did not succeed in establishing a regional union, they contributed important ideas to the development of German economic unification. After List's fertile mind had once conceived the possibility of a separate union, he promoted his idea with characteristic vigor, although he did not bother at all about details. Various South German cabinets became immensely interested in this scheme, in spite of all its vagueness, but apparently none of them formally initiated the negotiations. These were started privately by a few diplomats during the Vienna Final Conferences. The common opposition to Prussia, as well as the failure of a general German solution, furthered this movement, and toward the end of the Vienna Final Conferences all South German and many Central German governments reached a provisional agreement. The subsequent Darmstadt and Stuttgart Conferences continued formally what had begun as a private conversation in Vienna. The divergent political interests made impossible an agreement without some development of the technical aspects. Up to 1824 only two major schemes had been considered. The larger states worked for a common customs system, while the smaller ones favored a system of mutual preference. Neither system would have been workable. It was not an easygoing adaptation of earlier schemes, but a clear analysis of the underlying difficulties, combined with an extraordinary technical knowledge, which brought forth the basic principles of a customs union. Public opinion and economic conditions forced the governments to keep up what seemed to be a hopeless enterprise. When a point of mental exhaustion had been reached, a way finally was found to solve the problem by neutralizing the political factors. Without emphasizing technical details, the plan for a customs union did not share the vagueness in theory of earlier schemes. By hard thinking a solution had been evolved which had drawn the abstract concepts of the age into the reality of everyday life. The new plan was not immediately adopted since the direct effect of these negotiations was a general distrust among the participants. Nevertheless, the foundations had been laid.

CHAPTER V

PRUSSIA'S CUSTOMS REFORM OF 1818 AND HER ATTITUDE TOWARD ECONOMIC UNIFICATION IN GERMANY, 1815–25

THE attempts which various German governments made from 1819 to 1825 to form a regional union had been confined primarily to South and Central Germany. The Prussian government had held aloof from the Darmstadt and Stuttgart Conferences. Although it was not until after 1825 that it embarked on the policy which subsequently led to the formation of the Zollverein under its leadership, the developments in Prussia during the decade following the Napoleonic wars are of importance for the understanding of the origin of the Zollverein. Prussia thoroughly reformed her customs administration in 1818, and she successfully adopted a modern tariff policy. It was this new commercial system of Prussia which was later to be taken over by the Zollverein. Thus the history of Prussian customs institutions and economic policies between 1815 and 1825 forms an important link in the origin of the Zollverein. For this reason this chapter will be devoted to a critical discussion of the principles underlying the Prussian customs reform of 1818. Since it has frequently been charged that the Prussian government planned the subsequent Zollverein as early as 1818,[1] special attention will be given to Prussia's attitude towards German economic unification prior to 1825. The development of the Zollanschluss, that peculiar institution by which Prussia incorporated small territories belonging to other German states into her customs system, will be taken up in the next chapter, since its technical details contributed relatively little to the general development of that period.

THE UNDERLYING PRINCIPLES OF THE PRUSSIAN CUSTOMS REFORM OF 1818

IN ORDER TO understand the Prussian customs reform one must go back to the Prussian administration of the

[1] For the earlier literature see Fischer, "Über das Wesen . . . ," *Jahrbücher für Nationalökonomie und Statistik*, II (1864), 341, n. 48; 342–43.

eighteenth century. In 1776 Frederick the Great had introduced a system of customs supervision along the boundaries of his kingdom. Up to then customs had been collected primarily at the city gates, through which all commerce had to pass. The new boundary control was not a
substitute for this earlier system, but only supplemented it,[2]
and so the system of border protection remained incomplete.
By 1815 it was altogether inadequate, since many sections
of the frontier were without guards while others were under-
staffed.[3] Although the reform of 1766 was an important
step toward a modern customs system, it did not do away
with the technical disadvantages of the older system. The
system of indirect taxation continued to distinguish between
rural and urban districts, and the various and complicated
provincial tariffs were maintained as well as many other
awkward features.[4] The period of wars which followed the
French Revolution showed how inadequate the Prussian
system of taxation was. The frequent territorial changes
especially had added to the confusion, and a general reform
became a necessity. Some attempts to effect it were made
during the Napoleonic period.[5] However, the system still
remained so complicated that even Bülow, the Prussian
minister of finance, stated officially that nobody could possibly know all the tariffs, regulations, modifications, and practices.[6]

Under such conditions the Prussian government not only

---

[2] Mamroth, *Geschichte*, pp. 283–85; Reinhold [Carl Bernhard Alexander]
Koser, *Geschichte Friedrichs des Grossen* (4th and 5th eds.; Stuttgart:
J. G. Cotta'sche Buchhandlung Nachfolger, 1913), III, 227.

[3] [Prussia, Staatsrath] Gutachten des preussischen Staatsraths über den
Entwurf eines neuen Steuergesetzes 1817, dated Berlin, July 20 [sic], 1817,
unsigned MS copy, General Library, University of Michigan, [f. B3ʳ]: "Die
Grenzen sind theils nicht hinreichend theils garnicht besetzt und die innere
Fabrikation genieset [sic] dort einen sehr unvollständigen, hier gar keinen
Schutz, worunter insbesonderheit die fabrikreichen rheinischen und säch-
sischen Erwerbungen ausserordentlich leiden"; cf. *ibid.*, [f. C4ᵛ]. This
document will hereafter be cited as [Prussia, Staatsrath] Gutachten . . . 1817.

[4] Rural districts paid the *Kontribution*, a land tax, while the cities paid
the *Accise*, a consumption tax. Both had been introduced by the Great
Elector in order to finance a permanent army (G. von Below, "Kontribution,"
Handwörterbuch der Staatswissenschaften, IV (1892), 847.

[5] [Prussia, Staatsrath] Gutachten . . . 1817, [f. B12ᵛ].

[6] Bülow to Friedrich Wilhelm III, Berlin, January 14, 1817, Oncken
and Saemisch, I, 39, No. 8.

undertook to reform the customs administration, but tried to put the whole system of taxation on a new footing. This was the only possible course it could have taken in view of the close ties which existed between the customs revenues and the taxes on consumption, and in view of their peculiar relation to the direct taxes. Although the higher financial bureaucracy took the leading rôle in shaping the new system of taxation,[7] the social implications of its measures were well considered. Naturally, technical, financial, and administrative reasons predominated. It is necessary to stress the internal aspect of the customs reform.

When the Prussian government started to reform its customs system, it had no intention of solving the German Question, but, rather, was continuing the period of reform, which had begun after the downfall of 1806, as well as consolidating the recently enlarged state. In abandoning her antiquated system of taxation Prussia took another step in breaking down the paternalistic methods of eighteenth-century political economy and thus continued the earlier reforms of the Stein-Hardenberg era. The reforms of the years 1807–10 had expressed the growing belief of government circles in individual freedom and local self-government, a tendency which was to prevail in spite of temporary relapses. The financial reforms of the postwar period reflected in a similar way the trend toward private initiative in business.[8] The tax reform was not the only reorganization undertaken by the Prussian government. The year 1817, for instance, saw a fundamental change in the organization of the provincial administration, a reform which can be directly linked to the legislation of 1808.[9]

For this reason the tax reform should not be looked upon as a purely departmental affair. Although the Minister of Finance had taken the initiative and worked out the program for the reform, Friedrich Wilhelm III and Hardenberg should receive credit for securing the passage of the new customs law. The instructions given to the Minister of Finance in-

---

[7] The following officials were primarily responsible for the customs reform: Bülow, Maassen, Kunth, Hoffmann, Humboldt, Klewiz, and Schütz.

[8] Brinkmann, *Die preussische Handelspolitik*, p. 8.

[9] Treitschke, *Deutsche Geschichte*, II, 202.

cluded only general directions.   The burden of taxation was
to be reduced, the rates were to be just and fair, and the
tariffs of the old and new provinces were to be put on the
same footing.[10]   After the reform had got under way, Friedrich Wilhelm and Hardenberg frequently urged that it be
hurried up.[11]   The financial reform was a part of the general
program the Prussian statesmen had begun after 1806;[12] it
tried to follow the same. concepts of equality and justice
which had been the basis of the general program, and it
sought a larger popular basis for this branch of the government.   Thus it tried to win the support of the people by
reasonable regulations, fair tariffs, and just enforcements.[13]
The reform was designed to unify the monarchy and break
local forces obstructing the progress of the nation,[14] without,
however, abandoning the happy balance of provincial and
central authorities attained in the other reforms.   Tradition
received due consideration, and the nature of the new organization differed from the French system of centralized
administration.[15]

These basic political ideas determined the general tendency of the economic principles to be followed.   As early as
1815 Hardenberg had opposed a system of prohibition, but
he nevertheless favored some protection for Prussian industries.[16]   These   economic   principles,   however,   were
thoroughly reconsidered at each stage of the reform legislation.   The query has often been put whether the Prussian
customs reform reflected the administrative experience of the
higher Prussian officials or whether it primarily showed
Adam Smith's influence.   The assertion has been advanced
that the Prussian reformers of 1817–18 were blind doctrinaires
who tried to realize Adam Smith's theories without sufficient

---

[10] Friedrich Wilhelm III to Hardenberg, Berlin, January 31, 1816,
Oncken and Saemisch, I, 33, No. 5.

[11] Cf. Bülow to Friedrich Wilhelm III, Berlin, January 14, 1817, *ibid.*,
p. 35, No. 8.

[12] *Ibid.*, p. 39; [Prussia, Staatsrath] Gutachten . . . 1817 [f. B12ᵛ].

[13] *Ibid.*, [f. C5ᵛ]; Brinkmann, *op. cit.*, p. 23.

[14] Büloy to Friedrich Wilhelm III, Berlin, January 14, 1817, Oncken
and Saemisch, I, 38, No. 8; Treitschke, *Deutsche Geschichte*, II, 195.

[15] Bülow to Hardenberg, Berlin, February 7, 1816, Oncken and Saemisch,
I, 33–34, No. 6; cf. Treitschke, *Deutsche Geschichte*, II, 188, 205–6.

[16] Hardenberg to manufacturers of cotton goods in Reichenbach, Wien,
May 15, 1815, Oncken and Saemisch, I, 26–29, No. 2.

knowledge of the actual situation.[17]   Undoubtedly, the Prussian officials were deficient in theoretical knowledge as well as in practical experience.[18]

The ideas expressed by the reformers primarily reflected the experience of fiscal and political administrators.   It is true that they were not first-class academic theorists in political economy; but there was hardly anybody in Germany at that time from whose knowledge of theory they might have benefited.   Although Adam Smith's doctrines were generally known and commonly taught in German universities, the study of economics in Germany had as a whole not yet risen to a position comparable to that of later times.   For this reason the Prussian statesmen, most of whom had been subjected to Adam Smith's influence in their student years, did not benefit as fully from their studies as one might expect.[18a]

Nevertheless, the reformers' lack of economic experience was a definite handicap.   However, the fact that they had not been associated with any economic group, kept them from rationalizing the interests of one particular class.   For this reason they were much better followers of Adam Smith than subsequent generations of free traders who can be identified with certain commercial interests.[19]   Moreover, they were not bureaucrats pure and simple, but exhibited on many occasions considerable concern for the common welfare.   It is also remarkable that the Prussian leaders, only a few years after having experienced their struggle for national resurrection, showed so little of that type of nationalism which believes in economic retaliation.   No traces of Fichte's *Closed Commercial State* or Jahn's isolationism can be found in the thought of the financial reformers, although their work was closely connected with the reforms leading up to the Wars of Liberation.   On the other hand, the reactionaries were the ones who took the same position which many of their much suspected "German revolutionaries" were holding by also favoring economic isolation.[20]

---

[17] Treue, *Wirtschaftszustände*, p. 242; see the review by E. N. Anderson, *The American Historical Review*, XLIV (1939), 374.

[18] Brinkmann, *op. cit.*, pp. 29–30.

[18a] *Ibid.*, pp. 7–8.   [19] *Ibid.*, pp. 24, 28.

[20] It should be remembered that party lines were not yet clearly cut and that this division applied particularly to the Prussian capital; cf. Borcken-

Theoretical training and practical experience constituted important factors in the background of the Prussian reformers. They also had acquired a considerable amount of knowledge by studying the administrative history of Prussia and of other countries.[21] Although more knowledge and more experience would undoubtedly have been of value to them, they undertook to make the best of the difficult situation in which they found themselves. They should receive credit not only for their training and experience, but also for what they were themselves and for the use they made of their abilities.

To understand the Prussian customs reform one has to take up the reasons which motivated the reformers. The antiquated system of collecting revenue unquestionably needed a complete reorganization.[22] Moreover, that mass of complicated territorial divisions and constitutional oddities which was the Prussia of 1815 obviously had to be consolidated.[23] These reasons, which need no further elaboration here, are basic and explain sufficiently why a general reform was undertaken.

The precarious situation of the Prussian state finances and the economic depression which had hit private enterprise in Prussia made it almost mandatory that the reforms should have a double aim: to make the collection of indirect taxes more economical and to help business. The Prussian reformers therefore never considered complete free trade and the abolition of all customs as an immediate possibility. They were concerned with the question of protection, and especially with the degree and type of protection to be established. They decided to abolish all prohibitions.[24] They

hagen, *National- und handelspolitische Bestrebungen,* pp. 9–10; committee of the Prussian Staatsrath, memorandum, Berlin, April 3, 1817, Oncken and Saemisch, I, 59, No. 10.

[21] Cf. Bülow to Friedrich Wilhelm III, Berlin, January 14, 1817, *ibid.,* p. 40, No. 8.

[22] Bülow to Friedrich Wilhelm III, Berlin, December 28, 1815, *ibid.,* p. 29, No. 3; Bülow to Friedrich Wilhelm III, Berlin, January 14, 1817, *ibid.,* p. 39, No. 8.

[23] Bülow to Friedrich Wilhelm III, Berlin, December 28, 1815, *ibid.,* pp. 29–30, No. 3; Bülow to Friedrich Wilhelm III, Berlin, January 14, 1817, *ibid.,* p. 39, No. 8.

[24] Only the trade with playing cards and salt remained restricted because they were state monopolies (Law of May 26, 1818, Art. IV, *ibid.,* p. 72, No. 14).

also did away with high tariffs. They were willing to grant Prussian industry what they considered adequate protection, but they did not want to grant a virtual monopoly.

Many reasons were given in support of this decision. It was argued that it was difficult to enforce any system of prohibition and that in particular Prussia's boundaries made it almost impossible.[25] Any such attempt would result in large-scale smuggling and in public and private corruption.[26] The customs system was to gain the support of the people by charging reasonable rates and by avoiding anything which might remind them of Napoleonic methods.[27] Especially valuable goods were to enjoy low tariffs.[28] Just as industry was to receive a certain amount of protection, so the interests of the other classes were considered. The reformers felt that the consumer should receive equal consideration and that the welfare of large groups should not be sacrificed for the sole benefit of one class, the manufacturers.[29] They were afraid that such a protectionist policy would cause the rise of an impoverished industrial proletariat.[30] Neither were any privileges which had exempted certain classes from contributing their share to be tolerated any further.[31] Another argument pointed out that many of the industries in Prussia had developed without the protection of a tariff.[32]

The Prussian reformers also considered the positive side

[25] Bülow to Friedrich Wilhelm III, Berlin, January 14, 1817, ibid., p. 40, No. 8; Hardenberg to manufacturers in Rheydt, Süchteln, Gladbach, Viersen, and Kaldenkirchen, Berlin, June 3, 1818, ibid., p. 79, No. 15; [Prussia, Staatsrath] Gutachten . . . 1817 [f. B9ᵛ].

[26] Ibid., [f. B11ʳ]; Hardenberg to manufacturers of cotton goods in Reichenbach, Wien, May 15, 1815, Oncken and Saemisch, I, 27, No. 2; Bülow to Friedrich Wilhelm III, Berlin, January 14, 1817, ibid., p. 43, No. 8.

[27] Ibid., pp. 36, 43; [Prussia, Staatsrath] Gutachten . . . 1817, [f. C5ᵛ].

[28] Bülow to Friedrich Wilhelm III, Berlin, January 14, 1817, Oncken and Saemisch, I, 42, No. 8.

[29] Ibid., p. 41; Hardenberg to manufacturers of cotton goods in Reichenbach, Wien, May 15, 1815, ibid., p. 26, No. 2.

[30] Hardenberg to manufacturers in Rheydt, Süchteln, Gladbach, Viersen, and Kaldenkirchen, Berlin, June 3, 1818, ibid., pp. 81–82, No. 15.

[31] Law of May 26, 1818, Art, XXVII, ibid., p. 76, No. 14; Treitschke, "Die Anfänge des deutschen Zollvereins," Preussische Jahrbücher, XXX (1872), 418–19.

[32] Bülow to Friedrich Wilhelm III, Berlin, January 14, 1817, Oncken and Saemisch, I, 41, No. 8.

of the problem, namely, that of finding markets for Prussian goods. The abolition of internal customs duties was to improve the home market. In this way the Rhenish manufacturers especially were to be compensated for their loss of the French market.[33] Furthermore, the reformers expected that Prussia would gain access to those foreign markets on which many of the recently acquired territories were dependent.[34] It was expected, however, that Prussian exports could not develop without a corresponding increase of imports.[35] Although the reformers reserved the right for Prussia to pass retaliatory measures, they believed that she would be able to promote her trade through commercial treaties of reciprocity.[36]

Besides these general economic benefits specific advantages for the state treasury were expected. In order to achieve them the system of collection was to be unified and simplified as much as possible.[37] All internal customs lines were to be abolished and one line established along the boundaries of the monarchy. This line, however, did not coincide with the political frontier since odd pieces of territory were to be excluded.[38] The tariff was standardized, although each of the two main parts of the monarchy was subject to different rates. The tariff did not go into any great detail, and its classification of goods was rather general.[39] In order to facilitate the collection of duties all rates were set up according to weight or number.[40] As a rule, industrial goods had to pay a 10 per cent ad valorem duty when imported, and

---

[33] Hardenberg to Bülow, Berlin, February 12, 1816, *ibid.*, pp. 34–35, No. 7.

[34] Bülow to Friedrich Wilhelm III, Berlin, January 14, 1817, No. 8, *ibid.*, pp. 39–40, No. 8.

[35] *Loc. cit.*; Hardenberg to manufacturers in Rheydt, Süchteln, Gladbach, Viersen, and Kaldenkirchen, Berlin, June 3, 1818, *ibid.*, pp. 80–81, No. 15.

[36] Bülow to Friedrich Wilhelm III, Berlin, January 14, 1817, *ibid.*, p. 40, No. 8; Law of May 26, 1818, Art. V, *ibid.*, p. 72, No. 14.

[37] Bülow to Friedrich Wilhelm III, Berlin, January 14, 1817, *ibid.*, p. 45, No. 8.

[38] Law of May, 1818, Art. XXIV, *ibid.*, p. 76, No. 14.

[39] Law of May 26, 1818, appendix, [Prussia] *Gesetz-Sammlung für die königlichen preussischen Staaten,* 1818, No. 9 (September 5), pp. 70-101, No. 482.

[40] Bülow to Friedrich Wilhelm III, Berlin, January 14, 1817, Oncken and Saemisch, I, 44, No. 8.

the export of certain raw materials was also taxed in order to help the home industries. The rates on other imported goods, especially on those for consumption, and the duties on transit were designed as financial tariffs.[41] Technically the law called for the collection of customs duties and consumption taxes on imports, the consumption taxes being generally heavier than the regular tariff. This distinction had little practical value in the operation of the customs administration and is noted only because it was applied later to determine the amount to be refunded to various enclaves. Particular care was to be taken to select honest and efficient officials, and all authorities were to coöperate with them.[42]

This new system of collection, which constituted a complete break with the past,[43] was expected to yield a greater revenue than the old one had done without considerably increasing the burden of the taxpayer.[44] Although the law was part of the program reorganizing and consolidating the Prussian monarchy, its primary purpose was to safeguard the state finances. Its secondary aim was to help Prussian industry and commerce. The reform, however, did not constitute a victory of the tax authorities over the common man. Although the change brought many hardships, the law was fair in its own way, and opportunities for petty official spite did not have much chance to develop.[45]

THE CUSTOMS LAW OF 1818 AND THE QUESTION OF GERMAN ECONOMIC UNIFICATION

THE main question in the study of Prussia's economic policy of these years was her attitude toward her German neighbors. The first phase which should be considered is the period before May 26, 1818, the date of her new customs law.

[41] *Ibid.*, pp. 42–43.
[42] [Prussia, Staatsrath] Gutachten . . . 1817 [f. C5ᵛ–C6ʳ].
[43] Law of May 26, 1818, Art. XXVIII, Oncken and Saemisch, I, 76, No. 14.
[44] Friedrich Wilhelm III to Hardenberg, Berlin, January 31, 1816, *ibid.*, p. 33, No. 5; Bülow to Friedrich Wilhelm III, Berlin, January 14, 1817, *ibid.*, p. 45, No. 8.
[45] Cf. Benzenberg's opinion as quoted by Oncken, *ibid.*, p. xxi; Brinkmann, *op. cit.*, p. 113, n. 28; [Prussia] Zoll- und Verbrauchs-Steuer-Ordnung, May 26, 1818, Art. CVII, [Prussia] *Gesetz-Sammlung* 1818, No. 9 (September 5), pp. 130–31, No. 483.

The first problem which the Prussian Ministry of Finance had to meet in executing the Law of May 26, 1818, bearing on Prussia's relation to other German states was the question of how to deal with those various non-Prussian territories which were completely surrounded by Prussia. These territories, known as enclaves, were to constitute the chief objects of Prussian tariff policy after the reform of her customs system had been effected.

During the preparation of the new customs law, however, no definite policy toward the enclaves was formulated, nor was much thought given to German economic problems as a whole. King Friedrich Wilhelm III was opposed to any measure which might be interpreted as putting pressure on weaker allied neighbors. The reason for this position has to be sought in his monarchical convictions.[46] The King's intentions were known to the Foreign Office as well as to the Ministry of Finance.[47] Throughout the discussions of the new customs system the monarch was kept ignorant of the problems the enclaves might cause. It was not until the end of January, 1819—after the law had become effective—that he was informed about the difficulties the Prussian administration was encountering.[48] He charged the Minister of Finance with neglect of his duty for not bringing up this matter while the customs law was under consideration.[49] The evidence is, however, inconclusive on the problem whether the King was intentionally kept in the dark by the officials.[50]

Hardenberg, also, favored a good-will policy toward Prussia's smaller German neighbors. His reasons, however, were political. Ever since the Congress of Vienna he had known how little coöperation he could expect from his German allies in economic matters. Being well aware that pressure would achieve nothing, he resigned himself to a passive policy.[51] Now and again Hardenberg spoke in favor-

[46] Brinkmann, op. cit., p. 113.   [47] Loc. cit.

[48] Klewiz to Friedrich Wilhelm III, Berlin, January 28, 1819, Oncken and Saemisch, I, 91–94, No. 22.

[49] Friedrich Wilhelm III to Klewiz, Berlin, February 8, 1819, ibid., pp. 97–98, No. 24.   [50] Cf. Brinkmann, op. cit., p. 113.

[51] Benzenberg to Gneisenau, Berlin, December 25, 1816, Julius Heyderhoff (ed.), Benzenberg, der Rheinländer und Preusse, 1815–1823 (Rheinisches Archiv, Vol. VII; Bonn: F. Klopp, 1928), p. 58.

able terms of a general German customs system,[52] but he seems to have given the problem little thought and less care. He nevertheless used all his influence to keep the financial authorities from pursuing a policy of oppressing smaller German neighbors. Thus he opposed suggestions made by Hoffmann of the Foreign Office for an inclusion of enclaves into the Prussian system of taxation and won him over to his point of view.[53]   He also reprimanded the Ministry of Finance for introducing such harsh measures in the collection of duties on goods shipped by mail to Anhalt[54] and intervened on other occasions in favor of this small neighbor.[55]

Besides Hardenberg other high officials gave the problems of the enclaves some consideration. Hoffmann continued to follow the State Chancellor's ideas.   During the preparation of the customs law he also tried to persuade the Ministry of Finance to adopt a more liberal policy toward all countries and especially toward the German neighbors.[56] Once he even intervened for one of the Thuringian states against the oppressive policy of the Ministry of Finance.[57]

Bülow was squarely confronted with the issue when the government of Saxe-Hildburghausen asked Prussia to take common measures with her against the Bavarian customs system.   Although Hildburghausen had asked for "a common or at least a uniformly organized countertariff,"[58] Bülow in his answer to Saxe-Hildburghausen gave a precise analysis of the advantages Prussia would receive if the enclaves should join her customs system.[59] He advised, however, against starting negotiations at that moment because Prussia was not yet ready.   The incident seems to have had very little if any influence on the subsequent developments.

---

[52] Loc. cit.; Joseph von Görres, Die Übergabe der Addresse der Stadt Coblenz an Se. Majestät den König in öffentlicher Audienz bei Sr. Durchl. dem Fürsten Staatskanzler am 12. Januar 1818, reprinted in Görres, Gesammelte Schriften, XIII (1929), 20.

[53] Hoffmann to Klewiz, Berlin, November 20, 1818, Oncken and Saemisch, I, 88–89, No. 19.   [54] Brinkmann, op. cit., pp. 113–14.

[55] Ibid., pp. 112–13.   [56] Loc. cit.   [57] Ibid., pp. 111–12.

[58] Government of Saxe-Hildburghausen to Prussian Government at Erfurt, Hildburghausen, March 6, 1817, Oncken and Saemisch, I, 312–13, No. 158.

[59] Bülow to Prussian Ministry of Foreign Affairs, Berlin, May 20, 1817, ibid., p. 314, No. 160.

What the ideas of the financial experts on the enclaves were during that period it is difficult to determine. Their main concern seems to have been the financial interests of the state. The matter was formally discussed once in the tax committee of the State Council; but no decision was reached.[60] The reasons why the financial officials neglected this problem can only be guessed at.

There are, however, a number of indirect indications as to the intentions of the Ministry of Finance. During all the incidents of 1816–17 it favored a much harsher policy than the Foreign Office, and it primarily followed its narrow fiscal interests.[61] No policy seems to have been thought out, and none of the future problems were foreseen. Thus even after the promulgation of the new law the Ministry of Finance opposed any measures intended to suppress the smuggling of Prussian goods into neighboring countries,[62] and it also stated during the deliberations of the State Council that Prussia could not interfere with the transit traffic on the Elbe.[63] Later on, however, when the negotiations with the Anhalt duchies failed, Prussia taxed the goods imported by way of the Elbe and justified this step by stating that the small duchies had allowed themselves to become smuggling centers against Prussia.[64] It also seems very strange that the Law of May 26, 1818, made specific mention of Prussian enclaves and other territories which could not be efficiently included in the new system, but did not deal at all with the enclaves of other German states within Prussian territory.[65]

The tariffs of the new law hit the German neighbors hardest and were denounced throughout Germany. There is nothing to show that the rates were purposely designed to favor non-German goods. On the contrary, the highest duties were to be collected from nonindustrial goods imported from overseas. The new customs law had a devastating effect on the smaller German states, because their economic and fiscal systems were weak, so far as they existed.

[60] *Ibid.*, p. 97, n. 2, referring to the meeting of May 22, 1817.
[61] Brinkmann, *op. cit.*, pp. 111–14.   [62] *Ibid.*, pp. 25–26.
[63] [Prussia, Staatsrath] Gutachten . . . 1817, [f. B12ʳ].
[64] Cf. Bernstorff to Anhalt-Köthen, Berlin, June 30, 1820, Oncken and Saemisch, I, 135–39, No. 44.
[65] Law of May 26, 1818, Art. XXIV, *ibid.*, p. 76, No. 14.

The collection of customs according to weight and piece and the refusal to introduce differential tariffs were the two innovations which gave the Prussian financial policy its anti-German character in the eyes of contemporaries, since it discriminated against the low-grade goods which were the main products of German industry. These measures, however, had been adopted on principle and were a matter of conviction to the reformers. Hence the tariffs were not designed to discriminate against German goods. On the other hand, Prussia's German neighbors received no special consideration.[66]

The new law provided for two different sets of tariffs, one for the eastern and one for the western provinces. If there had been any intention in the minds of the Prussian reformers to follow a German customs policy, they would have first tried to join the two main divisions of the monarchy into one economic unit through a union with the territories lying in between. If they did not plan to unite the monarchy, they were obviously not thinking of uniting Germany. A common tariff for both sections of the monarchy would seem to have been the first step for a policy of German economic unification.

The meaning of Article V in the new law presents a special problem. This article stated that Prussia intended to follow a commercial policy of treaties of reciprocity with other states. It was to apply to all states, since the non-Prussian German states are not especially mentioned.[67] There is nothing to show that this article was designed to be the basis of a policy of German economic unification. The

<hr/>

[66] Prussian Ministry of Foreign Affairs to the three Anhalt governments, Berlin, December 23, 1819, *ibid.*, p. 128, No. 39; Bernstorff to Friedrich Wilhelm III, Berlin, July 13, 1824, *ibid.*, II, 71–72, No. 317; Brinkmann, *op. cit.*, p. 117; cf. Treitschke, "Die Anfänge," *Preussische Jahrbücher*, XXX (1872), 415–16, on the fiscal reasons for high tariffs.

[67] "Die vorstehend ausgesprochene Handelsfreiheit soll den Verhandlungen mit anderen Staaten in der Regel zur Grundlage dienen. Erleichterungen, welche die Untertanen des Staats in anderen Ländern bei ihrem Verkehre geniessen, sollen, soweit es die Verschiedenheit der Verhältnisse gestattet, erwidert und zur Beförderung des wechselseitigen Verkehrs sollen, wo erforderlich und zulässig, besondere Handelsverträge geschlossen werden. Dagegen bleibt es aber vorbehalten, Beschränkungen, wodurch der Verkehr der Untertanen des Staats in fremden Ländern wesentlich leidet, durch angemessene Massregeln zu vergelten." Law of May 26, 1818, Art. V, Oncken and Saemisch, I, 72, No. 14.

two drafts which had been considered during the deliberations stated the same ideas as the final version.[68]   This article had its origin in the belief of the Prussian reformers that a country could do nothing but gain through an increase in trade and that a policy of commercial treaties for the removal of trade restrictions on an international scale was the best method to achieve this aim.[69]   Later, official comments on the Prussian policy of these years only confirm this interpretation.[70]   Article V, however, was cited by contemporaries, especially by non-Prussian Germans, in order to bring Berlin to adopt a more pro-German tariff policy.[71]

So far the Prussian character of the Customs Law of 1818 has been described, and it has been shown that it was not planned as a basis for German economic unification.   Later developments, however, bound up the Prussian reform inseparably with German economic unification.   Since the Zollverein was to adopt many technical details from the Prussian system, the Law of May 26, 1818, deserves a brief evaluation.   Many important items, like the boundary customs line, the abolition of internal lines, and the rates of tariff according to weight, were not new, and the Prussian Ministry of Finance cannot be given credit for entirely new devices in the collection of customs.   The new system was, nevertheless, adapted to specific Prussian needs and was not an outright copy of an existing system.

The effect of this reform has been evaluated differently by various writers.   Although the Law of 1818 has been esteemed very highly for a considerable length of time, a recent study of it charges that it had a detrimental effect on Prussian business and that it would have been a failure had its tariff policy not been amended a few years later.[72]

[68] Zimmermann, *Geschichte,* pp. 30, 35.

[69] Bülow to Friedrich Wilhelm III, Berlin, January 14, 1817, Oncken and Saemisch, I, 39–40, No. 8.

[70] Bernstorff to Otterstedt, September 22, 1820, Köhler, *Problematisches,* p. 31; Bernstorff to Friedrich Wilhelm III, Berlin, July 13, 1824, *ibid.,* pp. 34–35, and Oncken and Saemisch, II, 71, No. 317; Bernstorff, February 19, 1819 [Eduard Arno] Wilhelm Thieme, *Eintritt Sachsens in den Zollverein und seine wirtschaftlichen Folgen* (Doctor's dissertation, Leipzig, 1914), p. 16.

[71] Cf. List to Diet, Frankfurt, April 14, 1819, List, *Schriften,* I, Part II, 495, No. 17.

[72] Treue, *op. cit.,* pp. 343–44.

It should be pointed out, however, that the experts had expected an increase in unemployment[73] and that a country whose interests were so interwoven with those of her neighbors could not withdraw completely from the depression which followed the Napoleonic wars and which affected all of Europe.   How much Prussia would have suffered without the reform, it is difficult to estimate.   Undeniably the Prussian reformers entertained a number of mistaken notions and made several wrong decisions.   But one should not forget that they had experienced one of the great upheavals of Europe and that in 1815 they were confronted with an entirely new situation which they were able to transform into a new era of steady progress.   They were not content to resurrect the good old days.

Although the Prussian government was soon obliged to grant a higher degree of protection than it had originally intended, no fundamental change in policy occurred.   It remained hesitant and skeptical in adopting a more aggressive policy against protectionist neighbors.   It tried to promote Prussian interests by negotiating trade agreements, and only occasionally did it resort to reprisals.[74]   This policy of commercial treaties failed as such, and the little successes it enjoyed were not gained purely on its own merits, but were often due to independent developments in other countries.[75] A cautious policy was probably the wisest course the Prussian government could have taken.   Being the least stabilized of the great powers, she could only have lost in an economic war.   This careful, but determined, policy of following moderate free-trade principles was responsible for the economic progress made by her in the twenties.

There may also be raised the question of how much the slight immediate success of the new system owed to the personality of the new minister of finance.   Klewiz, who held this key position from 1819 to 1825, was incapable of conducting a farsighted fiscal policy.   Although he was otherwise an able official, his administration lacked initiative and imagination, so that he was finally replaced by Motz

---

[73] [Prussia, Staatsrath] Gutachten . . . 1817, [f. Cl^r].
[74] Brinkmann, op. cit., pp. 152–97, especially 159–60, 163, 166–67.
[75] Ibid., pp. 167, 186.

in 1825, who succeeded in using the Customs Law of 1818 to the greater advantage of the state finances.

The economic liberalism of the customs reform of 1818 continued to dominate Prussian fiscal policy and subsequently became an important component element of the Zollverein.

Thus the new customs law did not work miracles for Prussian commerce. In the long run, however, it proved to be an excellent piece of administrative legislation. The system worked so well that no major reforms needed to be introduced for a long time to come. It put Prussian state finances on a sound basis. Perhaps the best indication of its efficiency was the fact that only 14 to 15 per cent of the total revenue was used for collection. The cost even decreased later and compared favorably with that of other German states of this period.[76]

PRUSSIA AND GERMAN ECONOMIC
UNIFICATION, 1819-25

ALTHOUGH the basic principles of the Prussian customs policy remained unchanged, her attitude toward her German neighbors underwent some modifications.

First of all, the Prussian government came to terms with the governments of those small dominions which were surrounded by her territory. She developed the institution of the Zollanschluss in order to incorporate these enclaves, as these parcels of land were called, into her customs system. Although the Zollanschluss was later taken over by the Zollverein, it had little bearing on Prussia's attitude toward German economic unification, and for this reason it will be treated separately in the next chapter.

In the second place, from 1819 on the statesmen in Berlin became increasingly aware of the problem underlying German economic unification. The degree to which the slow evolution of their ideas tended toward German economic unification must be examined in order to describe clearly the

[76] Gustav Schmoller, "Das preussische Handels- und Zollgesetz vom 26. Mai 1818," *Beilage zur Allgemeinen Zeitung* [Munich], No. 177 (August 10, 1898), p. 5; Fischer, *op. cit.*, p. 364.

process by which Prussia achieved economic hegemony in Germany.

Shortly after the first enclave treaty had been signed in 1819 the Prussian government was obliged to define its policy in relation to the question of general German unification. List's propaganda had put this problem squarely up to the German governments, and public opinion had forced them to tackle the task. Until then Hardenberg had spoken favorably of this idea, but only in general terms. The Prussian Ministry of Foreign Affairs had stated Prussia's willingness to include neighboring territories in her customs system, but had been ready to conclude treaties with enclaves only and even then only after a great deal of hesitation.[77]

When, however, the Karlsbad Conferences put the execution of Article XIX on the program of the Vienna Final Conferences, the Prussian government was obliged to define its stand. The instructions the Prussian representative, Graf Bernstorff, received on this point advised caution.[78]   A number of difficulties were pointed out, such as those caused by the difference in financial institutions and industrial interests. They also stated that the constitution of Germany was not

---

[77] Oncken and Saemisch, I, 91, n.; Bernstorff to the three Anhalt governments, Berlin, March 11, 1819, *ibid.*, p. 100, No. 25; Bernstorff to Gotha, June 13, 1819, Treitschke, "Die Anfänge," *Preussische Jahrbücher*, XXX (1872), 426. Treitschke quotes certain passages from this document, while others are only paraphrased.   This makes it difficult to arrive at a correct analysis of this document. Bernstorff apparently defended Prussia's new customs system as being designed primarily against non-German goods and stressed that Prussia must have guarantees from the smaller territories against the importation of non-German goods. He suggested the formation of a special union by these smaller states, which in turn was to ally itself with the Prussian system.   The difficulty arises if one tries to harmonize this common customs federation ("gemeinsamer Zollverband") thus to be founded with Bernstorff's specification that certificates of origin alone would not suffice (Treitschke's paraphrase: ". . . Sicherstellung der Zolleinahmen, wozu Ursprungszeugnisse allein nicht genügen").   It seems that Bernstorff was thinking not so much of a common customs line as of the hole in the Prussian line which a free-trade treaty would create and which would have to be stopped. Bernstorff, moreover, was apparently not aware of the geographical principles underlying economic unification when he spoke of individual states reaching an agreement with Prussia, an agreement which was to cover all the territories constituting them.   This seems to indicate a rather legalistic construction of Article V of the Law of May 26, 1818.

[78] Dated Berlin, November 10, 1819, Oncken and Saemisch, I, 356, No. 180.

adaptable to such a reorganization, and guarantees were demanded for a regular execution of the once adopted plan. Hardenberg, when writing these instructions, believed that the increased clamor for economic unification had been caused by the new Prussian customs law, and for this reason he injected so many reservations against a general agreement. He probably foresaw only too well that it would be used indirectly to attack the Prussian system. He also offered some positive suggestions, however, when he instructed Bernstorff that individual complaints could be eased by separate agreements and that thus internal barriers could gradually be abolished. Hardenberg's statement on this last point was very indefinite, but it seems to have followed the same trend of thought as that expressed in Article V of the customs law. He was apparently more concerned with the creation of a free-trade area than with the foundation of a customs system. The instructions, moreover, should not be taken to mean that the Berlin officials had agreed on a definite program on these matters. The Ministry of Foreign Affairs and the Ministry of Finance did not see eye to eye on this issue, and it might be questioned to what extent Hardenberg's phrases were intended to cover up this dilemma.[79]

This same formula was used in the answer which was given to the representatives of List's League when they came to Berlin shortly before the opening of the Vienna Final Conferences in order to present a petition to Friedrich Wilhelm III.[80] Although this formal reply was somewhat cool and vague, the private opinions expressed by various Prussian officials were much more friendly. They were so friendly, indeed, that the overoptimistic delegates thought that they had been received in Berlin as saviors of Prussia and Germany.[81] Except for Hoffmann, who took the formalistic conservative view against their organization, all the Prussian officials upon whom the delegates called showed their sympathy for their cause. They all praised the idea of general German unification as proposed by List, and Maassen even admitted that a general German customs system would be

---

[79] Cf. Brinkmann, *op. cit.*, pp. 125–26.
[80] Oncken and Saemisch, I, 356, n. 2.
[81] Schnell to List, Gera, December 8, 1819, List, *op. cit.*, VIII, 153, No. 69 *bis*.

able to develop a better tariff policy than Prussia had done so far, while Klewiz stated that fiscal interests should not be the main consideration in approaching such a problem. The objections raised were primarily political. Hardenberg pointed to the fact that Prussia was not able to take the initiative in these matters and advised the delegates to present their case directly at Vienna. Maassen objected on principle to retortions and reprisals of any kind and showed himself to be more of a free trader than the delegates.[82]

The contrast between the official policy which was so cautiously pursued and the friendliness of the officials in Berlin indicated the difficult situation Prussia found herself in. These men were still the patriots of the Napoleonic wars, as well as liberals of the eighteenth century. On the other hand, since a more closely knit German federation had not been achieved in 1815, Prussia was compelled to follow her own interests and stand up for her sovereign rights as much as any other German state. Moreover, Prussia had learned only too well with what delicacy German matters had to be handled, and she had also seen her popularity in Germany wane. Both the delegates as well as the officials had that enthusiasm in common which was characteristic of the period of good will. General ideas dominated, while specific questions, although recognized, stood in the background. If such a meeting could have been repeated a generation later, the degree of protection, specific tariffs, and definite political actions would have been discussed, and a feeling of general agreement would not have been reached so easily.

At the Vienna Final Conferences, however, Prussia was not able to make friends over economic questions. Bernstorff was not an expert in these matters, and his conservatism prejudiced him against reform in general. But he had no intention of abandoning the Prussian Law of May 26, 1818, as some German statesmen had hoped who believed that it had been the work of the revolutionary party in the Berlin offices.[83] Bernstorff did not display much

---

[82] *Loc. cit.;* League delegation to Berlin, report, n.d., n.p., Olshausen, *Friedrich List,* pp. 262–66, No. 64; Schnell to Bauereis, Gera, December 6, 1819, *ibid.,* pp. 267–68, No. 66; cf. *ibid.,* p. 81.

[83] Menn, *Zur Vorgeschichte,* pp. 53–54.

diplomatic ability at the conferences; he was either too passive or, if he finally took action, too blunt to achieve anything positive. The two methods of general economic unification which were considered in Vienna were not acceptable to Prussia. A system of retaliation against non-German goods was against the liberal economic beliefs of the Prussian reformers, while a general German customs system within the framework of the Confederation was opposed by Prussia because it would have cut her territories in two. But many German states were not looking for such general institutions, since they wanted to see the new Prussian system modified. The numerous and often naïve attacks against the Prussian customs law only stiffened Bernstorff's attitude and embittered him. Such personal friction, as well as the lack of a common basis for the discussion, made these negotiations a complete failure. As chairman of the commerce committee Bernstorff had a fine opportunity to show Prussia's policy at its best, but he lacked any new or positive suggestion of how to solve the problem, and he just stood by his instructions. He stated that Prussia was willing to conclude treaties with individual states, but that she was unable to modify her customs system. This point was not elaborated by Bernstorff, and there is no indication that he had a separate customs system in mind. For some time he even opposed the proposal that the Diet should be allowed to hear experts on economic matters.[84] How ill prepared he was in reality to deal with such problems can be seen from the fact that he referred to Berlin the Saxe-Weimar-Eisenach representative when he attempted to discuss the situation of certain enclaves under the new Prussian customs law.[85]

Prussia's policy during the Vienna Final Conferences was not more enlightened than that of the other German states, and for years to come this passive rôle was not changed. Although Bernstorff continued to assert the willingness of his government to admit to the Prussian customs system those German states whose geographical position tied them closely to Prussia, the statesmen in Berlin were in reality not

[84] Aegidi, *Aus der Vorzeit*, pp. 25–26, 34–35, 38–39, 45–47, 54–60, 85–87.
[85] Brinkmann, *op. cit.*, pp. 125–26.

ready for an extensive policy of economic unification. In particular, the Prussian government was not interested in reaching an agreement with the more industrialized South German states.[86] This policy was only reconsidered occasionally, as, for instance, when the South German negotiations seemed to promise success. And it was primarily the possible danger arising from an anti-Prussian coalition which set off lengthy discussions in Berlin. The first of these scares occurred in the early summer of 1822, when the Darmstadt Conferences appeared to be achieving a separate union in South and Central Germany. At the same time a Thuringian government inquired about the possibilities of joining the Prussian system if the negotiations for a separate union should fail.[87] The considerations which determined the Prussian government to remain passive were based on the belief that a non-Prussian union in Germany would be unable to pursue a concerted policy against Prussia, since many discrepant interests would be represented in such a union. No commercial or financial losses were to be expected. Other territories, therefore, should be admitted into the Prussian system only if that could be done without endangering existing Prussian institutions. The Ministry of Finance formulated a three-point minimum requirement for safeguarding the Prussian tax administration. It demanded (1) security for the Prussian consumption taxes, (2) Prussian preponderance in determining tariffs, and (3) direct control of the customs organization in the territories to be included. Prussia's special interest in Hesse-Kassel as a link between the two main parts of the monarchy was recognized, and it was recommended that she should be treated "without coolness."[88] The reserve expressed in this attitude should be ascribed, not to hostility to other German governments, but to the general inertia in Berlin circles. Thus no objection was raised by Klewiz against Prussian enclaves joining other

---

[86] Bernstorff to Küster, Laibach, February, 1821, Oncken and Saemisch, I, 409–11, No. 209.

[87] Bernstorff to Bülow and Klewiz, Berlin, June 8, 1822, *ibid.*, II, 45, No. 300; Klewiz to Bülow, Berlin, June 27, 1822, *ibid.*, p. 46, No. 301.

[88] *Ibid.*, pp. 46–49.

customs systems,[89] and Prussia's policy toward the Darmstadt Conferences continued to be benevolently tolerant.[90]

When two years later the Hesse-Kassel government suggested negotiations for a customs agreement,[91] the idea was taken up favorably by Bernstorff;[92] but the Electoral Hessian government had apparently not meant the offer seriously, since it caused difficulties as soon as Prussia tried to bring about an understanding.[93]

At the same time Prussia's position toward economic unification with other German states was again discussed in Berlin. Developments in South Germany had caused Otterstedt, the Prussian representative in southwestern Germany, to warn Friedrich Wilhelm III of the bad effects that a continued policy of isolation would have on Prussia's relation with South Germany. For political reasons he suggested a reconsideration of the whole problem.[94] The Ministry of Finance made a thorough analysis of it.[95] Prussia, it claimed, should not fear a South German union, but rather welcome it, since a large union would be least dangerous. Only a number of smaller territories bordering Prussia were considered as possibilities for a customs unification with Prussia. They comprised sections of Hesse-Darmstadt and of Hesse-Kassel, the districts between Rhenish Prussia and the Bavarian Palatinate, and Thuringian and other small Central German territories. The memorandum conceded that between equals a customs union would be ideal, but that, since all the territories in question were considerably smaller than Prussia, a number of guarantees for Prussian

[89] Ibid., p. 48.

[90] Bernstorff to Friedrich Wilhelm III, Berlin, July 13, 1824, ibid., p. 70, No. 317.

[91] Haenlein to Prussian Ministry of Foreign Affairs, Kassel, December 16, 1824, ibid., pp. 75–76, No. 319.

[92] Bernstorff to Haenlein, Berlin, December 25, 1824, ibid., pp. 76–77, No. 310.

[93] Haenlein to Prussian Ministry of Foreign Affairs, Kassel, December 30, 1824, ibid., pp. 98–99, No. 322.

[94] Otterstedt to Friedrich Wilhelm III, Darmstadt, March 3, 1824, ibid., pp. 59–63.

[95] Ministry of Finance, memorandum, Berlin, December 28, 1824, ibid., pp. 77–98, No. 321.

preponderance would have to be insisted on. These guarantees were the adoption of the Prussian customs system, Prussian administration, and the introduction of Prussian consumption taxes if complete free trade was to be established. Prussia would gain only if the new customs boundary meant a considerable simplification of her administration. If she could not shorten her tariff lines, she would make no financial profits, since she would lose her transit trade in any case and would have to admit at the same time a new competitor to her home market. Such were the considerations which led to the selection of the territories mentioned above as being suitable for economic unification. Since it was improbable that Electoral Hesse would accept a complete subordination of her administration, some modifications of the guarantees were suggested for her. No formal right to vote on the common tariff was to be granted, but she should be heard before any changes were made and have an opportunity to end the arrangement if no agreement was reached. Moreover, the customs administration in the Electorate was to be handled by a mixed commission which was to guarantee Prussian interests. Hesse-Kassel was to be compensated for all duties collected at the boundaries.

The Ministry of Finance was finally willing to make concessions in cases where Prussia's gain was unquestioned. But no territory to be admitted was to be treated on the basis of equality, and only those parts of neighboring states were to be considered which would serve Prussia's immediate financial interests. The aim was to consolidate the Prussian system by including neighboring and intermediate territories. A connection of the eastern and western parts of the monarchy was particularly desired, and for this reason concessions to Electoral Hesse were made. The Ministry of Finance's dilemma lay in the fact that, even if a medium state agreed to join on a basis of inequality, such a step would have been opposed by Friedrich Wilhelm III for legitimistic reasons.[96] Prussia, even at the end of this decade of economic reform, had not adopted a definite policy toward German economic unification.

[96] Brinkmann, *op. cit.*, p. 223, especially n. 7.

During the decade following the Congress of Vienna the Prussian government succeeded in developing a coherent general commercial policy, but failed to apply it to the particular problem German economic unification presented. The customs reform of 1818 was part of the general revival the Prussian monarchy had undergone since 1806. The thoughtful adaptation of new liberal ideas, both political and economic, took older values and existing realities into careful consideration. Its program of universal trade through commercial treaties anticipated the subsequent development of a world-wide economy. It constituted a rare combination of detailed technicalities with general theories. By formulating and executing a definite fiscal program the Prussian government did valuable groundwork for the subsequent Zollverein at a time when such advanced thought was seldom found in Germany.

On the other hand, the statesmen in Berlin failed to combine Prussia's fiscal and commercial interests with her foreign policy so as to present a well-integrated program for German economic unification. Not until they had worked out the whole problem were they able to embark on the Zollverein policy.

CHAPTER VI

THE ORIGIN AND EARLY HISTORY OF THE ZOLLANSCHLUSS, 1818–33

A BY-PRODUCT of the Prussian customs reform of 1818 was an institution which provided economic unification for small territories enclosed in larger states. An arrangement which provided for the accession of a small territory to the fiscal system of a larger enclosing or neighboring dominion has been called in technical literature Zollanschluss.[1] It was to become the standard method by which the Zollverein dealt with enclaves and other small territories. The early history of this institution is important not only for its peculiar administrative aspects, but also for the light it throws on the origin of the Zollverein.

For many years the first and foremost problem Prussia's new commercial policy had to face arose from the difficulties created by the enclaves of other German states within Prussian territory. Little thought had been given to this question while the reforms were being discussed. These enclaves had always represented a special problem for Prussia's commercial and financial policy. It was not a new field of foreign policy she was entering, but merely a different phase of it.[2]

THE YEARS 1818-19

WITHIN a month after the new customs law had been passed the authorities in Berlin began to realize the new situation, and the official machinery was slowly put in motion. The largest enclaves were the Anhalt duchies which were almost entirely surrounded by Prussian territories.[3] It was with regard to these states that the Prussian Ministries of

---

[1] This meaning of the word should not be confused with the use the term Zollanschluss, or simply Anschluss, has received in recent years in connection with the proposed Austro-German customs unification. Such a union would have been a customs union and not a Zollanschluss.

[2] Brinkmann, Die preussische Handelspolitik, p. 112.

[3] The Upper Duchy of Anhalt-Bernburg was not completely surrounded by Prussian territory; it had a short common boundary with Brunswick.

Commerce and Finance submitted on June 27, 1818, a number of suggestions to Hardenberg.

A brief and simple program of some six points was developed.   Prussia was to leave all traffic between her own territories and the Anhalt enclaves unmolested.   She would collect on her exterior frontier all the tariffs and taxes on all the goods going to Anhalt or coming from the duchies as if they were imported into a Prussian district or exported from such a district.   If necessary, she would call the import revenues transit duties, which she could claim legally by her sovereign rights.   It admitted that Prussia had no right to charge her consumption tax in this way on goods going to Anhalt through Prussian territory.   For this reason Prussia was to compensate Anhalt for the losses caused by this consumption tax.   The main compensation for Anhalt was the fact that she could export into Prussia without any restriction and that Prussia was not collecting any export tariffs on goods going from Prussia into Anhalt.   If this compensation should prove insufficient, then the Prussian government was to offer Anhalt the "payment of a definite, moderate sum of money."   In order to make the Prussian system of internal revenue airtight, the Anhalts were to collect in Anhalt consumption taxes at the Prussian rate.   Moreover, a separate understanding was to be reached with regard to salt.   The experts estimated that the Prussian exchequer would save between 34,000 and 39,000 talers by not having to patrol the Anhalt-Prussian frontier and would gain an additional 37,000 talers from the import and consumption duties collected from goods sent through Prussian territory into the Anhalts.[4]

In many ways this proposal is significant.   It showed only too clearly the purely fiscal intentions of the Prussian Ministry of Finance.   It demonstrated the Ministry's ignorance of German affairs, since it did not take into account the mentality prevalent in the governments of the small states. It also proved that it had no conception of the principles underlying a customs union or even a Zollanschluss policy. It entirely lacked the basic criterion of either type of eco-

---

[4] Prussian Ministries of Commerce and Finance to Hardenberg, Berlin, June 17, 1818, Oncken and Saemisch, I, 83–84, No. 17.

nomic unification, namely, the principle of dividing the joint income in proportion to the population or some other similar factor. Whatever value the Hildburghausen incident of 1817 might have had, this later scheme certainly shows that it was only an episode and that the statesmen in Berlin had to begin from the bottom. They, however, started tackling this problem on their own account before they were swamped with complaints from all over Germany.[5]

But Hardenberg, being in no hurry to make a decision, shelved the matter and finally referred it to the Cabinet on August 14. He gave the question a significantly different formulation. Instead of asking for an opinion on how to treat the enclaves, he wanted to be advised whether the government district (*Regierungsbezirk*) of Erfurt was to be excluded from the new Prussian customs system.[6] Hardenberg's retreat in this matter contrasts with Treitschke's claim that on June 3, 1818, the Prussian State Chancellor had already outlined the future policy of economic unification.[7] Treitschke, however, based his opinion on a quotation from which one very significant clause had been omitted.[8] Moreover, Hardenberg's terminology must be used with caution. There is no proof that such terms as "the union of several German states into a common manufacturing and trading system"[9] or as "a neighborly getting together for a common interest"[10] expressed anything more than a vague concept of some kind of system of commercial treaties.

The Cabinet, to which Hardenberg had referred the problem, reported on September 23, 1818, the following deci-

[5] It should be noted that the Law of May 26, 1818, was not published until September 9, 1818, and that it took effect in the western provinces of the monarchy almost immediately after copies had arrived by special delivery (*ibid.*, pp. 76–77, n. 1; Menn, *Zur Vorgeschichte*, p. 33, n. 1).

[6] Cabinet to Hardenberg, Berlin, September 23, 1818, Oncken and Saemisch, I, 85, No. 18.

[7] Treitschke, "Die Anfänge des deutschen Zollvereins," *Preussische Jahrbücher*, XXX (1872), 422.

[8] Cf. Hardenberg to manufacturers in Rheydt, Süchteln, Gladbach, Viersen, and Kaldenkirchen, Berlin, June 3, 1818, Oncken and Saemisch, I, 79–80, No. 15, where the passage is quoted in its entirety.

[9] "Vereinigung mehrerer deutschen Staaten zu einem gemeinschaftlichen Fabrik- und Handelssystem."

[10] "Nachbarliches Anschliessen an ein gemeinsames Interesse."

sions:[11] Prussia should try to include the main bulk of the
Erfurt district in her customs line. This would have been
profitable only if some agreement had been reached with the
enclaves. Such understandings should follow the plan outlined by the Ministries of Commerce and Finance on June 27,
except that no consumption tax should be charged for goods
imported through Prussian territory to be used in the enclaves. In a similar way exports through Prussian territory
were to be free. This trade, however, was to be restricted to
certain roads and only to be permitted under certain conditions. Such an arrangement would be just, and Prussia had
a moral right to ask for special considerations, since her
finances were the basis for the protection she granted the
small German states. The Cabinet formally resolved that
the Foreign Office be instructed to approach the various
Anhalt and Schwarzburg governments with the purpose of
concluding such agreements.

Still no trace of a Zollanschluss can be found in this
resolution. The technical suggestions were impractical, but
two features are worth emphasizing. Prussia was to take
the initiative by starting the negotiations, and it was declared
that she was entitled to preserve the integrity of her finances
in order to fulfill her military obligations toward the smaller
members of the Confederation.

The Prussian Foreign Office, however, being disinclined
to start negotiations, remained inactive. It soon received
an inquiry from the Ministry of Finance asking how it was
carrying out the resolution.[12] The Foreign Office allowed
a whole month to pass before it finally answered.[13] Hoffmann, director of German affairs in the Office, found himself
in a difficult position. He had been in sympathy with a
revenue agreement with the enclaves, but he knew only too
well the obstacles any negotiations on such a topic with the
other German states would have met. Moreover, Hardenberg, who had pursued a policy of moderation in German

---

[11] Cabinet to Hardenberg, Berlin, September 23, 1818, *ibid.*, pp. 88–89,
No. 19.   [12] *Ibid.*, p. 87, n. 2.
[13] Hoffmann to Klewiz, Berlin, November 20, 1818, *ibid.*, pp. 88–89,
No. 19.

affairs, was attending the conferences at Aachen with Bernstorff, his successor as foreign minister. Since Bernstorff had not yet taken over his office in Berlin,[14] Hoffmann, understandably, did not want to commit himself. He therefore advanced a number of valid arguments: A royal decision should be secured on some of the disputed points. He had not been authorized by Hardenberg to start negotiating. It would be almost impossible to reach an agreement with other German governments, as the negotiations about the military constitution showed, and nobody could expect these governments to submit to the Prussian system of indirect taxation before this system was set up.

The Ministry of Finance, however, went ahead and without waiting any further for diplomatic negotiations, it ordered, on December 14, 1818, that the enclaves should be treated as if they were Prussian territory in the application of the new customs law.[15]

Subsequently two reasons were given for this decision. It was argued that, if negotiations had been started before the law went into full effect, many merchants would have taken advantage of the following loophole: All goods stored in the eastern provinces of the Prussian monarchy on January 1, 1819, the date the Law of May 26, 1818, was introduced, had to pay a supplementary tax before being retailed. This special tax could not be enforced in the enclaves, especially since agreements would not have been reached so soon, and there would have been no way of preventing goods from being stored up in these enclaves before the new system was functioning and from having them later exported into Prussia over an open boundary. By keeping quiet on this point the Ministry of Finance had expected to escape this

---

[14] [Anonymous] "Christian Günther Graf v. Bernstorff, Königl. preuss. Geh. Staats- und Cabinets-Minister," *Politisches Journal*, LVI (1835), 454.

[15] Ministry of Finance to Government at Erfurt, Berlin, December 14, 1818, Oncken and Saemisch, I, 89, No. 20. This order meant that all goods shipped through Prussian territory into these enclaves were to pay the same rates when first entering Prussian territory as goods to be consumed in Prussia. No direct invasion of the sovereignty of these enclaves was planned. This was not an entirely new procedure; the Kingdom of Westphalia had done the same to the enclaves in its territory (*ibid.*, p. 94, n. 1).

dilemma.[16]   The other reason was indicated by Maassen when he voiced the expectation that the new regulation would force the smaller states to open the negotiations with Prussia.[17]

When the customs law took effect in the eastern section of the Prussian monarchy on January 1, 1819, Maassen had not yet worked out a plan of how to deal with the enclaves. He looked forward to reaching some kind of compromise on the customs and perhaps also on the consumption taxes.[18] No common policy had been developed, and, a more important consideration, no understanding had been reached with the Foreign Office.   Moreover, no decision had been made by either Friedrich Wilhelm III or Hardenberg.   Thus Prussia, being without plan or policy, had to face the flood of protests which were soon to come from her German neighbors.

The German governments affected by the new customs law were not long in sending complaints to Berlin.   The Anhalt duchies and Schwarzburg-Sondershausen were among the first to point out the difficulties the system was imposing on their territories.[19]   Stirred by these remonstrances, the Prussian government finally decided on a policy toward the enclaves.   Klewiz brought the matter up again by submitting a detailed report to Friedrich Wilhelm III in which he discussed three different ways of settling this problem.[20]   He argued that (1) the enclaves could be treated as foreign territory and surrounded by a Prussian customs line; (2) they could be allowed a certain quota for their import; (3) they could be asked to pay full rates for all goods imported through Prussia and receive a fixed sum of money as an indemnity for the consumption tax collected by Prussia. Klewiz advocated the third system, since the two others were impractical and expensive. Friedrich Wilhelm III followed

---

[16] Klewiz to Friedrich Wilhelm III, Berlin, January 28, *ibid.*, p. 92, No. 22.

[17] Maassen to Hoffmann, Berlin, January 11, 1819, Irmgard Kamlah, *Karl Georg Maassen und die preussische Finanzreform von 1816–1822* (Doctor's dissertation, Halle, 1934), pp. 31–32.   [18] *Loc. cit.*

[19] L'Estocq to Bernstorff, Berlin, January 22, 1819, Oncken and Saemisch, I, 89–91; three Anhalt governments to Prussian Ministry of Foreign Affairs, Bernburg, January 29, 1819, *ibid.*, pp. 94–97, No. 23.

[20] Klewiz to Friedrich Wilhelm III, Berlin, January 28, 1819, *ibid.*, pp. 91–94, No. 22.

this suggestion and ordered the Ministry of Foreign Affairs to conduct negotiations along that line.[21]

From that point on the Prussian Ministry of Foreign Affairs stood ready to answer the complaints of the enclaves by offering their inclusion into the Prussian revenue system against a fair monetary compensation. Although Bernstorff declared himself willing to enter into such an agreement with any German state,[22] actually negotiations were taken up only with a few of the states which had enclaves in Prussian territory. A somewhat conciliatory note was sent to the Anhalts,[23] but no such efforts were made with other states. Schwarzburg-Sondershausen's frequent notes were left unanswered by Bernstorff; although Klewiz seems to have been willing to negotiate, he was without authority to do so.[24] On the other hand, when Nassau suggested a special arrangement, the Ministries of Commerce and Finance went into opposition.[25] Weimar also seems not to have received a conciliatory note.[26] The result of this poorly coördinated policy was obvious. Most governments had been aggrieved by the way the enclaves had been included in the Prussian system without any previous notification. Their resentment against paying the consumption tax was only too understandable. Prussia's highhanded procedure was condemned even by Friedrich Wilhelm III.[27]

When a policy was finally adopted, it was carried out by diplomats who were not in touch with the economic and fiscal problems of the monarchy. They had therefore to rely on the advice of the competent government authorities in these matters, who, in turn, were interested only in the immediate effects on their departments and who were little aware of the damage their decisions might cause to Prussia's foreign relations. Thus the actions taken by the Ministry of Finance frequently interfered with established treaty rela-

---

[21] Friedrich Wilhelm III to Klewiz, Berlin, February 8, 1819, *ibid.*, pp. 97–98, No. 24, p. 98, n. 1.

[22] Bernstorff to the three Anhalt governments, Berlin, March 11, 1819, *ibid.*, p. 100, No. 25.   [23] *Loc. cit.*

[24] *Ibid.*, p. 91, n. 1.

[25] Menn, *op. cit.*, pp. 40–41.

[26] Kamlah, *op. cit.*, pp. 32–33.

[27] Friedrich Wilhelm III to Klewiz, Berlin, February 8, 1819, Oncken and Saemisch, I, 97–98, No. 24.

tionships.[28] The Foreign Office was opposed to such infractions, but was in most cases unable or unwilling to conduct the negotiations on a sound basis. In their complaints most of the governments had asked both to have their treaty or other rights reëstablished and also to have modifications made in the new system in their particular case.[29] Most answers limited themselves to the points brought up in the complaint. Hence Marschall, Nassau's minister, proposed a mutual free-trade agreement for goods from Prussia and Nassau which was to work with certificates of origin.[30] The Ministries of Commerce and Finance opposed such a plan since they were afraid of the legitimate competition of Nassau wines and also of the illegitimate one of French and Italian wines, which could be imported via Frankfurt under such an agreement.[31] A system of certificates of origin can easily be abused by fraud. But this objection, as well as an earlier demand for guarantees against imports into Prussia through a free-trade inlet of this kind,[32] showed that the Prussian statesmen had worked out a plan for enclaves only, but not for other adjacent territories. Otherwise they would have made counterproposals. Moreover, they were ready to conclude agreements only in their own financial interest, but were unwilling to make a deal in trade which included a *quid pro quo*, as their rather naïve opposition to the possible import of Nassau wines indicated. No particular effort was made to resume older negotiations[33] or to follow up new complaints. Negotiations were continued with the Anhalts;

---

[28] For Nassau's case see Brinkmann, *op. cit.*, p. 115; for Schwarzburg-Sonderhausen's case see *ibid.*, p. 118.

[29] L'Estocq to Bernstorff, Berlin, January 22, 1819, Oncken and Saemisch, I, 89–91, No. 21; three Anhalt governments to Prussian Ministry of Foreign Affairs, Bernburg, January 29, 1819, *ibid.*, pp. 94–97, No. 23; Brinkmann, *op. cit.*, pp. 115, 118.

[30] Marschall to Otterstedt, Wiesbaden, March 6, 1819, Oncken and Saemisch, II, 28, No. 288.

[31] Bülow and Klewiz to Bernstorff, Berlin, April 14, 1819, *ibid.*, pp. 28–29, No. 289.

[32] Bernstorff to three Anhalt governments, Berlin, March 11, *ibid.*, I, 100, No. 25.

[33] Treitschke, however, claims that the Prussian Foreign Office sent out a general invitation to all states with enclaves in Prussian territory for negotiations ("Die Anfänge," *Preussische Jahrbücher*, XXX [1872], 424). There is no independent supporting evidence for this statement (cf. Oncken and Saemisch, I, 100).

but as discussions centered around the legal aspects, for years to come they achieved anything but a closer coöperation between the governments.

Flaws can easily be found in the arguments which were brought forward against Prussia and in the suggestions which she refused. But that is not sufficient to justify Prussian policy or to conclude that she was working for German economic unification. If she had had a higher aim, she would have been able to make something out of Nassau's well-meaning offers instead of rejecting them. Prussia would also have taken up Bavaria's offer to come to an understanding concerning the commerce between the Palatinate and the Prussian Rhine provinces.[34] The Prussian Foreign Office served as a complaint department and seems to have been satisfied with curing the symptoms. It was, however, not in Prussia's financial interest to have the unsettled conditions of the enclaves continued.

Nevertheless, Prussia's relative success in 1819 should be credited, not to her new policy,[35] but to the persistent efforts of the Schwarzburg-Sondershausen government, which finally managed to gain consideration in Berlin. Its notes and memoranda of January 22, February 27, March 23, April 22, and May 29, 1819, had been left unanswered by the Prussian Ministry of Foreign Affairs.[36] It was not until Weise, the chancellor of this small principality, came in person to Berlin that he was able to elicit a reply, which, however, did not reach him until he had returned home.[37] The change was due to Hardenberg's intervention for Weise.[38] In the ensuing negotiations the Ministry of Finance was given an equal share, so that the monopoly of the Foreign Office was broken down and the conflict between the departments was diminished. The new task was assigned not to the ministers, but to two of their subordinates. Maassen, the Prussian general tax administrator (General-Steuer-Direktor), represented the new spirit of the financial reform, while Hoffmann, of

---

[34] Brinkmann, op. cit., p. 120.
[35] Cf. Treitschke, "Die Anfänge," Preussische Jahrbücher, XXX (1872), 428, and Zimmermann, Geschichte, pp. 48–49 for a different view.
[36] Oncken and Saemisch, I, 91, n. 1.   [37] Ibid., p. 107, n. 1.
[38] Loc. cit.

the Foreign Office, was an expert on German affairs. Both had participated in drafting the Law of May 26, 1818, and now that they were given a free hand, they took the clumsy policy Prussia had hitherto pursued toward the enclaves and transformed it into a marked success.

The attitude adopted by these two men toward Schwarzburg-Sondershausen was to be firm on matters of principle but liberal in details. This policy was well designed to take care of Prussian state interests and at the same time to consider the sensitiveness of the smaller governments about their sovereignty. The same method later proved successful in the foundation of the Zollverein.

Maassen and Hoffmann insisted on an Anschluss of the Schwarzburg-Sondershausen enclave, i.e. on its inclusion in the Prussian customs system on unequal terms. The enclave was as a rule to be subjected to Prussian indirect taxation and receive a proportional compensation for the consumption tax collected by the Prussian government. A firm stand was taken against any system employing an import quota for the enclaves. Most of the details were left to the little principality to decide.[39] Schwarzburg-Sondershausen did not easily assent to an Anschluss, but no other choice was given.[40] After a brief period of negotiation the first Anschluss treaty was signed on October 25, 1819.[41]

This treaty contained a number of general provisions which were to be used as the basis for later and similar agreements; it also included some arrangements designed in particular for Schwarzburg-Sondershausen. Three principles were established. (1) Complete free trade was allowed, as a rule, between the Prussian and the Schwarzburg-Sondershausen territories enclosed within the exterior Prussian customs line. On the other hand, Prussia was to continue to enforce the new law along the frontiers as she had done before and to treat the enclave in this respect as if it were Prussian territory. (2) Schwarzburg-Sondershausen was to be compensated for the consumption tax collected by Prussia

---

[39] Maassen and Hoffmann to Weise, Berlin, October 10, 1819, *ibid.*, pp. 108–11, No. 31.

[40] Weise to Maassen and Hoffmann, Berlin, October 12, 1819, *ibid.*, p. 113, No. 34.

[41] Dated Berlin, *ibid.*, pp. 116–19, No. 35.

on imports going through Prussian territory. (3) The rate was to be fixed according to the proportion which the population of the enclave bore to that of the eastern part of the Prussian monarchy.[42]

These principles were elaborated and modified by a number of more detailed provisions. In order to safeguard the taxes on consumption collected on goods produced in both states, only goods which paid an equal rate in both territories were allowed complete free trade. All other goods, when passing from a state in which they were less taxed into one with a higher tax rate, had to pay an import tax, called transfer duty, amounting to the difference between the two rates. Moreover, both salt and playing cards were excluded from the free-trade privilege, since both commodities were Prussian state monopolies. They could, however, be exported from the enclave through Prussian territory. The rate of compensation was to be revised every three years. In order to enforce the treaty Prussian officials had the right of hot pursuit in Schwarzburg-Sondershausen territory. But the assistance of local officials had to be enlisted, and searches, seizures, and arrests were to be executed within the enclave solely by officials of the principality. The Schwarzburg-Sondershausen authorities could refuse to comply with a request for such action, if it was against the provisions of the Law of May 26, 1818. Moreover, all such cases were to be tried in the courts of the principality, and all fines went into its exchequer.[43]

A number of articles took cognizance of certain peculiar conditions existing in Schwarzburg-Sondershausen's case. Since the prince's residence was in the enclave, all goods for the use of his household were not to pay duty at the time of importation, if properly certified. The amount thus evaded was to be deducted from the next payment of compensation. Moreover, all goods shipped by mail to Sondershausen were not to pay duty until they reached that town, since it had a Prussian postoffice where the tax could be collected. A clause of an earlier treaty providing for free trade in certain goods was modified to allow Schwarzburg-Sondershausen to ship free of charge through Prussian territory all products of

[42] *Ibid.*, Preamble, Arts. I, VII.   [43] *Ibid.*, Arts. I, V, VIII, IX.

the state-owned mines. Since the new Prussian system had not been in operation long enough to determine the three-year average income, a temporary provision stipulated a fixed sum of 15,000 talers per annum up to December 31, 1821.[44]

The importance of this treaty lay in the three main principles on which it was based and in the more specific provisions on transfer duties, monopolies, and enforcement. Not all of its provisions were ready to be taken over by any subsequent Anschluss agreement, since some articles were especially designed to meet particular problems. The treaty was apparently concluded for an indefinite time, since the problem of expiration was not mentioned at all. On the other hand, it provided only for the smoother operation of the Law of May 26, 1818, which was specifically mentioned,[45] and nothing was said about a possible modification of this law.

The principle of proportional compensation was apparently evolved by the Prussian representatives very early during the negotiations.[46] This idea was the essence of the understanding. Prussia had recognized at an earlier date the necessity of including the enclaves in her system of taxation and the right of the enclaves to compensation. As early as 1819 it was proposed that this compensation should be in money.[47] But no reference to proportional compensation can be found before the opening of the negotiations with Schwarzburg-Sondershausen in the fall of 1819. There is also no indication that this idea originated outside the Berlin offices. The Nebenius memorandum had not yet been published.

Apparently, the Prussian officials arrived at the idea of awarding compensation in proportion to the populations involved when they were immediately confronted with the problem of how much they owed the government of an enclave. The practice was not uncommon to base similar

---

[44] *Ibid.*, Arts. II, III, IV, VI.   [45] *Ibid.*, Preamble, Art. V.

[46] Maassen to Hoffmann and Weise, Berlin, October 10, 1819, *ibid.*, pp. 108–11, No. 31.

[47] Ministries of Commerce and Finance to Hardenberg, Berlin, June 27, 1818, *ibid.*, pp. 83–85, No. 17; Klewiz to Friedrich Wilhelm III, Berlin, January 28, 1819, *ibid.*, p. 92, No. 22; Bernstorff to three Anhalt governments, Berlin, July 28, 1819, *ibid.*, p. 105, No. 28.

calculations—especially those on tax expectancies—on a population census. As early as 1818 the income to be derived by Prussia from the Anhalt enclaves under the new law had been calculated by this method.[48] Over a whole year, however, passed before this idea was tied more closely to that of compensation in order to establish the principle of proportional compensation for a common tax revenue.

But this principle was applied only to the consumption tax and not to the customs duties proper. Thus neither a customs union nor even a Zollanschluss in a technical sense was established. All taxable goods entering the Prussian customs system had to pay an import duty and a consumption tax. The latter was refunded when goods were exported again.[49] The combined import and export duties constituted the transit duties. Although the customs duties were technically separated from the consumption revenues, for all practical purposes the latter had the character of a customs revenue because the import rates were relatively low in comparison with the consumption rates which constituted the bulk of revenue paid by the importer. Nevertheless, the agreement cannot be called a Zollanschluss because Schwarzburg-Sondershausen did not share in principle in all the revenues derived from her trade.

This distinction showed the fiscal and legalistic tendencies of the Ministry of Finance. The reason which can be assigned was the belief of the responsible tax administrators that Prussia had a sovereign right to collect the customs from goods sent to the enclaves, but that this right did not apply to the revenue derived in a similar way from the consumption tax.[50]

The territorial principle was fully recognized in the agreement. The system was not based on certificates of origin or on corridors. The enclave became a part of the free-trade

---

[48] Ministries of Commerce and Finance to Hardenberg, Berlin, June 27, 1818, *ibid.*, p. 84, No. 17.

[49] Law of May 26, 1818, Arts. VI, VII, VIII, XII, XXIII, *ibid.*, pp. 73–76, No. 14.

[50] Ministries of Commerce and Finance to Hardenberg, Berlin, June 27, 1818, *ibid.*, p. 83, No. 17; Bernstorff to three Anhalt governments, Berlin, July 28, 1819, *ibid.*, p. 105, No. 28; Maassen and Hoffmann to Weise, Berlin, October 10, 1819, *ibid.*, p. 108, No. 31; this distinction was not made in Bernstorff to three Anhalt governments, March 11, 1819, *ibid.*, p. 101, No. 25; cf. Brinkmann, *op. cit.*, p. 129, n. 59.

area created by the new Prussian customs line. Goods were
allowed to pass freely from and to the enclave as if it were
Prussian territory. The Law of May 26, 1818, became ap-
plicable in the enclave. And if it had not been for minor
exceptions, one might say that the enclave had been completely absorbed into the Prussian commercial system.

Although the enclave lost its commercial identity, it nevertheless retained its political personality. The sovereignty
of the small principality was to be left undiminished.[51] As
a rule, Prussian customs officials were not allowed to execute
the Prussian tax laws within the boundaries of the enclave.
Only two exceptions to this rule were stipulated. Prussian
officials had the right of hot pursuit, and the Prussian post-
master in Sondershausen was allowed to collect duties for
the convenience of the inhabitants of the enclave. Otherwise, the Prussian Law of 1818 and the treaty were solely enforced in the enclave by Schwarzburg-Sondershausen
through her own police and her own courts. Perhaps nothing can indicate the extreme homage paid to the little
sovereign better than the provision which allowed him to
charge the duties on goods for his own household by having
them deducted from the next payment of compensation.

Naturally a relationship like the one this treaty established was more than a mere legal edifice. It involved a
great deal of trust, coöperation, good will, and tact. The
negotiations must have brought a close understanding; otherwise the various references to coöperation found in the treaty
would be empty phrases.[52] The treaty was concluded to the
satisfaction of both parties. Prussia went ahead and made
similar treaties with other enclaves. Both parties to the
Treaty of October 25, 1819, derived great advantages from
it. Schwarzburg-Sondershausen was assured a steady income for little, if any, additional expense. Prussia, on the
other hand, had her new customs system recognized and was
able to obtain the coöperation of the enclave against attempts to break down this system. Moreover, she still had
all the important controls, and her revenue machine remained
intact. No privileges were granted which might easily have

---

[51] Treaty of October 25, 1819, Berlin, Oncken and Saemisch, I, 116–119,
No. 35; cf., in particular, Preamble.

[52] Good faith was involved in Arts. III, V, VI, VIII, X (loc. cit.).

led to abuse.   Prussia had to make a financial sacrifice for it, although it was not a great one.   But the assurance that smuggling would not become the national industry of Schwarzburg-Sondershausen was worth 15,000 talers.

Primarily, this last consideration helped to persuade the Prussian Ministry of Finance to allow the enclave a cash indemnity.   If it had wanted to pacify its own conscience, it would have incorporated the consumption tax into the customs duties—as it actually did two years later—and so would have been able to refuse to its own satisfaction all claims for compensation.   There is nothing to indicate that it aimed at German economic unification through a customs union or otherwise.   The very fact that Schwarzburg-Sondershausen was not compensated for customs duties proper makes this evident.   Moreover, all provisions of the treaty applied either to Prussia or to Schwarzburg-Sondershausen.   The possibility of third parties changing the condition of certain stipulations was not even mentioned. Thus the amount of consumption tax collected in the eastern provinces of the Prussian monarchy was to be used as a basis for calculating the compensation due to Schwarzburg-Sondershausen.[53]   Free transit of certain Schwarzburg goods was granted through Prussian territory only.[54]

The treaty was never intended as a step toward German economic unification, but was a product of the fiscal policy of the Prussian state.   Its provisions clarified a complicated situation of conflicting commercial and fiscal claims.   Prussia's solution of these particular problems displayed, for its time, a high standard of administrative ability and furnished valuable experience to be used for the formation of the Zollverein.   Moreover, the confidence growing out of the mutual coöperation was one step, however slight, toward economic unification.

THE YEARS 1822-24

OTHER German governments followed the example set by Schwarzburg-Sondershausen, so that by 1834 almost all the enclaves in Prussian territory had been included.[55]

[53] *Ibid.*, Art. I.   [54] *Ibid.*, Art. VI.
[55] The Brunswick district of Calvörde was the most notable exception.

The greatest difficulties were encountered by the statesmen in Berlin in their negotiations with the three Anhalts, especially with Anhalt-Köthen. Almost a whole decade passed before this controversy was settled, and the strife absorbed the best energies of those concerned. Most of these negotiations contributed relatively little to the institutional growth of the Prussian customs system, since a basic understanding was reached comparatively late. For years political moves and minor issues gave this relationship the character of a diplomatic fight. The controversy does not fall, therefore, within the scope of the present study,[56] although the agreements finally reached are of interest and are considered later. On the other hand, very little is known about the negotiations with the other governments having enclaves in Prussia. But most of the treaties concluded have been published.

Difficulties within the Prussian government continued. In a short time the negotiations were almost exclusively conducted by the Ministry of Foreign Affairs.[57] The first difficulties arose because neither King nor Chancellor provided the necessary coördination of the various departments. Hardenberg seems to have been primarily interested in stopping the complaints.[58] Since after his death in 1822 the position of state chancellor remained vacant,[59] Friedrich Wilhelm's stagnating influence in these matters was only increased. His desire for good relations with his smaller neighbors was based on his strict monarchical and legal convictions. For him the whole problem was very simple: Prussia just had to pay what it owed the governments of the enclaves without attaching any conditions to it. While such conditions prevailed, Hardenberg and others naturally tried their best to keep complaints away from him. And after the King had intervened in 1823 in favor of the Anhalts by having certain measures revoked, the Foreign Office adopted a

---

[56] Documents pertaining to this issue have been reprinted *ibid.*, Nos. 23, 25–28, 36–155.

[57] The treaty with Schwarzburg-Rudolstadt was still negotiated by Hoffmann and Maassen; the negotiations with Anhalt and others were primarily conducted by Bernstorff and H. von Bülow of the Foreign Office.

[58] Hardenberg to Hoffmann, December 12, 1820, *ibid.*, p. 145, n. 1.

[59] Treitschke, *Deutsche Geschichte*, III, 361–62.

more cautious policy and rarely resorted to anything else but negotiations.[60]

These treaties which incorporated the enclaves into the Prussian system of taxation varied according to circumstances. Existing treaty relations, diplomatic considerations, size and location of the territories involved seem to have been the main factors determining the nature of these agreements. Besides these individual differences a steady improvement in technical aspects can be observed. New institutions and new safeguards were developed, and the turn of the Prussian policy toward economic unification by the Zollverein was also reflected in a different attitude toward the enclaves. Within fifteen years the treaty concluded with Schwarzburg-Sondershausen in 1819 was outdated and had to be replaced.

The treaty made by Prussia with Schwarzburg-Rudolstadt in 1822 was modeled after the earlier one with Schwarzburg-Sondershausen. There were, however, a number of modifications. The provisions directed against the circumvention of the internal consumption taxes were tightened. Thus Schwarzburg-Rudolstadt was obliged to impose a fine of twice the amount evaded on all attempts to break the monopolies of salt and playing cards and the other internal revenue laws dealing with beer, wine, liquor, and tobacco. Moreover, she had to introduce a tax on distilled liquor within the enclave. The rate of this tax had to conform with the Prussian one.[61]

Since with regard to the revenues collected from the goods entering her customs system Prussia had given up the distinction between customs duties and consumption taxes, there was no way to determine the exact proportion of the consumption taxes to the total yield. The treaty therefore presumed that they constituted five eighths of the total amount, and Schwarzburg-Rudolstadt's share was to be figured accordingly.[62]

The next treaty expressed still more clearly Prussia's

---

[60] Brinkmann, op. cit., pp. 119, 130.

[61] Treaty, dated Berlin, June 24, 1822, [Prussia] Gesetz-Sammlung, 1822, No. 22 (December 19), pp. 225–29, No. 765; cf., in particular, Arts. I, VII, IX.   [62] Ibid., Art. I.

growing concern about the enforcement of the internal revenue laws. This treaty was concluded with Saxe-Weimar-Eisenach on June 27, 1823, and added the districts of Allstedt and Oldisleben to the Prussian system. No excise tax was to be levied at the border, since distilled liquor was to be taxed in the enclaves according to the Prussian rates, since tobacco and wine were not produced, and since beer was taxed sufficiently high in the enclaves. In return, Prussia would not deduct the cost of her own administration from the compensation paid to the grand duchy. Many other provisions were also improved. The right of hot pursuit and the obligation to enforce the other's revenue laws were made mutual. Up to then Prussia had received all the privileges and none of the obligations on these points. Saxe-Weimar-Eisenach, however, had not only to adopt the Law of May 26, 1818, for the enclaves, but also to do likewise with all its amendments, past and future. On the other hand, the treaty was limited to a period of eleven years. In addition, the grand duchy obtained some minor privileges. Her compensation had to be paid partly in gold, in the same proportion that this metal was collected by the Prussian customs officials.[62a] She had the right to a refund of the revenue collected on such liquor as was exported from the enclaves through Prussia to non-Prussian territory. Special provision was made for the salt supply of the enclaves.[63] Secret clauses provided for complete exemption of goods belonging to the grand duke and guaranteed a minimum compensation.[64] That Saxe-Weimar-Eisenach was able to obtain such favorable terms should be credited to her astute

---

[62a] Since each German state was sovereign, there was no guarantee against any of them debasing their currency. Moreover, the years 1818 to 1821 had seen a violent fluctuation of the value of gold in relation to silver in Germany. This measure was designed to secure Saxe-Weimar-Eisenach her fair share of the intake.

[63] Treaty dated Berlin, June 27, 1823, *ibid.*, 1823, No. 18 (December 9), pp. 169–74, No. 830; cf., in particular, Arts. I, III, IV, VII, VIII.

[64] Brinkmann, *op. cit.*, pp. 133–34. I am unable to follow Brinkmann's statement that Article I of the open agreement excluded all Prussian customs officials from Saxe-Weimar-Eisenach soil and that it was therefore different from the respective treaties with the Schwarzburgs. The only difference I can see is that the later treaty provided for reciprocity.

diplomacy. This was especially remarkable since the enclaves in question were rather small.[65]

The two treaties which Prussia concluded shortly afterward with Anhalt-Bernburg were of even greater importance, since they marked the crumbling of Anhalt resistance. That dealing with the enclave of Mühlingen contained no innovations and followed the patterns of the older agreements with the Schwarzburgs and with Saxe-Weimar-Eisenach.[66] The other treaty, signed on the same day, is important because the district involved was not completely surrounded by Prussian territory. The Upper Duchy, as this odd piece of land was called, had a common boundary of about four and one-half miles with the Duchy of Brunswick. It was thus the first time that a territory which was not an enclave joined the Prussian customs system. The problem was solved as follows. The customs line along the frontier between the Upper Duchy and Prussia was to be abolished, and a new line was to be set up along the Anhalt-Brunswick border. Except for the customs collector or collectors the whole personnel of this new line was to be appointed by Prussia. All officials had to swear obedience to both the king of Prussia and the duke of Anhalt-Bernburg, and they wore the insignia of both states on their caps. The official buildings likewise were to display both coats of arms and also a sign reading "Royal Prussian and Ducal Anhalt-Bernburg Second-Class Customs Office" (*Königlich-Preussisches und Herzog-lich-Anhalt-Bernburgisches Neben-Zollamt*). The officials were paid by Prussia, and for all official acts were under Prussian jurisdiction, but they were otherwise subject to Anhalt-Bernburg courts. Prussia had to maintain the customs line, while Anhalt-Bernburg was obliged only to make certain facilities, like office space, available for rent. All the money collected went into the Anhalt-Bernburg exchequer, but the amount was later subtracted from the compensation paid by Prussia. The Law of May 26, 1818, with its amend-

---

[65] They had a population of about 6,500 people, while the Schwarzburg-Rudolstadt enclaves had 13,484 and the Schwarzburg-Sondershausen 30,078 (official survey of enclaves in Prussian territory [1819], Oncken and Saemisch, I, 113, No. 33).

[66] Treaty dated Berlin, October 10, 1823, [Prussia] *Gesetz-Sammlung*, 1823, No. 19 (December 23), pp. 177–79, No. 834.

ments past and future, was to be introduced in the Upper Duchy, but no changes of its principles were to be made without the consent of Anhalt-Bernburg. Moreover, ducal police and ducal courts were to enforce the Law in the Upper Duchy. Since on account of its geographical location the Upper Duchy had hitherto been able to import without paying Prussian customs duties, Anhalt-Bernburg was to receive its proportional share from three fourths of the Prussian customs revenue in the eastern provinces. Moreover, the cost of administration was not to be deducted, because Anhalt-Bernburg was to introduce the same taxes on liquor, beer, and tobacco in the Upper Duchy that were enforced in Prussia. The moment the Upper Duchy joined the Prussian customs system a supplementary tax was to be collected by Anhalt-Bernburg on all goods stored in it and subject to the Prussian revenue laws. The receipts were to be deducted from the compensation payments made by Prussia. A number of special privileges were granted for the trade between the Upper and the Lower Duchy, and a secret agreement provided for compensation for the taxes collected previous to the treaty.[67]

This treaty of 1823 constituted the first Zollanschluss Prussia concluded. The employment of a few Anhalt officials in the customs administration and the collection of the revenue by Anhalt-Bernburg against further account were two features which bore a relationship to certain characteristics of the Zollverein. This Zollanschluss, incomplete as it was from a technical point of view, represented, nevertheless, a great improvement, since it furnished a solution for the inclusion of territories which were not enclaves. The Prussian negotiator of this treaty was not conscious of this progress at the time, but he looked upon the provisions which took care of the new situation as "more burdensome conditions."[68] He arrived at this solution by taking the previous treaties with the Schwarzburgs as his basis and by changing

---

[67] Treaty between Anhalt-Bernburg and Prussia, Berlin, October 10, 1823, ibid. 1824, No. 1 (January 5), pp. 1–9, No. 837; cf., in particular, Arts. I, II, III, IV, VII, VIII, IX, X, XI, XII, XIV, XVI, XVII, XIX, XX; Brinkmann, op. cit., p. 130.

[68] "Unter lästigeren Bedingungen," H. von Bülow to Bernstorff, Berlin, January 27, 1823, Oncken and Saemisch, I, 206, No. 84.

them to meet the special problems that confronted him.[69] This explains the many half-developed stipulations of the treaty.

The growth of the Prussian enclave system was not without effect on the development of a similar system by Württemberg. The first step was taken by Württemberg when in 1824 she concluded treaties with Hohenzollern-Sigmaringen and Hohenzollern-Hechingen, according to which the bulk of these principalities was to join the Württemberg customs system. The treaties were styled a "temporary and partial fulfillment" of the treaty concluded on May 19, 1820, in Vienna. The principalities were to introduce the Württemberg customs laws with all future amendments, but had the right to be heard before such changes were promulgated. The customs administration within the principalities was to be called a common one. It was to be set up by a mixed commission, and the customs houses were to have the sign "Royal Württemberg and Princely Hohenzollern-Sigmaringen (or Hechingen) Customs Office." All officials were to be appointed, directed, and paid by Württemberg; the principalities were obliged only to make office and storage space available to be rented by Württemberg. Württemberg was to give subjects of the principalities preference in the employment of the common service. She was to collect all revenues and give the principalities their shares, which were to be computed according to the proportion of the populations. All consumption taxes were to be equally applied to each other's subjects. The ruling families of the states involved were to be exempted from all customs duties. The courts of the principalities were to enforce the Württemberg customs laws for the territories included. Road tolls in the principalities could not be raised above those collected in Württemberg. The principalities were to participate in all commercial treaties that Württemberg would enter into while the agreement was in force. They had, moreover, the right to be heard before such treaties were concluded. The customs treaties were to expire at the earliest after eleven years.[70]

---

[69] *Loc. cit.*

[70] Württemberg treaties with Hohenzollern-Sigmaringen and Hohenzollern-Hechingen, n.p., n.d. [published July 18, 1824], Geo. Fred. de [i.e. Georg Friedrich von] Martens, *Nouveau recueil de traités d'alliance, de*

A number of provisions in these treaties seem to have been taken from the arrangements Prussia had developed. Thus the introduction of the Württemberg customs law in the principalities and the employment, direction, and payment of the officials by Württemberg closely followed Prussian practice. The stipulation that the customs houses should be joint offices and should show both coats of arms was taken almost literally from the Prussian treaty with Anhalt-Bernburg.[71] The enforcement of the system in the smaller territories was also identical. It was left entirely to the local authorities. Other provisions, such as the regulation of road tolls and the reciprocity to be granted in the collection of consumption taxes, seem to have originated in the Vienna and Darmstadt Conferences.[72] Moreover, the style of a common administration seems to have been taken from the results of the South German conferences. On the other hand, the equal rights of commerce or trade granted to each other's subjects and the extension of the commercial treaties to the territories included were new provisions. As a whole, the Württemberg treaties were clearer, touched more points, and did have fewer special provisions than the Prussian agreements had had.

Thus the institution of the Zollanschluss had become common knowledge by 1824.

THE YEARS 1825-33

WHEN Motz took over the administration of the Prussian Ministry of Finance in July of 1825, a more energetic policy toward the enclaves was pursued than under his prede-

---

paix, de trêve, de neutralité, de commerce, de limites, d'exchange etc. et de plusieurs autres actes servant à la connaissance des relations étrangères des puissances et ètats..., VI (Gottingue, 1828), pp. 560–72, No. 117; cf., in particular, Preamble, Arts. I, II, III, VI, VIII, IX, X of both treaties; Arts. XI, XII, XIII, XIV, XV, XVI of the Hohenzollern-Sigmaringen treaty; and Arts. XI, XII, XIII, XIV, XV of the Hohenzollern-Hechingen treaty.

[71] Art. XIII of the Hohenzollern-Sigmaringen treaty and Art. XII of the Hohenzollern-Hechingen treaty; ibid.; treaty between Prussia and Anhalt-Bernburg, Berlin, October 10, 1823, Art. X, [Prussia] Gesetz-Sammlung, 1824, No. 1 (January 5, 1824), No. 837.

[72] Bavarian Cabinet, protocol, München, May 1, 1820, Arts. II, III, Oncken and Saemisch, I, 382–84, No. 195; Nebenius draft Section I, Arts. XV, XVI, XX, Darmstadt Conferences, protocol, November 27, 1820, ibid., pp. 399–401, No. 207.

cessor. By using all means at his disposal Motz was able to end the feud with the Anhalts. He also put pressure on the governments of Lippe-Detmold and Mecklenburg-Schwerin and forced them to join the Prussian customs system with their enclaves, which had been smuggling centers. He also proceeded against Schwarzburg-Sondershausen for negligent fulfillment of her Anschluss treaty.[73]

The treaty which included the Lower Duchy of Anhalt-Bernburg in the Prussian customs system in 1826 contained substantially the same provisions that had been applied earlier to the Upper Duchy. There was a new provision that both parties reserved their rights to collect customs duties on the rivers Elbe and Saale.[74]

The principality of Lippe-Detmold was, however, unable to conclude such a favorable agreement with Prussia when she joined the customs system of the western Prussian provinces with the three small enclaves of Lipperode, Cappel, and Grevenhagen. The rate of compensation was calculated in proportion to the total customs receipts of these provinces. Lippe obliged herself not only to introduce the Prussian taxes on the production of liquor, beer, and vinegar, but also to permit Prussian officials to check the collection of the revenue. These officials had to swear obedience to both rulers, and they wore the coats of arms of both states. The revenue derived from the beer, tax in Westphalia and in the enclaves was to be divided proportionally between the two states. The erection of new distilleries and breweries in the enclaves was restricted, and a salt quota for these territories was set up.[75] A number of other stipulations followed the pattern of the earlier treaties. According to a secret clause, Lippe was to be compensated for the loss of revenue she had incurred through the Prussian system prior to the treaty.[76]

---

[73] Herman von Petersdorff, *Friedrich von Motz, eine Biographie* (Berlin: Reimar Hobbing, 1913), II, 94–107.

[74] Dated Berlin, June 26, 1826, [Prussia] *Gesetz-Sammlung*, 1826, No. 11 (August 14), pp. 65–70, No. 1017; cf., in particular, Art. XII.

[75] Treaty between Lippe-Detmold and Prussia, Detmold, June 9, 1826, Minden, June 17, 1826, *ibid.*, No. 15 (November 9), pp. 101–5, No. 1029; cf., in particular, Arts. I, IV, V, VI, VII, VIII, IX.

[76] Brinkmann, *op. cit.*, p. 124.

The importance of this agreement lay in the fact that it distinguished between collecting the revenue and checking this collection.   It also reflected the growing desire of Prussia to control the administration of the internal revenue. Lippe probably offered less resistance, since the territories involved were rather small.[77]

The treaty concluded with Mecklenburg-Schwerin in 1826 went even further.   It dealt with the Mecklenburg-Schwerin enclaves of Rossow, Netzeband, and Schönberg, which had a total population of less than 900 people.[78] Mecklenburg was obliged to introduce the Prussian Law of February 8, 1819, which taxed the consumption of liquor, wine, beer, and tobacco, and she had to allow Prussian officials to collect the revenues derived from it in the enclaves. Moreover, in theory, Mecklenburg's share in the receipts was to be determined according to the proportion of the populations; in practice, however, it was to be a fixed sum paid periodically for the duration of the treaty.[79]

As a whole, Mecklenburg-Schwerin's treaty was the least favorable.   The grand duchy was not compensated for losses of revenue incurred on account of the Prussian customs system prior to the Anschluss treaty, and she was also obliged to give up the Dransee toll.[80]

Of the inclusions during the two following years only those of the main territories of Anhalt-Köthen and Anhalt-Dessau will be taken up.[81]   The treaty which finally ended the bitter and long-standing controversy bore all the signs of a compromise.[82]   Prussia was obliged to yield on a number of points.[83]   The two duchies had to introduce the Law of

---

[77] These districts had 852 inhabitants in 1831 (Viebahn, Statistik, I, 152).   [78] These enclaves had 890 inhabitants in 1831 (loc. cit.).

[79] Treaty dated Berlin, December 2, 1826, [Prussia] Gesetz-Sammlung, 1827, No. 1 (January 16), pp. 1–6, No. 1042; cf., in particular, Arts. VII, IX.

[80] Brinkmann, op. cit., p. 196.

[81] The treaty between Prussia and Anhalt-Dessau, dated March 30, 1827, and April 5, 1827, concerning the enclaves of Sandersleben and Gross-Alsleben, and the treaty between Prussia and Anhalt-Köthen, dated July 17, 1828, concerning the enclave of Warmsdorf were not available to me.

[82] Treaty dated Berlin, July 17, 1828, [Prussia] Gesetz-Sammlung, 1828, No. 15 (September 16), pp. 99–106, No. 1160.

[83] Cf. Köthen's proposal of compromise, Köthen, May 26, 1827, Oncken and Saemisch, I, 272–74, No. 143; Prussia's comments on this proposal [June, 1827], ibid., I, 277–82, No. 146.

May 26, 1818, with all amendments, into their territories, but reserved the right to consent to all changes affecting their interests. They were to receive a proportional share of the revenues collected at the frontier of the seven eastern Prussian provinces. They were allowed to import freely over the Elbe certain goods, mostly of non-German origin, to store them under bond at Rosslau, and to collect the import duties themselves as soon as these goods were taken out of storage for consumption. The amount thus collected was to be checked yearly by a mixed commission and deducted from the compensation to be paid to the duchies by Prussia. Goods shipped by mail were allowed to be imported free through Prussia and were taxed in Anhalt by Anhalt officials. The duchies were not obliged to join the Prussian system of internal revenue. All commercial treaties concluded by Prussia were to apply to the subjects of the duchies if their interests were affected, a point which was probably taken from the customs union treaty with Hesse-Darmstadt.[84] The duchies reserved the right to pardon transgressions against the customs system, but were to inform Prussia when doing so.

These provisions showed how the idea of a customs union exerted an influence on the Anschluss treaties. The enclaves were granted a more independent position than in any of the previous agreements of this kind.[85]

The treaties by which the district of Volkenroda, an enclave of Saxe-Koburg-Gotha, joined the Prussian system closely followed earlier patterns. The internal revenue was to be collected by Saxe-Koburg-Gotha; but Prussia had the right to check this administration with her own officials.[86]

It was not until 1831 that other enclaves joined what was now the Bavaria-Württemberg Customs Union. A number

---

[84] Treaty between Anhalt-Köthen and Prussia, Berlin, July 17, 1828, [Prussia] Gesetz-Sammlung, 1828, No. 15 (September 16), pp. 99–106, No. 1160; cf., in particular, Arts, I, II, III, IV, V, VI, VII, X, XII, XIV, treaty between Hesse-Darmstadt and Prussia, Berlin, February 14, 1828, Art. V, Oncken and Saemisch, II, 197, No. 376.

[85] This convention, however, did not have the character of a customs union, since equality was not established as a matter of principle.

[86] Treaty dated Berlin, July 4, 1829, [Prussia] Gesetz-Sammlung, 1829, No. 17 (November 21), pp. 121–25, No. 1217; cf., in particular, Art. VI.

of Baden enclaves were to be included in this customs system, while certain Württemberg enclaves were incorporated in the Baden administration. The treaty covering this transaction was outstanding for its simplicity and .brevity.[87] Article I described the district affected and the date the arrangement was to take effect. The next article introduced the customs law, the customs administration of the other state, and their enforcement in the respective enclaves. The income was to be divided according to the proportion of the populations, which was to be fixed every three years. Article V excepted salt from the arrangement, and Article VI allowed the governments the right to end the treaty by giving notice three months in advance.

The two other agreements concerning Ostheim and Königsberg did not introduce any new provisions, were more elaborate, frequently followed earlier Prussian treaties in their wording, and were closely interdependent.[88]

The treaties concluded by Prussia during these years showed a closer coördination of the new territories into the system of the Prusso-Hessian Customs Union. The agreement by which the Saxe-Koburg-Gotha district of Lichtenberg joined the system contained a number of new provisions. The duchy was to receive from the income collected in the western provinces of Prussia a full proportional share of all the customs duties and other revenues in which she participated. Hitherto Prussia had paid only a fraction of this proportional share. The customs officials in the district were to be appointed by the duchy, but had first to pass an examination given by the Prussian provincial tax administrator at Cologne. The tax administration of Lichtenberg was to be set up by a mixed commission, and the revenue officials were to be under Prussian jurisdiction for their official acts. The duchy was to collect the customs as well as those internal revenues which had been introduced to conform to

[87] Treaty between Württemberg and Baden [n.p., n.d.], [Baden] *Grossherzoglich badisches Staats- und Regierungsblatt*, 1831, No. 8 (May 27), pp. 57–59.

[88] Treaty between Bavaria/Württemberg and Saxe-Weimer-Eisenach [Munich], January 25, 1831, Martens, *Nouveau recueil de traités*, IX (1833), 193–200, No. 36; treaty between Bavaria/Württemberg and Saxe-Koburg-Gotha [Munich], June 14, 1831, *ibid.*, pp. 369–75, No. 52.

the Prussian system. Both governments abolished all dis-
criminations against the employment of each other's subjects,
another feature characteristic of the Prusso-Hessian Customs Union and of the earlier Württemberg Anschluss
treaties.[89]

The district of Birkenfeld belonging to Oldenburg joined
the Prusso-Hessian system in 1830 on substantially the same
conditions as Lichtenberg,[90] and only slight changes were
made in the treaty by which Waldeck (without Pyrmont)
acceded to the system.[91]

At the end of 1831 a number of Brunswick enclaves and
other odd territories joined the Hanoverian customs system.
The Anschluss treaty was modeled after the earlier Prussian
agreements, but contained a number of deviations. Thus
Hanover was obliged to pay only a "fair compensation" to
the Brunswick exchequer. Offenses against the customs
laws committed in the enclaves were to be prosecuted by
Hanoverian officials before Brunswick courts. All Hanoverian customs officials operating in Brunswick were to enjoy
exemption from all taxes, except for burdens on real estate.
In addition, Brunswick surrendered all rights to pardon
offenders against the customs regulations. Existing export
prohibitions were to remain in force in both states.[92]

When Prussia renewed the various treaties with Anhalt-
Bernburg in 1831, she saw to it that the duchy's system of
taxing liquor, beer, and tobacco was coördinated.[93] In connection with the organization of the Zollverein in 1833 the
earlier arrangements dealing with the enclaves of Schwarz-

---

[89] Treaty between Saxe-Koburg-Gotha and Prussia, Berlin, March 6,
1830, [Prussia] Gesetz-Sammlung, 1830, No. 8 (May 8), pp. 57–62, No. 1241;
cf., in particular, Arts. I, II, III, VI, XI, XII; treaty between Prussia and
Hesse-Darmstadt, Berlin, February 14, 1828, Art. XIII, Oncken and Saemisch, II, 203, No. 376.

[90] Treaty dated Berlin, July 24, 1830, [Prussia] Gesetz-Sammlung, 1830,
No. 17 (September 22), pp. 121–28, No. 1265.

[91] Treaty dated Berlin, April 16, 1831, ibid., 1831, No. 12 (August 26),
pp. 159–68, No. 1303.

[92] Treaty between Hanover and Brunswick, Hannover, December 9,
1831, Martens, Nouveau recueil de traités, IX, 559–74, No. 70; cf., in particular, Arts. II, XIII, XIV, XVI, XX.

[93] Treaty dated Berlin, May 17, 1817, [Prussia] Gesetz-Sammlung, 1831,
No. 7 (June 6), pp. 53–56, No. 1288.

burg-Rudolstadt, Saxe-Weimar-Eisenach, Schwarzburg-Sondershausen, and Saxe-Koburg-Gotha were thoroughly revised.[94] All the provisions for these enclaves were made
very much alike. They were to receive a proportional share
from the total income of the whole Zollverein. The enclaves
were to join the Prussian system of internal revenue on liquor,
beer, wine, and tobacco. In matters of road tolls, employment restrictions, coinage, and measures they were to conform to Zollverein standards.

Two tendencies can be observed in the Prussian policy
toward the enclaves. One was a growing interest in extending her internal revenue system; the other and later development was that of coördinating the inclusion of these territories with her customs union policy. The proceeds from
the customs duties, as defined by Prussia, were at the beginning not restored to the enclaves. The first Zollanschluss occurred in 1823, when this principle was modified. The conditions granted to these odd pieces of territory which joined
the Prussian tax system varied according to their size and
location and according to diplomatic considerations or political convenience. There is no indication that the aims of
fiscal security and good neighborly relations were supplemented by higher political aims before the adoption of the
customs union policy. Prussia's fiscal policy often led her
to harsh measures which cannot be justified as such. One
must, however, consider the military protection Prussia was
obliged to give to her smaller neighbors and the difficulties
her territorial conditions created for her financial system,
which in turn had to support her army. In many cases
Prussia was not so much fighting the rights of the smaller
states as the abuse of these rights by which neighboring territories transformed themselves into smugglers' paradises.[95]

---

[94] Treaty between Prussia and Schwarzburg-Rudolstadt, Berlin, May 25,
1833, ibid., 1833, No. 21 (December 5), pp. 269–73, No. 1479; treaty between
Prussia and Saxe-Weimar-Eisenach, Berlin, May 30, 1833, ibid., No. 21
(December 5), pp. 274–78, No. 1480; treaty between Prussia and Schwarzburg-Sondershausen, Berlin, June 8, 1833, ibid., No. 21 (December 5), pp.
279–83, No. 1481; treaty between Prussia and Saxe-Koburg-Gotha, ibid., No.
21 (December 5), pp. 284–88, No. 1482.

[95] Cf. Klewiz to Friedrich Wilhelm III, Berlin, January 28, 1819, Oncken

The Zollanschluss became the standard arrangement by which the Zollverein dealt with smaller territories. The first treaties of this kind gave the Prussian officials experience in problems arising out of this small-scale economic unification. The early Zollanschluss developed some few features, like the complete control of all internal revenue, which can be identified as original contributions to the Zollverein. When the Zollanschluss was taken over by the Zollverein certain technical aspects were changed to conform with Zollverein practice. Although it always remained of secondary significance, it was an important part of the Zollverein machinery, since it dealt with territories which were too small to be able to participate effectively and on equal terms in a customs union.

---

and Saemisch, I, 92, No. 22; Prussian Foreign Office to three Anhalt governments, Berlin, December 23, 1819, *ibid.*, p. 128, No. 39.

CHAPTER VII

POPULAR VIEWS ON ECONOMIC
UNIFICATION, 1820-33

THE reactionary wave which swept over Germany in 1819-20 reduced popular influence on public affairs to a minimum. The German governments under Austria's leadership combined to fight the subversive elements and to suppress all liberal thought. The governments did not hesitate to employ extreme measures, and they soon succeeded in establishing the new order by an arbitrary system of censorship and police investigation. Patriots of 1812-15, like Arndt and Jahn, were silenced, and the censorship was so strictly enforced in Prussia that even a reprint of Fichte's *Speeches to the German Nation* was prohibited. At the same time less important men and their works were suppressed with the same arbitrary vigor. Austria went so far as to allow only a very limited number of encyclopedias to be imported, while Prussia forbade a translation of Hutten's works to appear.[1]

The triumph of the reactionary forces in 1819-20 did away with the last vestiges of that alliance between people and cabinets which had won the Wars of Liberation. This break extended to economic as well as political matters, with the result that no popular movement participated in the founding of the Zollverein. After 1820 the important work on economic unification was exclusively performed by the cabinets, who frequently acted against the expressed will of the people.

Although popular thought between 1820 and 1833 did not contribute to the institutional origin of the Zollverein, its history is important for two reasons. First of all, the ever-increasing economic dissatisfaction stirred up the masses so much as to cause many a government to consider economic unification seriously. Secondly, the thought of the period furnished the background against which the events leading

[1] Treitschke, *Deutsche Geschichte*, III, 433–53.

to the foundation of the Zollverein took place. The end of List's agitation in 1820–21, the subsequent quiet years up to 1827, and the movements and discussions during the immediate foundation of the Zollverein (1828–33) form the three major aspects which must be considered for the period 1820–33.

THE END OF LIST'S AGITATION, 1820–21

THE reaction did not at first hit economic liberalism so hard as it did political liberalism. Thus List was tolerated during the Vienna Final Conferences. When he left Vienna in May of 1820, his League was planning to carry on at the South German conferences which had been scheduled for the near future. All during the summer the League was active holding meetings, and it evolved a definite program. The industrial interests received most consideration, and a protective tariff was demanded. All goods that could compete with South German industries were to pay a 10 per cent ad valorem duty if they originated in other German states, and a 30 per cent duty if they came from non-German countries.[2] This program was officially adopted by the League. At the same time various leading members of the League attempted to establish personal contacts with officials who were likely to be sent to the South German conferences by their governments. Great efforts were made to have Bavaria and Württemberg delegate the Bavarian official, Brunner, to these conferences.[3] In this way the League prepared itself by agreeing on a program and through extensive lobbying in a way which seemed to indicate that they had profited from their previous experiences.

The Darmstadt Conferences opened on September 13, 1820, and List left Darmstadt on September 16, turning his back on the South German aspirations. He continued to edit the *Organ* for some time, but did not participate in any other activity of the League beyond that date.

List's reasons for this decision are not quite clear. He had come to Darmstadt with every intention of working for

---

[2] Weber, circular, Gera, November 16, 1820, Olshausen, *Friedrich List,* pp. 329–30, No. 168.   [3] *Ibid.,* pp. 158–60.

a South German customs unification. He had elaborated two memoranda, one on the revenue to be expected from a South German customs system, the other a draft of a treaty for this system. Neither work was ever used. The first memorandum proved to the governments that they need not fear a loss of revenue when establishing such an organization. The draft treaty was a logical exposition of a common customs system. Although it contained a number of original ideas, it remained without any influence on the subsequent development.[4]

There seems to be no question that in early September List wholeheartedly supported a South German economic unification. But this made his sudden change of mind the more difficult to understand. There was some personal friction with officials of the League and with certain diplomats at the Darmstadt Conferences. The two other League delegates began to intrigue against List, and soon further quarrels were to end all its organized activities. The chief causes of conflict were personal jealousy and the matter of finances and compensation. Some delegates of the League continued to claim money from the League for over two decades without ever achieving a settlement.[5]

On the other hand, the Darmstadt Conferences themselves declared as early as September 18, 1820, that they could not recognize the League officially,[6] and Nebenius even told List privately that his presence in Darmstadt was superfluous.[7] Metternich had exerted all his influence with the conservative cabinets at Karlsruhe and Wiesbaden to combat any influence List might possibly gain in the course of the negotiations.[8] There is also some evidence that List changed his mind about Wangenheim, with whom he had consulted rather closely before the conferences started. List

---

[4] Überschlag des Ertrags einer gemeinschaftlichen Douane der Süddeutschen Staaten, List, *Schriften/Reden/Briefe*, I, Part II, 662–666, No. 43; Skizze eines Präliminarvertrages für einen Handelsverband der süddeutschen Staaten, *ibid.*, pp. 667–72, No. 44.

[5] Olshausen, *op. cit.*, pp. 180–84.   [6] *Ibid.*, p. 177.

[7] Nebenius to Berstett, Darmstadt, September 22, 1820, Oncken and Saemisch, I, 395–96, No. 205.

[8] Berstett to Nebenius, Karlsruhe, September 13, 1820, *ibid.*, pp. 389–90, No. 200; Marschall to Metternich, Wiesbaden, September 20, 1820, Olshausen, *op. cit.*, pp. 312–16, No. 152.

supported South German economic unification as a step toward general German unification, while Wangenheim wanted the Third Germany to be strengthened. Thus List may have left the South German conferences because he realized the extent to which trialistic forces were furthering them.[9] At any rate, he withdrew to Stuttgart, where he continued to edit the *Organ* of the League. It was in this magazine that he published his article "Ideen über den süddeutschen Handelsverband."[10] In it he stressed the need of a general German economic unification in the face of non-German competition, and little attention was given to the proposed South German system. List never published his more detailed memoranda on a South German customs system and referred to this system in general terms only.[11]

During the fall of 1820 List's relation to the League became more and more estranged. He now entered Württemberg politics and was elected to the Württemberg House of Representatives. He still worked for the German economic cause,[12] but he almost completely withheld his support from the Darmstadt Conferences.

Personal conflicts drove List out of the League, but a change of mind occurred at the same time about the value of the South German separate negotiations. List would probably have continued his campaign for the betterment of German economic life if he had not been suppressed by the Württemberg government. He had printed a petition in which he frankly criticized the whole administration of Württemberg. The authorities took this as a pretext for trying and convicting him. He was finally pardoned on the condition that he would immediately emigrate to America.

---

[9] Cf. *ibid.*, pp. 177–178. Although List seems to have established close contacts with Wangeheim before the supposed break (*ibid.*, p. 176), he left hurriedly without seeing the Württemberg representative (*ibid.*, p. 168). Subsequently he desired all League representatives to withdraw from the Darmstadt Conferences (Schnell to List, Darmstadt, September 24, 1820, *ibid.*, p. 318, No. 154), while Wangenheim wished List's absence from these negotiations continued (Weber to List, Gera, November 16, 1820, *ibid.*, p. 328, No. 166).

[10] Reprinted, List, *op. cit.*, I, Part II, 647–56, No. 41; cf. *ibid.*, IX, 294.

[11] List to Arnoldi, Stuttgart, December 23, 1820, *ibid.*, p. 51, No. 118a.

[12] *Ibid.*, pp. 294-96; List, speech in the Württemberg Diet, December 13, 1820, *ibid.*, I, Part II, pp. 673–75, No. 45.

He was to return many years later, but for a long time his voice had been effectively silenced in Germany.

THE QUIET YEARS 1820-27

IT WAS not so much the outright reactionary forces of the Holy Alliance that brought about the downfall of Friedrich List as his having become a victim of the trialistic elements in the Württemberg government. The underlying ideas of this ideology were publicized in extreme form in the *Manuscript aus Süd-Deutschland*. This pamphlet, which appeared first in Stuttgart in September, 1820, had been written to order by Lindner, a political publicist, according to an outline given to him by King Wilhelm I of Württemberg.[13] The *Manuscript* contained a chronological interpretation of German history, laying particular stress on the Napoleonic period. Its main theme was the assertion that Austria, Prussia, and Hanover would not represent German interests and that the South Germans were the only true Germans. This position was defended through a one-sided array of facts with an even more biased discussion. It blamed the distress the Napoleonic era brought to Germany on Prussia and Austria, and at the same time praised this period as a particularly progressive one.[14] Austria, Prussia, Hanover, Holstein, and Luxemburg were not truly German states, and only the remainder was the pure Germany.[15] But that was not enough. The North Germans (i.e. those living north of the Thuringian Forest) were entirely different from the South Germans, who were the salt of the earth. The North Germans were in every respect inferior.[16] Such were the arguments on which Lindner based his statement that "Germany could not become a Reich during the nineteenth century."[17] Not only the "half-breed" and the North Germans were ex-

---

[13] [Friedrich Ludwig Lindner] *Manuscript aus Süd-Deutschland*, "Herausgegeben von George Erichson" (2d ed.; "London, bei James Griphi. 1821"), xviii + 276; Treitschke, *Deutsche Geschichte*, III, 55.

[14] For anti-Prussian passages see [Lindner] *op. cit.*, pp. 43, 69, 157–60, 173–75, 177–78, 186, 206–12; for anti-Austrian passages see *ibid.*, pp. 41, 69, 74–75, 105, 156–57, 173–74, 186; for pro-*Rheinbund* passages see *ibid.*, pp. 109, 112, 114, 116–17, 128–30, 138, n.; Napoleon was primarily criticized for his low origin and his lack of etiquette, *ibid.*, p. 134.

[15] *Ibid.*, p. 234.   [16] *Ibid.*, pp. 236, 241–45.   [17] *Ibid.*, p. 247.

posed to these vituperations, but also the smaller territories and courts, the former Imperial knights, the Mediatized Estates, the former ecclesiastical states, and the patriots of 1813, and the liberal movement were subjected to a similar treatment.[18]   The South German medium states and their constitutions alone received unconditional praise.[19]   Lindner even went so far as to claim that Austria and Prussia imposed these constitutions in order to weaken the Third Germany.[20] The pamphlet did not set up a detailed program.   Pure Germany was to remain pure, and also independent of Austria and Prussia.   It denied, however, that South Germany could be united politically.[21]

The economic ideas were presented on a similar level. Napoleon's commercial system was praised, and English "sea despotism" condemned.[22]   But, above all, the commercial interests of Hamburg and Bremen were attacked, and the merchants of these cities were referred to as British agents.   "The seaports were to be returned to Germany," and in this connection the Hanseatic cities were even called the "German Barbary States."[23]

Although the *Manuscript* was dictated by personal spite, it remained the prototype of certain South German ideas. Condemnation of the pamphlet was general, and even men like Wangenheim did not want to be identified with it.   Its opposition to almost everything did not win new friends to the cause of trialism.   Nevertheless, the *Manuscript* did not stir up many answers.[24]   A few Hanseatic writers took up the fight.   Hess wrote a lengthy protest, which he called *Aus Nord-Deutschland kein Manuscript*.[25]   All major points of the original *Manuscript* received a full answer.   Prussia's sacrifices in the Wars of Liberation received due credit, and Austrian and Prussian policies during the Napoleonic era were defended.   Hess turned particularly against the Francophile character of the *Manuscript* and its trialistic ideas.

---

[18] *Ibid.*, pp. 49-50, 54, 138, 141, 189, 221, 248.
[19] *Ibid.*, pp. 33, 109, 112, 170, 218–21.   [20] *Ibid.*, pp. 173–74.
[21] *Ibid.*, pp. 247, 254.   [22] *Ibid.*, pp. 117–65.   [23] *Ibid.*, p. 249.
[24] Treitschke, *Deutsche Geschichte*, III, 57–60.
[25] [Jonas Ludwig von Hess] *Aus Nord-Deutschland kein Manuscript* (Hamburg, 1821), xvi + 408.

At the same time a liberal and constitutional development in Germany was favored.[26]

A large part of this pamphlet was devoted to defending the Hanseatic cities and their trade interests. Hess argued that Hamburg's trade—like any trade—was increasing the wealth of the nation,[27] and he tried to show that it would be impractical to introduce a protective tariff system in Germany.[28] He also turned against the introduction of German fashions and argued that it was the duty of the manufacturers to persuade the German consumers to buy German cloth.[29] The abolition of internal German customs lines was favored.[30]

Hess remained objective throughout his reply, although he took particular care to answer all the spiteful accusations which had been made against Hamburg.[31] The absence of a personal element is best illustrated in his treatment of List and his League. Even though he disagreed with this protectionist movement, Hess was able to understand its position.[32]

A similar careful distinction between List and the *Manuscript* was not made by Hess's fellow citizen Haller, who used his reply to the *Manuscript* for an attack on List and the League.[33] The method was not mere demagogy, since it was seriously believed by many people in Hamburg that List was the author of the *Manuscript*.[34] Haller dealt with all opponents of Hamburg's trade interests with the same vigor, although the particular aversions of the *Manuscript* received special attention. While Hess's work had treated the subject thoroughly and comprehensively, this pamphlet limited itself to Hamburg's interests, and its refutations were more lively. Another Hanseatic pamphlet also turned against the accusations made in the *Manuscript* and argued for the preservation of the German intermediary trade. It attacked List's League both as representing the manufactur-

---

[26] *Ibid.*, pp. 10–12, 18–19, 20–23, 38–39.
[27] *Ibid.*, pp. 222–63, 290–91.   [28] *Ibid.*, pp. 279, 389.
[29] *Ibid.*, pp. 400–2.   [30] *Ibid.*, pp. 391–95.
[31] *Ibid.*, pp. 258, 290.   [32] *Ibid.*, pp. xi, 337, 403.
[33] [M. J. Haller] *Sechs Briefe über den Handel der Hansestädte besonders mit Beziehung auf die Angriffe des Manuscripts aus Süd-Deutschland* (Bremen, 1821), 70 pp.   [34] Blume, *Hamburg*, p. 57.

ing interests and on the ground that its businessmen were not political economists and that its experts lacked practical experience.[35]

The low level on which public discussions were conducted had been observed by others, but Hess made the following interesting observation.[36] He said that it had become almost impossible in Germany to hold any political opinion without being accused by the opposite side of being an extreme reactionary or an extreme liberal. If one tried to steer a middle course, one would be accused by both sides. The growing tendency of objecting to anything the opponent did or said can be noticed primarily in the criticism the Prussian Customs Law of 1818 received. The promulgation and enforcement of this law aroused general protests all over Central Germany. Most of the hostile opinions were complaints made by business interests.[37] There is no evidence that the Prussian tax reform directly caused the foundation of List's League.[38] This movement, however, tended to organize the anti-Prussian sentiment and frequently attacked the Prussian customs reform.[39] Popular opinion did not complain half so much about other German customs systems or about the Austrian system of prohibitions. The German cabinets carried the tendency further by trying to deprive Prussia of a right which all other larger German states exercised in their own interest. Marschall's naïve suggestion made at the Vienna Final Conferences represented the extreme. He proposed that all customs which had been introduced in Germany after January 1, 1814, should be abolished.[40] Nevertheless, Marschall's plan reflected the desires of the average German statesman.

The objections to the Prussian system were supported on

[35] [Storck] Über das Verhältnis, pp. 53, 55, 58–91, 136; for further details of this feud see Blume, op. cit., pp. 63–64.

[36] [Hess] op. cit., pp. iii-iv; cf. Benzenberg's case, Treitschke, Deutsche Geschichte, III, 114–15.

[37] Müller, Die Berichterstattung, pp. 96–99; Menn, Zur Vorgeschichte, pp. 34–38.   [38] Olshausen, op. cit., p. 15.

[39] List to Confederate Diet, Frankfurt, April 14, 1819, List, op. cit., I, Part II, 494–95, No. 17; List to Metternich [Vienna], March 9, 1820, ibid., pp. 553–54, No. 27; List, speech, Württemberg Diet, December 13, 1820, ibid., pp. 674–75, No. 45.   [40] Menn, op. cit., pp. 57–58.

various grounds. Marschall argued that it constituted an illegal destruction of private property,[41] while the Hildburghausen Diet objected to both the new Prussian and the Bavarian tariffs and recalled the legal protection the old Empire had given in such instances.[42] It should, however, be stated emphatically that Prussia had blundered in not giving her customs law the necessary diplomatic preparation. The clamor increased when the enclosed territories became aware of their situation and when the Prussian government was unable to settle some of these disputes amicably. The situation was not improved when Prussia's feud with the Anhalts was fought out in public.[43]

The official Prussian press had all along supported the customs law,[44] but it was one against many, since only a few publicists would defend the Law of 1818. Thus Benzenberg reviewed the law from a purely Prussian point of view and found that as a whole it followed Prussian interests.[45] Benzenberg criticized a number of technical details, such as the relative height of the tariff, the partially inadequate boundary supervision, and the regulation which called for the payment of certain duties in gold.[46] Here Benzenberg followed to some extent the arguments submitted by various businessmen from the Lower Rhine to Friedrich Wilhelm III in 1818; these had tried to show that it was impossible for Prussia to set up an effective boundary patrol.[47] Benzenberg used a similar approach when he asked List about the details of his plan.[48] He pointed out that a common protective tariff for

[41] Aegidi, Aus der Vorzeit, p. 28.
[42] Resolution and negotiations, March 30, 1819, [Saxe-Hildburghausen] Landtags-Verhandlungen im Fürstenthum Hildburghausen (Hildburghausen, 1819), pp. 179–80, 192–93.
[43] Eisenhart Rothe, in Oncken and Saemisch, I, 10.
[44] Müller, op. cit., pp. 96–97.
[45] Benzenberg, Über Preussens Geldhaushalt, pp. 279–94; cf., Benzenberg, quoted by Oncken, in Oncken and Saemisch, I, xxi.
[46] Benzenberg, op. cit., pp. 289–97.
[47] Manufacturers in Rheydt, Süchteln, Gladbach, Viersen, and Kaldenkirchen to Friedrich Wilhelm III, Rheydt, April 27, 1818, Oncken and Saemisch, I, 69–71, No. 13; cf. ibid., p. 69, n. 1, on Benzenberg's authorship of this petition.
[48] Benzenberg to List, Brüggen, August 20, 1819, Benzenberg, op. cit., pp. 314–20.

Germany would call for a customs administration of French proportions. He stated that internal free trade would only be possible if all internal revenues were unified and that a common administration was the only way to enforce a common tariff along Germany's boundary. But, asked Benzenberg, how can anybody expect to persuade the various states to give up such an essential part of their sovereignty as the customs administration? Benzenberg recognized the main problem of a customs unification between equal and independent states. List never answered the query. Benzenberg, however, discontinued his work as publicist and confined himself purely to scientific works. In spite of his strong Prussian loyalty he lost favor with the government in Berlin for his avowed liberalism.[49]

The *Manuscript aus Süd-Deutschland* originated the last great controversy to be discussed publicly in Germany for a number of years. Pamphlets and articles were still published on German economic problems, but their number declined, and none of them had the universal appeal Görres, List, and others had been able to instill into their work. The best that was written was not intended for immediate publication. The political poems of this period were the work of men who had lived through the Wars of Liberation and who had absorbed the best that German idealism had to give.[50] Such idealism retained a cosmopolitan character through its interest for the Polish and Greek causes.[51] There were also attacks on the reactionary bureaucracy of the Holy Alliance. The abuses of this system were generally con-

---

[49] Bruhns, "Benzenberg," *Allgemeine deutsche Biographie,* ed. by the Historische Commission bei der Königlichen Akademie der Wissenschaften [at Munich], II (1875), 349.

[50] Johann Georg Kramer, *Erinnerung ans Rütli* (1820), in Ernst Volkmann (ed.), *Um Einheit und Freiheit 1815–1848 (vom Wiener Kongress bis zur Märzrevolution)* "Deutsche Literatur, Politische Reihe," Vol. III; Leipzig: Philipp Reclam jun., 1936), pp. 62–63; Adalbert von Chamisso, *Schiller* (1821–22), *ibid.,* pp. 70–71; Wilhelm Hauff, *Hoffnung* (about 1824), *ibid.,* pp. 80–81; Hans Ferdinand Massmann, *Winter* (1825), *ibid.,* p. 83.

[51] Wilhelm Müller, *Die Griechen an die Freunde ihres Altertums* (1821), *ibid.,* p. 69; W. Müller, *Die Griechen an den österreichischen Beobachter* (1821), *ibid.,* p. 70; Karl von Holtei, *Der alte Feldherr* (1825), selection, *ibid.,* pp. 81–83.

demned by all independent intellectuals, most of whom, however, remained monarchists. Highly seasoned satires of contemporary officialdom were written by two prominent Prussian administrators, E. T. A. Hoffmann and Eichendorff.[52] These political writers retained the spirit of the preceding decade, without, however, being active political writers as Arndt, List, and Görres had been. The enthusiasm for Greek liberation was the only sentiment which swept all Germany. But no political program or issue was formulated on the German Question.

The decline in public discussion of economic problems was similar. Some of the old issues were occasionally revived. Thus free trade continued to be advocated for philosophical as well as practical reasons.[53] As late as 1824 Germany's economic problem was formulated by giving her the choice between "enforcing free trade" or abandoning all foreign trade in order to give up all luxury.[54] Moreover, one pamphlet still argued that customs duties infringed on citizens' rights.[55] Young professionals in the field of political economy, like Karl Heinrich Rau, would deal with the subject only from the purely academic point of view.[56] His positive suggestions included the establishment of a German consular system, the adoption of a German flag, and internal integration of economic life through common trade (*Gewerbe*) and patent legislation.[57]

The period is best characterized by those magazines which covered at the same time literary, economic, and gen-

---

[52] E. T. A. Hoffmann, *Meister Floh* (1821), selection, *ibid.*, pp. 64–69; Joseph Freiherr von Eichendorff, *Ratskollegium* (1824), *ibid.*, pp. 73–74.

[53] H. F. Hopf, *Meinungen von der Handelsfreyheit und dem Prohibitionssysteme in Beziehung auf die Industrie in den deutschen Bundesstaaten* (Wien, 1823), pp. 15, 132–33, 223–25, 230.

[54] Ernst Gottfried Georg von Bülow-Cummerow, *Betrachtungen über Metall- und Papiergeld, über Handelsfreiheit, Prohibitiv-Systeme, den gegenwärtigen Zustand der ersten europäischen Reiche, Verschuldung der Grundbesitzer* . . . (Berlin, 1824), p. 97.

[55] [Anonymous] "Über Gewerbe- und Handelsfreiheit," *Hermes*, 1827, p. 206.

[56] Rau's appendix to his translation of Malthus and Say, *Über die Ursachen der jetzigen Handelsstockung* (Hamburg, 1821), pp. 264–301.

[57] *Ibid.*, pp. 297–99.

eral subjects with changing depths of treatment.[58]   During the period pamphlets were published which in different ways reflected the spirit of the age.   Some appeared on controversial subjects in such a complex form and filled with so much specious material that it is difficult to analyze their major position.[59]   A Marburg professor dedicated a work in which he recommended prohibitive tariffs on all French and English goods to King Charles X of France for his restoration of a free press.   This professor still argued in 1825 along the 1819 lines for a common German customs system with a prohibitive tariff in order to enforce general free trade.[60]

While many minds thus continued to think in earlier patterns, some contemporary problems were discussed in public.   The South German negotiations for a regional customs unification received some attention in the press, but they did not inspire anything that might have resembled a controversial discussion.   The reports in the *Augsburger Allge-*

---

[58] Cf. G. A. v. Mt., "Die Accise":

> " 'Was giebt's Neues in der Stadt?'
> Fragte Peter jüngstens Kunzen—.
> 'Nichts, Gevatter! Toll und matt
> Rennt man sich, und alle hunzen
> Sich herunter, nach wie vor.
> Nur am neuen Gänsethor
> Hört' ich sonderbare Dinge,
> Wie's mit der Accise ginge!—
> Ja—so ist es! Nicht genug,
> Dass wir jede Elle Tuch
> Noch besteuern und plombieren—
> Nein, Gevatter, wir verlieren
> Immer mehr am Tagelohn:
> Man p l o m b i e r t ohn' Erbarmen—
> Denk' Dir! Reichen so wie Armen—
> Jetzt sogar die Z ä h n e schon!' "

Der Gesellschafter, 1821, No. 183 (November 16), p. 855, quoted from a facsimile reprint in Herbert Eulenberg (ed.), *Der Anlauf, Zeitschriften der Jahre 1817–1821 mit den ersten dichterischen Veröffentlichungen von H. Heine in naturgetreuen Wiedergaben* (Hamburg: Hoffmann & Campe, 1921).

[59] Cf., e.g., "Chlodwig Bunder" [pseudonym of Ludwig Basedow], *Beleuchtung der Verhältnisse Anhalts zu Preussen in Bezug auf das von letzterm angenommene und auf ersters ausgedehnte Zoll- und Verbrauchs-steuer-System* ("Deutschland" [i.e. Dessau], 1819) 113 pp.

[60] [Michael] Alexander Lips, *Über den gegenwärtig tiefen Stand der Getraide-Preise in Deutschland, ihr nothwendig immer tieferes Sinken, die Ursachen dieser Erscheinung und die Mittel, sie zu heben* (Nürnberg, 1825), pp. [1], 60, 68, 70–71.

meine Zeitung were meager and discouraging, although the business interests continued to complain bitterly about the economic anarchy and although some of them went even so far as to wish for a return of Napoleon's Continental System.[61] A few former members of the League continued to publish their views,[62] but, to judge from one of Miller's pamphlets, did not get beyond an elementary exposition.[63] At least one author, anonymous, however, dealt with the technical aspects of a customs unification and argued for a common customs system and against a customs union.[64]

Other topics which attracted a number of publicists were the coinage reform[65] and the dispute over the navigation of the Rhine.[66]

During the years from 1821 to 1827 economic problems were not discussed publicly to any extent in Germany, since the reactionary forces had succeeded in suppressing almost all liberal thought. One has to search for reflections on contemporary questions in order to find the few comments which were published. Occasionally, older ideas were revived, but even they received only rare expression.

MOVEMENTS AND DISCUSSIONS, 1828–33

THE conclusion of the Bavaria-Württemberg and of the Prussia-Hesse-Darmstadt Customs Unions early in 1828 marked the beginning of a new period of public interest in the question of economic unification. The July Revolution

---

[61] Müller, *op. cit.*, pp. 133–55.

[62] Franz Miller, *Über ein Maximum der Zölle zwischen süddeutschen Staaten und die Ausführung gemeinsam verabredeter Maasregeln gegen fremde feindliche Douanen-Systeme* ... (Darmstadt, 1822), p. 34, n.

[63] *Op. cit.*

[64] [Anonymous] *Kurze Ansichten über die Vereinigung mehrerer süd- teutschen Staaten zu einem gemeinsamen Zoll- und Maut-Sisteme als Heil- mittel für den Druck der Zeit* ... (Mannheim, 1826), 48 pp.

[65] Cf., e.g., [Anonymous] *Materialien für Münzgesetzgebung und dabei enstehende Erörterungen* (Frankfurt a.M., 1822), xiv + 494; L[udwig] A[ugust] Brüel, *Materialien für die zu erwartende Reform des deutschen Münzwesens* (2d ed.; Hannover, 1831), 60 pp.; Johann Ludwig Klüber, *Das Münzwesen in Teutschland* ... (Stuttgart, 1828), vii + 296.

[66] Cf., e.g., [Anonymous] *Neue Organisation der Schifffahrts- und Handelsverhältnisse auf dem Rheinstrome*, Part I (Basel, 1822), viii + 180; [Prussia, Rhine Province, Landtag] *Bericht des dreizehnten Aus- schusses an die Plenar-Versammlung der rheinischen Provinzialstände über die ihm unter dem 6[.] November 1826 zugewiesenen Anträge in Betreff der Freiheit der Rheinschiffahrt* (Düsseldorf, 1826), 54 pp.

in Paris and the Polish as well as the Belgian fight for freedom inspired German liberals with new ideas.   During the same years various German cabinets negotiated for the formation of the Zollverein, successfully concluding their work in 1833.   This interval from the conclusion of the Bavaria-Württemberg customs treaty (January, 1828) to the introduction of the Zollverein on January 1, 1834, formed a period with common characteristics in its publicly expressed thought.   It was more complex than the six preceding years, and its thought reflected the new political movements, the greater economic forces, and the keener diplomatic rivalry of this age.

Thus the cabinets attempted to control public opinion to such a degree that the relationship between government and press forms the key for understanding the public thought of this period.   The governments continued to supervise the press so strictly that actually no independently expressed public opinion existed.[67]   Not only did the public censor suppress any publication displeasing to his government, but the cabinets also wrote and distributed articles and pamphlets defending their policies.   This did not mean that only pro-government ideas were printed.   Academic and apparently objective discussions and presentations were, as a rule, not prohibited.   Petitions, complaints, and free speech in legislative bodies were, in general, not interfered with.   But any polemic attack which tended to undermine the position of the government was suppressed.   Although many German governments had to obtain the approval of their diets for the ratification or the execution of any customs union treaty, the individual parliaments exercised relatively little influence on the course of events.   Nevertheless, the governments watched public opinion carefully and were anxious to have their policies favorably considered.

Naturally, each government's power to censor ended at its boundaries. The attempts of the Prussian government to overcome this dilemma and to exert an influence in other German states were characteristic.   Not only did high-ranking Prussian officials write articles for non-Prussian newspapers,

[67] Bab, *Die öffentliche Meinung*, p. 5.

but Prussia was also able to have the Bavarian government promise to suppress any articles or pamphlets with a malicious tendency toward Prussia.[68] But even in these matters the old conflict between the Prussian Ministry of Foreign Affairs and the Ministry of Finance persisted. The Foreign Office was opposed to any propaganda and felt that Prussia was not interested in concluding a union with a country whose public opinion was opposed to such a step. In some instances it advised reserve in such matters to Prussian representatives.[69]

Any Prussian propaganda would have lost its effectiveness if its source had been known. For this reason a great number of the pro-Zollverein pamphlets appeared anonymously.[70] To make the situation more complicated, newspapers would freely reprint articles from each other without always verifying their source. Thus a Prussian article was copied by a Frankfurt paper from the *Karlsruher Zeitung*, apparently without realization of its true origin.[71] In some instances public feuds arose between two governments. The most famous of these was caused by Lindenau's article on the Central German Union.[72] The Bavarian government hired Lindner, the author of the *Manuscript aus Süd-Deutschland*, to write an exposition of its commercial policies.[73] Lindner had so few scruples that he reversed his opinion on the North Germans completely and spoke favorably of the Prussian

---

[68] *Ibid.*, pp. 8–9, 12.

[69] *Ibid.*, pp. 6–8, 12–13; Treitschke, *Deutsche Geschichte*, IV, 372.

[70] Cf., e.g., [Anonymous] *Beleuchtung der Opposition des Herrn Zais gegen den preussischen Zollverein* (Stuttgart, 1833), 60 pp.; [Anonymous] *Denkschrift über Zollwesen und Zoll- und Handels-Vereine in Deutschland;* ... (Stuttgart, 1831), 74 pp.; [Anonymous] *Einige Worte über Handel und freien Verkehr im Allgemeinen und insbesondere zwischen den verschiedenen Bundesstaaten* ... (Mainz, 1833), 48 pp.; [C. J. Bergius] *Betrachtungen über die Finanzen und Gewerbe im preussischen Staate* ... (Berlin, 1830), 77 pp.; [Reinwald] *Kurze Betrachtungen über Deutschlands Einigung in seinen Merkantilinteressen* (Mainz, 1830), 34 pp.; [Speyerer] *Die Frage der Zollvereinigung deutscher Staaten* (Heidelberg, 1831), 30 pp.; Bab., *op. cit.*, p. 11. [71] *Ibid.*, p. 8; other examples, *ibid.*, pp. 16, 18, 34.

[72] Oncken and Saemisch, III, 434–36, No. 505, 436, n. 2, extending to p. 438.

[73] [Friedrich Ludwig] Lindner, *Considérations sur le Traité d'Union commerciale entre la Prusse, la Bavière, le Wurtemberg, et Hesse-Darmstadt* (Munic, 1829), 26 pp.; cf. Müller, *op. cit.*, pp. 149–50.

government, with which Bavaria was allied at the time.[74] Naturally, since the public was not informed who had sponsored this pamphlet, it had the desired effect.[75] Newspaper morale was very low; even the *Augsburger Allgemeine Zeitung*, Germany's leading newspaper, would sell its influence.[76]

Considering these circumstances, it is easily understood why so many pamphlets and articles were published anonymously, although not every anonymous piece was government-inspired.

The class from which the pamphlets originated can be determined in most cases where the author was known. Professional and business men were responsible for a large majority of them.[77]

In particular, the government and the upper classes expressed their ideas most frequently in print and so dominated the controversial literature of the period. The common people very rarely appeared in print. Moreover, what was printed apparently had a relatively small effect since there was very little exchange of ideas. One finds no instance of a publicist changing the course of events or of a government convincing a publicist by arguments alone. The intellectual leaders of the nation, like Goethe and Stein, expressed themselves favorably in private about the trend of the time, but did not attempt to influence the public.[78] Even a man like Arnoldi, who had helped List in 1819-20, remained silent in public, much as he favored Prussia's economic leadership.[79] Only Ranke devoted time to the Zollverein and wrote its early history.[80]

---

[74] Lindner, *Considérations*, p. 10: "En Prusse, un gouvernment sage . . ."

[75] Müller, *op. cit.*, pp. 150–51.   [76] *Ibid.*, p. 127.

[77] Thus Amsberg, Böhmer, Hundeshagen, Lindner, Lips, Pfizer, Raumer, Rudhart, and Nebenius belonged to these classes.

[78] Goethe to Eckermann, October 28, 1828, Johann Peter Eckermann, *Gespräche mit Goethe in den letzten Jahren seines Lebens* (9th ed.; Leipzig, 1909), pp. 558–59; Stein to Gagern, August 28, 1827, March 20, 1828, May 6, 1828, June 14, 1828, January 22, 1829, Stein to Cotta, March, 1830, Stein, *Briefwechsel*, VI [1934?], 518, 563, 576, 630, VII (1937), 137.

[79] Emminghaus, *Ernst Wilhelm Arnoldi*, pp. 160, 171.

[80] Ranke's article in *Historisch politische Zeitschrift* (about 1832–33), quoted from Alfred Dove, "Ranke," *Allgemeine deutsche Biographie*, XXVII (1888), 255.

Although these economic problems were neglected by the leading men of the age, economic forces were among the most important factors in the history of the period. The unrest of the masses in Central and Southwest Germany between 1830 and 1832 was caused primarily by economic conditions. While the middle and upper classes were influenced by political considerations, the common people were stirred up by the effects of the existing economic anarchy. Such reasons made the lower classes participate in the Brunswick Riots (September, 1830), which drove the Duke away and during which his castle was destroyed.[81] One of the slogans of the Kassel Revolution, which occurred a few days later, was that the "toll was a child of darkness."[82] When the mob tried to ransack the bakeries, order was restored by a citizen guard. In the southern districts of the Electorate customs houses were attacked, and all documents, including the money, were burned, because nobody wanted to be contaminated with customs money.[83] The new customs line of the Prussia-Hesse-Darmstadt Union, as well as the Electoral Hessian customs policy, had created an unbearable situation. There was serious dissatisfaction in the Upper Province of Hesse-Darmstadt, but much more so in Hesse-Kassel. Electoral mobs even tried to attack customs houses of the Prussia-Hesse-Darmstadt Union. The chief complaint was the customs system. Revolutionary songs dating back to 1790, which called for the "demolition" ("Zertrümmert Mauth") of all customs duties, were revived.[84] Treitschke claims that the Electoral Prince (*Kurprinz*) was able to stop the riots by a simple promise to abolish all customs duties.[85] It was characteristic of the period that smugglers who saw their business endangered by the strict Prussian system of enforcement participated in these riots. When Hesse-Kassel joined the Prussia-Hesse-Darmstadt Cus-

---

[81] Treitschke, *Deutsche Geschichte*, IV, 100–1.

[82] "Die Mauth ist ein Kind der Finsterniss," *ibid.*, p. 128.

[83] *Ibid.*, pp. 129–30.

[84] Christoph Crössmann, *Die Unruhen in Oberhessen im Herbste 1830* ("Quellen und Forschungen zur hessischen Geschichte," Vol. VIII; Darmstadt: Hessischer Staatsverlag, 1929), pp. 4, 7, 10–11, 41–52, 69.

[85] *Deutsche Geschichte*, IV, 130.

toms Union on July 1, 1832, the people tried again to destroy the customs houses.[86]

Similar movements were on their way in some of the large states, like Saxony or Hanover, but never won the upper hand, as they did in Brunswick or Hesse-Kassel.[87]

Radicalism was best organized in the Bavarian Palatinate. The Bavarian government had introduced a boundary tariff in this separate possession in 1830 for diplomatic reasons. It had hoped by this means to obtain another bargaining point. The new institution had little financial or commercial benefit for the people of the Palatinate. The quick temper of the population, together with French influence, did its part to stir popular sentiment, especially since two capable agitators made good use of the existing grievances. Dr. Siebenpfeiffer and Dr. Wirth were men of good intellectual capacity who had been in public service before persecution by the more conservative elements had driven them to become the prime exponents of a radical liberalism.[88] Siebenpfeiffer published a periodical called *Rheinbayern,* which attempted to discuss contemporary problems in a seemingly dignified tone. The economic abuses were exploited to the fullest extent. He not only criticized the customs administration in the Palatinate[89] and deplored the bad effect smuggling had on the public morale, but was also opposed to the commercial treaty Bavaria had concluded with Prussia and to any extension of the Bavaria-Württemberg Customs Union.[90] He was in particular opposed to any association with Prussia, which state was, in his opinion, not German at all and which tried only to exploit the other German states through her Zollverein policy. Prussia wanted political influence and her political system was compared with "Russian barbarism." Siebenpfeiffer also argued against protection. Although he favored a general German customs system, he was fully aware of the

[86] Crössmann, *op. cit.,* p. 40: Treitschke, *Deutsche Geschichte,* IV, 142.

[87] *Ibid.,* pp. 142–44, 152–58.

[88] Ney, "Siebenpfeiffer," *Allgemeine deutsche Biographie,* XXXIV (1892), 176–77; Max Mendheim, "Wirth," *ibid.,* XLIII (1898), 531–33.

[89] [Philipp Jakob] S[iebenpfeiffer], "Schriften über die Mauth im Rheinkreise," *Rheinbayern,* II (1831), 51–52.

[90] [Philipp Jakob] S[iebenpfeiffer], "Die Thron-Rede," *ibid.,* pp. 228–30.

ineffectiveness of the Confederate Diet, and he finally advocated a common customs system of all German constitutional states, in order to spread free trade.[91]

In a similar way his collaborator Stromeyer argued for South German solidarity and against Prussian leadership. Stromeyer was, however, against the Bavaria-Württemberg Customs Union, and he favored Baden's system of low tariffs. He tried to show that Württemberg had suffered through the Union, since she had been compelled to open her market to Bavarian products, but that general free trade would alleviate this condition.[92] Siebenpfeiffer stressed in particular the suffering of the poor under the new system[93] and in one instance went so far as to state that literary attacks would have no results.[94] He went still further in the revolutionary republicanism of his other writings. Here he even advocated the assassination of the Nassau minister Marschall.[95]

The Bavarian government prosecuted Siebenpfeiffer and Wirth who, however, were able to evade the authorities for a number of years with the help of minor officials and through the popular support they enjoyed.[96]

The movement in the Palatinate culminated in the Hambach Festival held near Neustadt in May of 1832. Some 25,000 people attended it, and among the chief speakers were Siebenpfeiffer and Wirth.[97] Political ideas dominated the scene, but the "oppressive" customs policy of the cabinets was denounced throughout the festival. It was claimed that the princes had disunited Germany through the customs lines,[98] and that Prussia was using her customs policy as a decoy for her arbitrary rule.[99] Much as the leaders of this

---

[91] [Philipp Jakob] S[iebenpfeiffer], "Handels- und Zollvereine," *ibid.*, III (1831), 154, 159–65, 167–71.

[92] Franz Stromeyer, "Über Handel und Mauthen in Süd-Deutschland," *ibid.*, IV (1831), 213, 216, 221, 224.

[93] [Philipp Jakob] S[iebenpfeiffer], "Die Mauth," *ibid.*, I (1830), 24.

[94] S[iebenpfeiffer], "Schriften," *ibid.*, II, 52.

[95] Treitschke, *Deutsche Geschichte*, IV, 252.

[96] *Ibid.*, pp. 252–53; Ney, "Siebenpfeiffer," *Allgemeine deutsche Biographie*, XXXIV, 176–77; Mendheim, "Wirth," *ibid.*, XLIII, 531–33.

[97] Treitschke, *Deutsche Geschichte*, IV, 261–65.

[98] J[ohann] G[eorg] A[ugust] Wirth, *Das Nationalfest der Deutschen zu Hambach* (Neustadt a/H., 1832), pp. 1–2, 95.   [99] *Ibid.*, p. 24.

movement were willing to appeal to the economic grievances of the people, there was, nevertheless, little unity among them with respect to solving Germany's economic difficulties. While Siebenpfeiffer and Stromeyer tended toward free trade and South German regionalism, Wirth, in order to establish world-wide free trade, favored the abolition of internal obstacles to free trade and a common German system of retortion against foreign restrictions.[100]

Such differences were of little consequence to the movement they led, since the masses were primarily interested in immediate relief from the vexations of the existing customs anarchy. The songs of the period are the most striking records of these sentiments which have been preserved. Whether they were folk songs, originated by the people themselves, or whether they were written by professionals for popular consumption, they all stressed two ideas, that the customs system was devised to impoverish the common man and that the customs administration and procedure constituted an intolerable nuisance.[101] The latter motive was very drastically used in the only folk song which has come down to our time dealing with the foundation of the Zollverein. It expressed its relief at having been liberated from all the inconveniences which the steady contact with the various customs systems had brought.[102] These contemporary songs also expressed the helplessness of the common people against the patriarchical practices of the cabinets. When one song exclaimed that "the princes have divided and encircled (umzingelt) the country with customs duties,"[103] or another called for a free press, because "a free press would certainly liberate them from the customs duties,"[104] one can form some idea of the state of mind the reactionary system of the Holy Alliance with the economic anarchy had created among the

---

[100] J[ohann] G[eorg] A[ugust] Wirth, *Die politischen Reformen Deutschlands* (Strasburg, 1832), p. 18.

[101] Johannes Bühler, *Das Hambacher Fest* (Ludwigshafen a. Rh.: J. Waldkirch, 1932), p. 37; song, Hambach festival, Wirth, *Das Nationalfest*, p. 57.

[102] Franz Wilhelm Freiherr von Ditfurth (ed.), *Historische Volkslieder von der Verbannung Napoleons nach St. Helena 1815, bis zur Gründung des Nordbundes 1866* (Berlin; F. Lipperheide, 1871), pp. 56–57.

[103] Wirth, *Das Nationalfest*, p. 57.   [104] Bühler, *op. cit.*, p. 44.

masses. Even intellectuals succumbed occasionally to similar feelings.[105]

The masses concentrated their interest on the immediate abolition of customs lines and houses. Their leaders were so much opposed to the trend toward the Zollverein that they never seriously considered the problem or developed a consistent program. Their thoughts centered around a revolutionary republicanism, and their basic ideas were political. Nevertheless, they became the leaders of a movement whose mainspring was to a large degree economic. The literary record this movement left is not very extensive, but its force should not be judged solely by this criterion. The masses believed less in paper feuds than in outright action, as the various riots showed.

Aside from the movements among the lower classes, there was a literary discussion of the problems arising during the founding years of the Zollverein. The problem generally considered was the question whether a certain German state should join a customs union dominated by Prussia. Prussian public opinion did not concern itself with the problem whether Prussia should pursue a Zollverein policy. And even Prussia's tariff policy was never seriously questioned by her own subjects. Only rarely did Prussian business interests petition the government against a proposed Zollverein treaty.[106] It was for these reasons that the vast majority of pamphlets were published outside of Prussia.[107] Naturally, as has been pointed out previously, many pamphlets and articles originated in Prussia, but their main purpose was to influence public opinion in South and Central Germany.

In all these regions there was strong opposition to a customs union with Prussia.[108] These anti-Zollverein groups

---

[105] Anastasius Grün, *Mauthkordon* (1830-31), in Otto Rommel (ed.), *Der österreichische Vormärz 1816–1847* ("Deutsche Literatur, Politische Reihe," Vol. IV; Leipzig: Philipp Reclam jun., 1931), pp. 39–40.

[106] Petition from Mülheim a. d. Mosel to Friedrich Wilhelm III, March 30, 1828, Oncken and Saemisch, II, 269–73, No. 410.

[107] The two following pamphlets were the only ones published in Prussia considered for this section: [Bergius] *Betrachtungen* (Berlin, 1830); Pet[er] Kaufmann, *Rheinpreussen und seine staatswirthschaftlichen Interessen in der heutigen europäischen Staaten-Krise, oder vergleichende Betrachtungen* ... (Berlin, 1831), xii + 200.

[108] The later sections will substantiate the general ideas expressed in this and subsequent paragraphs.

based their stand primarily on political beliefs.[109] Their trend of thought was very close to that of Siebenpfeiffer and Wirth, except that they lacked the revolutionary element. The ideological foundation of these movements was the same wherever they occurred, although there was very little organization. Thus no separate anti-Zollverein parties were organized within the individual states, and contacts between the movements in the various regions remained informal. This opposition was in most states identical with the extreme liberal groups.

The supporters of the Zollverein policy, on the other hand, did not have such a straight party ideology to fall back on, and in most cases did not show the fervor which political doctrinairianism lends to a cause.

Moreover, there were writers who neither entirely opposed nor entirely defended the Zollverein. Others were actuated by their economic beliefs when they chose sides or formed their opinion according to what they believed to be their immediate business interest. Most writers did not confine their arguments to one field, but based them on political principles and economic theory, as well as on business and other local interests. Nevertheless, the great majority were either for or against the Zollverein, and their opinions were founded primarily on political reasons. The gap between the liberals and the conservatives had widened during the twenties to such an extent that both parties almost talked different languages.

This split was understood fully by a few contemporaries and a synthesis of both ideologies was attempted. Paul Pfizer, a Württemberg liberal, turned against the doctrinairianism of his fellow liberals and tried to show them the realities of German politics. At the same time he retained his political convictions and hoped for a synthesis of the liberal idealists and the Prussian realists. He used a very ingenious way of presenting his views by putting his ideas in the form of a correspondence between a theorist and a realist.[110] His analysis of contemporary politics produced

---

[109] Treitschke, *Deutsche Geschichte*, IV, 370–71.

[110] Paul Achatius Pfizer, *Briefwechsel zweier Deutschen*, collation of first and second editions of 1831 and 1832 by Georg Künzel ("Deutsche Literaturdenkmale," No. 144; Berlin: Behr's Verlag, 1911), pp. 1–330.

results which must have perplexed his liberal readers. Thus he argued very realistically that an absolute Prussia was desirable, since a popular government in Prussia would lead to a greater unification of Prussia and to a domination of Germany by the Prussian people, to which a purely dynastic preponderance of the Hohenzollerns was preferable.[111] Like most prophets, he was thoroughly misunderstood. Although Pfizer had preached Prussian leadership as no other had done, even the Prussian minister in Stuttgart had no sympathy with him, because he had retained his fundamental belief in constitutional government.[112]

Pfizer described his aim as a synthesis, not of liberalism with conservatism, but of the theoretic with the practical.[113] These words characterized the hostile political camps in Germany only too well. Each side used almost exclusively its own way of thinking. The liberal opponents of the Zollverein based their beliefs primarily on theory, while their opponents argued with realities.

South German liberalism had developed during the twenties. Constitutional government had given to it the opportunity to participate in legislation and to its leaders parliamentary experience. The constitutional liberties had survived a period during which the reaction had triumphed in the remainder of Germany, and the impact of reactionary pressure had only accentuated the difference between the two camps. The Holy Alliance, the conservative international, was supplemented by a liberal internationalism. The South German liberal became more interested in the victory of constitutionalism than in greater unification of Germany. In theory, all writers of the period supported some kind of German nationalism, but most of them were only for greater unification under certain conditions. Rotteck, the liberal theorist, when confronted with the problem of whether to prefer German unification to a realization of his liberal ideas, stated that he would rather have "liberty without unity, than unity without liberty."[114]

---

[111] *Ibid.*, pp. 164–65.

[112] Treitschke, *Deutsche Geschichte*, IV, 258–59.

[113] "Die vorliegende Schrift hat zur Aufgabe, den unausgeglichenen Gegensatz des Theoretischen und Praktischen . . . auszusprechen," Pfizer, *op. cit.*, p. 3. [114] Treitschke, *Deutsche Geschichte*, IV, 265.

The liberals therefore took as a first line of defense the threat the Zollverein would constitute for South German constitutionalism. They charged that Prussia intended to have the constitutions of the South German states abolished through the influence she would gain by the Zollverein.[115] Other authors would not go thus far, but would state in general that a close union like that of the Zollverein with a larger autocratic state would not further the liberal cause in South Germany.[116]   In some instances the claim was made that the Zollverein would infringe on the constitutional right of the legislatures to control and supervise the collection of taxes,[117] and in particular that the Prussian customs system was incompatible with the Württemberg constitution.[118]   It was even charged that the Zollverein would do away with the principle of equality, since certain classes would be more affected than others by the Union tariff.[119]   This opposition to Prussian absolutism had curious limitations.   Some liberals would not support a customs union with any absolute monarchy.   Many would not join with Prussia because her size would give her an undue preponderance over the smaller constitutional states.   But such considerations did not prevent some liberals from advocating at the same time a customs system of the German Confederation.[120]   There were still serious publicists who looked for the Diet at Frankfurt to give Germany economic unification.[121]

This claim that liberal institutions were threatened was closely allied with the desire to preserve the independence of the German states.   Particularistic sentiment also turned

---

[115] [Anonymous] *Über den Anschluss Badens an den Preussisch-Hessischen Zollverein. Einige triftige und beherzungswerthe Motive gegen diesen*... (Freiburg in Brsg., 1833), pp. 20–21; Engel, *Wirtschaftliche und soziale Kämpfe*, p. 11; Bab, *op. cit.*, pp. 22–23, 27, 30.

[116] *Ibid.*, pp. 23–24; Treitschke, *Deutsche Geschichte*, IV, 370.

[117] J[ohann] Chr[istian] Hundeshagen, *Die Staatskräfte des Grossherzogthum Hessens* (Tübingen, 1832), p. 275; Bab, *op. cit.*, pp. 21–23.

[118] Motion by Zais in the Württemberg Diet, [Anonymous] *Beleuchtung* (Stuttgart, 1833), p. 11.   [119] *Ibid.*, p. 41.   [120] *Ibid.*, p. 28.

[121] [Anonymous] *Die Zollverhältnisse Kurhessens* (Leipzig, 1830), p. 45; A. von Amsberg, *Über die Einigung der Handels-Interessen Deutschlands* (Braunschweig, 1831), pp. 63–73; [Michael] Alexander Lips, *Deutschlands National-Ökonomie. Ein Versuch zur Frage: "wie kann Deutschland zu lohnendem Ackerbau, . . . gelangen?"* (Giessen, 1830, pp. 549–56).

toward the Confederation in order to offer a positive solution to the problem of economic unification. The defenders of states rights feared that the Zollverein would overshadow the Confederation, and remembered how much they had gained through the weakness of the Diet. Such were the reasons on which some South German publicists based their demand that the power of the Confederate Diet be increased in order to balance the influence of the Zollverein.[122]

While the liberals had conceded a general German solution as a theoretical point, they undoubtedly preferred the Diet as the lesser evil only. The simultaneous interest of the particularists in the Confederation was in a similar way an eleventh-hour solution.

The defenders of the Zollverein tried to minimize its political importance. They did not organize their ideas around basic ideological conceptions, but took up various lines of defense according to practical considerations. As a result, the feud over the Zollverein did not turn into a discussion of the relative merits of constitutionalism versus absolutism, but the extent of political disadvantages the South German states might suffer was debated.

It was first of all argued by Zollverein supporters that Prussia really had a liberal system of administration, although it could not be denied that she was not a constitutional monarchy.[123] In particular, the benefits the Prussian people had enjoyed through the reform of the customs administration were pointed out.[124]

The other argument used to quiet the constitutionalists claimed, with little logical connection, that there was no evidence that Prussia was attempting to spread her form of government and that the Zollverein would not change the political relations between its members, unless a member desired to surrender a political right.[125]

In some instances the pro-Zollverein publicists would

---

[122] Bab, *op. cit.*, pp. 16–18, 29–31.
[123] [Anonymous] *Denkschrift* (Stuttgart, 1831), pp. 18–19; Friedrich von Raumer, *Über den Anschluss Sachsens an die deutschen Zoll- und Handelsvereine*, reprinted from *Blätter für literarische Unterhaltung* (Leipzig, 1833), pp. 16–19. [124] [Bergius] *Betrachtungen* (Berlin, 1830), pp. 163–64.
[125] Bab., *op. cit.*, pp. 26–29.

counterattack those who hoped for a general German solution, by showing that the Diet of the Confederation was too weak and ineffective to accomplish such a task.[126]

The defenders of the Zollverein appealed strongly to national feelings when they tried to show that economic unification through the Zollverein would contribute to political unification.[127]   In most cases this national sentiment was vague.   Those who resorted to it were not conscious of a solution of the German Question under Prussian leadership and would have poured oil on the fire of the particularists if they had been.   One author who used this national appeal believed that it was not natural to consolidate Germany into an empire,[128] while another thought that the Zollverein would be the realization of Article XIX of the Acts of Confederation.[129]   An appeal to national sentiment was also made by calling all those who were opposed to the Zollverein traitors to the national cause.   Frequent reference was made to the "non-German" Hanover and the "Anglophile" Hamburg.[130] Austria was regarded by many writers as being incapable of participating in the Zollverein, and few directly favored a solution which would include the Hapsburg monarchy.[131]

Those who were afraid that the smaller states would lose their independence were answered that for all practical purposes these governments were not sovereign,[132] and in a diametrically different line of argument it was shown that these states were not independent if they could not enter a customs union.[133]   In some instances this defense was carried to extremes.   One writer fully explained why high

---

[126] *Ibid.*, pp. 18–22; [Reinwald] *Kurze Betrachtungen* (Mainz, 1830), pp. 7–8.

[127] [Anonymous] *Einige Worte* (Mainz, 1833), pp. 8–11; [Speyerer] *Die Frage* (Heidelberg, 1831), pp. 26–27; Bab, *op. cit.*, pp. 34–40.

[128] Raumer, *op. cit.*, p. 7.

[129] [Anonymous] *Einige Worte* (Mainz, 1833), p. 29.

[130] [Anonymous] *Denkschrift* (Stuttgart, 1831), p. 43; [Anonymous] *Über die Handelspolitik der teutschen freien Städte, insbesondere Hamburgs und Frankfurts*, reprint from *Teutsche Vaterlands-Zeitung* (Darmstadt, 1833), pp. v–vi; [Reinwald] *Kurze Betrachtungen* (Mainz, 1830), p. 30; Raumer, *op. cit.*, p. 24; Müller, *op. cit.*, p. 162.

[131] [Anonymous] *Denkschrift* (Stuttgart, 1831), p. 23; Bab, *op. cit.*, pp. 85–89.   [132] Bab, *op. cit.*, p. 32.

[133] [Anonymous] *Ansichten über Zollvereine unter südteutschen Staaten. Veranlasst . . .* (München, 1828), pp. 26–30.

tariffs would not be harmful to constitutional government.[134]

The defense of the Zollverein on political grounds consisted of a number of separate arguments, most of which were of a practical nature. Although some lines of arguments contradicted each other, most of them were powerful because they were realistic. They failed, however, to shatter the foundations of the liberal opposition since they did not take the opposite stand on fundamentals.

While the divisions according to political beliefs were clearly drawn, economic theories and interests did not form such a regular pattern. Immediate business interests were in many cases the only basis for a pro- or anti-Zollverein attitude.[135] The old feud between the commercial and the industrial interests continued with undiminished vigor. In some instances it seems to have overshadowed even the larger Zollverein issues.[136] Only a few were able to remain impartial in this conflict and to condemn the extremes of either side.[137] The predominance of economic interests explains to some extent the fact that both free traders and protectionists opposed the Zollverein. All those who believed in complete free trade were opposed to the Zollverein on principle.[138] Here economic thought relied on an absolute doctrine which frequently had close ties with the beliefs in the other liberties.[139] These theorists did not see the large internal market which the Zollverein was offering. At the same time, many writers opposed the Zollverein be-

---

[134] F. L. Runde, *Auch ein Wort über Sachsens Anschluss an den preusischen* [sic] *Zollverband, als Beleuchtung der jüngst von mehrern Kaufleuten dargestellten Schattenseite* . . . (Freiberg, 1833), p. 39.

[135] E.g. Geo. Meyenn, appendix to his translation of [Anonymous] *Bemerkungen über die Handels-Politik Englands gegen Preussen und andere nordische Staaten* (Rostock, 1833), pp. 81–84.

[136] For defenders of commercial interests cf. [Anonymous] *Über die Handelspolitik* (Darmstadt, 1833); [Anonymous] *Denkschrift über die nachtheiligen Folgen des hohen bayrischen Eingangszolltarifs und der bayrischen Zollordnung vom Jahre 1828* [Nuremberg] 1831), viii + 38; Johannes Scharrer, *Bemerkungen über den deutschen Zollverein und über die Wirkung hoher Zölle in nationalökonomischer Hinsicht* (Nürnberg, 1828), pp. 10–26; Bab, *op. cit.*, pp. 78–79. For defenders of industrial interests see *ibid.*, pp. 64–65, 68–69, 73–74; [Anonymous] *Beleuchtung* (Stuttgart, 1833), pp. 20–21.

[137] [Anonymous] *Über die Handelspolitik* (Darmstadt, 1833), pp. vi, 13.

[138] Bab, *op. cit.*, p. 61.   [139] Hundeshagen, *op. cit.*, pp. 273–75.

cause it would lay the South German industries wide open to Prussian competition. Some went so far as to use both arguments—that of complete free trade and that of the threatening Prussian competition within the same article.[140] Prussian sympathizers would not derive their arguments to that extent from any school of economic thought, but would prefer to emphasize facts. They would stress the advantages of a large free-trade area and of collective bargaining with other national economic systems.[141]   The first point was well taken, since the internal German customs lines were generally unpopular.[142]   Much as this pro-Zollverein discussion centered around facts, it was, nevertheless, also torn between free-trade and protectionist theories, although to a lesser degree.[143]   In some instances these realistic arguments were rebutted by the opponents of the Zollverein.   Thus a learned study tried to show that Hesse-Darmstadt had not benefited from the Customs Union with Prussia.[144]

The confusion in economic thought was in part due to the preference which the age entertained for general and theoretical ideas.   This tendency was accentuated by the deep gulf which separated the governing from the governed classes.   In many instances there was also outright provincialism.   There had been, however, some progress during the twenties.   Many a writer was quite conscious of the development of the preceding decade and gave a historical and critical exposition of List's activities in 1819–20.[145]

The period was also capable of self-criticism.   There were occasionally sarcastic characterizations of the intellectual level of the opponents.   For instance, one article in the

---

[140] Bab, *op. cit.*, p. 67.

[141] *Ibid.*, pp. 49–53, 56–59, 63–64; [Cunow] *Sachsens Anschluss an den preussischen Zollverband; nebst der davon abhängigen Gestaltung anderweitiger innerer und äusserer Verhältnisse* (Dresden, 1833), p. 11.

[142] Bab, *op. cit.*, p. 53.

[143] *Ibid.*, p. 62; [Anonymous] Denkschrift (Stuttgart, 1831), pp. 2–8; [Anonymous] *Einige Worte über Handel und Industrie in Deutschland, mit besonderer Rücksicht auf Bayern* (München, 1830), p. 120.

[144] Hundeshagen, *op. cit.*, pp. 306–9.

[145] [Anonymous] *Denkschrift* (Stuttgart, 1831), pp. 6–11; [Reinwald] *Kurze Betrachtungen*, pp. 3–12; Scharrer, *op. cit.*, pp. 8–9; Friedrich Schmidt, *Unter welchen Bedingungen kann ein allgemeiner Zollverband allen deutschen Staaten nützlich seyn?* ... (Zittau, 1832), pp. 5–9.

Augsburger Allgemeine Zeitung attacked with bitter satire the obscure motivations of many a Zollverein opponent.[146] In particular, the moralists, the legalists, the smuggling interests, and all those who had a purely personal grievance were described. Exaggerated as such polemic writings were, they contained, nevertheless, a good deal of truth. There appeared among the pamphlets of these years a learned legalistic treatise which tried to show that the dissolution of the Empire had not given the various governments full control over their customs policies.[147] Another legalist claimed that the Zollverein transit tariffs were against international law and tried to make a more than subtle distinction between *Mauth* and *Zoll;* these two terms are synonyms for "customs duty" in German. He claimed that all *Mauth* should be abolished, while a *Zoll* might be restored.[148] The trading interests especially seem to have shared his condemnation of the transit tariffs.[149]

Even minor contemporary details did not escape misinterpretation. One pamphlet claimed that a Baden citizen paid on the average more customs duties than a Prussian one, because more articles were taxable under the Baden tariff.[150] He forgot to mention that Baden had maintained a low tariff for years in order to promote smuggling into neighboring states. Another commentator on contemporary institutions was not aware of the difference between a Zollanschluss and a customs union.[151] This period had also its share in fantastic schemes. Thus one writer suggested that the army of the Confederation should act as boundary patrol in a Confederate customs system. Not only was the author unaware of the problematical nature of this military establishment, but he proceeded naïvely to reason that such service would give the troops valuable experience.[152] In a way, this

---

[146] Müller, *op. cit.*, pp. 156–58.
[147] [Böhmer] *Das Zollwesen*, pp. 83–84.
[148] Hundeshagen, *op. cit.*, pp. 272, 231.
[149] *Hamburger Börsen-Halle* quoted by [Anonymous] *Untersuchung der Frage: "Ist es an der Zeit, und den allgemeinen Handels-Interessen Teutschlands angemessen, dass man dem Preussisch-Hessisch-Waldeckschen Zollverbande entgegenwirke . . ."* (Bremen, 1832), pp. 7–8.
[150] [Speyerer] *Die Frage*, p. 4. [151] [Bergius] *Betrachtungen*, p. 72.
[152] Lips, *Deutschlands*, pp. 552–54.

idea was not very bad, if one considers the regular war which was waged between smugglers and customs officials all over Germany. In a similar way, Amsberg, the leading states- man of the Duchy of Brunswick, solved within a single footnote the problem of Austria's and Prussia's participa- tion in a general German customs system.[153] He would have offered Austria and Prussia the choice of joining either a closer-knit or a more general union. His ideas had certain merits, but completely overlooked the political interest both powers had in German affairs. The loose thinking which was typical of the period expressed itself also in other ways. One pamphlet included an ardent appeal to all legalists to reform and become true Christians.[154]

The temper of the age can be well illustrated by the atti- tude many publicists showed toward smuggling. The an- archy the various customs systems had created in Germany resulted in a widespread circumvention of customs regula- tions. Many writers lamented the general decline of morality such a condition had brought over Germany;[155] but suggestions for remedying the situation varied. One writer saw the solution in increasing the penalties on smuggling,[156] while another believed that the Zollverein would rid the country of this nuisance.[157] Still another publicist con- demned smuggling very strongly, because it led the lower classes to lawlessness, but with the same breath he called customs officials a most detestable group of people.[158] Smuggling had taken such proportions in certain sections that the welfare of the population depended on it. For this reason a pro-Zollverein publicist assured his Saxon readers that the Zollverein would not interfere with their illegitimate trade with Austria.[159]

---

[153] Amsberg, op. cit., pp. 72–73.

[154] [Anonymous] Über Bayerns Mautsystem, Erörterung der Frage: Ist ein hoher Mauttarif eines Binnenlandes geeignet die Industrie desselben zu heben? (Nürnberg, 1831), p. 15.

[155] [Anonymous] Über den Anschluss (Freiburg, 1833), pp. 14–15; [Anonymous] Die Zollverhältnisse (Leipzig, 1830), pp. 42–43.

[156] [Anonymous] Einige Worte (München, 1830), pp. 127–28.

[157] [Anonymous] Einige Worte (Mainz, 1833), p. 38.

[158] [Anonymous] Über den Anschluss (Freiburg, 1833), pp. 14–15.

[159] Runde, op. cit., pp. 28–29.

Anti-Zollverein pamphlets tried to stir up the lower classes by claiming that the upper classes had designed the Zollverein in order to enrich themselves.[160] Such statements were denied by the defenders of the Zollverein, but the political danger which continued unrest would bring to Germany was understood by many contemporaries.[161]

These revolutionary tendencies had been furthered by the inefficiency and natural limitations of the various customs administrations. The complaints about the bureaucratic methods of the customs collectors were general and were shared by high and low.[162] It was in this matter that the work of the Prussian reformers stood its final test. There were not many complaints against the technical and administrative details of the Prussian Customs Law of 1818 and its application. Its merits, however, were widely recognized. Not only did pro-Zollverein writers point to the saving a Zollverein administered according to Prussian principles would bring to various member states,[163] but impartial observers paid homage to the fine qualities of the Prussian administration.[164] One Bavarian free trader went so far as to advocate the adoption of the Prussian principles by the Bavarian administration.[165]

The years from 1828 to 1833 saw a slow recovery of the publicly expressed thought from the blows it had received during the preceding decade from the reactionary forces. A new generation of publicists gradually tried to pick up where the older writers had left off. The artificial break which the reaction had brought about in the normal continuation of thought from 1819-20 on separated the old

---

[160] [Anonymous] *Einige Worte* (München, 1830), p. 56; [Anonymous] *Über den Anschluss* (Freiburg, 1833), pp. 11–12; Bab, *op. cit.*, pp. 82–83.

[161] *Ibid.*, pp. 39–40, 83–84; [Anonymous] *Einige Worte* (Main, 1833), pp. 42–44; Amsberg, *op. cit.*, p. 28.

[162] [Ignanz] Rudhart, *Rede des Abgeordneten Dr. Rudhart über den Gesetzesentwurf zu einer Zollordnung* . . . (Nürnberg [1828]), pp. 4, 7, 36, 40–41, 43; [Anonymous] *Denkschrift* ([Nuremberg] 1828), pp. 13–21; [Anonymous] *Was soll und was kann Deutschland in Beziehung auf seine Zoll- und Mauthverhältnisse?* (Kassel, 1830), pp. 36–38.

[163] [Anonymous] *Untersuchung* (Bremen, 1832), p. 21; [Cunow] *Sachsens*, pp. 9–10, 12; Raumer, *op. cit.*, pp. 11, 29–31.

[164] [Anonymous] *Denkschrift* ([Nuremberg] 1828), p. 21.

[165] Scharrer, *op. cit.*, p. 42.

thought from the new. The younger writers would rarely go back beyond 1815 in their reflections, while the few older ones still lived in the Empire. At the same time the expression of certain sequences of ideas was prohibited by force, and such measures tended to widen the gap between the conservative and the liberal elements. The fact that a large class did not participate in public affairs only increased the growth of theoretical knowledge which this age had been predisposed to enjoy. The lack of economic unity made it difficult for the average intellectual to think in terms of nation-wide economy. This theoretical side found its supplement in the old-fashioned administrative practices current in most of the small states and in the pettiness in outlook displayed by many officials of minor princes. A similar provincialism developed in political thought, as both conservative and liberal institutions consolidated themselves in the various territories. The widespread cosmopolitanism was in many instances caused by reactionary suppression of a normal national life, and for this reason was in a sense also provincial. The value of the Prussian reform of 1818 can be best appreciated if one keeps these ideological divisions in mind. This customs law established a system which used the best contemporary theories and practices it could find and combined them into a workable unit. The intellectual leaders of the nation were not apt to study the technicalities of such a customs system, as they also remained unaware of the solid thought the smaller governments had contributed during the South German conferences to the development of the institutional aspect of the Zollverein. The damage the reaction had done to a normal growth of public thought in Germany should not be underestimated. Many oddities of the period can be attributed to nothing but this large-scale perversion of the public mind. Although the few outstanding syntheses between necessity and theory, like the Prussian reform or the conception of a customs union, made the Zollverein possible, the desperate economic situation did its part in urging the governing classes into action. But the Zollverein did not end the political discord between reaction and popular movements, but economic unrest disappeared as a serious political factor for many years to come.

CHAPTER VIII

THE FOUNDING OF THE ZOLLVEREIN, 1828–34

GERMAN economic unification had made little visible progress during the decade which followed the Congress of Vienna. The South German conferences had failed to organize a regional union, and in the North, Prussia had seemingly obstructed general German unification by consolidating her fiscal system. Although the South German governments had not reached an agreement, their negotiations brought forth valuable ideas on economic unification among equal and independent states. It was here that the principles of a customs union were developed. The Prussian government, on the other hand, had done important groundwork through its customs reform of 1818. This reorganization provided Prussia with a well-integrated fiscal as well as commercial policy. The statesmen who founded the Zollverein relied on both the South German and the Prussian achievements. But they also contributed their own ideas. Details had to be worked out, and many political difficulties had to be overcome.

The history of the immediate origin of the Zollverein deals primarily with political and administrative problems, all of which were solved by the cabinets. The German people did not exercise any extensive influence on the events between 1825 and 1833 which led to the establishment of the Zollverein. The year 1825 witnessed the rise of two new men to responsible positions. Ludwig I succeeded to the Bavarian throne, and Friedrich von Motz became Prussian minister of finance. Both men changed the policies of their governments, with the effect that in 1828 Bavaria concluded a customs union with Württemberg and Prussia entered into a union with Hesse-Darmstadt. These successes of the second and third largest states led most Central German states to form a union against all customs unions. Their attempts did not, however, have the desired results, since

Bavaria and Prussia were drawn closer to each other and even allied themselves to fight the smaller states. This alliance led directly to the establishment of the Zollverein in 1834. Ludwig I and Motz were primarily responsible for uniting the North and the South. In the following sections of this chapter the events surrounding the foundation of the Zollverein between 1825 and 1833 will receive a critical discussion, and special emphasis will be laid upon the motivating ideas and the development of the administrative technicalities.

THE BAVARIA-WÜRTTEMBERG CUSTOMS UNION OF 1828

WHEN Ludwig I ascended the Bavarian throne in the fall of 1825 one of his first steps was to dismiss Rechberg, the minister of foreign affairs. Thus the latent conflict in the Bavarian government was ended. Moreover, Armansperg became minister of finance, and a serious effort was made to put the state finances on a sound basis.[1]

Ludwig I's reforms during the first year of his reign included a revision of the Bavarian customs tariff. Wilhelm I of Württemberg took this opportunity to ask for a better understanding in commercial matters,[2] a suggestion which was taken up by Ludwig.[3] The Württemberg government immediately sought to put the negotiations on a definite basis.[4] For a time Ludwig hesitated to establish a common customs system,[5] but finally approved of a plan after hearing the arguments of the new ministers, who recommended a common customs system not only for economic, but also for political reasons. Better relations with Württemberg were expected to follow, and it was hoped that this step would

---

[1] Doeberl, *Entwicklungsgeschichte*, III (1931), 11.

[2] Wilhelm I to Ludwig I, Stuttgart, December 23, 1826, Oncken and Saemisch, I, 522–23, No. 269.

[3] Ludwig I to Wilhelm I, München, December 29, 1826, *ibid.*, pp. 523–25, No. 270; Trautmannsdorff to Metternich, München, December 29, 1826, *ibid.*, pp. 525–27, No. 271.

[4] Schmitz-Grollenburg and Herzog to Bavarian Ministry of Foreign Affairs, München, January 18, 1827, *ibid.*, pp. 527–28, No. 272; Doeberl, *Bayern*, p. 26.   [5] *Ibid.*, p. 27.

make a favorable impression on public opinion.[6] Bavarian officials were looking forward to Bavaria leading the "purely German" states.[7] Once the negotiations were begun, an agreement was reached in short order.

The preliminary treaty of April 12, 1827, provided that both kingdoms should in the near future form a common customs system and that until then certain goods were to be introduced free of duty, while others were to pay a special low tariff. The new customs system was to be based on a draft which had been worked out during the Stuttgart Conferences.[8] The final negotiations abandoned the idea of a common customs system, and a customs union was concluded. This innovation apparently originated in the Bavarian Ministries of Finance and the Interior.[9] Such a modification was expected to prevent misunderstandings, simplify matters, and give due consideration to Württemberg's position as a sovereign state. The fact that Württemberg had been willing to base the common customs regulation and tariff on the Bavarian system had contributed to this change of position.[10]

Moreover, Württemberg was to have the same amount of influence in the customs union as Bavaria. Both had the same number of votes in the governing body of the union. The immediate history of this provision remains obscure. It is known that there was strong opposition in Bavarian government circles to all attempts to "mediatize" Württemberg.[11]

---

[6] Armansperg and Thürheim to Ludwig I, München, March 5, 1827, Oncken and Saemisch, I, 528–31, No. 273; Armansperg to Ludwig I, München, March 12, 1827, *ibid.*, pp. 531–34, No. 274.

[7] Treitschke, *Deutsche Geschichte*, III, 629.

[8] Bavaria-Württemberg negotiations, protocol, München, April 4, 1827, Oncken and Saemisch, I, 534–35, No. 275; draft of preliminary treaty [early April, 1827], *ibid.*, pp. 536–37, No. 276; treaty, München, April 12, 1827, Martens, *Nouveau recueil de traités*, VII (1829), 167–77, No. 39.

[9] Bavarian Ministries of the Interior and Finance to Ministry of Foreign Affairs, München, December 27, 1827, Oncken and Saemisch, I, 544–45, No. 280.

[10] Cf. treaty, München, April 12, 1827, Art. II, Martens, *Nouveau recueil de traités*, VII, 168, No. 39; Zentner and Armansperg to Ludwig I, München, January 17, 1828, Oncken and Saemisch, I, 548–49, No. 282.

[11] Cf. Zentner to Ludwig I, München, December 30, 1827, *ibid.*, p. 546, No. 281.

On the other hand, this parity did not constitute a complete break with the earlier basic draft and other attempts to establish a fixed ratio of votes for the member states, since it never had been maintained that one state should have an absolute majority, and since only a relative one had been considered.

The final treaty of January 18, 1828, contained a careful elaboration of the system by which the customs union was to operate. The Bavaria-Württemberg Customs Union included Württemberg, the Hohenzollern territories which had joined the Württemberg customs system previously, and Bavaria without the Palatinate. Moreover, all enclaves of the contracting parties lying outside this customs territory were to be excluded. The regular customs line along the Bavaria-Württemberg frontier was to be dissolved. Both states, however, retained all rights to protect their internal revenue laws along this border. Neither government was allowed to conclude separate commercial treaties with outsiders. But if it should grant privileges to other states, it had to reimburse the Customs Union for the losses incurred on account of such an agreement. The law, procedure, tariff, and administration of the Union were to be uniform and to be based on the existing Bavarian regulations. The net income was to be divided according to the proportions of the respective populations. This ratio was to be revised every three years in accordance with the results of the census.[12]

The customs administration of each state was to be directed by a separate, central, office (*Oberzoll-Administration*). Each government was to send a plenipotentiary to the central office of the other state. This official had to see all orders and regulations which were to be sent out to the offices in the field. No order was valid unless he had inspected it. He was not entitled, however, to veto measures he did not agree with, for he possessed only the right to protest. If his objections were not heeded, he could appeal to the annual congress of the Union. This representative had

---

[12] Treaty between Bavaria and Württemberg, München, January 18, 1828, Martens, *Nouveau recueil de traités*, VII, 529–46, No. 107; cf., in particular, Arts. II, III, IV, V, VI, VII, VIII, IX, XIV.

the right to inspect all documents, books, and accounts of the customs administration to which he was sent. He was allowed to delegate this authority. He also had the right to be present at all proceedings dealing with accounts (*Aufnahme der Zoll-Rechnungen*).[13]

Both governments agreed to issue all additional regulations jointly and uniformly except in case of emergency. Fundamental changes could be made only by the annual congress of the Union. Bavaria and Württemberg retained, however, the following rights. They were to publish the common regulations in their own territory in their own name, and to appoint the officials in their separate administration. These officials owed allegiance not only to their sovereigns but also to the Customs Union. A special oath was drafted for this purpose. These officials remained under the jurisdiction of the state which had appointed them. On the other hand, each government was to bear certain costs. It had to pay out of its own treasury all the expenses incurred by the central customs office in its state, all pensions and similar items of all the officials it had appointed, and the cost of maintaining all the buildings used by its administration. But all other regular salaries, office supplies, rents, travel allowances, fuel, and similar expenses were to be borne by the Customs Union. These costs were to be standardized.[14]

The main agency of the Union was the annual *General-Congress*. It was to meet every year on May 1 in Munich. Each government was to be represented by two plenipotentiaries, that is, a first and a second plenipotentiary. The chairmanship was to alternate annually between the two first plenipotentiaries. In case of a tie the chairman had the decisive vote. The representatives at the central state administrative offices were always to be appointed as the second plenipotentiaries. This congress had the right to change the fundamental laws of the Union, to conclude its accounts, and to set up the budget for the following year. Each member was bound by the instructions he had received from his government, and all decisions were subject to ratifi-

---

[13] *Ibid.*, Arts. X, XI.   [14] *Ibid.*, Arts. XIV, XV, XVII, XVIII.

cation by the governments. If the governments were not able to agree, or if there was a complaint against the central state offices, or if any temporary or administrative regulations were to be reviewed, the congress transformed itself into a board of arbitration through the coöption of three experts. In that case no member was bound by instructions. However, no fundamental law of the Union could be changed without the consent of all parties. Both governments reserved the right to call a special congress or to change existing arrangements through diplomatic negotiations.[15]

Each government had the right to terminate the agreement after three years. The Customs Union was to be superseded or amended if the German Confederation should set up a system of its own or introduce special provisions for the free trade with foodstuffs.[16]

These general provisions were supplemented by a number of special regulations. The ruling families and other privileged classes were obliged to pay customs duties like anybody else, but the individual governments were allowed to refund them. Each member state had also to pay indemnifications which had been granted to certain private persons for the condemnation of their rights to collect customs duties. Moreover, each state had to pay for all the exemptions and reductions it might grant in customs duties on certain goods. The Union, however, was to pay for the refunds of revenues collected from diplomatic representatives.[17]

A number of provisions endeavored to eliminate other trade restrictions. Tolls for roads and waterways were not to exceed certain maxima. The movement of goods and their sale were to be free. Nobody could be forced to offer his goods for sale nor could anyone interrupt their shipment. Tradesmen, however, remained subject to state regulations, but the governments were to favor each other as much as possible. The collection of internal revenue was not to interfere with free trade, and the commerce in

---

[15] *Ibid.*, Arts. XXXVI, XXXVII, XXXVIII, XXXIX.
[16] *Ibid.*, Art. XLI.   [17] *Ibid.*, Arts. XX, XXI, XXII, XXIII, XXIV.

transit was to be exempted completely. In all other respects the member states reserved their sovereign rights. They obliged themselves only to publish their internal revenue tariffs and to coöperate with each other on the maintenance of their systems. The trade in salt was subjected to a special regulation.[18]

Some minor administrative details were also settled by the treaty. A number of articles described the procedure for dissolving the Union and provided for a division of the joint obligations. The Bavarian standard of weight was to be the official one. All officials were to wear the insignia of the state that employed them. The seals for bonds were to bear on one side the coat of arms of the state whose official affixed it, together with the name of that particular office. The reverse was to have the current number and the inscription *Zoll-Verein*. A special clearance office for all customs invoices was to be established in Munich by both governments.[19]

The treaty set up a customs union or *Zoll-Verein*, as it was called in various articles.[20] The key to the working of this union was the position of the two representatives at the central offices. They were the links between the state administrations and the general congress, and between the governments. Their position was so strong because they knew all the business transacted in one administration and in the annual conferences. Their authority was based on personal contact rather than on official power. It is also interesting to note that these representatives were to start working three months before the Union was to commence.[21] Many articles in the treaty recognized the principle of equality between the member states. Each state had the right to veto all fundamental changes. The annual conference had

---

[18] *Ibid.*, Arts. XIX, XXV, XXVII, XXVIII, XXIX, XXX, XXXII, XXXIII, XXXIV, XXXV.

[19] *Ibid.*, Arts. XII, XLII, XLIII, XLV, XLVII, XLIX.

[20] The document must have been drafted rather hastily or carelessly, since Article I (*ibid.*) states that the two governments were to form a common customs system in accordance with the agreement dated Munich, April 12, 1827: "Die Königreiche Württemberg und Baiern vereinigen sich in Gemässheit des zu München unter dem 12. April abgeschlossenen Vertrags zu einem gemeinsamen Zoll-Systeme...."   [21] *Ibid.*, Art. XI.

the nature of a diplomatic congress in its legislative and administrative aspects, while it assumed the character of an international arbitration commission for its judicial functions. The treaty did not mention whether or in what manner the congress could conclude treaties with third parties. The agreement limited itself strictly to provisions which were necessary for a customs union. No attempt was made to extend it to similar and related fields of taxation or administration. Its technical elements were sound, and neither government was given much opportunity for abusing it. The treaty was so designed as to allow for the accession of six other states without making a change of the arrangement necessary. Each additional member was to have only one plenipotentiary at the annual conferences.[22] The obvious conclusion is that the Union was to be enlarged to include the medium and smaller states of Central and Southwestern Germany. However, Prussia and Austria could never have adhered to such a treaty. Probably for this reason the treaty did not aim at general German economic unification, but was intended to promote a regional agreement among the medium and smaller states under Bavaria-Württemberg leadership. While the negotiations were still pending, the Bavarian government had made serious efforts to gain the adherence of the Hesse-Darmstadt and the Hesse-Kassel governments.[23]

The union treaty was executed in various steps. Württemberg raised her tariffs on February 12, 1828, to the level of the Bavarian rates in order to prevent speculators from storing less highly taxed goods in her territories before the final introduction of the new system. The new Union had been scheduled to start July 1, 1828; but since the Bavarian Diet had not approved the Customs Union as soon as expected, on June 26, 1828, Württemberg had to introduce

---

[22] *Ibid.*, Arts. XXXVI, XXXVIII. Many of the provisions about the conduct of the annual conferences are not understandable unless one keeps in mind that they were designed to take care of a union with more than two governments.

[23] Ludwig I did not, according to Treitschke ("Die Anfänge," *Preussische Jahrbücher*, XXX [1872], 495–96), pursue an anti-Prussian policy, but desired to connect the leadership of the "purely German" states with a friendship with Prussia.

temporarily the Bavarian customs law and customs tariff. In both Bavaria and Württemberg the Union tariff and customs law were not promulgated until September 26, 1828, after the consent of the Bavarian Diet had been received.[24]

THE PRUSSIA-HESSE-DARMSTADT CUSTOMS UNION OF 1828

WHILE the first customs union treaty was being concluded in South Germany a similar development occurred in the North. The appointment of Friedrich von Motz as Prussian minister of finance (July 1, 1825) marked the beginning of a new era in Prussia's economic policy. Klewiz, his predecessor, had finally given up his attempts to balance the Prussian state budget and had asked to be relieved of his position.[25] Motz had worked himself up in the Prussian administration. He had been *Landrat* of a district in Central Germany, vice-president and president of the Prussian Government at Erfurt, and, finally, governor (*Ober-Präsident*) of the Province of Saxony. He was an expert administrator by training and experience, and anything but a bureaucrat. He had a practical conception of government matters, which is best illustrated by the long trip he took through the Prussian monarchy in order to acquaint himself better with his task as minister of finance.

Motz's first and main concern was to put the state finances on a sound basis. Prussia's financial situation was so bad in 1825 that the new minister did not dare to promise a surplus, because nobody believed such an achievement possible.[26] Unification and simplification of the fiscal administration were the means by which he was able not only to eliminate the deficit, but also to show a surplus within three years.[27]

---

[24] J. D. G. Memminger (ed.), *Württembergische Jahrbücher für vaterländische Geschichte, Geographie, Statistik und Topographie, Jahrgang 1827* (Stuttgart, 1829), Part I, pp. 129–30; customs regulation for the Bavaria-Württemberg Customs Union, Martens, *Nouveau recueil de traités*, VII, 703–731, No. 140; cf. Weber, *Der deutsche Zollverein*, p. 53, who states that these measures did not become operative until early 1829.

[25] Treitschke, *Deutsche Geschichte*, III, 453–55.

[26] *Ibid.*, p. 457.

[27] Heinrich von Treitschke, "Aus den Papieren des Staatsministers von Motz," *Preussische Jahrbücher*, XXXIX (1877), 406.

The dualism which had existed in the higher financial administration between the Ministry of Finance and the *General-Controlle* was abolished, and the minister of finance received full control of the state finances. The accounts (*Kassen*) were unified, and thus a survey of the actual financial state was made possible. Minor reforms were introduced in collection of indirect taxes, and great gains were made by clever handling of the money market. The personnel of the customs administration was improved. Motz was not the man to increase the revenues by a drastic reduction of the expenses or by a narrow fiscal interest in the immediate revenue. He was not disturbed when the collection fell off from taxes on liquor, since he welcomed its decreased use. He reinvested the surplus his tax administration yielded and started an extensive road-building program.[28]

Naturally, a man who showed his energy in so many different phases of his work would embark on a more determined customs policy. As a native of Hesse-Kassel Motz was well acquainted with the conditions of the smaller states. He had shown contempt for the sovereign aspirations of their princes.[29] He had realized very early the importance of a connection between the western and the eastern parts of Prussia and had submitted to the Berlin government a plan to effect this union.[30] During his Erfurt period he had a good opportunity to familiarize himself with the absurdities of the existing territorial divisions in Central Germany and to form his opinion accordingly.[31] After having been called to Berlin in 1825, Motz stiffened the attitude of the Prussian Ministry of Foreign Affairs toward the enclaves and used legal and extralegal means to end their existence as smuggling centers.[32]

---

[28] Petersdorff, *Friedrich von Motz*, II, 5–12, 15–20, 69–71, 76–78; Treitschke, *Deutsche Geschichte*, III, 464.

[29] Motz to Elector Wilhelm I of Hesse-Kassel, Erfurt, January 22, 1821, *ibid.*, pp. 771–773, No. 14; Petersdorff, *op. cit.*, II, 88–89.

[30] *Ibid.*, I, 67–86.

[31] *Ibid.*, II, 106; Treitschke, *Deutsche Geschichte*, III, 456–57.

[32] Petersdorff, *op. cit.*, II, 88–107; Motz to Bernstorff, Berlin, February 4, 1825, Oncken and Saemisch, I, 230, No. 108; Motz to Bernstorff, Berlin, July 24, 1825, *ibid.*, pp. 233–34, No. 112; Motz to Bernstorff, Berlin, October 24, 1825, *ibid.*, pp. 237–38, No. 115; *ibid.*, p. 239, footnote 1; Menn, *Zur Vorgeschichte*, p. 149.

The Prussian customs policy toward the medium states did not undergo such a marked change during the first period of Motz's administration.   Years before he had recognized the geographical factors affecting the execution of the Tariff Law of 1818.   At that time he had been afraid that the law was premature, because Prussia's trade between the two main sections of the monarchy remained subject to the tax sovereignty of the intermediary states.[33] In 1822 he had advocated that all Thuringian states should, instead of forming a separate union, join the Prussian customs system.[34]   In 1825 Motz was thus predisposed to consider favorably an expansion of Prussia's tariff system so as to allow the union of the whole monarchy within one customs boundary.   For the time being, however, he retained the traditional reserve of his predecessor on this subject.

The initiative had to come from without, and it came from that capital, Darmstadt, which had been the scene of a most important conference for South German economic unification.   It might seem more than paradoxical that the Darmstadt government was to be the first to enter into a customs union with Prussia. In 1819–20 Hesse-Darmstadt had participated in the negotiations for free trade and subsequently in those for a separate South German union.   It had known the anti-Prussian character of this movement, and it played such a leading part in these developments that for years to come it was to be credited with having originated them.   Darmstadt was for a long period the meeting place for the conferences dealing with a South German union. Moreover, the Hesse-Darmstadt government had contributed the idea of a separate administration to these negotiations as a bulwark against any *capitis deminutio* of the smaller states.   It is even more amazing that the same du Thil who stood for free trade in Vienna and the same Hofmann who insisted on a customs union were to take charge of the negotiations with Prussia.

A closer examination will show that neither du Thil nor Hofmann was a political adventurer; on the contrary, both

---

[33] Motz to Otterstedt, March 16, 1819, Brinkmann, *Die preussische Handelspolitik*, p. 120.   [34] Petersdorff, *op. cit.*, II, 106.

were capable administrators. They had maintained a clean record during the South German negotiations. They had not entertained ulterior political ambitions and had held themselves aloof from trialistic or reactionary intrigues. They were not dominated by their personal feelings, like a Nebenius, nor did they adhere to a fanatical political or economic doctrine. They were practical statesmen who concentrated on major issues. They had introduced a system of boundary customs into the grand duchy when circumstances made it necessary. They had a clear insight into the interest of the state, and it was such self-analysis which produced Hofmann's customs union program. Hesse-Darmstadt's geographical position tied her interests very closely to those of Baden, Nassau, and Hesse-Kassel. Her economic interests pointed north. Under such circumstances an economic union with Bavaria and Württemberg alone was not advisable. The Darmstadt officials were fully aware of the situation, and when Baden, Nassau, and Hesse-Kassel refused to join a South German union, Hesse-Darmstadt was in no position to continue negotiations with the South German kingdoms.[35] Darmstadt insisted on an extension of the agreement to neighboring territories along the Rhine or on an understanding with Prussia as the conditions of her participation in a South German union.[36] For these reasons the grand duchy dropped out of the South German negotiations, although there had been a genuine desire in Darmstadt to effect such a regional union.

Primarily for political reasons, her relations with Baden, Nassau, and Hesse-Kassel had reached a low ebb at about the same time, which made a separate *rapprochement* of these states more than unlikely.[37] The first step taken in this direction had been a complete failure when Baden and Hesse-Darmstadt ended their ill-advised experiment of eco-

---

[35] Hofmann to ZuRhein, Darmstadt, August 24, 1825, Oncken and Saemisch, I, 515–17, No. 265; Baden declaration, Stuttgart, July 4, 1825, *ibid.*, p. 509, No. 259; Roentgen to Nebenius, Stuttgart, July 6, 1825, *ibid.*, p. 510, No. 260; Stuttgart Conferences, tenth session, August 6, 1825, *ibid.*, pp. 513–14, No. 263; Maltzan to Bernstorff, Darmstadt, June 23, 1825, *ibid.*, II, 100–1, No. 324.

[36] Hofmann to ZuRhein, Darmstadt, August 24, 1825, *ibid.*, I, 515–17, No. 265.   [37] Cf. Menn, *op. cit.*, pp. 137–39.

nomic coöperation. This agreement of September 8, 1824, had called for a system of mutual preference, based on certificates of origin, although both governments had been aware that such a plan was not the final solution.[38] The system did not work, and the Darmstadt government charged that Baden had abused it by issuing fraudulent certificates of origin.[39] Hesse-Darmstadt therefore gave notice of termination on October 31, 1825, a little over a year after the agreement had been concluded, and thus ended the experiment.[40]

Finally, the constant decline of Hesse-Darmstadt's economic strength made the abandonment of her isolation policy more and more urgent. The introduction of a boundary tariff system had not helped to alleviate her straits, business continued to decline, and costs of maintaining the customs line absorbed a large percentage of the revenue collected.[41] Smuggling began to flourish and to compete seriously with legitimate trade. These hopeless conditions were in the final analysis responsible for du Thil's change of policy.[42]

In the summer of 1825 Hofmann and du Thil approached the Prussian minister in Darmstadt with an inquiry whether Prussia would be inclined to consider the negotiation of an economic agreement. They suggested a commercial treaty as the least difficult solution and a customs union as a second choice. They also offered their good services to persuade Hesse-Kassel to join the negotiations.[43] The Prussian Minis-

---

[38] Treaty, Carlsruhe, September 8, 1824, Martens, Nouveau recueil de traités, VI (1828), 575–87, No. 120; supplementary convention, November 22, 1824, ibid., pp. 656–57, No. 129.

[39] H. Schmidt, Die Begründung, p. 15; Lerchenfeld to Ludwig I, Frankfurt, July 23, 1827, Oncken and Saemisch, I, 541, No. 278.

[40] Dated Darmstadt, October 31, 1825, Martens, Nouveau recueil de traités, VI [8]24, No. 163.

[41] Christian Eckert, "Zur Vorgeschichte des deutschen Zollvereins. Die preussisch-hessische Zollunion vom 14. Februar 1828," Schmoller's Jahrbuch für Gesetzgebung, Verwaltung und Volkswirtschaft im Deutschen Reich, XXVI (1902), Part II, 58–59.

[42] Eisenhart Rothe, in Oncken and Saemisch, II, 12; Lerchenfeld to Ludwig I, Frankfurt, July 23, 1827, ibid., I, 540–43, No. 278; Treitschke, Deutsche Geschichte, III, 629–30.

[43] Maltzan to Bernstorff, Darmstadt, June 23, 1825, Oncken and Saemisch, II, 100–2, No. 324; Maltzan to Bernstorff, Darmstadt, July 20, 1825, ibid., pp. 102–3, No. 326.

try of Foreign Affairs was willing to look into the matter, especially if Electoral Hesse would be included in the agreement. It accepted du Thil's offer to sound out the Kassel government, although it doubted the success of such an action. The Berlin Foreign Office was guided by a desire not to offend the good will of a German neighbor. At that time it pursued the policy which had been outlined in the memorandum of the previous year and which called for a possible program by unifying the Prussian monarchy economically by an agreement with Central and Southwestern German governments.[44] When Hesse-Kassel refused du Thil's offer to participate,[45] Bernstorff consulted Motz, who was of the opinion that an agreement with Hesse-Darmstadt alone was of no particular value, but that her government should be given an opportunity to show the merits of her plan.[46] The Prussian Foreign Office therefore did not press the matter any further, and the negotiations came to a standstill.[47]

The history of these first Hesse-Darmstadt attempts to reach an agreement with Prussia shows that the Prussian government still held the same position in 1825 and 1826 it had adopted in 1824 and that it did not even take the trouble to reëxamine its policy. It is also significant for the reserve exercised by Prussia in her pursuit of this policy that both du Thil and Hofmann had serious doubts whether the Prussian government would be willing to consider their offer. When Maltzan, the Prussian minister in Darmstadt, told these two Hessian officials that their doubts were without foundation, a most significant scene occurred. Both du Thil and Hofmann freely showed their happy feelings, while Maltzan in turn was very much surprised about this sudden

[44] Prussian Ministry of Foreign Affairs to Maltzan, Berlin, July 5, 1825, ibid., p. 102, No. 325; Prussian Ministry of Foreign Affairs to Maltzan, Berlin, August 6, 1825, ibid., pp. 104–5, No. 327; cf. Prussian Ministry of Finance, memorandum, Berlin, December 28, 1824, ibid., p. 88, No. 321.

[45] Meyerfeld to du Thil, Frankfurt, January 27, 1826, ibid., p. 109, No. 331.

[46] Schuckmann and Motz to Prussian Ministry of Foreign Affairs, Berlin, March 25, 1826, ibid., pp. 111–12, No. 333.

[47] Prussian Ministry of Foreign Affairs to Maltzan, Berlin, April 16, 1826, ibid., p. 112, No. 334.

outburst, realizing that they had actually been ignorant of this aspect of Prussian policy.[48]

There was undoubtedly no direct economic or fiscal gain for Prussia in a commercial treaty or a customs union with Hesse-Darmstadt. The indifference she showed in 1825-26 to the Hesse-Darmstadt proposals, is, therefore, only too understandable. When, however, the Prussian government was approached again in 1827, it was able to take a broader view and to give a different answer.

Here again it was Hesse which took the initiative,[49] but this time du Thil had spent more thought on the possibilities of a commercial alliance with Prussia. There was no question in his mind about the economic advantage of such an agreement for Hesse-Darmstadt.[50] The fundamental problem for du Thil lay in the political implications of his step.[51] Until then Hesse-Darmstadt had maintained excellent relations with Austria, and du Thil's main worry was how Metternich would receive an economic alliance of the grand duchy with Prussia. Austria had always been hostile to a South German union because of the political aspirations behind this movement. Stuttgart and Munich were suspected not only of liberalism and of obstructing the Powers, but also of intrigues with France. Metternich was not opposed to a customs union between Hesse-Darmstadt and her neighbors in Southwestern Germany; but attempts in that direction had failed completely.[52] Du Thil therefore concluded that, if he should be able to reach an agreement with Prussia, he would then have effectively stopped the further extension of the South German union. But if his negotiations with Prus-

---

[48] Maltzan to Prussian Ministry of Foreign Affairs, Darmstadt, July 20, 1825, *ibid.*, p. 103, No. 326.

[49] It is not certain whether du Thil approached Bernstorff by correspondence before getting in touch with Maltzan in Darmstadt; cf. Eisenhart Rothe in *ibid.*, p. 12, n. 2.

[50] Du Thil, memorandum, Darmstadt, August 16, 1827, *ibid.*, p. 123, No. 341.

[51] For the following discussion see Grolmann to du Thil, Darmstadt, August 13, 1827, *ibid.*, pp. 121-22, No. 340; du Thil, memorandum, Darmstadt, August 16, 1827, *ibid.*, pp. 122-27, No. 341.

[52] It seems interesting to reflect to what extent Austria's anti-South German pressure was contributory to the Heidelberg Protocol and, later, to the foundation of the Prusso-Hessian Customs Union.

sia failed, his very attempt would give him a clean bill so as to enable him to join Bavaria and Württemberg without being subjected to the same odium as the other participants. Moreover, as long as Prussia and Austria maintained their entente, Austria could not complain about a Prusso-Hessian economic alliance. Although du Thil stated that Austria's attitude toward the grand duchy would not change, he nevertheless did not want this theory confirmed through an inquiry in Vienna; he certainly realized that Prusso-Hessian relations would become closer.

Du Thil's arguments to justify such an alliance with Prussia were very ingenious. He admitted that all small states had to rely on other states and that they were wiser to ally oneself with a strong power than with a number of minor states, which were likely to overplay their hand in the diplomatic game. He pointed out, moreover, that the political consequences of an economic union with Bavaria and Württemberg were not necessarily advantageous. Although it is not quite clear whether he subscribed completely to the Austrian viewpoint of these South German aspirations, he certainly regarded the Prussian danger as the smaller evil. He was aware of the general opinion of Prussia's ambitions, but discounted their importance. First of all, he felt assured that Hesse-Darmstadt would be able to maintain her independence against Prussian political pressure. The commercial alliance could be dissolved at any time. In the event of a Prusso-Hessian war the grand duchy would be no worse off than without such an agreement. On the other hand, there was every reason to believe that Prussia would develop a thoroughly friendly attitude toward Hesse-Darmstadt. The Berlin government would appreciate such a diplomatic conquest, take interest in the grand duchy, have its ambitions in that direction satisfied, and even be willing to pay for the political gain through economic concessions. Moreover, there was a decided advantage in being the first government to join the Prussian economic system this way.

The change in policy was actually greater than du Thil wished to admit. Both Nassau and Baden had turned away from the South German political tendencies, but both had remained in the Austrian camp. The Darmstadt government, however, shifted its policy toward Prussia, without necessarily breaking with Austria or making a *rapproche-ment* with South Germany impossible. It seems to have done so, because it believed that in the long run Prussia's leadership would be the more intelligent and that her actual direction of German affairs would completely supersede Austria's formal presidency.[53]

Du Thil, however, in approaching the Prussian government, made no mention of these political considerations and believed that Prussia had enough delicacy not to bring them up either.

When du Thil proposed to negotiate a commercial agreement, he discussed two different types. On the one hand, Hesse-Darmstadt could join the Prussian customs system the same way the enclaves had done; on the other hand, both states could enter an arrangement which would lower the tariffs and still give each a separate administration. The first plan would have meant the Zollanschluss of Hesse-Darmstadt, and was not regarded as feasible by du Thil, since it was against the policy of both Prussia and Hesse-Darmstadt.[54]

Du Thil no longer suggested a choice between a customs union and a treaty of commerce, as he had done in 1825, but proposed a hybrid institution, which apparently was neither a customs union nor a simple commercial treaty.[55] The possibility of a Zollanschluss was only mentioned, to be immediately refuted.

While du Thil's chief proposals remained vague, his

---

[53] "Die Bemerkung, die in dem Schreiben gemacht wird, dass wenige Ereignisse vielleicht hinreichen dürften, um das reelle Präsidium von dem formellen zu trennen und die Leitung der deutschen Angelegenheiten dahin zu übertragen, wo sich die grösste Intelligenz nach einer temporären Abwesenheit vielleicht wieder einfinden würde, hat sehr viel Wahrscheinliches für sich . . . ." Du Thil, memorandum, Darmstadt, August 16, 1827, *ibid.*, p. 125, No. 341; the *Schreiben* referred to in this passage is not identified; cf. Grolmann to du Thil, Darmstadt, August 13, 1827, *ibid.*, p. 121, No. 340.

[54] Maltzan to Prussian Ministry of Foreign Affairs, Darmstadt, August 29, 1827, *ibid.*, p. 128, No. 342.

[55] Du Thil is not at all explicit about this second scheme. The lowering of tariffs seems to indicate that it was not going to do away with customs completely. The fact that each government was to retain its own administration seems to indicate that he had something more than a commercial treaty in mind. If he had wanted a commercial treaty, he would not have needed to mention a separate administration.

technical diplomatic suggestions were very concrete. He refused to be asked again to gain Hesse-Kassel's coöperation, since he saw no hope for success in such a move; but he inquired formally whether a representative duly authorized to negotiate a commercial agreement would be welcome in Berlin and whether such a mission could be kept secret.[56]

The Prussian Foreign Office wanted to accept this offer for political reasons, although it was undecided on the economic factors involved.[57]   It therefore asked for the opinion of the financial authorities on this matter.[58]   Since Motz was away from Berlin, Maassen, the general tax administrator, took care of the inquiry. First of all, he referred to the memorandum of December 28, 1824, as the fundamental exposition of this problem. While du Thil had only pointed to the impossibility of a Zollanschluss of Hesse-Darmstadt for political reasons, Maassen went further by erroneously interpreting him as refusing any extension of the Prussian customs line. Du Thil had not closed the door to negotiating a customs union, regardless of how ambiguous some of his terms might have been. The obvious conclusion is that Maassen was unaware at that time of the difference between a customs union and a Zollanschluss. Anyway he was opposed not only for political reasons, but also because of the geographical situation of the grand duchy. Maassen was not averse, however, to attempts to negotiate a treaty of commerce, because the Prussian enclave of Wetzlar was partially dependent on Hesse-Darmstadt and because the grand duchy might become a market for Prussian industrial products.[59]

The Prussian Foreign Office acted accordingly and declared that it would welcome a Hessian representative in Berlin and agreed to keep this mission secret.[60]

It was not until December, 1827, that Hofmann was able

---

[56] Maltzan to Prussian Ministry of Foreign Affairs, Darmstadt, August 29, 1827, Oncken and Saemisch, II, 128–29, No. 342.

[57] Eichhorn to Maassen, September 7, 1827, ibid., p. 129 f., n. 1.

[58] Loc. cit.

[59] Maassen to Prussian Ministry of Foreign Affairs, Berlin, September 9, 1827, ibid., pp. 133–34, No. 344.

[60] Prussian Ministry of Foreign Affairs to Maltzan, Berlin, September 13, 1827, ibid., pp. 134–35, No. 345.

to go to Berlin as the Hessian negotiator. In the meantime
both sides made preparations. Du Thil elaborated the instructions for Hofmann, which reverted to the dual proposal
of 1825, of concluding either a customs union or a treaty of
commerce. Du Thil assumed that Prussia would distrust
a customs union and therefore gave only detailed instructions for the commercial treaty. Hofmann was instructed
to accept the Zollanschluss of the Prussian Wetzlar district
into the Hessian system and to leave the grand duchy at
liberty to join a South German union, if nothing more than a
treaty of commerce was concluded.[61]   Du Thil had previously
demonstrated the serious intentions expressed in these instructions when he intervened in Kassel and prevented the
Elector from joining the South German system.[62]   On the
other hand, he informed Metternich about the impending
negotiations.[63]

The Prussian Foreign Office in the meantime collected
information on the economic condition of Hesse-Darmstadt[64]
and also informed Motz about the state of negotiations.[65]   It
remains obscure why and when Motz changed his policy and
began to strive actively for a customs union with Central
German states. It is well established that, when Hofmann
made his first call on Motz on January 3, 1828, Motz took
the initiative and suggested a customs union with Hesse-
Darmstadt, after stating that a treaty of commerce would be
only a partial solution.[66]   But this was not the first attempt
of its kind. Early in October, 1827, he had tried to persuade
Saxe-Weimar to form a customs union with Prussia.[67]   The

---

[61] Instruction for Hofmann, Darmstadt, December, 1827, *ibid.*, pp. 145–
52, No. 356.

[62] On Wittgenstein's mission see Maltzan to Prussian Ministry of Foreign
Affairs, Darmstadt, October 1, 1827, *ibid.*, pp. 137–38, No. 347; Maltzan
to Prussian Ministry of Foreign Affairs, Darmstadt, October 29, 1827, *ibid.*,
p. 139, No. 349.

[63] Du Thil to Metternich, Darmstadt, December 31, 1827, *ibid.*, pp.
153–55, No. 358.

[64] Maltzan, memorandum, November, 1827, *ibid.*, pp. 139–41, No. 350.

[65] Prussian Ministry of Foreign Affairs to Motz, Berlin, October 12, 1827,
ibid., p. 138, No. 348.   [66] Hofmann's diary, *ibid.*, p. 160, No. 361.

[67] Petersdorff, *op. cit.*, II, 142; Karl August declined the Prussian offer
on October 15, 1827, because he did not want to take such a step without
the other Thuringian governments or without Hesse-Kassel. The documents
of this episode are not reprinted, and very little is known about it.

question about the date and cause of this change of mind remains unsettled. It is possible that Maassen informed him about the Hessian overture after his return to Berlin and that the change occurred some time in September or early in October.[68] But there is no evidence to suggest such a conjecture, and Motz might have adopted the new policy earlier.

Whatever the cause and the date of this change may have been, certainly by January, 1828, Motz had developed a plan for Prussian economic expansion. Hesse-Darmstadt was going to be one link in this chain. Motz counted on Hesse-Kassel's adhesion to the new customs system and told Hofmann that he foresaw Hesse-Darmstadt's free access to Prussia's Baltic Sea ports.[69] Moreover, Motz was offering the grand duchy a considerable increase in revenue if she joined the Prussian system.[70] He was figuring that Prussia would not gain by a treaty of commerce with Hesse-Darmstadt, but that a customs unification would pay in the long run.[71] Such an agreement would also have some very desirable political effects for Prussia. It would put in a better light her fiscal policy, which had received such a bad reputation through the Anhalt-Köthen feud, and would show that the Prussian government was able to distinguish between enclaves and neighboring territories and that the latter could join the Prussian system without having to fear for their independence.[72]

---

[68] It seems unlikely that this was caused by Prussian Ministry of Foreign Affairs to Motz, Berlin, October 12 (Oncken and Saemisch, II, 138, No. 348), because this is too close to Karl August's answer of October 15, 1827 (Petersdorff, *op. cit.*, II, 142).

[69] Hofmann's diary, Oncken and Saemisch, II, 162, No. 361.

[70] *Ibid.*, pp. 160–61.

[71] *Ibid.*, pp. 161–62; Motz to Prussian Ministry of Foreign Affairs, Berlin, January 4, 1828, as interpreted by Eckert, "Zur Vorgeschichte des Zollvereins," Schmoller's *Jahrbuch*, XXVI, Part I, 82.

[72] "Das Aufsehen, welches der Streit mit Anhalt-Köthen errege, bestimme Preussen, der Welt zu zeigen, dass es in Handelssachen zwichen enklavierten und angrenzenden Staaten zu unterscheiden wisse, und dass letztere sich ohne alle Gefahr für ihre Selbständigkeit in Verbindungen mit Preussen einlassen könnten." Hofmann's diary, Oncken and Saemisch, II, 176, No. 367. Note that Motz distinguished erroneously between enclaves and neighboring territories; the difference in status was really determined by size. Thus the small Upper Duchy of Anhalt-Bernburg, which was not enclaved by Prussia, had joined the Prussian system under an Anschluss agreement.

This motivation should show, if anything, how slight was the connection which existed between the Zollanschluss development and this new direction of Prussian policy and how revolutionary Motz's change was.   Motz was able to follow this policy because his fiscal administration had yielded a surplus.

The technical workings of Motz's proposed union remained rather vague. He was not opposed in principle to the Hessian demands for equality and separate administration, but seems to have favored a common and joint customs direction for the grand duchy and the Prussian Rhine Province.   Once an agreement had been reached on the essential points, he was willing to give in on matters of form. He also denied having any intention of presenting "improper demands," i.e. demands affecting the sovereignty of the grand duchy, to Hesse-Darmstadt.[73]

The importance of Motz's step lies in the fact that finally a Prussian statesman tried to combine the monarchy's foreign and fiscal policy, which until then had remained at odds with each other.   His offer to Hofmann had been more than a political gesture of good will, which had been the main objective of the Prussian Foreign Office; it had been a part of a general, although somewhat vague, plan of economic policy. He should be credited with the coördination of Prussian policy.   This, however, did not give him any claim of priority over Hesse-Darmstadt's similar suggestion, which had not been pushed on that occasion, probably owing to the negative response received previously.

It is in keeping with this picture that it was not Motz but Hofmann who elaborated the basic principles for the negotiations.[74]   This draft provided for a customs union in which both parties would be equal as a matter of principle and in which the smaller Hesse-Darmstadt would receive her due share of influence.   Some consideration was given to Prus-

---

[73] Hofmann's diary, *ibid.*, pp. 160–61, No. 361.

[74] Hofmann, in writing his memoir on a customs union (*ibid.*, pp. 168–72, No. 365), took a defensive position in many matters in which he feared Prussian claims.   It was for this reason that he frequently stated Hesse-Darmstadt's rights when he really meant both parties to exercise such rights in their respective spheres.

sia's preponderant interests.   Hesse-Darmstadt was to adopt
the Prussian customs law and customs tariffs and organize
her customs administration according to the Prussian pattern.
The other suggestions followed more strictly the principles
of equality characteristic of a customs union.   Thus all legislative changes had to be approved and introduced by both
parties.   The customs organization of the grand duchy was
to be administered by a board (*Direktion*) to be located in
Darmstadt.   This board was to have purely executive functions and was to consist of three members, two of whom were
to be appointed by Hesse-Darmstadt and one by Prussia.   In
a similar way Hesse-Darmstadt was to appoint one of the
members of the Prussian Provincial Customs Board at Cologne.   Both boards were to keep in touch with each other
to insure uniformity.   All appeals were to be taken from
these boards to the central governments; in issues arising in
the grand duchy, to the Ministry of Finance at Darmstadt,
which had the right to make temporary decisions in doubtful
cases.   All real difficulties were to be ironed out by a conference of plenipotentiaries, two from each state.   These
representatives were to meet once a year to divide the income, settle the accounts, and straighten out difficulties
which came to their attention.   The contracting parties were
to exchange information about their accounts every month
and divide the net income once a year in proportion to their
populations.   The revenues went temporarily into the exchequer of the collecting state, subject to the adjustments
of the final annual settlement.   The regular current expenses
of the customs administration were to be pooled and deducted from the total revenue.   Pensions, however, were
not to be chargeable to the union.   Each government was to
pay for any damage done to the union through the neglect
or gross inefficiency of its officials.   Each party was entitled
to check the customs administration of the other government
through its own officials.   Both governments were to audit
each other's records on the collection of customs revenue,
but Hesse-Darmstadt was to adopt the Prussian auditing procedure.   The regular Hessian courts were to retain jurisdiction over defraudations committed in the grand duchy.[75]

---

[75] In accordance with the Hessian constitution.

Each government was to have the right of pardoning offenses against the revenue law,[76] and all fines were to go to the party imposing them. Hesse-Darmstadt was to participate "somehow"[77] in Prussian commercial treaties, and special provisions were to be made to suit local conditions in the grand duchy. A special arrangement was to be made for the Prussian district of Wetzlar. The collection of other revenue, such as consumption taxes, was not to be affected by the agreement, and each government was to retain the right of using customs officials for this purpose.

The only instructions Hofmann had received in case the question of customs unification was raised consisted of a general insistence on a separate administration, that is, a customs union.[78] Hofmann's outline of such a union was apparently drawn up by him after his first interview with Motz. Hofmann did not follow any ready-made plan or earlier pattern, but combined the principles of Hesse-Darmstadt's policy and his own experience with the Prussian demands into a new and specific plan for a customs union with Prussia. His suggestions bore rather the nature of his private opinion than of a formal draft, and they lacked all technical rigidity or legalistic formalism. They were, nevertheless, well thought out and were free from inconsistencies. Without pressing any point unduly, they represented a rare unity of purpose and thought.

The main thesis of Hofmann's outline, that of a customs union, went back to the Heidelberg Protocol of 1824 and, more specifically, to the instruction he received for his Berlin mission. The advantages of such a union were argued by him in the introductory paragraphs of his outline.[79] He tried to show how it would be impossible to divide administrative functions, such as the appointment of officials, proportionally in a common customs administration. This point was not directed entirely against the Prussian suggestions, for it referred to the Bavarian scheme of 1825.[80]

Hofmann, however, recognized that the relative small-

---

[76] Notices of all pardons were to be communicated to the other party in order to avoid abuses.   [77] "In irgendeiner Form."
[78] Hofmann's instructions, Darmstadt, December, 1827, *ibid.*, p. 146, No. 356.   [79] Dated January, 1828, *ibid.*, pp. 168–69, No. 365.
[80] Cf. basic draft, Stuttgart, February 16, 1825, *ibid.*, I, 486–87, No. 248.

ness of Hesse-Darmstadt in comparison with Prussia made impossible a logical extension of this doctrine of equality to all parts of the agreement.   He therefore conceded in principle the adoption of the Prussian customs law and administrative practice by the grand duchy.   Even though he tried to fulfill Prussian desires with this and other suggestions vital to Prussian fiscal interests, he insisted on all those provisions which would secure Hesse-Darmstadt's independence and sovereignty.   He might have been influenced in this attitude by Motz's general remarks; there seems to be no doubt that the idea of mixed regional boards was elaborated from the suggestion made by Motz at their first meeting.   Motz had suggested at that time that Hesse-Darmstadt should appoint a minority member to the Provincial Customs Board at Cologne.   Hofmann took this idea of a minority member and extended it to the board at Darmstadt, on whose creation he insisted, by giving Prussia the same rights she had offered the grand duchy in relation to the Cologne board.

The majority of the technical provisions can be traced back to earlier suggestions and practices.   The idea that the regional administrative office should have executive functions only had been elaborated during the South German negotiations by the smaller governments as a compromise solution to preserve the essential principles of the Heidelberg Protocol.[81]   The idea of yearly conferences, of the appointment of officials by each party to check the administration of the other party, and of the right of each government to pardon or commute sentences arising within its jurisdiction, originated also during the South German conferences and in part had been favorite ideas of Hofmann's.[82]   The Bavaria-Württemberg preliminary treaty of 1827 had declared that Württemberg was to adopt the Bavarian customs law and regulations.[83]   It is not certain whether the corresponding

---

[81] ZuRhein to Max I, Stuttgart,.May 16, 1825, *ibid.*, p. 505, No. 255.

[82] On the yearly conferences cf., e.g., basic draft, Stuttgart, February 16, 1825, *ibid.*, p. 489, No. 248; on the mutual checking system cf., e.g., ZuRhein to Max I, Stuttgart, March 11, 1825, *ibid.*, p. 495, No. 251; on the right to pardon cf., e.g., Hofmann to ZuRhein, Stuttgart, May 20, 1825, *ibid.*, p. 507, No. 256.

[83] Dated München, April 12, 1827, Art. II, Martens, *Nouveau recueil de traités*, VII, 168, No. 39.

proposal in Hofmann's outline was taken from this treaty or from earlier Prussian Anschluss treaties. Possibly, it was taken from both sources or from neither.

Hofmann seems to have adapted himself to Prussian practice and taken over certain elements from the Anschluss treaties. The peculiar system by which all revenue collected was immediately transferred into the treasuries of both parties, subject to certain modifications, was first developed in the Zollanschluss of the Upper Duchy of Anhalt-Bernburg.[84] This same agreement was also the first to grant the smaller territory the right to withhold its consent from fundamental changes on the Prussian customs law.[85] Both of these provisions can be found again in Hofmann's draft in a more developed stage, since Hofmann applied the principle of equality to them. Thus both governments were to retain the amounts collected, subject only to the final settlement of distribution, and both were to have the same degree of influence on future legislation of the union.

Hofmann, however, contributed some new ideas. The plan of informing each other of all pardons and commutations of penalties imposed in accordance with the customs law cannot be found in any of the previous schemes.

Until then the Anschluss treaties and unification proposals had contained a general clause stipulating mutual support of the common customs law. Hofmann injected a concrete element into this idea when he suggested that each government should be financially responsible for all losses incurred through the defects in its own administration.[85a]

Hofmann's memorandum served as basis for his subsequent conferences with the Prussian representatives. The negotiations proceeded rather rapidly, although some minor provisions of the treaty had to be changed after it had been signed. Hofmann was more and more successful in his ef-

---

[84] Treaty, Berlin, October 10, 1823, Art. XVI, [Prussia] *Gesetz-Sammlung* 1824, No. 1 (January 5), pp. 1–9, No. 837.

[85] *Ibid.*, Art. I. Hofmann refers nowhere directly to this treaty, although he undoubtedly must have known of it. It should, however, be noted that du Thil referred to it directly (Du Thil to Hofmann, Darmstadt, January 29, 1828, Oncken and Saemisch, II, 190, No. 375).

[85a] Hofmann suggested this scheme as early as 1824; cf. *supra*, p. 98.

forts to convince the Prussian government of the desirability
of a separate administration for Hesse-Darmstadt.[86] As a
whole, the memorandum was received favorably by Motz
and his assistants. The main objection was raised against
the necessity for Hessian consent for all legislative changes.[87]
However, both parties were able to work out a new formula
which was to be attached in a secret article to the treaty.
Hesse-Darmstadt was to give her consent to all changes be-
forehand, except raises in tariff and fundamental changes.
In a similar way the problem of commercial treaties was to
be settled in a secret clause. Moreover, Prussia demanded
that if Wetzlar joined the Hessian customs administration,
Hesse-Darmstadt territories which were in a similar position
in relation to Prussia were to be included in the Prussian system. Motz also demanded that, if a separate regional office
was to be created at Darmstadt, it should be audited by the
Prussian office at Cologne. Major difficulties presented
themselves in the method of distributing the joint income
and in the coördination of the customs duties with the consumption taxes. The first question was not definitely settled until after the treaty had begun operating, since an
optional solution had been agreed on, while the latter problem was settled by compromise. All goods—except monopolies, like salt or playing cards—produced in one state and
subject to a consumption tax in the other were allowed to be
imported into this other state against the payment of a transfer tax (Übergangsabgabe). After that they were to be
treated like native goods which had conformed to the corresponding excise regulations. The transfer dues were set at
a rate which made possible fair competition with the native
goods.[88]

During the course of the negotiations both Hofmann and
Motz had received additional instructions. Du Thil proposed that Hesse-Darmstadt's consent should be necessary

[86] Hofmann to du Thil, Berlin, January 12, 1828, ibid., p. 179, No. 368.
[87] Cf. Hofmann's diary, ibid., pp. 177–79, No. 367, for this and the
narrative following in this paragraph.
[88] Hofmann to du Thil, Berlin, January 22, 1828, ibid., pp. 184–86, No.
372; Hofmann to du Thil, Berlin, February 6, 1828, ibid,, pp. 193–94, No.
376; treaty, Berlin, February 14, 1828, Art. IX, ibid., pp. 200–1, No. 378.

if Prussia concluded any commercial treaties with the states neighboring the grand duchy.[89]   He also objected to the introduction of administrative courts for the trial of offenses against the customs regulations.[90]   Motz, on the other hand, was advised by the Ministry of Interior to withdraw his consent to having the proportional distribution derived from the total revenue of the Prussian customs system.   Instead, only the revenues of the western provinces and of the territories incorporated in the customs system of these provinces were to be used.[91]

These ideas, taken primarily from the South German conferences and the Prussian Anschluss policies, were the main influences which can be determined through the study of the negotiations leading to the conclusion of the treaty.[92]

The institution founded in the Treaty of February 14, 1828, was called a "common customs and commerce system," although really a customs union was set up.   Hesse-Darmstadt was to adopt the Prussian customs legislation and execute it for a common Prusso-Hessian account.   Since it is nowhere stated that Prussia was to execute her legislation for the same account, the Customs Union, strictly speaking, existed in the grand duchy only.[93]

Hesse-Darmstadt was to administer the customs collection in her territory, but according to the Prussian pattern. As soon as the treaty was ratified, a mixed commission was to supervise the reorganization of the Hessian administration prescribed in the agreement.   This idea was new and was probably introduced to keep the treaty free from detailed and minor clauses.   All future changes in the common legislation had to be approved by both sides, but a secret article limited Hesse-Darmstadt's participation to the points brought out during the negotiations.   Article V gave the grand duchy equality in the negotiation of joint commercial treaties, while

---

[89] Du Thil to Hofmann, Darmstadt, January 29, 1828, *ibid.*, p. 191, No. 375.   [90] *Ibid.*, pp. 189–90.

[91] Hofmann to du Thil, Berlin, February 10, 1828, *ibid.*, p. 195, No. 377.

[92] The protocols and other documents have not been published in full, but apparently all important sections have been included in Oncken and Saemisch (cf. *ibid.*, p. 183, n. 3).

[93] Prusso-Hessian treaty, Berlin, February 14, 1828, Art. I, *ibid.*, pp. 196–211, No. 378.

a secret article limited this to treaties with states neighboring on Hesse-Darmstadt and to all extensions of the Customs Union. It was expected that both governments would endeavor to extend all other treaties to each other through coöperation. Free trade was to be established between the two partners on the day the Union started functioning, and only certain consumption taxes could be levied at their joint boundaries. Subjects of Hesse-Darmstadt were to receive both equal rights with Prussian subjects in Prussian ports and Prussian consular protection abroad. This provision was also original with the treaty and showed the advantages Prussia was able to offer.[94]

The customs agreement did not include those territories of either party which, owing to their geographical location, could not easily be surrounded by the common customs line. The Prussian enclave of Wetzlar was to join the Hessian customs administration, while certain sections of the grand duchy were to be incorporated into that of the Prussian Province of Westphalia. In both cases the home states retained the right of appointing the customs officials of these odd pieces of territory.[95]

Both governments reserved their rights to collect other revenues besides customs duties, but limited their consumption taxes collected on goods shipped between each other's territories to certain commodities and certain maximum rates.[96] However, all the net income from the customs duties from Hesse-Darmstadt and the western provinces of Prussia was to be divided annually among these territories in proportions equal to those of the populations.[97] The ratio of distribution was to be revised every three years according to the last census. A special arrangement was made for cus-

---

[94] *Ibid.*, Arts. II, III, IV, VI, Secret Arts. II, III.   [95] *Ibid.*, Art. VII.
[96] Special prohibitions and regulations were inserted in regard to salt and playing cards.
[97] Cf. du Thil to Bernstorff, Darmstadt, February 29, 1828, *ibid.*, p. 219, No. 383. Hesse-Darmstadt had so strenuously objected to this treaty provision that a clause had to be inserted stating that it was a temporary measure. It is not quite clear whether political or fiscal reasons were the stronger motives. It should be noted that du Thil had instructed Hofmann to prefer a limitation of the commercial treaty to the western provinces (Instruction for Hofmann, Darmstadt, December, 1827, *ibid.*, p. 146, No. 356).

toms collected on goods shipped from one section of Prussia to the other. Moreover, any present or future Zollanschluss enlarging the customs system of the western provinces was to be considered in this calculation dividing the income.[98]

All customs duties were to go directly into the treasury of the state which had collected them, subject only to the final accounting and dividing. This revenue was to be used, preferably, for paying the costs of the customs administration. Any party taking more than its share of the revenue was to transfer the difference to the other.[99]

Hesse-Darmstadt obligated herself to set up an annual budget of the administrative expenses according to Prussian procedure and to forward one copy to the Prussian government. An attempt was to be made to lump all expenses into a quota consisting of a fixed percentage of the total income. Each government retained the right to restore all duties paid by diplomatic representatives or members of the ruling family, but could not charge such refunds to the common account. It could also issue free passes on certain goods, but had to make up for the loss the Union thus incurred. Moreover, each party had to pay out of its own treasury all compensations made for a condemnation of former rights of tax exemption. It was also stipulated that no pensions were to be charged to the Customs Union.[100]

Each government was to collect for its own account all fines imposed, but had the right of pardoning offenders or commuting sentences. On demand it was obliged to inform the other party of such action. All transgressions against the customs law were to be handled in Hesse-Darmstadt by the ordinary courts, but the grand duchy was to appoint a special fiscal prosecutor, who was to send every six months a report on his activities to the Prussian tax administrator at Cologne.[101]

The treaty followed Hofmann's suggestion for a separate administrative board at Darmstadt with two Hessian members and one Prussian. The grand duchy in turn appointed one member of the Prussian board at Cologne. It also was

---

[98] Prusso-Hessian treaty, Berlin, February 14, 1828, Arts. VI, VIII, IX, ibid., pp. 196–211, No. 378.   [99] Ibid., Art. X.
[100] Ibid., Arts. XI, XII, XVI.   [101] Ibid., Arts XIV, XV.

to send three auditors to the Prussian auditing office at Cologne, which was to audit the Hessian customs administration. Each of the representatives at Cologne and Darmstadt had the right to communicate all points of difference to the director of his state board and was encouraged to do so. This provision was introduced to insure uniformity in the administration of both boards. A secret article required that these representatives should see all transactions of the board of which they were a member, and it set up the following procedure for settling differences. First, the members of the board were to try to settle the difference among themselves. If that failed, the question was next to be referred to the superior ministry of finance, which was to effect at least a temporary settlement and which reported it finally to the plenipotentiaries of the annual conference.[102]

Each government had the right through its own officials to check the local administration of the other, but Hesse-Darmstadt was restricted in the number of officials she could thus employ. A special provision for the inspection of the boundary service was also inserted.[103]

Both governments retained the right to use customs officials for the collection of consumption taxes and were financially responsible for the actions of their officials. All data on collection and expenses were to be exchanged every three months. An annual conference of plenipotentiaries was to divide the income, settle the accounts, and straighten out all other difficulties. Both governments were to provide for as many opportunities as possible to subjects of the other party seeking trade or employment in their territories. The treaty was to last until September 30, 1834, when either party could give a year's notice of intent to terminate the agreement. If no notice was given, the Union was to last another six years. The secret additional treaty considerably modified certain articles of the main agreement, and also contained supplementary provisions. In order to insure uniformity of customs collection, a definite rate of exchange for both currencies was to be established, and general provisions for a similar coördination of measures and weights were made.

[102] *Ibid.*, Arts. XVII, XVIII, XIX, Secret Art. VII.
[103] *Ibid.*, Arts. XX, XXI

Road tolls and similar revenues were to be standardized. Each state had the right to collect for all enclaves within its own territories in the annual distribution. Special provisions were made for an adjustment tax (*Nachsteuer*) in the grand duchy.[104]

This treaty set up the first customs union into which Prussia entered, and her lack of experience with such an institution can be seen all the way through the document. Although the treaty was not purely experimental, one can observe how Motz was feeling his way through an unexplored field of administrative complication. One is first struck by the maze created through secret clauses, supplementary clauses, and an additional secret treaty. There were all those provisions which were not to become operative with the treaty, but only after an additional agreement had been reached or if demanded by one party.[105] There were obvious shortcomings, like the technical limitation of the Union to Hesse-Darmstadt.[106] Compared with the Bavaria-Württemberg treaty, procedure was not so clearly formulated, and the treaty did not guard so effectively against possible circumventions. The reason for these deficiencies did not lie in a lack of confidence between the two governments. Apparently all available material had been used and exchanged in the preparation of the treaty.[107] Primarily, the lack of experience was to blame. For this reason Prussia insisted on such a preponderant influence. Hesse-Darmstadt had to abandon her theoretical position of equality so frequently and extensively that she was obliged to keep many of these clauses secret.[108] The treaty was designed to effect a customs union between the two states, and its pattern could not

---

[104] *Ibid.*, Arts. XIII, XXII, XXIII, XXIV, XV, XVI, Secret Arts. I, VI, VIII, IX. Coinage and measures of both states had to be coördinated to maintain a joint customs system. In the case of coinage, both states used the Cologne standard (in Prussia 14 *Thaler* and in Hesse-Darmstadt 24½ *Thaler* were equivalent to a Cologne silver *Mark*); but owing to minor variations in their coinage practices, a rate of exchange had to be officially fixed.

[105] *Ibid.*, Arts. III, VII, VIII, XI, XIII, XXII, XXVII, Secret Arts. I, VI, IX.   [106] *Ibid.*, Art. I.

[107] Hofmann to du Thil, Berlin, January 12, 1828, *ibid.*, p. 180, No. 368; Hofmann to du Thil, Berlin, January 22, 1828, *ibid.*, pp. 183–84, No. 372.

[108] Prusso-Hessian treaty, Berlin, February 14, 1828, Arts. I, II, VIII, XI, XV, XVIII, XX, Secret Arts. I, II, III, IV, *ibid.*, pp. 196–211, No. 378.

have been used for the adherence of additional states without necessitating a new arrangement.   It should be remembered, however, that both Bavaria and Württemberg had undergone their most important administrative and territorial changes before 1815, while neither Prussia nor Hesse-Darmstadt had finished its postwar reorganization.   Moreover, Prussia was so much larger than Hesse-Darmstadt that a partnership on the basis of complete equality was impossible.

In spite of these fundamental differences between the two treaties, the possibility of interdependence must be examined.   Motz was quoted as stating by the end of 1828 that the essential provisions of the Prusso-Hessian agreement had been taken over from the Bavaria-Württemberg treaty.[109] It has also been intimated that Bavaria kept Hesse-Darmstadt informed about her negotiations with Württemberg and that for that reason Hesse-Darmstadt was able to follow the Bavaria-Württemberg pattern so closely.[110]   Naturally, it cannot be denied that the two agreements had certain points in common.   As a matter of fact, most customs unions would have certain similarities.   It can also be conceded that these two institutions agreed in such a peculiar way that some interdependence must have existed. Even that would have been natural if one recalls how actively Hofmann participated in the South German negotiations.   The ideas of these conferences were taken home by each participant, who was free to put them to any use he wanted to.   But the charge has been made that the Bavaria-Württemberg treaty, or at least the negotiations preceding it, directly influenced the subsequent Prusso-Hessian agreement.[111]

In order to examine this theory the main points of these negotiations must be restated.   Early in April of 1827 Bavaria and Württemberg agreed to set up a common customs system at some future date.[112]   Actual negotiations for the fulfillment of this obligation were not started before December 27, 1827, when the Bavarian Ministries of Finance

---

[109] Cotta to Armansperg, München, December 14, 1828, *ibid.*, III, 433, No. 728; cf. Doeberl, *Bayern*, p. 31.

[110] *Loc. cit.*   [111] *Loc. cit.*

[112] Bavaria-Württemberg negotiations, protocol, München, April 4, 1827, Oncken and Saemisch, I, 534–35, No. 275; draft of preliminary treaty [early April, 1827], *ibid.*, pp. 536–37, No. 276.

and the Interior urged the conclusion of a customs union.[113] Therefore, if the Prusso-Hessian treaty followed the Bavaria-Württemberg principles, such ideas must have reached Berlin between December 27, 1827, when these principles were adopted in Munich, and February 14, 1828, when the Prusso-Hessian treaty was concluded. The basic outline of this treaty went back to Hofmann's memorandum, which he wrote down between January 3 and January 9, 1828. Since it has been suggested that Hesse-Darmstadt was informed about the South German negotiations,[114] this should be interpreted as meaning that Hofmann's instructions or information about these developments must have reached him via Darmstadt. It seems to be unlikely that this could have been accomplished by January 9, 1828. Moreover, Hofmann's conferences during January, 1828, presented a coherent development, starting with his first interview with Motz. Du Thil, at first, gave only general advice and later remarked on various points in the draft as elaborated in Berlin. He even advised Hofmann that Hesse-Darmstadt could not ask for as much influence in a customs union with Prussia as in a South German union.[115] During this stage of the negotiations there is nowhere an indication that a pattern was superimposed from the outside.

The Bavaria-Württemberg treaty of January 18, 1828, became known to the negotiators in Berlin early in February, 1828. Hofmann examined it briefly during the conference of February 4, and remarked that Hesse-Darmstadt had not limited herself toward Prussia as Württemberg had toward Bavaria.[116] Apparently this was the first time Hofmann had received any detailed information on this treaty, and the only point he brought up was one of difference between the two systems. The draft of the Prusso-Hessian treaty had been completed on February 2, 1828;[117] the treaty itself was

---

[113] Bavarian Ministries of Finance and the Interior to Ministry of Foreign Affairs, München, December 27, 1827, *ibid.*, pp. 544–45, No. 280; *ibid.*, p. 544, n. 1; on this and the following discussion Treitschke, *Deutsche Geschichte*, III, 636.   [114] Doeberl, *Bayern*, p. 31.

[115] Du Thil to Hofmann, Darmstadt, January 10, 24, 29, 1828, Oncken and Saemisch, II, 174, 187–91, Nos. 366, 374, 375.

[116] Hofmann to du Thil, Berlin, February 6, 1828, *ibid.*, pp. 194–95, No. 376.   [117] *Ibid.*, pp. 191–92.

concluded on February 14, 1828. A number of provisions were changed before this final adoption, but there was no direct mention made of any changes caused by the Bavaria-Württemberg treaty.[118] For this reason one must look for internal evidence in the treaty itself. There is some conclusive evidence in the secret additional treaty. First of all, there was Article VII, which provided that the "foreign member" of the regional customs board was to see all orders originating from that office, a regulation obviously adopted from Article XI of the Bavaria-Wüttemberg treaty. Although the organization of the regional board was not entirely alike in the two customs unions, there has to be found an explanation why such a relatively harmless provision was not included in the public agreement. And in a similar way one can ask why such matters as coördination of coinage, weights, and measures or the standardization of road tolls were included in the secret agreement. These matters appeared here for the first time in the documents of the Prusso-Hessian negotiations, and their problems had been dealt with in the Bavaria-Württemberg treaty. Neither administration would have been able to keep these provisions secret for any length of time. It is therefore more than likely that these arrangements were suggested by the Bavaria-Württemberg treaty after the main agreement had been drafted and that they were inserted into the secret treaty at the last moment as a kind of afterthought.

Motz was therefore either misquoted or mistaken when he stated that the Prusso-Hessian treaty had followed the essential provisions of the Bavaria-Württemberg Union. The direct interdependence was very limited and extended to a few technical provisions only.

After the preliminary arrangements had been completed in the grand duchy, the Prusso-Hessian Customs Union began functioning on July 1, 1828. The Union greatly benefited Hesse-Darmstadt's economic life and state finances, and its administration proved to be quite efficient if one considers the geographical difficulties which were to be overcome.[119]

---

[118] Hofmann to du Thil, Berlin, February 10, 1828, *ibid.*, pp. 195–96, No. 377.

[119] Eckert, "Zur Vorgeschichte des deutschen Zollvereins," Schmoller's *Jahrbuch*, XXVI, Part I, 97–98. Thus Prussia collected 24 silver groschen

THE CENTRAL GERMAN UNION OF 1828

MOTZ had considered the customs union with Hesse-Darmstadt the first step toward the economic unification of Prussia. Prussia expected the intermediate territories, especially Electoral Hesse, to join the new system. Hesse-Darmstadt acted as mediator in Kassel, since Prussia had broken off diplomatic relations with the Electorate.[120] Prussia proceeded directly in Weimar and Nassau, and Motz tried to conclude a commercial treaty with Hanover.[121]   He had no particular interest in South Germany at that time and thought vaguely of cutting down trade restrictions, but still believed that matters like free trade in foodstuffs could be better handled by the Confederation.[122]   Motz had been instructed not to harm the interests of other German states, especially those of Baden,[123] and seems to have followed this instruction.   Moreover, he believed that all northern Germany would join the new union in a very short time.[124]

Simultaneously with Prussia, Bavaria tried to extend her system in Central Germany, and attempts were even made to prevent Hesse-Darmstadt from ratifying the union with Prussia.[125]   These attempts of both Prussia and Bavaria to enlarge their customs systems in Central Germany had the opposite effect.   Shortly afterward a movement among Central and North German statesmen got under way, having for its aim the economic independence of their territories.   In

per head, while the Bavaria-Württemberg received only 9½. Treitschke, *Deutsche Geschichte*, III, 642.

[120] This was due to the peculiar position the Countess of Reichenbach occupied at the Kassel court.

[121] Ritthaler, in Oncken and Saemisch, II, 297–99.

[122] Motz to Prussian Ministry of Foreign Affairs, Berlin, January 4, 1828, *ibid.*, pp. 155–56, No. 359; Hofmann's diary, *ibid.*, pp. 162, 176, Nos. 361, 367; Motz to Prussian Ministry of Foreign Affairs, Berlin, January 17, 1828, *ibid.*, p. 182, No. 369; cf. *ibid.*, p. 424, n. 1.

[123] Friedrich Wilhelm III to Bernstorff, February 3, 1828, as interpreted by *ibid.*, p. 187, n. 1.

[124] Motz to Crown Prince Friedrich Wilhelm, March 18, 1828, Petersdorff, *op. cit.*, II, 127.

[125] Cf. Lutzburg to Koenitz, Berlin, February 18, 1828, Oncken and Saemisch, II, 310–11, No. 422; Lutzburg to Fritsch, Berlin, February 21, 1828, *ibid.*, pp 311–12, No. 423; Ludwig I, order, München, February 24 and 25, 1828, *ibid.*, pp. 313–14, No. 425; Lerchenfeld to Ludwig I, Frankfurt, February 28, 1828, *ibid.*, pp. 317–18, No. 429; ZuRhein to Ludwig I, Darmstadt, March 1, 1828, *ibid.*, pp. 319–22, No. 431; Fahnenberg to Berstett, München, March 5, 1828, *ibid.*, pp. 239–40, No. 392.

the beginning one must distinguish between an exchange of ideas among Thomas of Frankfurt, Smidt of Bremen, and Rose of Hanover on the one hand, and a similar development among Saxon and Thuringian statemen. The results arrived at in each of these negotiations were very much alike. There is no conclusive evidence of a direct interdependence of ideas at this early stage, and the best modern opinion seems to support simultaneous evolution in both circles.[126] Similar as the immediate results of the discussions may have been, the motives of the men who conducted them varied. Men like Schweitzer of Saxe-Weimar were definitely anti-Prussian. Others, such as Smidt and Rose, had economic aims in mind. Thomas of Frankfurt was opposed to unifying anything in Germany, even the most trivial matter, since he believed that such a step would lead to complete political centralization. He argued that individualism was one of the basic German characteristics. Marschall was still dominated by his political conservatism. Although the tendency of this movement in Central Germany was anti-Prussian, men like Lindenau, who looked forward to an ultimate economic union with Prussia, could be found active in it.[127] It was naturally difficult to combine these different sentiments as well as the interests of the states involved in an active program. The oppositional character of the movement gave it from the beginning a conservative tone. Its main aim became the preservation of the *status quo*. It was characterized at a very early date as a "negative union."[128] The participants seem to have preferred the term "neutral" for this body—neutral between the conflicting aspirations of Prussia and Bavaria.[129]

These ideas received their first formulation in the Punctation of Oberschöna of March 26, 1828.[130] The Kingdom of Saxony and the Saxon states in Thuringia were to form a commerce union. This union was to be extended to include all the territories lying between the Prussian and the Ba-

---

[126] Based on Ritthaler's very competent discussion, *ibid.*, pp. 300–2.
[127] Petersdorff, *op. cit.*, II, 157–63.
[128] Oberkamp, report, March 6, 1828, Oncken and Saemisch, II, 301.
[129] Lindenau to Einsiedel, Frankfurt, March 17, 1828, *ibid.*, p. 342, No. 445.   [130] *Ibid.*, pp. 369–70, No. 461.

varian customs unions. Its purpose was to further the trade
of the participating states. For this reason the governments
were to treat each other's subjects on an equal footing with
their own. Moreover, the transit of goods was not to be
prohibited or charged higher dues than the Royal Saxon
tariff of 1822 had established. Each government was to
maintain the roads within its own territories. Article IV
stated the chief purpose of the punctation, namely, that no
member state was to join another customs system, or to conclude a customs or commercial treaty with a state "where a
customs system was in existence," unless the consent of the
Union had been secured. The purpose of this article was to
be covered up by another article, which stated that the new
Union was to decide after six months of its existence whether
it would join one of the existing customs systems, or fight
them or agree on some other policy. If no such agreement
was reached, the Union would last only one year; otherwise,
six years. The common affairs of the Union were to be
regulated by an annual congress of plenipotentiaries.

The only effective provision in this arrangement was the
prohibition of individual customs or trade agreements with
nonmembers. It was not intended to set up a customs
union immediately, even though such a result was ultimately
possible, but not likely. This, as well as its studied avoid-
ance of direct references to Prussia or Bavaria, was a poorly
attempted mystification of the real aims of this league.
These were described by one of the participants as "(1) the
erection of a commerce union among the states lying between the Prussian and Bavarian customs lines, (2) the construction of a road between Leipzig and Gotha circumvent-
ing Prussian territory, and (3) a treaty of succession among
the various Saxon states."[131] The Saxon government circulated at the same time a draft for a union to be extended
beyond the Saxon-Thuringian sphere. This proposal simply
provided for a prohibition of adherence to any outside customs system, a mutual trade preference, and a declaration
of adherence to the Vienna stipulations on the navigation

----

[131] Carlowitz to Einsiedel, Dresden, March 30, 1828, *ibid.*, p. 384, No.
469.

of rivers.[132]   These attempts very soon led to the Frankfurt
Declaration of May 21, 1828, which was signed by Saxony,
Hanover, Electoral Hesse, Weimar, Altenburg, Koburg, Nassau, Schwarzburg-Rudolstadt, and Frankfurt and was later
acceded to by Meiningen, Brunswick, Schwarzburg-Sondershausen, both Reuss principalities, Bremen, Oldenburg, and
Hesse-Homburg.[133]   Its contents substantially followed the
earlier Punctation of Oberschöna.[134]   The negotiations, however, had proceeded too rapidly to allow all the interests of
this rather extensive union to receive proper consideration.
Hanover, especially, objected to being dependent on the
small Thuringian states for permission to conclude any commercial treaty.[135]

In order to elaborate the earlier agreement a conference
of the participants was summoned to Kassel. With the
diplomatic support of a number of nonparticipating powers,[136] the Central German Union was set up, and a detailed
treaty was agreed upon on September 24, 1828.[137]   In its
twenty-one articles the agreement contained a number of
provisions for a coöperation in matters of economic policy, a
concrete obligation for every partner not to join another customs union without the consent of all the signatories of the
new Union, and a complicated and guarded clause limiting
transit dues. Each participant was allowed to conclude
commercial treaties so long as they did not conflict with its
obligation to the Union. All parties had to extend to the
members any tariff privileges granted to a nonmember. Although most of the negotiators had had experience in fiscal
and financial administration, the actual contents of the treaty
were somewhat insignificant. Its negative purpose was even

---

[132] Saxon draft for an agreement among Central German states [March,
1828], *ibid.*, pp. 390–91, No. 472.
[133] *Ibid.*, p. 428, n. 2.
[134] Draft, Frankfurt, April 30, 1828, *ibid.*, p. 421, No. 493; Frankfurt
Conferences, protocol, May 21, 1828, *ibid.*, pp. 390–1, No. 472.
[135] Ritthaler, *ibid.*, p. 303.
[136] The degree to which foreign, especially English, diplomacy furthered
the Central German Union was not so large as Treitschke describes it. Recent research has clarified the definite, but limited, rôle these influences
played (Henderson, *The Zollverein,* pp. 66–67; Ritthaler, in Oncken and
Saemisch, II, 302, 304, 307).
[137] Dated Kassel, *ibid.*, pp. 499–504, No. 532.

recognized by one of the participants.[138]   It was therefore only natural that the treaty itself should provide for a further expansion of the system.

After a year attempts were made to prolong to 1841 the treaty which was to expire in 1834 and to use the Central German Union as a collective bargaining agency for the negotiations with the real customs unions.[139]   As an institution the Central German Union was a failure.   Its members did not coöperate, and it was not able to bargain collectively.

Later on the northwestern members formed a regular customs union, abandoning the idea of a negative union.   A first attempt in that direction was made in the Treaty of Einbeck, dated March 27, 1830, which provided for a customs union between Hanover, Hesse-Kassel, Oldenburg, and Brunswick.[140]   Its technical contents can be traced back to the earlier customs negotiations and treaties.   But it represented an independent arrangement of these ideas, many of which were adapted and modified to suit the particular interests of the parties concerned.   There was, however, one provision which went beyond the scope of previous agreements of this kind.   Article XIV stipulated that all consumption taxes were to be standardized within the Union.   Until then an assimilation of internal revenues had been introduced only in the case of certain enclaves.   It was an innovation to attempt to do the same thing in a customs union.   When, after the defection of Hesse-Kassel from the Central German cause, Hanover and Brunswick, and subsequently Oldenburg, concluded a customs union a few years later, they developed this new principle, and it was for this reason that their union became known as the Tax Union (Steuerverein).   Still later the Zollverein attempted to unify its consumption taxes in a similar way.

During its best days the Central German Union even tried to induce Bavaria and Württemberg to join it.   The ideas behind this offer are not quite clear.   The Bavarian

[138] Hanover Cabinet to Münster, Hannover, July 15, 1828, ibid., p. 446, No. 510.

[139] Supplementary treaty of Kassel, October 11, 1829, ibid., III, 127–30, No. 614; Saxony and Weimar refused to ratify the extension of the treaty (ibid., p. 127, n. 1).

[140] Martens, Nouveau recueil de traités, VIII (1831), 334–49, No. 43.

government, however, declined, since it could not change its fiscal system, although the scheme had found advocates in the Bavarian camp.[141]

THE ECONOMIC ALLIANCE BETWEEN NORTH AND SOUTH AND THE END OF EFFECTIVE RESISTANCE IN CENTRAL GERMANY, 1828–31

ALTHOUGH Bavaria had been interested in enlarging her customs union in Central Germany, Ludwig I had also been looking forward to coöperation with Prussia in German economic matters.[142] He had been very much wrought up about the foundation of the Prussia-Hesse-Darmstadt Customs Union.[143] The Württemberg government sustained this crisis with fewer fluctuations, and it has been argued that Wilhelm I really harbored pro-Prussian sentiments behind his customary silence on political issues.[144] The Württemberg government realized that the Customs Union with Hesse-Darmstadt had put Prussia in a key position in South Germany. Although the statesmen in Stuttgart had opposed an undue extension of Prussian influence into the South, they now favored negotiations with Prussia about a political and economic understanding. They argued that Hesse-Darmstadt's defection from the South German cause had made any economic unification between South Germany and the Bavarian Palatinate impractical, and that the two South German kingdoms were unable to settle with Baden without Prussian mediation. Baden constituted the most vulnerable spot of their Customs Union. For these reasons Stuttgart attempted early in 1828 to prevail upon Bavaria to accept Prussian mediation in her dispute with Baden.[145]

---

[141] Kopp to Oberkamp, Kassel, September 29, 1828, Oncken and Saemisch, II, 517, No. 539; Bavarian Ministries of the Interior and Finance to Ministry of Foreign Affairs, München, October 10, 1828, *ibid.*, pp. 519–22, No. 542; Luxburg to Ludwig I, Koburg, October 17, 1828, *ibid.*, p. 528, No. 545.

[142] Statement made in 1824, quoted by Edwin Hölzle, "Der deutsche Zollverein. Nationalpolitisches aus seiner Vorgeschichte," *Württembergische Jahrbücher für Statistik und Landeskunde* 1932–33, ed. by Statistisches Landesamt (Stuttgart: Kohlhammer, 1935), p. 133.

[143] Treitschke, *Deutsche Geschichte*, III, 642–43.

[144] Hölzle, *op. cit.*, pp. 133–35.

[145] Instruction for the Württemberg minister at Munich, Stuttgart, March 6, 1828, *ibid.*, pp. 139–40, No. 4A.

Bavaria rejected this suggestion, claiming that it would interfere with pending Austrian mediation.[146] However, the lack of support Bavaria received from Austria and France in her Central German aspirations made Ludwig I and his cabinet reconsider their relation with Prussia. It was known in Stuttgart as well as in Munich that Motz had no hostile intentions against the South German Union and that he was willing to coöperate in economic matters.[147] But Ludwig I believed that Prussia's foreign policy was anti-Bavarian and complained about the cool treatment he received from Bernstorff. It was in this connection that there was conceived the idea of exploring the true political sentiments of the Prussian court by going over the head of the Prussian Ministry of Foreign Affairs.[148] This was another occasion when Prussia's policy was obscure, and the initiative to clarify it was not taken by Berlin. Both Bavaria and Württemberg seem to have participated equally in this *rapprochement* with Prussia.[149]

The intermediary for these negotiations was Johann Friedrich, Freiherr Cotta von Cottendorf, a famous publisher and a private citizen with no diplomatic position. While attending the Natural Science Congress at Berlin, in September of 1828, Cotta approached a few persons with decisive influence on Prussian government affairs and at first tried to straighten out the political differences and misunderstandings which had made Prussian relations with Bavaria difficult. He then sounded out Motz about the possibilities of a commercial alliance. Motz declared his willingness to discuss such a matter if Bavaria would take the initiative.[150] Negotiations

---

[146] Bavarian Ministry of Foreign Affairs to Württemberg Ministry of Foreign Affairs, München, March 19, 1828, *ibid.*, pp. 140–41, No. 4B.

[147] Armansperg to Zentner, München, November 10, 1827, Oncken and Saemisch, II, 141–42, No. 351; Beroldingen to Wilhelm I, Stuttgart, November 18, 1827, Hölzle, *op. cit.*, p. 138, No. 1; Motz to Prussian Ministry of Foreign Affairs, Berlin, January 4, 1828, Oncken and Saemisch, II, 156–57, No. 359; Blomberg to Beroldingen, Berlin, February 25, 1828, Hölzle, *op. cit.*, pp. 138–39, No. 3A; Beroldingen to Küster, Stuttgart, April 22, 1828, *ibid.*, p. 139, No. 3C.

[148] Schmitz-Grollenburg to Wilhelm I, München, October 11, 1828, *ibid.*, p. 142, No. 7A.

[149] *Ibid.*, p. 135; Doeberl, *Bayern*, p. 34.

[150] Cotta, memorandum, October, 1828, *ibid.*, pp. 73–75, No. 8.

were begun and were at first conducted informally, later formally and for a long time in secrecy.[151]

The agreement as originally planned was to consist of two parts, one setting forth a customs union of the Bavarian Palatinate with the western Prussian provinces, and the other being a treaty of commerce between Prussia and the South German Customs Union.[152]

The Bavarian government, however, objected to the separate inclusion of the Palatinate in the Prussian system. It was more interested in establishing a connection between its main territories and the Rhine District, and for this reason suggested a line of demarcation which would mark off all southern Germany for inclusion in the Bavaria-Württemberg Customs Union. Bavaria was particularly interested in persuading Prussia to give up her customs union with the southern part of Hesse-Darmstadt (Starkenburg and Rheinhessen) and in having these districts join the Bavaria-Württemberg Customs Union as links between the two sections of the Bavarian monarchy.[153] Prussia, however, objected to any line of demarcation, because she desired to avoid the appearance of prejudicing German governments in such a matter. She was supported in this opinion by Hofmann, Hesse-Darmstadt's representative, whose government did not want its territories to be divided between two different customs unions. Hofmann, however, proposed a customs union between the southern Union and the western Prussian system, including the Palatinate.[154] None of these ideas was executed in the final treaty, which primarily followed the principles Motz had outlined for a commercial treaty.

Motz had suggested the following points as a basis for the negotiations: (a) Bavaria and Württemberg were to as-

---

[151] For a detailed account see *ibid.*, pp. 34–48; Petersdorff, *op. cit.*, II, 199–254.

[152] Punctation between Motz and Cotta, Berlin, December, 1828, Doeberl, *Bayern*, pp. 76–77, No. 10.

[153] Bavarian proposal, Art. III, Oncken and Saemisch, III, 457, n. 2 on p. 456; Armansperg to Ludwig I, München, March 3, 1829, *ibid.*, p. 469, No. 752.

[154] Blomberg to Beroldingen, Berlin, March 10, 1829, *ibid.*, p. 470, No. 753; Cotta to Armansperg, Berlin, March 22, 1829, *ibid.*, p. 473, No. 754; Hofmann, memoir, Berlin, March 24, 1829, *ibid.*, pp. 477–80, No. 756.

similate their customs system to that of Prussia; (b) all goods—with certain exceptions, however—produced in the territories of the contracting parties were to be admitted duty-free by the other parties, if the origin of these goods could be proved through government certificates; (c) each system was to continue to levy customs duties on all other goods for its own account; (d) a special agreement was to be concluded for goods subject to a consumption tax; (e) all other tolls were to be standardized and were not to be levied discriminately on subjects of the contracting parties; (f) the governments were to assist each other in the execution of their customs system; (g) road tolls, measures, weights, and coinage were to be standardized and other trade restrictions were to be abolished; and (h) the Prussian consuls were to act as consuls for Bavaria and Württemberg also.[155]   The Bavarian and Württemberg governments accepted these proposals in principle[156] and, in general, the final Treaty of May 27, 1829, followed this outline.[157]

Although Article I of this convention set up the principle of duty-free import of each others' products, a number of detailed and complicated exceptions were stipulated in Article II.   In certain cases the reduction in tariff was to be gradual.   The principle of mutual exemption from import duties was analogously extended also to transit and export tariffs.[158]   A number of articles were devised in order to promote trade by standardizing tolls and other incidents, by setting up fixed proportions for weights, measures, and coinage, and by easing commercial legislation.[159]

The Prussian harbors were to be open to the subjects of all the other contracting parties on equal terms with the Prussian subjects.   On the other hand, Prussia's earlier one-sided proposals concerning the assimilation of the two systems and

---

[155] Punctation between Motz and Cotta, Berlin, December, 1828, Doeberl, *Bayern*, pp. 76–77, No. 10.

[156] Bavarian instructions, München, January 18, 1829, *ibid.*, pp. 85–91, No. 14.

[157] Treaty between Prussia, Bavaria, Württemberg, and Hesse-Darmstadt, Berlin, May 27, 1829, Oncken and Saemisch, III, 501–7, No. 766; separate articles, *ibid.*, pp. 507–13, No. 767.   In the subsequent references separate articles will be indicated as such.

[158] *Ibid.*, Arts. III, IV.   [159] *Ibid.*, Arts. V, VI, VIII, IX, X, XI.

the use of Prussian consuls were made mutual, and it was agreed that the two systems were to adopt identical principles, and all consuls were to help the subjects of all the signatories. All parties were to conclude a convention against smuggling. The treaty was also to extend to all those enclaves which had been incorporated in either system. The Palatinate was not to benefit from the treaty until the Bavaria-Württemberg customs system had been introduced in that district. A separate article restricted all partners in their right of concluding commercial treaties, and no new customs union treaty could be concluded without the consent of all the governments that were parties to the treaty. Prussia and Hesse-Darmstadt obligated themselves to negotiate with Bavaria and Württemberg, if requested to do so, for the establishment of a customs union between western and southern Germany. Yearly conferences were provided for the extension of the system set up by the treaty.[160]

The treaty did not establish a customs union, but it introduced a system which brought both customs unions into very close alliance. It went beyond the form of a simple commercial treaty, because it provided that each government could check certain aspects of the other's administration through its own agents. The treaty would not have had much practical value unless both parties had been certain that they would be able to secure the construction of duty-free roads through Thuringia to join the main bodies of the two systems.[161]

Moreover, the treaty was more than a *rapprochement* between the two systems, it was the first step toward a German customs union. Both systems had been regional, and this agreement meant a complete change in the economic policies of all the parties concerned. Bavaria and Württemberg gave up their economic regionalism, while Prussia took another step away from her previous, purely fiscal, policy. Among Prussia's assets which would make a union desirable Cotta listed her cultural standard, her strong fiscal position, especially Motz's surpluses, and her military strength.[162] It was

---

[160] *Ibid.*, Arts. VII, XIV, XV, XVI, XVII, XVIII, XIX, Sep. Arts. VI, IX.   [161] *Ibid.*, Sep. Art. V.
[162] Cotta, report, München, December 14, 1828, Doeberl, *Bayern*, pp. 83–84, No. 12.

hoped that the new union would provide the participants with increasing economic and fiscal strength as well as greater military protection.[163]

Motz was soon able to give the Treaty of May 27, 1829, its anticipated supplement through the conclusion of two agreements with Saxe-Meiningen and Saxe-Koburg-Gotha. Early in 1828 these two Thuringian governments had approached Prussia, and had asked for coöperation to improve highway communications in their region.[164] At that time the matter was of little importance for Prussia and was therefore delayed. But with the Bavarian *rapprochement* the road system of these small duchies became a matter of prime importance, since it could be used as a direct link between Prussia and Bavaria. An agreement was reached on the following terms. Prussia agreed to supply the capital for the construction of the roads, while the duchies obligated themselves to build and maintain them and not to collect any transit dues on them. Moreover, a number of goods were to be admitted free of duty into the territories of the contracting parties.[165] Secret agreements of the same dates provided that both duchies should join either the Bavarian or the Prussian customs system as soon as possible, i.e. as soon as they were released from their obligation toward the Central German Union not to join an outside customs system. Prussia promised Saxe-Meiningen that, if she joined the Prussian system, she would receive her proportional shares of the revenues and participate in the Treaty of May 27, 1829, while Prussia would preserve her sovereignty. A proportional share was also promised to Saxe-Meiningen in case Bavaria, Württemberg, Hesse-Darmstadt, and Prussia were to combine their unions into one union.[166] These two

[163] Cotta, report, October, 1828, *ibid.*, pp. 74–75, No. 8; Blomberg to Beroldingen, Berlin, April 6, 1829, Oncken and Saemisch, III, 481–84, No. 758; Motz, memoir, Berlin, June, 1829, *ibid.*, pp. 525–41, No. 775.

[164] Meiningen Ministry to Prussian Ministry of Foreign Affairs, Meiningen, March 12, 1828, *ibid.*, pp. 27–28, No. 562; *ibid.*, p. 60. n. 1.

[165] Treaty between Prussia and Saxe-Meiningen, Berlin, July 3, 1829, Martens, *Nouveau recueil de traités*, VIII, 111–17, No. 21; treaty between Prussia and Saxe-Koburg-Gotha, Berlin, July 4, 1829, *ibid.*, pp. 124–30, No. 23; Henderson, *op. cit.*, pp. 75–76.

[166] Separate articles of the Treaty of July 3, 1829, Oncken and Saemisch, III, 120–21, No. 608. The corresponding agreement with Saxe-Koburg-Gotha probably contained the same terms; cf. Eisenhart Rothe, *ibid.*, p. 141.

Thuringian governments broke, not the letter, but the spirit
of their obligations toward the Central German Union. For
all practical purposes Bavaria and Prussia had been economically unified. It was then only a matter of time for the
Central German Union to liquidate itself. Hanover tried to
come to terms with Prussia during the same summer.[167] Two
Reuss principalities followed the example set by Saxe-
Meiningen and by Saxe-Koburg-Gotha and promised to join
one of the customs unions as soon as possible.[168]

One main point of difference between Bavaria and Prussia
had been the Sponheim question. Bavaria believed herself
entitled to compensation from Baden, a claim arising from
the territorial negotiations of the end of the Napoleonic era.
Prussia had taken Baden's side, but after the Treaty of
May 27, 1829, had been concluded, was willing to help in
settling the matter. This problem was combined with the
question of Baden's entry into the South German Customs
Union. Negotiations were carried on for a long period until
a compromise was almost reached. At this point the Baden
Diet failed to support its government, and the negotiations
were broken off.[169] The aim of these negotiations was the
adhesion of Baden to the Bavaria-Württemberg Customs
Union, and the Baden government made a number of suggestions for the modification of this Union.[170] It first of all
insisted on equal representation at the annual conferences.
It wanted lower tariffs, if possible, and certain improvements
of the customs penal code. Baden also desired for herself a
larger number of places where goods could be stored under
bond, and she offered to trade a stronger border patrol
against release from the obligation to introduce a boundary
district. She argued that her peculiar geographical location
made these exemptions necessary. She also suggested the

---

[167] Hanover Cabinet to Bernstorff, Hannover, August 14, 1829, *ibid.*,
pp. 124–25, No. 611.

[168] Treaty between Prussia and Reuss-Schleitz and Reuss-Ebersdorf,
Berlin, December 9, 1829, Martens, *Nouveau recueil de traités*, VIII, 177–
80, No. 33.

[169] For an account of these negotiations see Ritthaler, in Oncken and
Saemisch, III, 409–14.

[170] Grand ducal instructions for Böckh and Franckenberg, Karlsruhe,
September 1, 1830, *ibid.*, pp. 601–2, No. 803.

adoption of the Prusso-Hessian regulations for pardons and similarly wanted to retain her weights and measures. Instead of having each state pay for all the pensions out of its own funds, it was proposed that each participant be given a lump sum every year for that purpose. While these demands were within the framework of a customs union, the proposal to erect a joint customs direction seems to abandon one of the most fiercely debated principles of a customs union. This central office was also to do all the inspecting, "in order to relieve the individual states of that duty." The contents of these suggestions showed the growing tendency to pool all technical ideas.

Saxe-Weimar followed the example set by some of the Thuringian governments in concluding a similar treaty with Prussia on February 11, 1831. Its main difference consisted in the definite promise to join the Prussian system on January 1, 1835.[171]

In the meantime the July Revolution had brought about changes in various German governments. Thus the Elector of Hesse-Kassel was virtually forced to abdicate. The revolutionary movement upset the Electorate's customs system and the anti-Prussian elements in the administration lost influence.[172] It was the Hesse-Kassel Diet which finally brought about the dispatch of a plenipotentiary to Berlin, and negotiations were soon under way.[173] Hesse-Kassel did not promise to join the Prussian system as soon as she should be released from her commitments to the Central German Union, but joined almost immediately, regardless of her treaty obligations to the Central German Union. For this purpose she signed a treaty with both Prussia and Hesse-Darmstadt. The Treaty of August 25/29, 1831, followed substantially the provisions and wording of the Prussia-Hesse-Darmstadt treaty of 1828. The Electorate was to join the Customs Union which existed between the western Prussian provinces and Hesse-Darmstadt on January 1, 1832.[174]

---

[171] Dated Berlin, February 11, 1831, *ibid.*, pp. 161–64, No. 632.

[172] Eisenhart Rothe, *ibid.*, pp. 16–17.

[173] Haenlein to Friedrich Wilhelm III, Kassel, February 10, 1831, *ibid.*, pp. 160–61, No. 631.

[174] Treaty, Berlin, dated August 25, 1831, signed, August 29, 1831, Arts. IX, XX, XXII, Martens, *Nouveau recueil de traités*, IX (1833), 496–517,

The eastern provinces remained outside the Customs Union. This was primarily a technical provision, since goods were allowed to pass as freely across the boundary separating Hesse-Kassel from the Prussian province of Saxony as over the border between the two Hesses.   Still it is significant that Prussia did not merge all her territories and those of the two Hesses into one single customs union after Electoral Hesse's adhesion had provided the geographical link.   The reason for this arrangement can be found in a secret clause which made provision for the ultimate establishment of a customs union between South Germany and the western Prussian provinces.[175]

The treaty of August 25/29, 1831, did not resemble in all respects the previous agreement between Hesse-Darmstadt and Prussia, since it contained the following modifications. As Hesse-Kassel had the same standards of coinage and of measures as Prussia, the treaty preserved this status and corrected minor differences.   The Electorate promised to introduce the same taxes on wine and tobacco that Prussia had, and all traffic in these articles was to be free between Prussia and Hesse-Kassel as soon as the new tax had been adopted. All parties, moreover, were to sign a convention against smuggling.   A special provision for the traffic on the Weser river was also included in this treaty.   Hesse-Kassel was able to obtain the privilege of importing all goods for the Kassel Fair under bond.   On the other hand, all goods stored in the Electorate on January 1, 1832, were to be taxed for the difference between the new and higher tariff and the old one.[176]   The treaty had also some secret articles which dealt, among other things, with transit tariffs.[177]   These differences between the treaties indicated the growing tend-

No. 61; concerning the date cf. Treitschke, *Deutsche Geschichte*, IV, 353.
    [175] Armansperg to Ludwig I, München, October 9, 1831, Oncken and Saemisch, III, 641, No. 822.
    [176] Treaty between Prussia, Hesse-Darmstadt, and Hesse-Kassel, Berlin, August 25/29, 1831, Arts. VI, VII, XI, XIII, XIV, XVIII, XXXVIII, Martens, *Nouveau recueil de traités*, IX, 496–517, No. 61.
    [177] W. Weber, *Der deutsche Zollverein*, pp. 88–89. These secret articles have apparently never been published.   Whether they contained in part provisions similar to those of the Treaty of February 14, 1828, can only be guessed.

ency to unify correlated matters—in this case, measures, coinage, and internal revenue.

Hesse-Kassel's open breach of her treaty obligations did not escape without protest. Hanover, especially, made representations and tried to induce the Confederation to intervene in favor of the Central German Union. The matter was never settled by the Diet, since Prussia had the procedure of the dispute stalled long enough for the whole question to become irrelevant.[178]

THE CONCLUSION OF THE ZOLLVEREIN TREATIES

WHILE negotiating with the Electorate, Prussia discussed possibilities of a customs union with Saxony, whose government had approached Berlin late in 1830. Moreover, Bavaria and Württemberg participated in all the major aspects of Prussia's negotiations by virtue of the Treaty of May 27, 1829, and from 1831 tried to establish a customs union with Prussia for themselves. But that was not all; discussions with Baden and, later, with the Thuringian governments tended to confuse the situation. Various differences on technical matters held up an early union with Saxony and South Germany. However, the coördination of these different diplomatic actions represented a major problem. The situation was complicated through the variety of obligations the governments had taken upon themselves. There were the duties of the members of the Central German Union. There were the commitments of the Treaty of May 27, 1829. There were all those temporary agreements improvised until everybody was free to conclude a customs union. For some time in 1831 the discussions between Prussia and Saxony centered around a hybrid institution which would give most of the advantages of a customs union to both parties, but still not be enough of a customs union to fall within the restrictions of the Central German agreements.[179]

The treaty with Hesse-Kassel brought the whole matter

---

[178] Eisenhart Rothe, in Oncken and Saemisch, III, 17–20.

[179] Zeschau's account of the negotiations between Saxony and Prussia, Berlin, March 10, 1831, *ibid.*, pp. 616–18, No. 809; Wietersheim to King Anton and Coregent Friedrich August of Saxony, Dresden, March 21, 1831, *ibid.*, pp. 618–22, No. 810.

of a partial or a complete customs union up for reconsideration in Munich, since it provided in a secret clause that the Electorate would join the Bavaria-Württemberg Customs Union together with Hesse-Darmstadt and the western Prussian provinces. This article had assumed that the Prussian tariff and Prussian administrative principles would be extended all over this contemplated union of South and Western Germany. The Bavarian government was very much interested in this union, because it hoped to gain a special position in it which would be transferred to the subsequent general customs union.[180]

The principal difficulty of the Prusso-Bavarian relationship lay in the poor territorial connection between Bavaria and Prussia's eastern provinces. The key to this connection was held by the Thuringian governments who wanted to join a customs union, but were forbidden to do so by the Central German Union. For this reason Prussia had concluded those tentative agreements with various Thuringian governments. But the question remained whether they were to join the South German or the Prussian customs system and, in the latter case, which section of the Prussian system. This would have been a very delicate subject to negotiate between Bavaria and Prussia, since it was not at all certain whether a line of demarcation would have solved the problem. Bavaria could refuse to sanction any customs treaty Prussia might enter upon in Thuringia. Naturally, such a rivalry could have been eliminated if the unions had merged. But in order to do so with profit, the adherence of Thuringia had to be secured. Eichhorn of the Prussian Foreign Office, realizing this dilemma, suggested that the Thuringian governments first form a customs union of their own and then join one or the other union, or both.[181]

It was for these and similar reasons that the Zollverein was established, not by one single act in 1833, but through a series of treaties. First Prussia and the two Hesses signed a treaty with Bavaria and Württemberg. These govern-

---

[180] Armansperg to Ludwig I, München, October 9, 1831, *ibid.*, pp. 641–46, No. 822.

[181] Eichhorn to Maassen, Berlin, July 24, 1832, *ibid.*, pp. 680–84, No. 837.

ments in turn came to terms with Saxony. Then the Thuringian Union organized itself, and it in turn entered upon an agreement with all the previous signatories. The Zollverein began functioning on one day, January 1, 1834, although it had taken a number of treaties, signed by various participants on different dates, to make it possible.

Besides the diplomatic difficulties, several technical matters had to be straightened out. These problems centered around the two different approaches Prussia and the other states used. Saxony, Bavaria, and Württemberg wanted to have the principle of equality carried out in the Zollverein to the greatest possible extent. They objected, in particular, to Prussian prerogatives and to a wholesale adoption of the Prussian tariff and the Prussian customs procedure. They did so not altogether because these were Prussian, but because they felt that the Zollverein would not have identically the same needs and interests that Prussia had. Prussia, on the other hand, wanted to keep all the advantages she had enjoyed in her eastern provinces. She was anxious to keep in her own hands the full control of her trade relations with Russia and Russian Poland. She wanted to retain the relatively higher revenues she had received from these provinces. Moreover, she did not desire any great change in her system of taxation. The negotiations were conducted in a frank and friendly manner. On one occasion they had to be broken off because some of the negotiators were not able to cope with the magnitude of the task. On most issues a satisfactory agreement was reached, since all parties seriously desired the Zollverein.[182]

---

[182] For the sources of the preceding narrative see Lindenau to King Anton and Coregent Friedrich August, Dresden, January 10, 1831, *ibid.*, pp. 612–15, No. 807; Bavarian Ministry of Finance to Ministry of Foreign Affairs, München, March 7, 1831, *ibid.*, pp. 615–16, No. 808; Wietersheim to Lindenau, Berlin, July 19, 1831, *ibid.*, pp. 630–31, No. 818; Wietersheim, memoir, Berlin, July 20, 1831, *ibid.*, pp. 631–38, No. 819; Armansperg to Ludwig I. München, October 9, 1831, *ibid.*, pp. 641–46, No. 822; Bever, diary, Berlin, December 31, 1831, *ibid.*, pp. 646–53, No. 823; Luxburg and Bever to Ludwig I, Berlin, January 10, 1832, *ibid.*, pp. 655–58, No. 825; Luxburg and Bever to Ludwig I, Berlin, January 15, 1832, *ibid.*, pp. 658–60, No. 826; Luxberg to Ludwig I, Berlin, February 21, 1832, *ibid.*, pp. 662–64, No. 828; Prusso-Hessian negotiations with Saxony [Berlin], April 12, 1832, *ibid.*, pp. 665–68, No. 830; Mohl the Beroldingen, Berlin, May 25,

When the final negotiations were begun, only relatively few points of difference remained. The following Prussian demands had not been accepted by Bavaria: (a) that the Zollverein should adopt the Prussian tariff and procedure, (b) that Prussia should be compensated with a lump sum for the loss of certain revenues in the eastern provinces, (c) that transfer dues were to be payable within the Zollverein on goods subject to different internal taxes in the various states, and (d) that Prussia was to have special rights in the conclusion of commercial treaties.[183]   During the final negotiations Prussia granted all members the right to conclude commercial treaties, and the other matters were settled by compromise. The principle of equality was generally carried out in the arrangements agreed upon, and most of the Prussian demands were reduced to a minimum.[184]

The three open treaties which established the Zollverein were almost identical in wording, and for this reason insured uniform operation.[185]   Article I declared the establishment of a customs union. Articles II and III gave the territorial extent of the Zollverein, including all the territories which had joined the contracting parties by Anschluss and excluding all those which could not easily be included in the new customs line. As a rule, the tariff, organization, and procedure were to be uniform throughout the Zollverein, but to a certain degree necessary local variations were allowed. All changes in the customs law, the tariff, and the procedure, and the introduction of new laws or norms were to be made

---

1832, *ibid.*, pp. 672–74, No. 833; Maassen and Eichhorn to Luxburg and Linden, Berlin, May 31, 1832, *ibid.*, p. 674, No. 834; Gise to Ludwig I, München, September 4, 1832, *ibid.*, pp. 687–89, No. 839.

[183] Open Bavarian instruction for Mieg, München, January 17, 1833, *ibid.*, pp. 704–9, No. 850.

[184] Mieg to Ludwig I, Berlin, February 26, 1833, *ibid.*, pp. 710–13, No. 852; Weber, *Der deutsche Zollverein*, pp. 96–98; Doeberl, *Bayern*, pp. 55–57; Treitschke, *Deutsche Geschichte*, IV, 367–69.

[185] Treaty between Prussia, Hesse-Kassel, and Hesse-Darmstadt on the one side and Bavaria and Württemberg on the other, Berlin, March 22, 1833, Martens, *Nouveau recueil de traités*, XI (1837), 525–45, No. 29; treaty between Prussia, Hesse-Kassel, Hesse-Darmstadt, Bavaria, and Württemberg on the one side and Saxony on the other, Berlin, March 30, 1833, *ibid.*, pp. 549–71, No. 31; treaty between Prussia, Hesse-Kassel, Hesse-Darmstadt, Bavaria, Württemberg, and Saxony on the one side and the Thuringian Customs and Commerce Union on the other, Berlin, May 11, 1833, *ibid.*, pp. 584–605, No. 34. The subsequent references will apply to all three treaties.

only with the consent of all contracting parties. All goods were to be shipped free of any duty from one member state to the other; only the following exceptions were recognized: All trade in playing cards and in salt was restricted, remaining under the jurisdiction of each member. All articles which were patented in one state could be excluded from that state if the importation infringed those patent rights. Certain products which were subject to a consumption tax in one Zollverein state could be shipped into another Zollverein state charging a higher internal revenue on them, but only after paying a transfer duty consisting of the difference between the two tariffs.[186]

No road tolls were to be levied as revenue, and they could not be higher than the Prussian tariff of 1828. Weights, measures, and coinage were to be standardized as much as possible, or at least the existing standards were to be put into a fixed proportion to each other. While the first two treaties were not definite about these provisions, the last treaty had a provision making the metric weight used in Hesse-Darmstadt the "customs weight" and standard for the whole union. Tolls on rivers were to be levied according to the provisions of the Congress of Vienna or on equal terms for all Zollverein subjects. The forced sale of goods was forbidden, and all such staple privileges, as they were called, were abolished. Charges for the use of technical improvements or implements, as canals, locks, docks, etc., were not to be raised, and all Zollverein subjects were to have the right to use them on equal terms. In a similar way, all trade restrictions were to be standardized. All Zollverein subjects were to have the right to use Prussian ports and resort to Prussian consuls on equal terms with Prussian subjects. A convention against smuggling was to be entered into by all participants.[187]

The Zollverein was to receive only the duties on imports, exports, transit, and certain water tolls, but no internal revenue, road tolls, or fines. Each state bordering on a nonmember was to be given a lump sum for maintaining a customs line along the boundary of the Zollverein, but the regu-

[186] *Ibid.*, Arts. IV, V, VI, VII, VIII, IX, X, XI, XII.
[187] *Ibid.*, Arts. XIII, XIV, XV, XVI, XVII, XVIII, XIX, XX.

lar administration had to be borne by each state individually. Each government had to pay for the maintenance of the office space it used. If any customs officials were assigned to other duties, a proportional deduction was made in the allowance of the state employing them. The Zollverein was to pay all refunds and special modifications which had been generally approved. The remaining net income was to be divided according to the proportion of the population, which was to be determined every three years. Each government had to pay to the Zollverein for all customs exemptions and modifications it had granted on its own account. All privileges which had been given to certain fairs were to be abolished as soon as feasible. The Zollverein was not to be charged with the customs privileges which certain persons, like diplomats, mediatized princes, and, in some instances, private citizens enjoyed. Each government had to pay for such exemptions as it might allow, but for purposes of accounting was permitted to issue free passes, the value of which was to be deducted from its share of the annual settlement.[188]

Each government had the right to pardon, but on demand had to communicate a record of all such pardons to the other members. Each government appointed and supervised all officials in its customs administration which was to be organized under one or more regional offices (*Zolldirectionen*). Each regional office was to prepare quarterly accounts for its district and forward them to the Central Bureau, which was to be the joint accounting agency. If these quarterly surveys showed that one government was collecting more than its share in revenues, it was to remedy this by making provisional payments from its surplus. Each government had the right to send inspectors to any customs office along the Zollverein frontier.[189] In a similar way officials could be sent to the regional offices. These officers were to enjoy all possible coöperation.[190]

A conference of all members was to be held every year in

---

[188] *Ibid.*, Arts. XXI, XXII, XXIII, XXIV, XV, XXX.

[189] This provision was omitted from the treaty with the Thuringian Customs Union, since this union did not border on a nonmember.

[190] *Ibid.*, Arts. XXVI, XXVII, XXVIII, XXIX, XXXI, XXXII.

the early days of June.   The meeting place was to be determined by the preceding conference, the first one meeting at Munich.   These conferences were to straighten out all difficulties, settle the accounts, discuss suggestions, and act as a legislative body.   Special conferences could be called if necessary.   In principle, other German governments were welcome to join the Zollverein.   The details of the treaty were to be worked out by a joint commission.   The Zollverein was to last for at least twelve years, unless a satisfactory substitute was introduced in accordance with Article XIX of the Acts of Confederation.[191]

The open part of the treaties set up an uncomplicated customs union in which the principle of equality was carried out systematically.   Its ideas can be traced back to earlier customs unions.   The treaties were free from technical detail, which was left to supplementary agreements.   Thus it was agreed that each member state should vouch for the integrity of its officials.[192]   Similarly, the regulations concerning the position of the representatives that each member was allowed to send to the various regional offices of the Union were elaborated in the separate agreements.   It was stipulated that not more than one representative should be accredited for any length of time to a regional office, and the distribution of these representatives was to be changed every three years.   But each member government had the right to authorize another government to take care of this function.[193]   This representative participated in all the business of the regional office he was accredited to.   He had the right to see all transactions, audit all books and accounts, and inspect the local offices in the district of his regional office. He had no veto power, nor could he give orders, but he could voice his objections, which had to be considered. Any differences which were not settled within the regional office had to be straightened out by the Zollverein govern-

---

[191] *Ibid.*, Arts. XXXIII, XXXIV, XXXV, XXXVIII, XL, XLI.

[192] Separate articles to the treaty of March 22, 1833, Art. X, [Zollverein, Central-Büreau (ed.)] *Verträge und Verhandlungen aus dem Zeitraume von 1833 bis einschliesslich 1836 über die Bildung und Ausführung des deutschen Zoll- und Handels-Vereins* (Berlin, 1845), I, 19, No. 2.

[193] *Ibid.*, Art. XI, pp. 19–20.

ments.[194]   Moreover, the governments agreed on the first distribution of these representatives.   Prussia was to send them to the offices at Munich, Kassel, and Dresden; Bavaria to those at Cologne and Erfurt; Saxony one to Magdeburg; Württemberg one to Darmstadt; Hesse-Kassel one to Münster; and Hesse-Darmstadt one to Stuttgart.[195]

The right of each member state to conclude commercial treaties was restricted by the provision that treaties of this kind were not to contravene the best interests of the Zollverein and that the other members were to be informed about pending negotiations.[196]   Any treaty extending the Zollverein was to be negotiated, as a rule, by a neighbor of the new member.   All other members were to be consulted during the negotiations.   These governments could not refuse their consent to such a treaty if it followed the provisions of the original Zollverein agreement.   No stipulation was made to meet the case if a non-German state should want to join.[197]

The annual conferences were the final authority for the settlement of all current business.   A special arbitration procedure was set up for the handling of disagreements. All new legislation, however, was to be negotiated by the plenipotentiaries according to their instructions, and it remained subject to ratification by the member states.[198]

The metric system of weights was adopted for the Zollverein.[199]   A number of minor technical details were incorporated in these separate agreements, as, for instance, a list of all the territories which belonged to the Zollverein by virtue of earlier Anschluss treaties,[200] a list of roads on which special transit dues could be introduced,[201] a provision to

---

[194] Final protocol of the treaty of March 22, 1833, on Art. XXXII of the open treaty, *ibid.*, pp. 27–28, No. 3.

[195] Final protocol of the treaty of May 11, 1833, Art. XVII, *ibid.*, p. 206, No. 42.

[196] Separate articles to the treaty of March 22, 1833, Art. XV, *ibid.*, p. 21, No. 2.

[197] *Ibid.*, Art. XIV, pp. 20–21.   [198] *Ibid.*, Art. XII, p. 20.

[199] Final protocol of the treaty of March 22, 1833, on Art. XIV of the open treaty, *ibid.*, p. 23, No. 3.

[200] Separate articles to the treaty of March 22, 1833, Art. I, *ibid.*, pp. 13–14, No. 2.

[201] *Ibid.*, Art. III, pp. 14–15.

regulate traffic in case of war or plagues,[202] and the rates of the transfer dues to be collected.[203] The Central Accounting Bureau was to be located at Berlin.[204] Special provisions were made for the navigation of the various rivers.[205]

The following privileges were granted. Prussia was to retain from the regular revenue the sum of 300,000 talers for having pooled her river tolls with other Zollverein collections,[206] and Württemberg was to be compensated for the excess amount of pensions she would have to pay in case Baden joined the Zollverein.[207] Detailed regulations were adopted for certain fairs.[208] Finally, Prussia succeeded in retaining full control of her commercial relations with Russia and Russian Poland.[209]

It was agreed to use the Prussian tariff, procedure, and other regulations as the basis for those of the Zollverein.[210] A common tariff was published before the Zollverein went into effect on January 1, 1834.[211] The other regulations were to follow slowly, although various provisional customs regulations established a fair amount of uniformity.[212] A con-

---

[202] *Ibid.*, Art. IV, p. 16.   [203] *Ibid.*, Art. VI, pp. 17–18.

[204] Final protocol of the treaty of March 22, 1833, on Art. XXIX of the open treaty, *ibid.*, p. 26, No. 3.

[205] *Ibid.*, on Art. XV of the open treaty, pp. 24–25; separate articles to the treaty of March 22, 1833, Art. VII, *ibid.*, pp. 18–19, No. 2.

[206] *Ibid.*, Art. VIII, p. 19.

[207] Final protocol of the treaty of March 22, 1833, on Sep. Art. X, *ibid.*, pp. 26–27, No. 3.

[208] Separate articles of the treaty of March 30, 1833, Art. VII, *ibid.*, pp. 134–36, No. 22.

[209] Separate articles of the treaty of March 22, 1833, Art. XV, *ibid.*, p. 21, No. 2.

[210] Final protocol of the treaty of March 22, 1833, on Art. IV of the open treaty, *ibid.*, p. 22, No. 3.

[211] With two introductory treaties of October 31, 1833, Martens, *Nouveau recueil de traités*, XI, 736–79, Nos. 50–52.

[212] Prussia kept her *Zollgesetz* and *Zollordnung* until a general Zollverein regulation was introduced in 1838. Bavaria, Württemberg, and Saxony introduced new regulations by 1833. These laws were different from the Prussian regulations, and the Saxon rules differed from the South German ones; but all contained a number of distinctly Prussian elements. For the details see [Zollverein] *Verträge*, I, 65–89, Nos. 10–14; Sächsische Zollordnung, December 4, 1833, [Saxony] *Sammlung der Gesetze und Verordnungen für das Königreich Sachsen vom Jahre 1833*, No. 27, pp. 301–40, No. 57; Zollgesetz of the same date, *ibid.*, No. 25, pp. 216–27, No. 53; [Württemberg] Provisorische Zollordnung, Stuttgart, December 15, 1833, [Würt-

vention to prevent smuggling was signed by all Zollverein states on May 11, 1833.[213] An additional secret treaty modified the public agreements and provided that the Zollverein might be dissolved by January 1, 1838,[214] if the revenues did not meet expectations.[215] Particular difficulty was caused by the stipulation that the Prussian tariff should be introduced in South Germany as a temporary measure before the treaty took effect, a provision which caused an upheaval in the Bavarian government and which finally had to be withdrawn.[216]

A number of supplementary treaties became effective on the same day that the Zollverein did. The Customs and Commerce Union of the Thuringian states was established by a treaty between Prussia, Hesse-Kassel, and the various Thuringian states.[217] Prussia and Hesse-Kassel participated actively in the Union because major portions of their territories were located in that region. Certain Saxon and Bavarian enclaves were included in the Thuringian Customs Union, but neither government was a member because the territories involved were relatively small.[218] Most of the provisions of the open treaty establishing the Thuringian Union were modeled on the Zollverein treaties. The principle of strict equality was not, however, carried out in the separate clauses. The formal presidency of the Union was given to Saxe-Weimar, while Prussia had the right to present one of her own officials for appointment by the member states as regional coördinator. Prussia was to furnish the office space for the regional office at Erfurt.[219] In a strict

temberg] *Der Zollvereinigungs-Vertrag zwischen Württemberg und Bayern einerseits und Preussen, den beiden Hessen, Sachsen u. s. w. andererseits nebst Zoll-Cartel, Zoll-Ordnung und Zoll-Tarif* (Stuttgart, 1833), pp. 45–108.

[213] Treaty, Berlin, Martens, *Nouveau recueil de traités*, XI, 606–614, No. 35.   [214] Oncken and Saemisch, III, 725–26, No. 861.

[215] Protocol about the signing of the special article, Berlin, October 31, 1833, [Zollverein] *Verträge*, I, 91, No. 16.

[216] Weber, *Der deutsche Zollverein*, pp. 110–11.

[217] Treaty, Berlin, May 10, 1833, Martens, *Nouveau recueil de traités*, XI, 574–83, No. 33.

[218] Kurt Wildenhayn, *Der Thüringische Zoll- und Steuerverein, sein Wesen und seine Bedeutung in völkerrechtlicher und staatsrechtlicher Hinsicht* (Doctor's dissertation, Jena, 1927), pp. 11–12.

[219] *Ibid.*, pp. 26–27; for further details see Wildenhayn, *op. cit.*, and [Zollverein] *Verträge*, I, 161–70, 192–209, 222–252, Nos. 33–35, 41–43, 48–52.

sense the erection of a joint regional office was a departure from standard Zollverein practices, which granted each member state at least one regional office, but the smallness of the Thuringian states would have made such an arrangement impractical. Technically, each Thuringian government was a member of the Zollverein, since the Thuringian Customs Union did not have enough of a legal personality to supersede them. Thus each Thuringian government could participate in Zollverein legislation and administration on an almost equal footing with any other member.[220] Moreover, both Saxony and the Thuringian Customs Union joined the Prussian system of consumption taxes and founded a tax union on Zollverein principles.[221]

Two attempts were made to forestall the conclusion of the Zollverein under Prussian leadership. Hanover introduced a motion in the Confederate Diet on August 9, 1832, that trade restrictions among German states should be modified according to Article XIX of the Acts of Confederation.[222] On the other hand, Metternich tried during the years preceding the foundation of the Zollverein to put Austria's economic policy on a more active basis and to meet Prussia on her own ground.[223] Both attempts failed.

The question may be raised to what extent was the formation of the Zollverein a conscious step toward excluding Austria from German affairs. Apparently members were more worried about the success of the Zollverein as established than about its expansion.[224] Moreover, the problem

---

[220] Thus only temporary officials could be sent by the Thuringian Customs Union to inspect regional offices as well as boundary offices (separate article of the treaty of May 11, 1833, Art. IX, *ibid.*, pp. 196–91, No. 41). The individual Thuringian governments had the right to veto major changes in the Zollverein arrangement, but not technical regulations or tariff amendments (final protocol of the treaty of May 11, 1833, Art. II, *ibid.*, pp. 201–2, No. 42; Wildenhayn, *op. cit.*, pp. 24–26).

[221] Treaty, Berlin, May 11, 1833, Martens, *Nouveau recueil de traités*, XI, 615–19, No. 36.

[222] Protocols, Oncken and Saemisch, III, 268–74, No. 676.

[223] Ritthaler, *ibid.*, pp. 419–20; see, in particular, Metternich to Franz I, Vienna, June, 1833, A. de Klinkowstroem (ed), *Mémoires documents et écrits divers laissés par le prince de Metternich chancellier de cour et d'état* (2nd ed.; Paris: Plon, 1908), V, 517–36, No. 1135.

[224] Cf. separate article of July, 1833 amending the Zollverein treaties, Oncken and Saemisch, III, 725, No. 826; documents relating to the reassurance treaty between Bavaria and Württemberg which provided for the

of a customs union with Austria was not at all acute, since, before any such agreement could have been negotiated, the Austrian customs system should have been thoroughly overhauled. It is quite possible that old anti-Austrian feelings influenced South German statesmen in their Zollverein policy, but one cannot discern a direct relationship between the two. The Thuringian states, Saxony, and both Hesses had joined the Zollverein for reasons of economic necessity. Many of them belonged to the Austrian camp. Ludwig I and his government had been motivated by patriotic feelings, although economic and fiscal expediency must have had some influence. He definitely wanted an economic union between the North and the South. He remembered only too well the unfortunate results which had been brought about by the division of Germany into two camps during the Napoleonic era.[225] He was willing to coöperate with Prussia, but not to subjugate Bavaria to the North. The Württemberg government, on the other hand, was not so enthusiastic about the political implications of the Zollverein, but did not have much choice. Prussia's intentions had, as long as Motz was alive, a certain anti-Austrian note. Motz was embittered by Austria's failure to contribute to German economic betterment, and criticized her for always following her own narrow fiscal interests. He was fully aware of the political gains Prussia would make through the Zollverein, and of how Prussia's military position toward Austria would be improved.[226] It is doubtful whether the Foreign Office and the court shared this extreme opinion. The officials responsible for Prussia's foreign policy had for years combined a political entente with Austria and a good-neighbor policy toward the smaller German states. There was no desire in the Prussian Foreign Office to start an anti-Austrian policy. Nobody in Prussia wanted to sacrifice es-

establishment of a South German Customs Union, in case the Zollverein should fail. Doeberl, *Bayern*, pp. 112–15, No. 22.

[225] "Eine Abtheilung in Süd und Nord-Teutschland finde ich heillos. Es darf die Demarcationslinie nicht vergessen werden, die sich dem Süden, dann dem Norden Teutschlands verderblich bewies." Ludwig I, order, München, May 10, 1834, *ibid.*, p. 114, No. 22B.

[226] Motz, memoir, Berlin, June, 1829, Oncken and Saemisch, III, 525–41, No. 775.

sential interests to Austria or to decline German economic leadership, which seemed to be the price Austria was obliged to pay for her entente with Prussia. The monarchical feelings of Friedrich Wilhelm III were as strong toward the Austrian throne as toward those of the other German princes.

The years 1828–33 saw the immediate foundation of the Zollverein. The basic principles of a customs union had been worked out previously in theory, yet the conclusion of each treaty brought new difficulties. Technical questions did not play such a rôle as previously, when whole conferences were stalled by them. Nor can it be said that there was a lack of serious intention on the part of the governments negotiating. The merging of two economic and fiscal systems into one proved to be a difficult task in itself. Even with all the theories of what a customs union should be, it was a different problem to be confronted with their practical application. Insufficient means of communication added their part to cause misunderstandings and prolongations.

All treaties establishing the Zollverein were bilateral treaties, although most of them were multipartite. One of the greatest obstacles the earlier conferences had encountered arose from the action of the least interested participant in setting the pace of the negotiations and in frequently sabotaging them.

Most governments were represented at the negotiations by high-ranking officials. Negotiations with either mere technicians or mere diplomats did not prove successful.

For details of their own organization and policy the customs unions either completely adopted, or somewhat modified, the existing customs system of their largest member. More minute points were always left to a technical commission to decide after the main agreement had been reached, but before it became effective. Most of the treaties had secret clauses, and most of the agreements had to be amended after signature and before ratification. The technical scope of the treaties increased, and their form improved with each succeeding treaty.

While the technical development was made possible

through constant revisions, the political problems were solved through careful analysis, mutual trust, and tact. Sheer economic necessity forced the smaller states to ask for the assistance of the larger neighbors. At the same time, men like du Thil, Motz, and Ludwig I were needed to pursue a farsighted program which preserved the independence of the medium and smaller states. This broader view was slow to permeate, and it was not until 1828 that the Prussian government fully understood its implications and began to integrate its foreign policies. Basic misconceptions about Prussia's foreign policy had to be removed in the minds of Hessian and Bavarian statesmen before negotiations could be undertaken. The statesmen participating in the foundation of the Zollverein were aware that an economic unification of this kind contained a number of political elements. Many negotiators believed that they were helping the German people, although hardly anyone desired or foresaw Prussia's political hegemony in German affairs.

Thus the establishment of the Zollverein was the work of the cabinets, which frequently acted under the pressure of popular discontent. The technical ideas of the new institution were taken directly from the South German conferences of 1820–25 and from the Prussian customs reform of 1818. As regards both its background and its execution the foundation of the Zollverein was the work of the South German as well as the Prussian statesmen.

CHAPTER IX

SUMMARY AND CONCLUSION

THE foregoing study has presented the slow evolution of the Zollverein. Although the Holy Roman Empire never formed an economic unit, there were many observers who suggested such a unification for Germany in 1813–15. These proposals always included economic unification as a by-product of political unification. At that time, however, German intellectuals lacked the theoretical and practical background to provide the Confederation with a customs system of its own. Even leaders like Stein were painfully ignorant concerning the administrative problems involved.

The idea of a customs union had not been conceived by 1815. The age had a peculiar preference for speculative thought and grandiose theories, and it liked to follow extremes. This tendency continued during the economic depression of 1816–17. The plans for general German economic unification which were proposed to remedy this crisis were poorly formulated. Although List was important as a leader of public opinion and succeeded in making the governments conscious of the necessity for reform, he failed to follow consistently a sound program and exhibited the intellectual instability which was so common during that period.

While List was still working for general economic unification, he conceived the idea of a separate union and urged the various German governments to adopt it. Although the origin of the separate negotiations during the Vienna Final Conferences remains obscure, the idea of a regional customs system came from those governments which had received List's idea with great interest. The Nebenius memoir of 1819 did not influence this early development of a regional union at all.

The principles of a customs union were evolved during the South German conferences (1820–25), although at that

253

time political factors prevented the application of the idea. Hofmann's suggestion for separate administrations had more the character of an independent elaboration than that of a wholesale adoption of earlier ideas.

Through the Prussian customs reform of 1818 the North contributed its share to the theoretical background of the Zollverein. Although this reorganization subsequently provided the Zollverein with a modern commercial policy, the Prussian reformers had not foreseen German economic unification. Neither the early Anschluss treaties nor the Customs Law of 1818 were steps consciously taken by the Prussian government toward the Zollverein. Prussia's fiscal and foreign policies were not coördinated until after 1825, and therefore it was not until then that Prussia was ready to enter upon a program of large-scale economic unification.

The suppression of liberal thought by the reactionary forces after 1819–20 excluded the German people from participating in the foundation of the Zollverein and caused an almost complete separation of liberal from conservative thought.

The Zollverein was founded between 1828 and 1833 by degrees. The Prussian and the South German administrative ideas of the preceding decade were combined and expanded. The result was that even the conclusion of the final treaties in 1833 was a major task in itself.

The account of the intellectual origin of the Zollverein which has been given in this work does not bring out much new information of a purely factual nature. If anything, this treatise is forced only too often to point painfully to important circumstances which are not known. However, by rediscovering interrelationships of ideas a new set of gauges is found by which to evaluate the thought of this period. A critical investigation of individual ideas reveals not only many elements which they have in common with each other, but also many deficiencies. These discoveries tend to push many a hero of earlier historiography back into the ranks of his contemporaries. The individual is shown in his intellectual environment, and thus many unevennesses of earlier evaluations are leveled off. On the other hand, this critical examination of ideas reveals the slow, but steady, progress which was made in perfecting plans and institutions. By relating each step forward to its background and by examining it critically a new setting is provided for its evaluation. Only by understanding the handicaps and difficulties this intellectual evolution had to overcome can one appreciate its achievements.

The slowly evolving intellectual history of the Zollverein has its definite place as the causal link between the basic political and economic conditions and the final outcome of economic unification. The intolerable economic situation did not automatically produce the solution, but it provided the stimulus. The intellectual environment was responsible for the shape which the desires for economic betterment assumed.

The movement for general German economic unification bore the mark of the vague theories which were so predominant in that period. As much as economic conditions made unification necessary, primarily political ideologies and not economic rationalism determined the extent of such a unification. However, nationalism was not the most powerful formative factor. Nationalistic groups exercised very little influence on the development toward the Zollverein. Nevertheless, there existed a national consciousness which manifested itself strikingly in the absence of any seriously considered scheme for unification with a non-German state. Particularism and trialism were much stronger forces. They dominated the South German negotiations, and the Berlin Cabinet pursued essentially a more or less enlightened policy of Prussian interests. Many a statesman who adhered loyally to the political precepts of the Holy Alliance supported at one time or another economic unification, partly in order to stabilize the existing order. Berstett, du Thil, Marschall, and Bernstorff belonged to this class. Moreover, they were also economic liberals in spite of their conservatism. The first separate negotiations aimed at the abolition of all customs duties, while the Prussian government followed a moderate free-trade policy in its customs reform of 1818.

Ideas were not static, but were developed. The Zollverein owed its existence to the coördination of practical and theoretical elements in the Prussian Customs Law of 1818; List's plan of economic unification, to be achieved through separate negotiations outside the framework of the Confederation; Hofmann's synthesis of particularism, with the necessity of a customs system; and Motz's integration of Prussia's fiscal and foreign policy.

At the same time the technical elements of economic unification were developed in order to eliminate as many political factors as possible. The institutional aspects of the Zollverein crystallized around the crosscurrents of thought.

The Zollverein occupies an important place in the formation of modern Germany. German nationalists after 1871, as well as Nazi writers in recent years, have hailed it as the cornerstone of Bismarck's Empire and the Third Reich respectively. What part did the Zollverein play in the genesis of German imperialism and totalitarianism? Did its founders make a Bismarck or a Hitler inevitable? Are the ideas which led to the Zollverein incompatible with Western thought and culture? Undoubtedly the Zollverein contributed heavily to the creation of modern Germany and not only to its economic aspects. To its founders, however, the establishment of the Zollverein was a move leading away from antiquated and partly feudal institutions and striving toward a modern economy in the Western sense. The Prussian reformers, with their moderate protection policies and their concept of a world economy by means of international trade agreements, were far ahead of their prohibitionist continental neighbors. Liberal economic thought was resorted to in order to overcome the economic anarchy of post-Napoleonic Germany. Fichte and Jahn, whose ideas were closest to modern nationalism and totalitarianism, did not influence this development.

Moreover, the Zollverein reflects only too well the desire of various German states to remain as independent as possible, and thus represents that form of German nationalism which believed in a certain degree of unity, but only if such unity was accompanied by the proper decentralizing checks and balances. For this reason the founders of the Zollverein can be called progressive in the Western meaning of this term. This is particularly borne out by the fact that the Zollverein served as the prototype for modern international functional organizations.

These principles of the early Zollverein disappeared gradually in Germany, as imperialism and totalitarianism rose. How different these new forces were can be seen from the two following examples: First, in 1866 almost all German medium states sided with Austria against Prussia, thus indicating how few members of the Zollverein wanted Prussia's exclusive political leadership in Germany. Second, National Socialism was never able to indoctrinate Luxembourg, which had belonged for over seventy-five years to the German customs system, while Hitler had relatively little trouble to win the Sudeten Germans, who had never been in the Zollverein.

The foundation of the Zollverein, which stands apparently at the beginning of Germany's unification and centralization in modern times, was guided by ideas which were not akin to either imperialism or totalitarianism. The liberal and progressive tradition of the early Zollverein may therefore still be worth remembering.

Thus action alone did not found the Zollverein either. Economic unification among independent and equal states is too complex a problem just to happen without some preliminary thought. In the case of the German Zollverein, the formative ideas emanated from the general background of the period, and it took hard work and bitter experience to mold these general concepts into the specific principles on which German economic unification was to rest.

APPENDIX A

THE NEBENIUS MEMORANDUM OF 1819

THE lithographed copy of the Nebenius memorandum did not bear the name of the author. There is no question about the authorship, but it was not generally known until 1833, when Nebenius published the memorandum. Berstett, however, when he distributed the memorandum in 1820, did not keep the author's name completely secret.[1]

TITLE

A title of the memorandum is not mentioned in the pertinent literature. If one accepts Nebenius's statement that the 1833 reprint followed the original word for word,[2] the memorandum did not have a title, since the reprint does not carry any title of its own.[3]

DATE

One must distinguish between the dates when the memorandum was written, handed to the government, lithographed, and distributed. Nebenius himself consistently maintained that it was written in 1819, and he also always linked its influence with the Vienna Final Conferences and with no earlier event.[4] This statement is supported by other evidence. A member of List's League printed sections of the memorandum in 1822, and referred to it as the very remarkable (*merkwürdig*) anonymous lithographed essay which was circulated about the time of the Vienna Final Conferences.[5]

---

[1] Du Thil, report No. 49, Wien, January 12, 1820, H. Schmidt, *Die Begründung*, p. ii; Miller, *Über ein Maximum* [p. 2]; Aegidi, *Aus der Vorzeit*, p. 35; Treitschke *Deutsche Geschichte*, III, 775; Menn, *Zur Vorgeschichte*, p. 60; Blume, *Hamburg*, p. 37, n. 113; Weech, *Correspondenzen*, p. 95, n.
[2] Nebenius, *Denkschrift*, p. 5, n.
[3] The memorandum was reprinted. *Ibid.*, Appendix, pp. 1–32.
[4] *Ibid.*, p. 5, Appendix, p. 32, n.; Nebenius, "Über die Entstehung und Erweiterung des grossen deutschen Zollvereines," *Deutsche Viertel-Jahrsschrift*, 1838, p. 326; Nebenius, letter draft [1819], Köhler, *Problematisches*, pp. 4–5.   [5] Miller, *op. cit.* [p. 2].

Concerning the movement in the Baden Diet, Nebenius only stated that the intentions of the government were not unknown to the representatives.   In 1864 Beck, his biographer, gave the following account: Nebenius wrote the memorandum as early as 1818, according to a statement found in his papers, and he showed the memorandum to Berstett, who had it lithographed and distributed among the members of the Baden Diet in April, 1819.   Beck conjectures that Nebenius influenced Lotzbeck and Liebenstein and that the memorandum was used in 1819 as a basis for negotiations with various German governments.   Beck also says that the memorandum was known in many circles in the first months of 1819, and he also claimed, rather inconsistently, that List only knew its general contents by the summer of 1819 and that Nebenius did not reveal any details to List.[6]   No published contemporary account mentions the memorandum prior to the Vienna Final Conferences, and there is coherent evidence to show that List influenced Lotzbeck, who in turn persuaded the Baden government to adopt his plan.[7]   Various historians have followed Beck's version of the origin of the memorandum, without giving a critical account of their thesis.[8]

Böhtlingk, who also examined the Nebenius papers, wrote in 1899 that he was unable to find any support for Beck's story about the distribution of the memorandum to members of the Diet in April, 1819[9]   Böhtlingk says that there is only proof that the representatives were informed privately by the government of its intentions, a version for which he finds additional proof in Nebenius's article of 1838.[10]   It should be noted that Beck alone had claimed to have found proof that the memorandum was written in 1818, a statement which he felt needed further confirmation, and that

---

[6] Beck, "Karl Friedrich Nebenius," *Unsere Zeit*, VIII (1864), 52–53.

[7] Cf. *supra*, pp. 56–57.

[8] Aegidi, *op. cit.*, Weech, *op. cit.*, p. 79, Treitschke, *Deutsche Geschichte*, II, 614; Ritthaler, in Oncken and Saemisch, I, 327, n. 1 of p. 326.

[9] *Nebenius*, p. 13, n.

[10] Nebenius, "Über die Entstehung," *Deutsche Viertel-Jahrsschrift*, p. 327. What Nebenius had in mind when he made his ambiguous statement that the representatives in the spring of 1819 were not unaware of the intentions of the government cannot be determined.

he is the only one who relates that the memorandum was lithographed and distributed to the Baden Diet in April, 1819; moreover, Beck does not give a source for this latter item.

The following conclusions seem to be reasonable: Beck's unreliable and uncritical account should be used with the greatest caution possible, and preference should be given to accounts of contemporaries. Böhtlingk's inability to find material in support of Beck's story and the absence of any visible influence that Nebenius's memorandum might have exercised prior to the Vienna Final Conferences make it more than likely that the memorandum was not circulated until the last months of 1819. There is not sufficient evidence to overcome Nebenius's own statement that he wrote it in 1819.[11] If Nebenius wrote the memorandum in the fall of 1819—which is not improbable—it might be suggested that he became again interested in the topic through the popular agitation at this time and through his official work on the new Baden customs law.[12]

[11] Nebenius, *Denkschrift*, Appendix p. 32, n.
[12] [Baden, Landtag] *Übersicht*, II, 217–51.

APPENDIX B

CHRONOLOGICAL TABLE

THE list of dates given below does not attempt to be in any way comprehensive, but includes only the major events pertaining to the evolution of the Zollverein. It is primarily intended for the general orientation of the reader, who may find further information by turning to the Index.

1523: Attempts to establish an Imperial customs system.

1806: Dissolution of the Holy Roman Empire.

1815: Acts of Confederation, Art XIX. Provisions of the Congress of Vienna on the navigation of certain rivers.

1818, May 26: Prussian Customs Law.

1819, summer of: Karlsbad Conferences.

1819, October 25: The first Anschluss treaty. The Lower Dominion of Schwarzburg-Sondershausen joins the Prussian customs system.

1819, November–1820, June: Vienna Final Conferences.

1820, September–1823, summer: Darmstadt Conferences.

1822: Arnstadt Conferences.

1824, November: Heidelberg Protocol.

1825, February-August: Stuttgart Conferences.

1825, July 1: Motz becomes Prussian minister of finance.

1828, January 18: Bavaria-Württemberg Customs Union.

1828, February 14: Prussia-Hesse-Darmstadt Customs Union.

1828, September 24: Treaty of Kassel among Central and North German governments.

1829, May 27: Commercial alliance between the Prussia-Hesse-Darmstadt and the Bavaria-Württemberg Customs Union.

1831, August 25–29: Hesse-Kassel joins the Prussia-Hesse-Darmstadt Customs Union.

1833, March to May: Final Zollverein treaties concluded.

1834, January 1: The Zollverein starts operating.

APPENDIX C

BIOGRAPHICAL SURVEY

Amsberg, Philipp August Christian Theodor von, 1789–1871; Brunswick statesman.

Aretin, Johann Adam, Freiherr von, 1769–1822; Bavarian diplomat.

Armansperg, Joseph Ludwig Franz Xaver, Reichsfreiherr von, 1787–1853; Bavarian statesman.

Arndt, Ernst Moritz, 1769–1860; German patriotic writer.

Arnoldi, Ernst Wilhelm, 1778–1841; business man.

Benzenberg, Johann Friedrich, 1777–1846; publicist and scientist.

Bernstorff, Christian Günther, Graf von, 1769–1835; Prussian minister of foreign affairs, 1819–35.

Berstett, Freiherr von, 1769–1837; Baden statesman.

Brunner, Hans Caspar Carl, fl. 1816–20; free trader and Bavarian customs official.

Bülow, Ludwig Friedrich Victor Hans, Graf von, 1774–1825; Prussian minister of finance, 1814–17.

Cotta von Cottendorf, Johann Friedrich, Freiherr, 1764–1832; publisher.

Du Thil, Karl Wilhelm Heinrich, Freiherr du Bos, 1778–1859; Hesse-Darmstadt statesman.

Eichendorff, Joseph Karl Benedict, Freiherr von, 1788–1857; German writer.

Eichhoff, J. J., fl. 1790–1820; general director of the Rhine Commission under Napoleon.

Eichhorn, Johann Albrecht Friedrich, 1779–1856; Prussian statesman.

Fichte, Johann Gottlieb, 1762–1814; German philosopher.

Franz, I, 1768–1835; emperor of Austria, 1804–35, German emperor (as Franz II), 1792–1806.

Frederick the Great, 1712–86; king of Prussia, 1740–86.

Friedrich Wilhelm III, 1770–1840; king of Prussia, 1797–1840.

Fritsch, Karl Wilhelm, Reichsfreiherr von, 1769–1851; Saxe-Weimar statesman.

Gentz, Friedrich von, 1764–1832; Austrian publicist.

Görres, Johann Joseph von, 1776–1849; German publicist.

Goethe, Johann Wolfgang von, 1749–1832; German author.

Hach, Johann Friedrich, 1769–1851; Lübeck senator.

Haller, Martin Joseph, fl. 1814–23; Hamburg publicist.

Hardenberg, Karl August, Fürst von, 1750–1822; from 1810 Prussian state chancellor.

Hess, Jonas Ludwig, 1756–1823; publicist.

Hoffmann, Ernst Theodor Amadeus, 1776–1822; German writer.

Hoffmann, Johann Gottfried, 1765–1847; Prussian statistician.

Hofmann, August Konrad, Freiherr von, 1778–1841; Hesse-Darmstadt administrator.

Humboldt, Karl Wilhelm, Freiherr von, 1767–1835; Prussian statesman.

Jahn, Friedrich Ludwig, 1778–1852; German writer and educator.

Klewiz, Anton Wilhelm von, 1760–1838; Prussian minister of finance, 1817–25.

Kotzebue, August Friedrich Ferdinand von, 1761–1819; German writer.

Lepel, von; Hesse-Kassel representative in Frankfurt during the early twenties.

Lerchenfeld[-Koefering], Maximilian, Reichsgraf von, 1779–1843; Bavarian minister of finance.

Liebenstein, L. A. F., Freiherr von, 1781–1821; liberal politician and administrator.

Lindenau, Bernhard August von, 1779–1854; Saxon statesman.

Lindner, Friedrich Georg Ludwig, 1772–1845; publicist.

Lips, Michael Alexander, 1779–1838; economist.

List, Friedrich or Frederick, 1789–1846; economist.

Lotzbeck, K. L., Freiherr von, 1786–1873; industrialist and politician.

Ludwig I, 1763–1830; grand duke of Baden, 1818–30.

Ludwig I, 1786–1868; king of Bavaria 1825–48.

Maassen, Karl Georg von, 1769–1834; Prussian tax administrator, 1818–30, Prussian minister of finance, 1830–34.

Maltzan, Mortimer, Graf von, 1793–1843; Prussian diplomat, between 1825 and 1829, Prussian minister at Darmstadt.

Marschall von Bieberstein, Ernst Franz Ludwig, Freiherr von, 1770–1834; Nassau statesman.

Metternich[-Winneburg], Clemens Wenzel Nepomuk Lothar, Reichsfürst von, 1773–1859; Austrian statesman.

Möser, Justus, 1720–94; German publicist.

Motz, Friedrich Christian Adolph von, 1775–1830; Prussian minister of finance, 1825–30.

Müller, Adam Heinrich, 1779–1829; German publicist and Austrian official.

Mülmann, von; Nassau diplomat at the Darmstadt Conferences.

Münster[-Ledenburg], Ernst Friedrich Herbert, Reichsgraf von, 1766–1839; Hanoverian statesman.

Napoleon, Bonaparte, 1769–1821; emperor of the French, 1804–14/15.

Nebenius, Carl Friedrich, 1784–1857; Baden economist.

Otterstedt, Georg Ulrich Joachim Friedrich, Freiherr von, 1769–1850; Prussian diplomat.

Pfizer, Paul Achatius, 1801–67; Württemberg official.

Ranke, Leopold von, 1795–1886; German historian.

Rau, Karl Heinrich, 1792–1870; professor of Political Economy at Heidelberg, 1822–70.

Rechberg und Rothenlöwen, Alois, Graf von, 1766–1849; Bavarian minister of foreign affairs, 1817–25.

Rose, Just Philipp, 1787–1849; Hanoverian administrator.

Rotteck, Karl von, 1775–1840; Baden liberal.

Schmidt, Karl Ernst; vice-president of the government of Saxe-Hildburg-hausen in 1814.

Schweitzer, Christian Wilhelm, 1781–1856; Saxe-Weimar official.

Seume, Johann Gottlieb, 1763–1810; German writer.

Siebenpfeiffer, Philipp Jakob, 1769–1845; German publicist.

Smidt, Johann, 1773–1857; Bremen statesman.

Smith, Adam, 1723–90; British economist.

Soergel, *fl.* 1800; publicist.

Stadion, Johann Philipp Karl Joseph, Graf von, 1763–1824.

Stahl, Philip von, 1762–1831; "Praesident der Kommerzhofkommission" in 1819.

Stein, Heinrich Friedrich Karl, Reichsfreiherr von und zum, 1757–1831; Prussian statesman.

Stromeyer, Franz, *fl.* 1831; Baden (?) publicist.

Thomas, Johann Gerhard Christian, 1783–1830; mayor of Frankfurt.

Trott, August Heinrich, Freiherr auf Solz, 1783–1840; Württemberg diplomat.

Wangenheim, Karl August, Freiherr von, 1773–1850; Württemberg diplomat.

Weber, Johann Friedrich Ernst, 1769–1834; business man.

Weise, von; chancellor of Schwarzburg-Sondershausen in 1819.

Wilhelm I, 1781–1864; king of Württemberg, 1816–64.

Wintzingerode, Heinrich Karl Friedrich Levin, Graf von, 1778–1856; Württemberg statesman.

Wirth, Johann Georg August, 1798–1848; German publicist.

APPENDIX D

GLOSSARY

Article XI of the Acts of Confederation.—This article gave each member of the German Confederation the right to conclude alliances and treaties, so long as they were not directed against the Confederation.

Central Germany.—The region comprising Upper Saxony, Thuringia, and Hesse.

Certificates of origin.—Documents showing the country of origin of certain goods in order to provide a lower rate of tariff.

Common customs system.—An administrative body set up by independent states or entities as a joint authority for their customs affairs. This authority has its own personnel, and each participant has a relative influence on the central agency of that authority.

Common measures.—Actions undertaken jointly by various governments, such as reprisal tariffs.

Customs union.—An administrative arrangement between independent states or entities for the purpose of levying tariffs upon nonmembers according to uniform principles and for allowing free trade among its members. Each state administers these common regulations within its own territory and through its own officials, and participates—as a rule—equally in the affairs of the union.

Dualism.—The rivalry between Austria and Prussia for leadership in Germany.

Economic unification.—The process by which a region becomes an economic entity, enjoying free trade for all parts so unified and maintaining a uniform attitude toward outsiders.

Enclave.—(a) A territory completely surrounded by that of another state; (b) A small territory separated from the main body of the state to which it belongs.

General-Controlle.—Central Prussian government agency which controlled a part of the state expenditures until 1825.

General German economic unification.—The economic unification of all German states or of all states belonging to the Empire or the Confederation.

German economic unification.—The economic unification of a large part of Germany.

German Question.—The question of German political unification.

Impost.—An indirect tax levy.

Internal German customs lines.—Customs lines between or within German states.

Landrat.—Prussian administrative official in charge of a *Kreis,* a district comparable to a county.

Mediatize.—(a) Before 1806: to deprive an estate of the Empire (*Reichsstand*) of its immediate position under the Empire (*Reichsunmittelbarkeit*); (b) After 1806: To derive a German state of its full sovereignty.

266

Medium states.—The medium-sized states of the German Confederation.

Mutual preference.—An arrangement by which two or more states agree to grant each other's goods a considerable reduction in tariff.

North Germany.—The territories of the north German plains.

Octroi.—A levy on the traffic of goods.

Organ.—Official periodical of List's League.

Particularism.—The movement for the political independence of the various German states; equivalent to states' rights.

Punctation.—A tentative program agreed upon by various states.

Purely German states.—A political slogan used to class those states with no non-German inhabitants and no foreign influences—in particular, Central and South Germany.

Regional Union.—*see* Separate union.

Retortion.—An act of economic reprisal.

Separate customs system.—A common customs system, established without the help of the Confederation and comprising only a part of Germany.

Separate (state) administrations.—Characteristic feature of a customs union by which each member retained its own (separate) customs administration.

Separate union.—Economic unification, established without the help of the Confederation and comprising only a part of Germany.

South Germany.—The region comprising Bavaria, Württemberg, Baden, the Hohenzollern principalities, and parts of Hesse-Darmstadt.

Territory.—A component part of the old Empire.

Third Germany, or third power in Germany.—*See* Trialism.

Trialism.—The idea of establishing a third German power (besides Austria and Prussia) by unifying South and Central Germany.

Zollanschluss.—An administrative agreement between independent states or entities by virtue of which a small piece of territory—it may be a state or a fraction of a state—is incorporated into the customs system of the other contracting party without retaining its separate administration and without having a decisive influence on the policies of the larger customs system.

Zollverein.—The customs union of a large number of German states which existed betweeen 1834 and 1871.

BIBLIOGRAPHY

PRIMARY SOURCES: PUBLIC RECORDS, EXCEPT PARLIAMENTARY
DEBATES

Unpublished Material

[Prussia, Staatsrath] Gutachten des preussischen Staatsraths über den Entwurf eines neuen Steuergesetzes 1817. Unsigned MS copy, General Library, University of Michigan, Berlin, July 20 [*sic*], 1817. [A1-2, B1-12, C1-12, D1-12, E1-6.] The Prussian State Council participated actively in the customs reform of 1818. Its memorandum of June 20 contains valuable material on the foundations of the new customs law. The memorandum of June 20, 1817, has been published only in part by Oncken and Saemisch.

Published Material

[Baden] *Grossherzoglich badisches Staats- und Regierungs-Blatt* [title varies]. 1803–.

[Central Rhine Commission] *Rheinurkunden, Sammlung zwischenstaatlicher Vereinbarungen, landesrechtlicher Ausführungsverordnungen und sonstiger wichtiger Urkunden über die Rheinschiffahrt seit 1803 . . . Rijndocumenten . . .*, 2 vols. S'Gravenhage: Martinus Nijhoff, 1918.

[Congress of Vienna, 1814–15] *Acten des Wiener Congresses in den Jahren 1814 und 1815,* ed. by Johann Ludwig Klüber. Second ed., Vol. I– Erlangen, 1815–.

Gebhardt, Bruno (Ed.). "Zwei Denkschriften Stein's über deutsche Verfassung," *Historische Zeitschrift*, LXXX (1898), 257–72.

[German Confederation] *Protokolle der deutschen Bundes-Versammlung* [1816–28], 19 vols. Frankfurt am Main, 1819–28.

[Holy Roman Empire] *Deutsche Reichstagsakten.* "Jüngere Reihe," ed. by the Historische Kommission bei der Königlichen Akademie der Wissenschaften [at Munich], Vol. I. Gotha: F. A. Perthes, 1893–. This valuable collection of documents was used for the study of the attempted customs unification of 1523.

Klinkowstroem, A., de (Ed.). *Mémoires documents et écrits divers laissés par le prince de Metternich chancellier de cour et d'état,* 8 vols. Various eds. Paris: Plon, 1881–1908. Includes Metternich's memoir of 1833.

L., M. (Ed.). "Der Ursprung des deutschen Verwaltungsrathes von 1813," *Historische Zeitschrift*, LIX (1888), 295–301. A reprint of a memorandum by Stein.

Martens, Geo. Fred. de [i.e. Georg Friedrich von]. *Nouveau recueil de traités d'alliance, de paix, de trêve, de neutralité, de commerce, de limites, d'exchange etc. et de plusieurs autres actes servant à la connaissance des relations étrangères des puissances et états de l'Europe tant dans leur rapport mutuel que dans celui envers les puissances et états dans d'autres parties du globe depuis 1808 jusqu'à présent,* 16 vols. Gottingue, 1817–41. A large number of treaties reprinted in this standard collection were used.

Martens, de [i.e. Georg Friedrich von]. *Nouveau recueil général des traités, conventions et autres transactions remarquables, servant à la* connaisance des relations étrangères des puissances et états dans leurs rapports mutuels, 20 vols. Gottingue, 1843–75.

NAU, B[ERNHARD] S[EBASTIAN] VON (Ed.). Beiträge zur Kenntniss und Beförderung des Handels und der Schiff-Fahrt, xii + 189. Mainz, 1818. A collection of documents on the navigation of the Rhine.

ONCKEN, HERMANN, AND SAEMISCH, F. E. M. (Eds.). Vorgeschichte und Begründung des deutschen Zollvereins 1815–34 Akten der Staaten des Deutschen Bundes und der europäischen Mächte, "Veröffentlichungen der Friedrich List-Gesellschaft E. V." Vols. VIII–X. Sections edited by W. von Eisenhart Rothe and A. Ritthaler. Berlin SW 61: Reimar Hobbing, 1934. This collection of documents illuminates like no other the origin of the Zollverein. It was relied on throughout this study.

[Prussia] Gesetz-Sammlung für die königlichen preussischen Staaten [title varies]. 1806–. An official collection of Prussian statutes, containing a large number of public treaties concluded by Prussia and thus furnishing material for the study of her Anschluss and Zollverein policies.

[Saxony, laws, etc.] Sammlung der Gesetze und Verordnungen für das Königreich Sachsen vom Jahre 1833, xxxvi + 586. 38 parts. Dresden [1833].

SCHMIDT, HERIBERT [HEINRICH ROBERT]. Die Begründung des preussischhessischen Zollvereins vom 14. Februar 1828, 19 + xxix. Doctor's dissertation, Giessen, 1925. Giessen, 1926. Schmidt reprints in his appendix invaluable documents on Hesse-Darmstadt's policy at the Vienna Final Conferences.

SCHMIDT, WILHELM ADOLF. Geschichte der deutschen Verfassungsfrage während der Befreiungskriege und des Wiener Kongresses 1812 bis 1815, ed. by Alfred Stern, vi + 497. Stuttgart: G. J. Göschen, 1890. Schmidt incorporates a number of valuable documents in his critical study.

[Württemberg] Der Zollvereinigungs-Vertrag zwischen Württemberg und Bayern einerseits und Preussen, den beiden Hessen, Sachsen u.s.w. andererseits nebst Zoll-Cartel, Zoll-Ordnung und Zoll-Tarif, 108 pp. Stuttgart, 1833.

ZIMMERMANN, ALFRED. Geschichte der preussisch-deutschen Handelspolitik aktenmässig dargestellt, 850 pp. Oldenburg: Schulzesche Hof-Buchhandlung und Hof-Buchdrukerei. A. Schwartz, 1892. This treatise has been superseded by Brinkmann's work. It contains, however, reprints from documents not otherwise available.

[Zollverein, Central-Büreau (Ed.)] Verträge und Verhandlungen aus dem Zeitraume von 1833 bis einschliesslich 1836 über die Bildung und Ausführung des deutschen Zoll- und Handels-Vereins, Vol. I, x + 471. Berlin, 1845. The official edition of the Zollverein treaties.

SECONDARY SOURCES: EXPRESSIONS OF CONTEMPORARY PRIVATE THOUGHT, INCLUDING PARLIAMENTARY DEBATES

COLLECTIONS

ARNDT, E[RNST] M[ORITZ]. Schriften für und an seine lieben Deutschen, 4 vols. Leipzig, 1845-55.

DITFURTH, FRANZ WILHELM, FREIHERR VON (Ed.). Historische Volkslieder von der Verbannung Napoleons nach St. Helena 1815, bis zur Gründung *des Nordbundes 1866,* viii + 224. Berlin: F. Lipperheide, 1871. Reprints one of the early songs on the Zollverein.

ECKERMANN, JOHANN PETER. *Gespräche mit Goethe in den letzten Jahren seines Lebens.* Ninth ed., 806 pp. Leipzig: F. A. Brockhaus, 1909.

EULENBERG, HERBERT (Ed.). *Der Anlauf, Zeitschriften der Jahre 1817-1821 mit den ersten dichterischen Veröffentlichungen von H. Heine in naturgetreuen Wiedergaben,* xvi pp. and 30 facsimile reproductions. Hamburg: Hoffmann & Campe, 1921. Eulenberg's reprint was used to illustrate the contemporary magazine *niveau.*

GÖRRES, [JOHANN] JOSEPH [VON]. Gesammelte Schriften, ed. by the Görres-Gesellschaft, Vol. 1–. Köln: Gilde-Verlag, 1926–. Includes a facsimile reprint from *Rheinischer Merkur.*

HEYDERHOFF, JULIUS (Ed.). *Benzenberg, der Rheinländer und Preusse, 1815-1823. Rheinisches Archiv,* Vol. VII, 169 pp. Bonn: F. Klopp, 1928. A collection of writings illuminating the life of this great liberal.

Johann Gottlieb Fichte's sämmtliche Werke, ed. by J. H. Fichte, 8 vols. Berlin, 1845–46.

KLEIN, TIM (Ed.). *Die Befreiung 1813·1814·1815, Urkunden Berichte Briefe mit geschichtlichen Verbindungen,* 534 pp. Ebenhausen bei München: W. Langewiesche-Brandt, 1913.

LIST, FRIEDRICH. *Schriften/Reden/Briefe,* ed. by Friedrich List Gesellschaft E. V. 10 vols. Berlin SW. 61: Reimar Hobbings, 1927–35. All major works written by List can be found in this excellent edition.

ROMMEL, OTTO (Ed.). *Der österreichische Vormärz 1816–1847,* Deutsche Literatur, Politische Reihe, Vol. IV, 334 pp. Leipzig: Philipp Reclam jun., 1931.

SEUME, J[OHANN] G[OTTFRIED]. *Prosaische und poetische Werke,* 10 vols. Berlin [1875].

STEIN, KARL, FREIHERR, VOM. *Briefwechsel, Denkschriften und Aufzeichnungen,* ed. by Erich Botzenhart, Vol. I–. Berlin: C. Heymann, 1931–.

VOLKMANN, ERNST (ED.). *Um Einheit und Freiheit 1815–1848 (vom Wiener Kongress bis zur Märzrevolution),* Deutsche Literatur, Politische Reihe, Vol. III, 332 pp. Leipzig: Philipp Reclam jun., 1936. This anthology proved useful for the study of political poems.

INDIVIDUAL PUBLICATIONS
Before 1815

JAHN, FR[IEDRICH]-[SIC] L[UDWIG]. *Recherches sur la nationalité, l'esprit des peuples allemands et les institutions qui seraient en harmonie avec leurs mœurs et leur caractère,* trans. by P. Lortet, xv + 432, Paris, 1825. The first German edition appeared in 1810.

LIPS, [MICHAEL] ALEXANDER. *Der Wiener Congress oder was muss geschehen um Deutschland vor seinem Untergange zu retten...,* 48 pp. Erlangen, 1814.

Möser, Justus. *Patriotische Phantasien*, ed. by J. W. J. v. Voigt. New and enlarged ed. Frankfurt, 1780. Vols. I-III. Berlin, 1786. Vol. IV.

1816

[Anonymous] "Über Englands Reichthum und Deutschlands Wohlstand in Beziehung auf staatswirthschaftliche Gesetzgebung," *Europäische Annalen*, 1816, Part VI, pp. 233–271, No. 7, pp. 3–44.

Cölln, F[riedrich Willibald Ferdinand] v[on]. "Keine Accise mehr?!" reprinted from *Freimüthige Blätter*, XIII (Berlin, 1816), 457–526. Cölln was a well-known Prussian publicist.

Brunner, Hans Caspar. *Was sind Maut- und Zollanstalten der Nationalwohlfahrt und dem Staatsinteresse?* vii + 135. Nürnberg, 1816. Although Brunner was a radical free trader, he became a Bavarian customs official.

Poppe, Johann Heinrich Moritz. *Deutschland auf der höchst möglichen Stufe seines Kunstfleisses und seiner Industrie überhaupt. Vorschläge, Wünsche und Hoffnungen zur Vermehrung des deutschen Wohlstandes*, vi + 58. Frankfurt am Main, 1816.

1817

[Anonymous] "Meinungen verschiedener Völker über den gegenwärtig bedrängten Zustand des Kunstfleisses und Handels, und Vorschläge ihm abzuhelfen," *Europäische Annalen*, 1817, No. 8, pp. 194–219. Contains a survey of current opinion.

[Anonymous] *Unterthänigste Vorstellung, der Bundes-Versammlung zu Frankfurt, von Deutschlands Fabrikanten und sämmtlichen Arbeitern, dem engl. Handelssystem Einhalt zu thun, zutrauungsvoll zugeeignet*, 15 pp. Reprinted from *Stafette*. "Germania, im Sommer 1817," A Francophile pamplet.

1818

[Anonymous] "Entwurf einer Rede die von einem der deutschen Gesandten am Bundestage zu Frankfurt am Main bey Wiedereröffnung der Sitzungen desselben am 3. November 1817 gehalten werde sollte," *Europäische Annalen* 1818, No. 3, pp. 321-53.

[Anonymous] "Über Kurzsichtigkeit in vaterländischen Angelegenheiten," *Europäische Annalen*, 1818, No. 5, pp. 265–76.

Nebenius, [Carl] Friedrich. *Bemerkungen über den Zustand Grossbritanniens in staatswirthschaftlicher Hinsicht. Nebst einem Worte über Deutschlands auswärtige Handelsverhältnisse.... Mit einer Übersetzung der französischen Schrift: Über England und Engländer, von J. B. Say*, xii, 59 + 158. Karlsruhe, 1818. Devotes some space to conditions in Germany.

1819

[Baden, Landtag] *Übersicht der ständischen Verhandlungen beider Kammern des Grossherzogthums Baden*, 2 vols. Karlsruhe, 1819.

"Bunder, Chlodwig" [pseudonym of Ludwig Basedow]. *Beleuchtung der Verhältnisse Anhalts zu Preussen in Bezug auf das von letzterm angenommene und auf ersters ausgedehnte Zoll- und Verbrauchssteuer-System*. "Deutschland" [i.e. Dessau], 1819, 113 pp.

[Saxe-Hildburghausen, Landtag] *Landtags-Verhandlungen im Fürstenthum Hildburghausen*, 1819–24, 4 vols. Hildburghausen, 1819–25.

1820

[Anonymous] *Schutz der einheimischen Industrie, eine Municipal-Massregel und keine Kriegs-Erklärung, als Antwort der in Leipzig erschienenen Schrift "Über das Retorsions-Princip etc. etc.,"* 39 pp. "Von dem Verfasser der Beantwortung der Bremer Vorlesung." Hamburg, 1820.

Benzenberg, J[ohann] F[riedrich]. *Über Preussens Geldhaushalt und neues Steuersystem*, xviii + 454. Leipzig, 1820. Benzenberg was a well-known Prussian liberal.

[Gruner, Karl Gustav Adolph] *Über das Retorsions-Princip als Grundlage eines deutschen Handels-Systems*, 84 pp. "Geschrieben im Februar 1820." Leipzig [1820]. Gruner attacked List's industrial interests.

[Lindner, Friedrich Ludwig] *Manuscript aus Süd-Deutschland*, "Herausgegeben von George Erichson." Second ed., xviii + 276. "London, bei James Griphi. 1821." The first edition of Lindner's famous pamphlet appeared in 1820.

Weber, Ernst. *Deutschlands Retorsions-System als Nothwehr und nicht als Zweck. Zur vorläufigen Erwiederung [sic] der Schrift: "Über das Retorsions-Princip etc.,"* 59 pp. Gera, "im Mai-Monat 1820." Weber was a member of List's League.

1821

[Haller, M. J.] *Sechs Briefe über den Handel der Hansestädte besonders mit Beziehung auf die Angriffe des Manuscripts aus Süd-Deutschland*, 70 pp. Bremen, 1821.

[Hess, Jonas Ludwig, von] *Aus Nord-Deutschland kein Manuscript*, xvi + 408. Hamburg, 1821.

Malthus [Thomas Robert], and Say. *Über die Ursachen der jetzigen Handelsstockung*, trans. by Karl Heinrich Rau, with an appendix by the translator, xviiii + 301. Hamburg, 1821. Rau discusses German conditions in his appendix.

[Storck, A.] *Über das Verhältnis der freien Hansestädte zum Handel Deutschlands*, 208 pp. "Von einem Bremer Bürger." Bremen, 1821.

1822

[Anonymous] *Materialien für Münzgesetzgebung und dabei entstehende Erörterungen*, xiv + 494. Frankfurt a.M., 1822.

[Anonymous] *Neue Organisation der Schifffahrts- und Handelsverhältnisse auf dem Rheinstrome*, Part I, viii + 180. Basel, 1822.

Miller, Franz. *Über ein Maximum der Zölle zwischen süddeutschen Staaten und die Ausführung gemeinsam verabredeter Maasregeln gegen fremde feindliche Douanen-Systeme ohne einen gemeinschaftlichen Handels- und Zoll-Verband*, 40 pp. Darmstadt, 1822. Miller quotes the Nebenius memorandum of 1819 a number of times.

1823

Hopf, Heinrich Friedrich. *Meinungen von der Handelsfreyheit und dem Prohibitionssysteme in Beziehung auf die Industrie in den deutschen Bundesstaaten*, x + 287. Wien, 1823.

274   THE EVOLUTION OF THE ZOLLVEREIN

1824

BÜLOW-CUMMEROW, ERNST GOTTFRIED GEORG VON. *Betrachtungen über Metall- und Papiergeld, über Handelsfreiheit, Prohibitiv-Systeme, den gegenwärtigen Zustand der ersten europäischen Reiche, Verschuldung der Grundbesitzer, Pfandbrief-System etc. und Landbanken,* viii + [196] pp. Berlin, 1824. Bülow was a Prussian publicist.

1825

LIPS, [MICHAEL] ALEXANDER. *Über den gegenwärtig tiefen Stand der Getraide-Preise in Deutschland, ihr nothwendig immer tieferes Sinken, die Ursachen dieser Erscheinung und die Mittel, sie [sic] zu heben,* 72 pp. Nürnberg, 1825.

1826

[ANONYMOUS] *Kurze Ansichten über die Vereinigung mehrerer südteutschen Staaten zu einem gemeinsamen Zoll- und Maut-Sisteme als Heilmittel für den Druck der Zeit, die Wohlfeilheit der Producte und den zunehmenden Geldmangel,* 48 pp. Mannheim, 1826.

[Prussia, Rhine Province, Landtag] *Bericht des dreizehnten Ausschusses an die Plenar-Versammlung der rheinischen Provinzial-Stände über die ihm unter dem 6[.] November 1826 zugewiesenen Anträge in Betreff der Freiheit der Rheinschiffahrt,* 54 pp. Düsseldorf, 1826.

1827

[ANONYMOUS] "Über Gewerbe und Handelsfreiheit," *Hermes* 1827, pp. 199-245.

1828

[ANONYMOUS] *Ansichten über Zollvereine unter südteutschen Staaten. Veranlasst durch die Schrift: Hingeworfene Gedanken über die Frage: ob Bayern mit benachbarten Staaten in eine gemeinschaftliche Mautlinie treten soll?* 30 pp. München, 1828.

KLÜBER, JOHANN LUDWIG. *Das Münzwesen in Teutschland nach seinem jetzigen Zustand, mit Grundzügen zu einem Münzverein teutscher Bundesstaaten,* vii + 296. Stuttgart, 1828.

RUDHART [IGNAZ]. *Rede des Abgeordneten Dr. Rudhart über den Gesetzesentwurf zu einer Zollordnung gehalten in der Kammer der Abgeordneten der bayrischen Ständeversammlung in München am 5. Juni 1828,* 60 pp. Nürnberg [1828]. Rudhart subsequently became a prominent figure in the Bavarian and Greek governments.

SCHARRER, JOHANNES. *Bemerkungen über den deutschen Zollverein und über die Wirkung hoher Zölle in nationalökonomischer Hinsicht,* 54 pp. Nürnberg, 1828.

1829

LINDNER [FRIEDRICH LUDWIG]. *Considérations sur le traité d'Union commerciale entre la Prusse, la Bavière, le Wurtemberg, et Hesse-Darmstadt,* 26 pp. Munic, 1829. Lindner wrote this pamphlet for the Bavarian government.

1830

[ANONYMOUS] *Einige Worte über Handel und Industrie in Deutschland, mit besonderer Rücksicht auf Bayern,* 134 and 39 pp. München, 1830.

[ANONYMOUS] *Was soll und was kann Deutschland in Beziehung auf seine Zoll- und Mauthverhältnisse?* 34 pp. Kassel, 1830.

[ANONYMOUS] *Die Zollverhältnisse Kurhessens,* 46 pp. Leipzig, 1830.

[BERGIUS, C. J.] *Betrachtungen über die Finanzen und die Gewerbe im preussischen Staate, veranlasst durch die Schrift des Herrn G. O. F. R. Ferber, über Preussens gewerblichen und kommerziellen Zustand,* 77 pp. Berlin, 1830.

LIPS, [MICHAEL] ALEXANDER. *Deutschlands National-Ökonomie. Ein Versuch zur Frage: "wie kann Deutschland zu lohnendem Ackerbau, zu blühender Industrie und wärksamem [sic] Handel gelangen?"* xvi + 655. Giessen, 1830.

[REINWALD, J.] *Kurze Betrachtungen über Deutschlands Einigung in seinen Merkantilinteressen,* 34 pp. Mainz, 1830.

1831

AMSBERG, A. VON. *Über die Einigung der Handels-Interessen Deutschlands,* 79 pp. Braunschweig, 1831. Amsberg was a high Brunswick official.

[ANONYMOUS] *Denkschrift über die nachtheiligen Folgen des hohen bayrischen Eingangszolltarifs und der bayrischen Zollordnung vom Jahre 1828,* viii + 38. [Nuremberg] 1831. This memorandum was submitted by a number of Nuremberg business men to the Bavarian Diet.

[ANONYMOUS] *Denkschrift über Zollwesen und Zoll- und Handels-Vereine in Deutschland; dann über die Klagen und Wünsche mehrerer Handelsstände in Bayern und Baden,* 74 pp. Stuttgart, 1831. This pamphlet has been ascribed to Cotta.

[ANONYMOUS] *Über Bayerns Mautsystem, Erörterung der Frage: Ist ein hoher Mauttarif eines Binnenlandes geeignet die Industrie desselben zu heben?* 21 pp. Nürnberg, 1831.

BRÜEL, L[UDWIG] A[UGUST]. *Materialien für die zu erwartende Reform des deutschen Münzwesens.* Second ed., 60 pp. Hannover, 1831.

KAUFMANN, PET[ER]. *Rheinpreussen und seine staatswirthschaftlichen Interessen in der heutigen europäischen Staaten-Krise, oder vergleichende Betrachtungen über den gegenwärtigen Zustand der königlich preussischen Rheinlande, mit volkswirthschaftlichen Vorschlägen und statistischen Nachweisungen,* xii + 200. Berlin, 1831.

PFIZER, PAUL ACHATIUS. *Briefwechsel zweier Deutschen.* Collation of first and second editions of 1831 and 1832 by George Künzel. Deutsche Literaturdenkmale, No. 144, pp. 1–330. Berlin: Behr's Verlag, 1911.

S[IEBENFFEIFFER, PHILIPP JAKOB]. "Die Thron-Rede," *Rheinbayern,* II (1831), 225–38.

S[IEBENPFEIFFER, PHILIPP JAKOB]. "Handels- und Zollvereine," *Rheinbayern,* III (1831), 153–81.

S[IEBENPFEIFFER, PHILIPP JAKOB]. "Die Mauth," *Rheinbayern,* II (1831), 21–26.

S[IEBENPFEIFFER, PHILIPP JAKOB]. "Schriften über die Mauth im Rheinkreise," *Rheinbayern,* II (1831), 51–54.

[SPEYERER] *Die Frage der Zollvereinigung deutscher Staaten,* 30 pp. Heidelberg, 1831.

STROMEYER, FRANZ. "Über Handel und Mauthen in Süd-Deutschland," *Rheinbayern,* IV (1831), 197–224.

1832

[ANONYMOUS] *Untersuchung der Frage: "Ist es an der Zeit, und den allgemeinen Handels-Interessen Teutschlands angemessen, dass man dem Preussisch-Hessisch-Waldeckschen Zollverbande entgegenwirke, oder dass man sich ihm, wenn irgend möglich, anschliesse . . . ?"* pp. i–vi, 7–30. Bremen, 1832.

[BÖHMER, JOHANN FRIEDRICH] *Das Zollwesen in Deutschland geschichtlich beleuchtet.* "Geschichtliche Beleuchtungen des deutschen Staatsrechts," Vol. I, 94 pp. Frankfurt am Main, 1832.

HUNDESHAGEN, J[OHANN] CHR[ISTIAN]. *Die Staatskräfte des Grossherzogthum Hessens,* viii + 334. Tübingen, 1832.

SCHMIDT, FRIEDRICH. *Unter welchen Bedingungen kann ein allgemeiner Zollverband allen deutschen Staaten nützlich seyn?* . . . , 108 and [4] pp. Zittau, 1832.

WIRTH, J[OHANN] G[EORG] A[UGUST]. *Das Nationalfest der Deutschen zu Hambach,* 104 pp. Neustadt a/H, 1832. Wirth gives a detailed account of that famous festival.

WIRTH, J[OHANN] G[EORG] A[UGUST]. *Die politischen Reformen Deutschlands,* 63 pp. Strasburg, 1832. Wirth published this book after he fled Germany.

1833

[ANONYMOUS] *Beleuchtung der Opposition des Herrn Zais gegen den preussischen Zollverein,* 60 pp. Stuttgart, 1833.

[ANONYMOUS] *Bemerkungen über die Handels-Politik Englands gegen Preussen und andere nordische Staaten,* vi + 84. Translated from the English by Geo. Meyenn, with an appendix by the translator. Rostock, 1833.

[ANONYMOUS] *Einige Worte über Handel und freien Verkehr im Allgemeinen und insbesondere zwischen den verschiedenen Bundesstaaten mit Hinblick auf den Art. 19 der deutschen Bundesacte und den neuen Preussich-Baierischen (Württemberg, beide Hessen, Sachsen und die Thüringischen Staaten) [sic] begreifenden Zollverband,* 48 pp. Reprint from *Archiv für die neueste Gesetzgebung aller deutschen Staaten.* Mainz, 1833.

[ANONYMOUS] *Über den Anschluss Badens an den Preussisch-Hessischen Zollverein. Einige triftige und beherzigungswerthe Motive gegen diesen von Herrn Staatsrath Nebenius in seiner bekannten Denkschrift empfohlenen Anschluss,* 22 pp. Freiburg im Brsg., 1833.

[ANONYMOUS] *Über die Handelspolitik der teutschen freien Städte, insbesondere Hamburgs und Frankfurts,* viii + 30. Reprint from *Teutsche Vaterlands-Zeitung.* Darmstadt, 1833.

[CUNOW] *Sachsens Anschluss an den preussischen Zollverband; nebst der davon abhängigen Gestaltung anderweitiger innerer und äusserer Verhältnisse,* 21 pp. Dresden, 1833.

NEBENIUS, C[ARL] F[RIEDRICH]. *Denkschrift für den Beitritt Badens zu dem zwischen Preussen, Bayern, Württemberg, den beiden Hessen und mehren andern deutschen Staaten abgeschlossenen Zollverein,* 62 and 32 pp. Karlsruhe, 1833. Nebenius's memorandum of 1819 is reprinted in 32 pages of the appendix of this pamphlet.

RAUMER, FRIEDRICH VON. *Über den Anschluss Sachsens an die deutschen Zoll- und Handelsvereine,* 32 pp. Reprinted from *Blätter für literarische Unterhaltung.* Leipzig, 1833. An article by the well-known Prussian historian.

RUNDE, F. L. *Auch ein Wort über Sachsens Anschluss an den preusischen [sic] Zollverband, als Beleuchtung der jüngst von mehrern Kaufleuten dargestellten Schattenseite dieser Anschliesung [sic] aufgenommen aus dem Standpuncte der sächsischen Landwirthe,* 54 pp. Freiberg, 1833.

TERTIARY SOURCES: STATISTICAL AND LEGAL AUTHORITIES, AND OTHER MISCELLANEOUS MATERIAL

KLÜBER, JOHANN LUDWIG. *Öffentliches Recht des Teutschen Bundes und der Bundesstaaten.* Third ed., xx + 880. Frankfurt a.M., 1831. Klüber is an authority on the Public Law of the German Confederation.

KLÜBER [JOHANN LUDWIG]. *Das Postwesen in Teutschland, wie es war, ist, und seyn könnte,* xii + 227. Erlangen, 1811. Klüber's monograph on postal administration is valuable for the study of institutions in his day.

MEMMINGER, J. D. G. (Ed.). *Württembergische Jahrbücher für vaterländische Geschichte, Geographie, Statistik und Topographie,* 1827, Part I, viii + 224. Stuttgart, 1829. Memminger's yearbook contains information on the execution of the Bavaria-Württemberg Customs Union of 1828.

PÜTTER, JOHANN STEPHAN. *Historische Entwicklung der heutigen Staatsverfassung des Teutschen Reichs.* Göttingen, 1786–87, 3 vols. An authoritative treatise on the Public Law of the old Empire.

VIEBAHN, GEORG VON. *Statistik des zollvereinten und nördlichen Deutschlands,* 3 vols. Berlin: G. Reimer, 1858–68. An excellent source of statistical information.

ZEDLER, JOHANN HEINRICH. *Grosses vollständiges universal Lexicon...,* 64 vols. Halle, 1732–50.

HISTORICAL TREATISES

AEGIDI, LUDWIG KARL [JAMES]. *Aus der Vorzeit des Zollvereins. Beitrag zur deutschen Geschichte,* 132 pp. Hamburg: Noyes & Geisler, 1865. A detailed study of the Vienna Final Conferences; based on archival material, much of which has not been used since.

ALBRECHT, CURT. *Die Triaspolitik des Frhn. K. Aug. v. Wangenheim,* x + 196. Doctor's dissertation, Leipzig, 1914. "Darstellungen aus der württembergischen Geschichte," Vol. XIV. Stuttgart: W. Kohlhammer, 1914. Describes the political activities of Württemberg's representative at Frankfurt.

[ANONYMOUS] "Christian Günther Graf v. Bernstorff, Königl. preuss. Geh. Staats- und Cabinets-Minister," *Politisches Journal,* LVI (1835), 445–62. This biography, written by a contemporary, preserves data which are otherwise not easily obtainable.

BAASCH, ERNST. "Die deutschen wirtschaftlichen Einheitsbestrebungen, die Hansestädte und Friedrich List bis zum Jahre 1821," *Historische Zeitschrift,* CXXII (1920), 454–85. Represents a valuable contribution to the understanding of the period after the Vienna Congress.

BAB, BERND. *Die öffentliche Meinung über den deutschen Zollverein zur Zeit seiner Entstehung*, 98 pp. Doctor's dissertation, Berlin, 1930. An excellent monograph; analyzes public opinion. The study relies primarily on the periodical literature of the period; but documents have also been consulted in order to clarify the relation between governments and instruments of public opinion.

BECK, JOS[EPH]. *Carl Friedrich Nebenius. Ein Lebensbild eines deutschen Staatsmannes und Gelehrten. Zugleich ein Beitrag zur Geschichte Badens und des deutschen Zollvereins*, 128 pp. Mannheim: J. Schneider, 1866. Follows substantially his earlier article on the same subject (cf. next entry).

BECK, J[OSEPH]. "Karl Friedrich Nebenius in Beziehung zur Geschichte Badens und des deutschen Zollvereins," *Unsere Zeit. Jahrbuch zum Conversations-Lexikon*, VIII (1864), 35–69. A pro-Nebenius account of the origin of the Zollverein. Although it cannot be called a reliable treatment of the topic, its suggestions are still widely accepted.

BEER, ADOLF. "Österreich und die deutschen Handelseinigungsbestrebungen in den Jahren 1817 bis 1820," *Österreichisch-Ungarische Revue*, III (New Series, 1887), 277–311. A competent study on Austria's economic policy after the Napoleonic era.

BEER, ADOLF. *Die österreichische Handelspolitik im neunzehnten Jahrhundert*, x + 618. Wien: Manz, 1891. A standard presentation of Austria's commercial policy in the nineteenth century.

BELOW, G. VON. "Kontribution," *Handwörterbuch der Staatswissenschaften*, IV (1892), 847.

BIBL, VIKTOR. *Der Zerfall Österreichs*, 2 vols. Wien: Rikola Verlag, 1922–24. A study of Austria's decline; includes independent investigations of her commercial policy.

BLUME, CARL J. H. *Hamburg und die deutschen wirtschaftlichen Einheitsbestrebungen 1814–1847*, 115 pp. [Hamburg, 1934.]

BÖHTLINGK, ARTHUR. *Carl Friedrich Nebenius. Der deutsche Zollverein, das Karlsruher Polytechnikum und die erste Staatsbahn in Deutschland*, 119 pp. Karlsruhe: Friedrich Gutsch [1899]. A pro-Baden account of the foundation of the Zollverein, Böhtlingk's monograph is nevertheless based on archival research.

BORCKENHAGEN, FRITZE. *National- und handelspolitische Bestrebungen in Deutschland (1815–1822) und die Anfänge Friedrich Lists.* "Abhandlungen zur mittleren und neueren Geschichte," ed. by Georg von Below and others, No. 57, 83 pp. Berlin: W. Rothschild, 1915. An excellent and indispensable treatise on the origins of German economic unification.

BRINKMANN, CARL. *Die preussische Handelspolitik vor dem Zollverein und der Wiederaufbau vor hundert Jahren*, vi + 242. Berlin: Verein Wissenschaftlicher Verleger, 1922. One of the great interpretations of nineteenth-century German history. It deals primarily with Prussia's commercial policy, and is not so much concerned about economic unification.

BRUHNS. "Benzenberg." *Allgemeine deutsche Biographie*, ed. by the Historische Commission bei der Königlichen Akademie der Wissenschaften [at Munich], II (1875), 348–49. A standard biography of Benzenberg.

BÜHLER, JOHANNES. *Das Hambacher Fest*, 197 pp. Ludwigshafen a. Rh.: J. Waldkirch, 1932. A good account of that famous festival.

CAHN, JULIUS [ALFRED]. *Münz- und Geldgeschichte von Konstanz und des Bodenseegebiets im Mittelalter bis zum Reichsmünzgesetz von 1559. Münz- und Geldgeschichte der im Grossherzogtum Baden vereinigten Gebiete*, ed. by Badische Historische Kommission, Part I, x + 460. Heidelberg: C. Winter, 1911. A description of coinage unions in South Germany during the late Middle Ages.

CRÖSSMANN, CHRISTOPH. *Die Unruhen in Oberhessen im Herbste 1830.* "Quellen und Forschungen zur hessischen Geschichte, ed. by Historische Kommission für den Volksstaat Hessen," Vol. VIII, [iv] + 82. Darmstadt: Hessischer Staatsverlag, 1929. A good narrative on one aspect of the disturbances in southwest Germany after the July Revolution.

DOEBERL, M[ICHAEL]. *Bayern und die wirtschaftliche Einigung Deutschlands.* "Abhandlungen der Königlich Bayerischen Akademie der Wissenschaften, Philosophisch-philologische und historische Klasse," Vol. XXIX, Part II, 117 pp. München, 1915. An excellent study of Bavaria's participation in German economic unification. It has a supplement consisting of the important documents on this problem.

DOEBERL, M[ICHAEL]. *Entwicklungsgeschichte Bayerns.* Third ed., 3 vols. München: R. Oldenbourg, 1916–31. A good standard history of Bavaria.

DOVE, ALFRED. "Ranke," *Allgemeine deutsche Biographie*, ed. by the Historische Commission bei der Königl. Akademie der Wissenschaften [at Munich], XXVII (1888), 243–69. Dove gives a lengthy account of the life of that great historian.

ECKERT, CHRISTIAN. *Rheinschiffahrt im XIX. Jahrhundert* "Staats- und socialwissenschaftliche Forschungen," ed. by Gustav Schmoller, No. 81, xix + 450. Leipzig: Duncker & Humblot, 1900. Eckert gives a thorough treatment of navigation on the Rhine.

ECKERT, CHRISTIAN. "Zur Vorgeschichte des deutschen Zollvereins. Die preussisch-hessische Zollunion vom 14. Februar 1828," *Schmoller's Jahrbuch für Gesetzgebung, Verwaltung und Volkswirtschaft im Deutschen Reich*, XXVI (1902), Part II, 51–102. A good account of the history of the Prussia-Hesse-Darmstadt Zollverein. His monograph is based on solid archival research.

EMMINGHAUS, A[RWED]. *Ernst Wilhelm Arnoldi. Leben und Schöpfungen eines deutschen Kaufmanns*, 369 pp. Weimar: Böhlau, 1878. A good biography of this leading German business man.

ENGEL, WILHELM. *Wirtschaftliche und soziale Kämpfe vor dem Jahre 1848 in Thüringen (insbesonderheit in Herzogtum Meiningen)*, viii + 30. Doctor's dissertation, Marburg, 1927. Jena, G. Fischer, Engel's work is a good monograph.

ENGELBRECHT, H[ELMUTH] C[ARL]. *Johann Gottlieb Fichte. A Study of His Political Writings, with Special Reference to His Nationalism.* "Studies in History, Economics and Public Law," ed. by the Faculty of Political Science of Columbia University, No. 383, 221 pp. New York: Columbia University Press, 1933. A thorough treatment of Fichte's political thought.

EULER, CARL [PHILIPP]. *Friedrich Ludwig Jahn, sein Leben und Wirken,* xv + 634. Stuttgart: Krabbe, 1881. This is a standard biography of the well-known educator.

FALKE, JOHANNES. *Die Geschichte des deutschen Zollwesens. Von seiner Entstehung bis zum Abschluss des deutschen Zollvereins*, xx + 426. Leipzig, 1869. An early general treatise of German tariff history prior to 1834.

FISCHER, GUSTAV. "Über das Wesen und die Bedingungen eines Zoll-vereins," *Jahrbücher für Nationalökonomie und Statistik*, II (1864), 317–85, 397–432; VII (1866), 225–304; VIII (1867), 252–360 (not completed). An analytical and systematic study of the nature of a customs union; based on the history of the Zollverein.

GOTHEIN, EBERHARD. *Geschichtliche Entwicklung der Rheinschiffahrt im 19. Jahrhundert.* "Schriften des Vereins für Sozialpolitik," No. 101, vi + 300. Leipzig: Duncker & Humblot, 1903. A standard presentation of the topic.

HASEK, CARL WILLIAM. *The Introduction of Adam Smith's Doctrines into Germany*, 157 pp. Doctor's dissertation, Columbia University, New York, 1925. A good survey of the beliefs held by German economists around 1800.

HENDERSON, W[ILLIAM] O[TTO]. *The Zollverein*, xvi + 375. "Cambridge Studies in Economic History," Cambridge: University Press, 1939. The best general presentation of the history of the Zollverein. Henderson relied not only on the best monographic material available, but also on archival research of his own.

HÖLZLE, ERWIN. "Der deutsche Zollverein. Nationalpolitisches aus seiner Vorgeschichte," *Württembergische Jahrbücher für Statistik und Landeskunde*, 1932–33, ed. by Statistisches Landesamt, pp. 131–45. Stuttgart: Kohlhammer, 1935. Deals primarily with Württemberg's part in the foundation of the Zollverein. The article is supplemented with documentary material.

Jahresberichte der Geschichtswissenschaft, 36 vols. Berlin, 1880–1916. This general bibliography was used in order to obtain information otherwise inaccessible.

KAMLAH, IRMGARD, *Karl Georg Maassen und die preussische Finanzreform von 1816–1822*, 64 pp. Doctor's dissertation, Halle, 1934. A good presentation of the topic, relying on Prussian archival material.

KÖHLER, CURT. *Problematisches zu Friedrich List. Mit Anhang: Lists Briefe aus Amerika in deutscher Übersetzung*, x + 259. Leipzig: C. Hirschfeld, 1908. An analytical study of the economic ideas of the young List. It is one of the best introductions to the complex character of this famous economist.

KOSER, REINHOLD [CARL BERNHARD ALEXANDER]. *Geschichte Friedrichs des Grossen.* Fourth and fifth eds., 3 vols. Stuttgart: J. G. Cotta'sche Buchhandlung Nachfolger, 1912–13. A good account of the life of this Prussian king.

LENZ, FRIEDRICH. *Friedrich List. Der Mann und das Werk*, x + 441. München: R. Oldenbourg, 1936. A general, but analytical study of List's life.

LERCHENFELD, MAX, FREIHERR VON. "Lerchenfeld," *Allgemeine deutsche Biographie*, ed. by the Historische Commission bei der Königlichen

Akademie der Wissenschaften [at Munich], XVIII (1883), 423–24. A standard account of the life of this Bavarian statesman.

MAMROTH, KARL. *Geschichte der preussischen Staats-Besteuerung 1806–1816,* xix + 766. Leipzig: Duncker and Humblot, 1890. A good account of Prussian taxation during the Napoleonic era.

MEERWARTH, HERMANN. *Die öffentliche Meinung in Baden von den Befreiungskriegen bis zur Erteilung der Verfassung (1815–1818),* 117 pp. Doctor's dissertation, Heidelberg, 1907. A standard description of the topic.

MEINECKE, FRIEDRICH. *Weltbürgertum und Nationalstaat. Studien zur Genesis des deutschen Nationalstaats,* Seventh ed., x + 558. München: R. Oldenbourg, 1928. An outstanding analysis of German thought in the nineteenth century.

MENDHEIM, MAX. "Wirth," *Allgemeine deutsche Biographie.* Ed. by the Historische Commission bei der Königlichen Akademie der Wissenschaften [at Munich]. XLIII (1898), 531–33. A standard account of the life of this well-known publicist.

MENN, WALTER. *Zur Vorgeschichte des deutschen Zollvereins, Nassaus Handels- und Schiffahrtspolitik vom Wiener Kongress bis zum Ausgang der süddeutschen Zollvereinsverhandlungen 1815–1827,* 159 pp. Greifswald: Ratsbuchhandlung L. Bamberg, 1930. An excellent and thorough monograph of Nassau's participation in the South German conferences. It is based primarily on unpublished documents.

MÜLLER, HANS FRIEDRICH. *Die Berichterstattung der Allgemeinen Zeitung Augsburg über Fragen der deutschen Wirtschaft 1815–1840,* 200 pp. Doctor's dissertation, München, 1934. (Printed in Berlin by Franz Linke) 1936. A good account of the attitudes expressed in the leading German newspaper.

NEBENIUS, [CARL] F[RIEDRICH]. "Über die Entstehung und Erweiterung des grossen deutschen Zollvereines," *Deutsche Viertel-Jahrsschrift,* 1838, part II, pp. 319–59. Includes a description of early events in the history of German economic unification.

NEY. "SIEBENPFEIFFER," *Allgemeine deutsche Biographie,* XXXIV (1892), 176–77. Ed. by the Historische Commission bei der Königl. Akademie der Wissenschaften [at Munich]. A biography of this popular leader.

OLSHAUSEN, HANS-PETER. *Friedrich List und der Deutsche Handels- und Gewerbsverein,* "List-Studien," No. 6, x + 357. Jena: Gustav Fischer, 1935. A thorough study of List and the League in 1819–20. Olshausen uses primarily unpublished material, much of which he cites or reprints. Since he tries to superimpose the concept of the *Führerprinzip* on List's relation to the League, his work has to be used with caution.

ORTH, PETER. *Die Kleinstaaterei im Rhein-Main-Gebiet und die Eisenbahnpolitik 1830–1866,* 121 pp. Doctor's dissertation, Frankfurt, 1936. Printed: Limburg an der Lahn, 1938. A good account of conditions in southwest Germany.

PERTHES, CLEMENS THEODOR. *Friedrich Perthes' Leben nach dessen schriftlichen und mündlichen Mitteilungen aufgezeichnet,* 3 vols. Gotha: F. A. Perthes, 1896. A comprehensive biography of this great publisher.

PERTZ, G[EORG] H[EINRICH]. *Das Leben des Ministers Freiherrn vom Stein*, 6 vols. Berlin: G. Reimer, 1849–55. An early comprehensive biography of this great statesman.

PETERSDORFF, HERMAN VON. *Friedrich von Motz, eine Biographie*, 2 vols. Berlin: Reimar Hobbing, 1913. A thorough and exhaustive history of Motz's life, using all available material.

RAPP, ADOLF. *Der deutsche Gedanke, seine Entwicklung im politischen und geistigen Leben seit dem 18. Jahrhundert*, 373 pp. Bonn: K. Schroeder, 1920. An important treatise on German thought.

RATHGEN, KARL. "Die Ansichten über Freihandel und Schutzzoll in der deutschen Staatspraxis des 19. Jahrhunderts," *Die Entwicklung der deutschen Volkswirtschaftslehre im neunzehnten Jahrhundert*. Memorial volume for Gustav Schmoller's seventieth birthday. Vol. II (Leipzig, 1908), contribution No. 17, 54 pp. A survey of one aspect of German economic thought.

ROSCHER, WILHELM [GEORG FRIEDRICH]. *Geschichte der National-Ökonomik in Deutschland.* "Geschichte der Wissenschaften in Deutschland, neuere Zeit," ed. by the Historische Commission bei der Königlichen Akademie der Wissenschaften [at Munich], Vol. XIV, viii + 1085. München: R. Oldenbourg, 1874. A general and detailed account of German economic theory.

ROSCHER, WILHELM. "Zur Gründungsgeschichte des deutschen Zollvereins," *Deutschland*, 1870, pp. 143–211.

SCHMOLLER, GUSTAV. "Das preussische Handels- und Zollgesetz vom 26. Mai 1818," *Beilage zur Allgemeinen Zeitung* [Munich], No. 175 (August 3, 1898), pp. 1–7; No. 176 (August 9, 1898), pp. 4–6; No. 177 (August 10, 1898), pp. 3–8. An analysis and evaluation of the Prussian Law of 1818.

SCHNELL, PHILIPP. *Das Frankfurter Handwerk von 1816–1848, ein Beitrag zur Wirtschaftsgeschichte*, 104 pp. Doctor's dissertation, Frankfurt, 1933. Frankfurt am Main, 1936. A good treatise; contains some valuable details.

SICK, PAUL. *Übersichtliche Geschichte der Entstehung des grossen deutschen Zollvereins*, 61 pp. Doctor's dissertation, Tübingen. Printed: Stuttgart, 1843. An early and impartial account of the foundation of the Zollverein.

SOMBART, WERNER. *Die deutsche Volkswirtschaft im neunzehnten Jahrhundert und im Anfang des 20. [sic] Jahrhunderts.* Fifth edition, xvi + 532. Berlin: Georg Bondi, 1921. An excellent general German economic history of the nineteenth century.

SRBIK, HEINRICH RITTER VON. *Metternich, der Staatsmann und der Mensch*, 2 vols. München; F. Bruckmann A.-G., 1925. A thorough reëvaluation of Metternich; includes many otherwise forgotten details.

SUCHEL, ADOLF. *Hessen-Darmstadt und der Darmstädter Handelskongress von 1820–1823.* "Quellen und Forschungen zur hessischen Geschichte," ed. by Historische Kommission für den Volksstaat Hessen, No. 6, vii + 109. Darmstadt: Hessischer Staatsverlag, 1922. A good monograph on Hesse-Darmstadt.

THIEME, [EDUARD ARNO] WILHELM. *Eintritt Sachsens in den Zollverein und seine wirtschaftlichen Folgen*, 99 pp. Doctor's dissertation, Leipzig, 1914. Printed: Liebertwolkwitz, 1914. The value of the study lies in the fact that it cites material which has not been used otherwise.

TREITSCHKE, HEINRICH VON. "Die Anfänge des deutschen Zollvereins," *Preussische Jahrbücher*, XXX (1872), 397–466, 479–571, 648–97.

TREITSCHKE, HEINRICH VON. "Aus den Papieren des Staatsministers von Motz," *Preussische Jahrbücher*, XXXIX (1877), 398–422.

TREITSCHKE, HEINRICH VON. *Deutsche Geschichte im neunzehnten Jahrhundert.* "Staatengeschichte der neuesten Zeit," Vols. XXIV–XXVIII. Second edition, Leipzig: S. Hirzel, 1879–89, Vols. I–III. Third edition, Leipzig: S. Hirzel, 1890–95, Vols. IV–V. Treitschke makes one of the most intensive studies on the origin of the Zollverein. He shows the important part Prussia, and especially Motz, played in this development. However, he frequently overshoots his mark, since he approaches the problem by applying the ideological standards of the nationalism which the new Empire had created. For this reason, his very detailed and vivid account of political events has to be used with caution.

TREUE, WILHELM. *Wirtschaftszustände und Wirtschaftspolitik in Preussen 1815–1825*, "Vierteljahrsschrift für Sozial- und Wirtschaftsgeschichte," Beiheft No. 31, 258 pp. Stuttgart: W. Kohlhammer, 1937. Reviewed by E. N. Anderson in *The American Historical Review*, XLIV, 2 (January, 1939), 374. Treue attempts to show that the Prussian Customs Law of 1818 was a failure since it did not have immediate success. This interpretation is not generally accepted.

WEBER, W. *Der deutsche Zollverein. Geschichte seiner Entstehung und Entwickelung.* Second ed., x + 503. Leipzig: Veit & Comp., 1871. A good general account, based on Bavarian documents. Weber, who was a Bavarian official, frequently takes the Bavarian point of view.

WEECH, FRIEDRICH [OTTO ARISTIDES] VON (ED.). *Correspondenzen und Actenstücke zur Geschichte der Ministerialkonferenzen von Carlsbad und Wien in den Jahren 1819–1822 und 1834*, xvi + 296. Leipzig: Vogel, 1865. A study primarily based on Baden archival material.

WILDENHAYN, KURT. *Der Thüringische Zoll- und Steuerverein, sein Wesen und seine Bedeutung in völkerrechtlicher und staatsrechtlicher Hinsicht*, [vi], 100 + vi. Doctor's dissertation, Jena, 1927. An excellent administrative history of the Thuringian Customs Union by a former official.

WIRSCHING, HEINZ AUGUST. *Der Kampf um die handelspolitische Einigung Europas, eine geschichtliche Darstellung des Gedankens der europäischen Zollunion*, 95 pp. Feuchtwangen: Sommer & Schorr, 1928.

WOLFF, KARL [THEODOR ALBERT]. *Die deutsche Publizistik in der Zeit der Freiheitskämpfe und des Wiener Kongresses 1813–1815*, xvi + 100. Doctor's dissertation, Leipzig, 1934. Plauen im Vogtland: Günther Wolff [1934–35]. A good survey of public opinion at the time of the Congress of Vienna.

INDEX

Aachen, Congress of, 134

Acts of the German Confederation, 19, 24, 29, 47, 66

Adjustment tax, see Supplementary tax

Allstedt, Saxe-Weimar-Eisenach enclave, 147, 148 n.

America, see United States

Amsberg, Philipp August Christian Theodor von, 1789–1871, Brunswick statesman, 188

Anhalt, North German duchies, 72, 116, 117, 142, 167; and Prussian policy, 130–33; complaints to Prussia, 135–37; controversy with Prussia, 145

Anhalt-Bernburg, North German duchy, 215; Zollanschluss treaties with Prussia, 148–50, 152, 156

Anhalt-Dessau, North German duchy, joins Prussian customs system, 153–54

Anhalt-Köthen, North German duchy, 145, 210; joins Prussian customs system, 153–54

Annual conferences, institution of, 94, 95, 102; in Bavaria-Württemberg Customs Union, 194–98; in Hofmann draft, 212; in Prussia-Hesse-Darmstadt Customs Union, 220; in Oberschöna Punctation, 227; in Prussia-Bavaria-Württemberg treaty, 234; in Zollverein, 244–45

Anschluss, see Zollanschluss

Antipiratical League, foundation of, 34

Aretin, Johann Adam, Freiherr von, 1769–1822, Bavarian diplomat, memorandum of 1819, 65–66

Armansperg, Joseph Ludwig Franz Xaver, Reichsfreiherr von, 1787–1853, Bavarian statesman, 192

Arndt, Ernst Moritz, 1769–1860, patriotic writer, 7, 159, 169; economic proposals of, 19

Arnoldi, Ernst Wilhelm, 1778–1841, business man, 174

Arnstadt Conference, draft proposal, 98–100

Article XI of the Acts of Confederation, 66, 69

Article XIX of the Acts of Confederation, 58, 95, 122, 249; origin of, 19; reconsidered, 37; in Zollverein treaties, 245

Auditing procedure, in Hofmann draft, 212; in Prussian proposal, 216; in Prussia-Hesse-Darmstadt Customs Union, 219–20; in Zollverein treaties, 245

Augsburger Allgemeine Zeitung, 187; on economic problems, 170–71; sells its influence, 174

Austria, leading German power, 39–40, 41, 47, 65, 67, 73, 78, 79, 87, 163, 164, 184, 188, 207, 231, 257; 1814 proposal, 17–18; at Vienna Final Conferences, 48–53; intrigues with Nassau, 89; fight against liberalism, 159; relations with Hesse-Darmstadt, 205–6; and Zollverein, 249–51

Baasch, Ernst, historian, 4

Bab, Bernd, historian, 4

Baden, South German grand duchy, 3, 4, 63, 70, 72, 73, 74, 75, 76, 78, 88, 95, 96, 104, 160, 161, 177, 206, 225, 239, 247, 260–61; economic policies 1818–20, 53–59, 69–70; Ministry of Finance instructs Berstett, 76–77; policy at South German Conferences, 82–84; commercial treaty with Hesse-Darmstadt, 86; octroi treaty with France, 101; enclaves, 154–55; commercial treaty with Hesse-Darmstadt, 202–3; dispute with Bavaria, 230–31; negotiates with Bavaria, 236–37

Barbary States, 34